MY TRINITY

My Trinity

by

Eric Howard

The Pentland Press Limited
Edinburgh · Cambridge · Durham · USA

© Eric Howard 1999

First published in 1999 by
The Pentland Press Ltd.
1 Hutton Close
South Church
Bishop Auckland
Durham

British Library Cataloguing in Publication Data.
A catalogue record for this book is available
from the British Library.

ISBN 1 85821 674 5

Typeset by George Wishart & Associates, Whitley Bay.
Printed and bound by Antony Rowe Ltd., Chippenham.

*To my wife Jean and son Chris,
I should apologize for my many
absences. I confess to placing the
job as a priority to my family on
occasions. Thanks to Donna for
unravelling my scribble.*

Contents

List of Illustrations   ix

Foreword   xi

Comments appertaining to those at 'the sharp end'   xiii

Prologue   xv

Chapter 1   The Early Days, the War and the Army   1
Chapter 2   Palestine   31
Chapter 3   Iraq Street Bombing   69
Chapter 4   Good Friday 1948, Jaba   73
Chapter 5   The Battle for Mishmar Ha'emek and
               HOP Involvement, 1948   77
Chapter 6   Approaching the End – July 1948   87
Chapter 7   Police 1948-56 – Preston and Kent   94
Chapter 8   May 1956 – Lydd ISG 108
Chapter 9   Battalion Training – Bodney North, Norfolk, 1957 . . . 113
Chapter 10   Windsor 1957-8 117
Chapter 11   Mons – Proposed Commission Candidate 135
Chapter 12   Mons – Ten-Mile Run 136
Chapter 13   Promotion to CSM 138
Chapter 14   Unlawful Discharge – Battle Camp 141
Chapter 15   HMS *Plover* 143
Chapter 16   1SG Gravesend – January 1961 154
Chapter 17   Gravesend and Maresfield 1961-2 160
Chapter 18   Wales 1962 165
Chapter 19   BAOR 1963-5 169
Chapter 20   British Embassy, Warsaw 175
Chapter 21   Cyprus 182
Chapter 22   Return to Duty – BAOR 228
Chapter 23   The Girl from Hameln 231
Chapter 24   Borneo – the Facts 242
Chapter 25   Borneo – the Job 246
Chapter 26   Intelligence Corps Commitment 259

Chapter 27 Initial Reactions 266
Chapter 28 Duties of FIO 278
Chapter 29 The Serious Work Begins 281
Chapter 30 The Saga of Manjar 2 320
Chapter 31 The Sheriff of Bau 330
Chapter 32 The Last Hours 346
Chapter 33 Hong Kong 350
Chapter 34 CI Section, HQ Scotland 388
Chapter 35 HQ 6 Infantry Brigade (Barnard Castle) 397
Chapter 36 22 Interrogation Coy, London 1970-3 404
Chapter 37 Preston North-West District HQ 1973-6 424
Conclusion 429

List of Illustrations

Mother and Father's wedding   5
Brother John and I, 1929 15
Wadi Rushmiya, Haifa 37
A Jewish casualty, Haifa 53
A Jewish victim of the massacre at the IPC oil refinery, Haifa 71
Kent County Constabulary, Ashford, 1954 103
Mons Officer Cadet School, 1959 124
George 'Spirou' Raftis 197
On the 'pad' prior to crossing the border 283
The disabled 'scout' 297
Bau 'town' and the police compound 303
'Fred' and me about to board the 'chopper' 316
Patrick and I with two 1/2 Gurkhas bring back two 'scouts'
   of the Indonesian incursion party 317
Indonesian SAS equivalent: 'Resemen Pelopor' with some
   Serikin villagers 331
Thirsty work crossing rivers 337
Our last 'op' 345
The border at Sha Tau Kok 356
In 1967 the Hong Kong Police were probably the finest riot
   control group in the world 372
Sha Tau Kok. My wasted eight days of 'China watching' 375
Two proud parents outside Buckingham Palace 430

Foreword

The relationship between the non-commissioned officers responsible for training would-be officers at Mons Officer Cadet School is a curious one. Perhaps it is best summed up in the old story of the sergeant major addressing his squad of officer cadets. 'You call me "Sir" and I call you "Sir". The only difference is that you mean it and I don't.'

Whatever the truth of the story, that is certainly the reality. No matter that within months the vast majority of these young men will be officers, not one of them will trespass upon the assumption. Everyone knows who is in charge.

Thus it was forty years ago that I met Eric Howard, then a sergeant in the Scots Guards. Memories fade and our paths were never to cross again, but I remember a tough but good humoured professional soldier, determined to ensure that if these largely young and inexperienced 18 year olds were going to command in a matter of months, then he would do all he could to fit them for the responsibility.

This is a soldier's book. Eric served in many of the most exposed trouble spots of the past half century. He tells it like it was and, in doing so, signposts a way of life that is one of challenge, excitement and no little danger. But there is the human side too of comradeship and shared experience, of reliance on colleagues and of the frailty that is inseparable from life itself.

For anyone interested to know what it is like to serve in one of our finest regiments, this book will prove a valuable insight.

Michael Heseltine
April, 1999

COMMENTS COLLECTED OR WRITTEN OVER THE YEARS APPERTAINING TO THOSE AT THE 'SHARP END', IN ANY ENVIRONMENT THE PEOPLE WHO REALLY DO THE HARD WORK.

'A real soldier is a bloke – he'll drink and swear – but he relies on himself; a bloke that can take care of himself.'

A General was quite contemptuous of 'bolt hole beetles who always cluster around the base, the queer little people who, when the war is won, re-emerge fresh and whole to figure so prominently in our organs of publicity, arrogantly, avidly and spitefully trying to drag others down to their deplorable level. There is far more "flap" in the rear areas than up front; they mouth each others rumours and vent their malice. Up front all a man can do is lose his life, way behind he may lose his kit. That prospect can be most worrying.'

An infantryman states: 'I'll tell you what hurts most of all – they call themselves soldiers . . . talking about their long service and whine about going home. Service! why God damn me! it's one long picnic for them. Bloody little small town nobodies doing the big shot act, it makes you cry. When you talk to them, they don't look you in the eye, but you know what they are thinking. Here's another bloody fool, a thick head, that wasn't clever enough to get a soft job like me. They think we all tried and missed because we weren't clever enough, they have the brains. That's what the base boys think of you.'

The stifling jungle with its carpet of swamp-ooze, rotting stumps and leaves and the perpetual stench of vegetable decay, this bog of trees, strangling vines and foliage that shut out the sunlight. In the mangrove swamps conditions were even worse, men having to live and move in a stinking jumble of twisted slime-covered roots and muddy soup. The humidity was so overpowering it hung heavily in the air, more like a material object than a weather condition. It brought out sweat from every pore with the slightest exertion, your clothing absorbed it and when it couldn't cope, it ran down your body and legs into your jungle boots and your feet wallowed in the wet as if you had waded a river.

The heat, humidity and at times altitude, even a slope, tends to reduce your legs to matchsticks and brittleness, despite good physical strength and constitution. You gasp for air which has difficulty entering your body, your stomach lacks the power, your heart pounds violently as if it's trying to leave you, and in desperation to avoid a temporary blindness, you continuously wipe the salt sweat tears from your aching eyes.

No man, however he may talk, has the remotest idea of what an ordinary infantry soldier endures.

I think that most men fear death and cowardice and would admit it. I was more scared of showing myself up under fire before a group or an individual than anything else, and in my private prayers to God I hoped he would spare me that terrible degradation; in retrospect I think he did.

And then there were the fighting troops who lived in a different world of which most of us know nothing. When we met them when they were resting we noticed they kept together and seemed to regard the life we led as being cut off from a greater reality. They were friendly but they made us feel that there were secrets that could only be known to those who shared their existence. They saw our comfort but didn't hold it against us as we might have been unlucky too. But since it hasn't, don't try to understand what you can't.

Some of us, despite being physically tough lost 3-4 stone in weight. It was not just the humidity, heat, rain, insects, fevers or starvation which all contributed, nor was it specific stomach diseases or a bloodstream infection but the whole organism of your body had been violently disrupted. In quieter, more reflective moments, I sometimes felt that my peers might regard me as expendable, that I might die, and my thoughts rushed to my family, but these moments were rare. My stress was not the constant danger but so much work to do. I never saw my body, only a thin, tired, gaunt face in a dirty mirror. I was being worn down by an aching, at times painful fatigue!

My own escapes from death are nothing short of miraculous. Over the years, I've chanced my arm but will I be spared, will all the prayers for me be answered? Does God ever recognise dedication?

It's like a battle: the first wave of assault troops is wiped out, the second is wounded and the third get the medals. You cannot recommend if you're dead.

Prologue

Why did I write this? Occasionally pushed into a corner by friends and certain matters discussed, it was mentioned several times that I should put my experiences down on paper, if not for publication at least for family posterity. This of course is true. How many grandsons of today know what grandfathers' and great grandfathers' or -mothers' experiences were in the late nineteenth century? Frequently, when discussed, the experience was either totally exaggerated or unfairly underplayed and the whole truth never known. I would have loved to have sensibly talked to my father about India and those first three terrible battles of World War I at Mons, Marne and Aisne in which he took part as a member of the North Lancashire Regiment and in the latter battle received a permanent injury.

Unless stated otherwise all the incidents recorded involved me, they are not secondhand. One has to be honest, but alas without documentary records the memory could be at fault. The facts are stated as recalled, those forgotten are not quoted because this could lead to exaggeration and embarrassment.

I could be accused of scepticism against military units, officers, comrades, and of personalities and organisations outside the military environment. If this should cause anger, indignation and thoughts of retribution, all I can say is: think about it through my eyes and thoughts. It could be said, 'Surely he suffers from sour grapes,' and you may be right, but may I add, with some justification, if these experiences have never happened to you in your adult life you have been most fortunate.

My life could have been so different but God decided otherwise. Looking back from a purely selfish and personal view I wouldn't have missed it for the world but I had the support of an understanding (not always true), loving wife and family. Jean did not appreciate duty first, family second, which you must accept when you sign on the dotted line; she just learned, like most police or service wives: a case of gritting your teeth and getting on with life.

I always attempted to do my work loyally, honestly and with dedication but must surely accept criticism and ridicule from whoever wishes to contribute. I have never suffered fools gladly; when advice has been requested, ignored, and disaster follows, I have no sympathy. When in charge I consider the facts and advice available, I make the decisions, then if anything goes wrong only I carry the can. That's life and I am grateful that I have been allowed the pleasure of reminiscence.

Jean has said both at the time and in retrospect that during my service career I was a fool to be so conscientious and loyal. I'm sorry; it must be in the blood, a touch of the 'Flashman' – 'I always tried to do my best at all times' that's what God expects. We should not automatically seek rewards for a job well done, that should be the aim of every man.

For the last fifteen years of Service life the necessity of secrecy and the 'need to know' forced me to be unsocially silent at times which annoyed Jean and no doubt others at times, but it had to be. In compiling my notes I experienced great difficulty in continually referring to myself. I have had many years compiling reports and actions, but found it embarrassing to recall matters totally in the first person. I have the advantage of a retentive memory and was assisted by maps, books, photographs, personal notes and a Borneo diary. Inaccuracies and omissions are inevitable but by honest endeavour I have recounted the truth as I saw it and I do not feel that apologies are necessary. Initials or blanks are used to avoid embarrassment. I hope these memoirs merit interest and could serve to be instructive and informative and invest pride in a family background. Maybe it could also show character not necessarily manifested in the person we think we know. I'm a listener and a watcher, not a speaker.

If these papers are to be published and I am still alive and kicking I will be available to remove any ambiguities raised by constructive critics. I found it sad that in my letter to and received from the Israelis concerning events in Palestine, the subject matter was effectively camouflaged by a well constructed verbal smokescreen which only drew the observer to obvious conclusions. At the time of writing I wonder what will be the result of my contact with a leading Arab historian now resident in Paris who is a self confessed supporter of 'Arab terrorists' (sic).

When I made notes for lecture purposes I copied facts and figures submitted by authors of military papers and magazines (e.g. BAR) and some of these are included in these memoirs, individuals unknown. To them my apologies and grateful thanks. I was not always in a position to obtain authentic information.

So, if I have annoyed or bored you with my pontifications please accept my apologies. Nothing personal, but I must admit it was fun to write, even in the middle of a murder trial!

Are you sitting comfortably? Then let's begin.

CHAPTER I

The Early Days, Home, The War and The Army

To begin this book now should be the time for self analysis of personal makeup, as family genes would show I descend on the Howard side with certain attributes and faults. The name is well established in English and Irish history and has origins from Cumbria and the French, in our Irish connections, from which country my grandparents emigrated to England in the late nineteenth century. All their children were born in this country, however, and brought up in a strict Catholic background, full of love, with lots of humour and music.

Physically, with the exception of Uncle Bill, all the brothers were tall and athletic in build and inclination, strong in body and will. With two exceptions all the brothers travelled extensively showing great courage and a spirit of adventure. Again with two exceptions, the five remaining brothers all had a military bent, covering India, Australia, South Africa, Belgium and France. All had a tendency to chauvinism yet showing great affection for family. The brothers were dour characters showing dogged determination in whatever they were confronted with; strong silent types, they could not be described as social animals. As children and later as adults the eight boys and two girls had a 'pot pease' of character like this: great humour and a strong sense of fun, independent, selfish, blunt, arrogant, self opinionated, quite a mixture.

Both my grandparents on the Howard side originated from Southern Ireland and from what background is not known, but I have no doubt that an hereditary check would give some indication. They originally settled in Bolton, and there are many Howards in that area so we could be looking at various cousins who settled there. Later the family moved to Preston and were members of St Ignatius's parish. Being of Irish Roman Catholic background, large families were the expected order of the day and ours was no exception. Ten children were born, two girls and eight boys, details as follows:

1

Norah died at birth or shortly after. This would probably be in 1879.

Tom was the eldest son and was killed in the First World War with North Lancs Regt.

Jim, whose son Jim still lives in Longton. By all accounts he was not a nice person to family and neighbours, being a male chauvinist pig, somewhat of a bully and with a drink problem. My earliest recollections of him were at a house with many steps on the south side of a street in Kirkham. I don't think my parents held him in great esteem. To my knowledge he never had any military service and he died in August 1955. He had a daughter Frances, who became involved with a married man and left home in disgrace to live with this person.

William (Bill). This was the one I knew best of all until he died in 1963 aged eighty-four. My father loved him as the last remaining brother, with the exception of Jim. During a serious illness my father slept with him each night for three weeks and worked as well. My Aunt Winifred was loving and generous to John and me. Both my parents liked her, but my mother thought Bill 'knew it all'. He was a very fit and capable person; self assurance oozed from him. At the beginning of the Boer War Bill was probably about twenty two years of age; he joined Baden Powell's Scouts and served well for three years. I wish I could remember all his tales. When World War I broke out he immediately rejoined and served as a Mounted Military Policeman for almost four years on the Western Front. Now, he could tell a tale or two and I have no reason to doubt their truth. He was never slow to pat himself on the back. He had a fetish about physical fitness as did my father, and he was big enough to admit that his younger brother was a far greater athlete than he was. Huge open-air PT sessions were held in Moor Park and most of the brothers attended, but Bill studied and became a part time PT instructor and masseur. He was good; his knowledge of physiology and the human body in general was extremely high. I think originally he worked in a clerical capacity at the Leyland Rubber Company, then moved to Leyland Motors Ltd. His skill as a masseur and PT instructor enabled him to obtain a post (part time) at Wellington House which catered for a number of potential managers who were known as 'Premiums'. They left school at seventeen or eighteen years with School Matriculation, were boarded out at Wellington and given four years in various Departments of Leyland. Uncle Bill kept them fit with PT and boxing.

In 1942 Bill left Leyland and became PT Instructor at King Edward

College, St Annes and I think this period of his life was his happiest. He was an ardent and knowledgeable Socialist, having endured, as an eight-year-old, the horrors of part time work in the mill. Justifiably he was extremely anti-Tory.

Here at a College full of learned teachers/Tories he was in his element and frequently described the passionate but good humoured arguments he enjoyed with his fellow teachers. He even achieved an award for rescuing a boy from drowning in the baths, when he was sixty six years old. He also had two bravery awards for rescues from the Ribble in flood when he was a young man. As a young person in the late 20s and early 30s he and my father, with a boat full of companions, used to enter the Ribble at Penwortham and swim to Nelson's Buoy near Lytham, some fourteen miles. Uncle Bill also had two unsuccessful attempts to swim across Morecambe Bay.

When he was in his late sixties and retired, Bill decided to apply for a temporary job at Ormskirk Grammar School as a PT teacher. To his delight he was successful and stayed for three terms.

I think it was 1962 when my brother moved from Preston to Whittle le Woods and Uncle Bill was not happy. I had left for Germany and Jean was still living in inaccessible Mid Wales, then Auntie Win died in 1963. I was not informed by John until the day before she was buried but I couldn't have attended the funeral anyway, so I sent a telegram; Jean had the children and could only send a wreath. Bill decided he wanted nothing further to do with John and me for reasons best known to himself. I felt very sad about this because since the death of my father he was the one person Mother, John and I could count on for support and I used to sit at his feet for hours in the house in Cheviot Street listening to fascinating tales of Australia, India, South Africa and France. He had become my proxy father which was as it should be, to replace a brother. I felt terribly hurt when I visited him at the old people's home on Ashton Park. I asked him for his reasons for refusing to see John and me. Very indignant, he said John had left him and I had not attended the funeral. No way would he accept that I would not have been given permission to leave Germany. He curtly dismissed me by turning on his heel and briskly as ever he walked away. He died some weeks later, on the same day as Churchill, collapsing in Friargate outside St Mary's Catholic Church. He had idolized Auntie Win and it was probably kinder that he died soon after her; it just grieves me that after all they had both done for me the parting had to be like that. A sad chapter of family life.

Charles (Charlie) was somewhat of a lad. He joined the Scots Guards, saw service in the Police in Australia, returned to UK and joined Lancashire Constabulary. He died in January 1915.

John (Jack) served in the South African Police then returned to UK and joined the Lancashire Constabulary. He died November 1914.

Frank: Nothing known. Died 1897.

Albert: This uncle was blind, following an attack of measles then a subsequent unsuccessful operation. I only have a vague recollection of him as a child; he died in May 1940. His competence with Braille was phenomenal, with hands and fingers the envy of any woman.

Edward (Ted): my memory of him is mixed because I was only eight years old when he died of a strangulated appendix owing to medical incompetence by our own doctor. In those days recourse to a higher authority was practically unknown and it wouldn't have brought him back. I have never met anyone of the family, close friends, neighbours or police colleagues who had a bad word to say about him, he was so well liked. It was only late in life that I could appreciate how deeply in love they must have been for my mother to miss him so, and for so long. Before they married he wrote her love poems which she treasured. My mother lived in Cold Bath Street on Maudland (which does not exist now); previously her family had a newsagency on Fylde Road facing the Polytechnic. They had had a burglary and my father investigated. My mother was an extremely beautiful woman but very shy and nervous and I think they had only 'been out' a few times when the war started and my father marched down Fishergate as a North Lancs reservist, to his delight as he proudly marched behind the band. Mary Alice Smith shouted to him, waving frantically. He left the ranks, as did many others, picked her up and kissed her for the first time; that takes some believing these days. Throughout those frightening early weeks of the war when the Germans were cock-a-hoop about their early successes having fought hard to try and break down that 'Contemptible Little Army' that faced them and of which my father was part.

    Through the battles of Mons, Marne and finally the Aisne my father was involved against this magnificent German Army. During the Aisne in No Man's Land my father was seriously wounded in the left foot. Initially he was brought back to hospital in Liverpool, but then later became the first soldier to be admitted to Mount Street Hospital in Preston. It was obvious he could never fight as a soldier again, as he would always need a special boot with a leg iron. Invalided from the Army he returned to the police: 'The Hero Returns'.

So as a mark of honour and respect they sent him out on the roughest and most tedious beats available, to drive this Constable, who had an almost indiscernable limp, off the job. So much for King and Country. But he dug in and finally they admitted defeat and he became what was known as 'on Reserve'; in other words he was permanently behind the desk at the Police Station and so hundreds, possibly thousands, knew him. I can remember him as a person with a passion for sport which now he could not play, and an eloquence with the pen. In fact senior officers of Preston Borough Police in my day, apparently used to ask him to write their reports when they were young constables; it was a travesty. He was also a very talented musician who could play piano, piano accordion, harmonica, flute and drums all by ear; not a note of music could he understand, but his memory of music was extraordinary. I recall his slim upright figure in dark suit and bowler hat sitting at the piano stool playing Gilbert and Sullivan while he waited for my mother to get ready.

His sense of humour was well known not only on the force but with friends and neighbours and each Christmas Day he prepared scripts and sketches for various humorous digs against the church, Council, State etc. and dressed for the part too. People chosen had to rehearse. He was a man of considerable talent in many ways, who, had he been born in my time, might have risen to greater heights with good secondary and University

Mother and Father's wedding.

education. I resemble my father physically in many ways, at a comparable age still being slim but taller, slightly heavier in build, with a great enthusiasm for sport and fitness. I am losing my hair as he did, but maybe not as fast, and for that I am grateful; I hope my son improves on that. Facially we are alike, could be described as hard, worn, craggy, grim in our later years; it changes with a smile. I love music but never had father's talent for instruments although I could probably sing better than he. I still have a sense of humour which I have frequently needed and I have enjoyed writing scripts and plots for exercises when I was an instructor. So it's nice to know that some things brush off.

In 1932 he underwent an operation for appendicitis, but due to incompetent surgery three years later a blockage was caused, coupled again with incompetent diagnosis. The surgeon at Preston Infirmary stated that had he been admitted two days earlier he could have saved him, but my father died on 19th March 1935. In an unprecedented show of affection for a comrade, the Chief Constable and all his officers plus fifty Constables (almost half of the Police Force) accompanied my father's coffin to the cemetery; it had never been done before nor since for any Police officer. It makes you think why a person so well respected in every way had to receive accolades to his personal contribution to the human race when he was dead!

Oh, how I wish that we had had him longer; would my life have been different? I expect it would; we just have to accept life as God's pattern for us, but it's frequently difficult, I just hope that my son and maybe his male successors inherit some of the fine qualities that appeared to be part of the Howard family makeup with possibly one exception. Like most families they originated from humble backgrounds but character came through and it's nice to know you can look back with some pride on one side of the family and the name you carry.

Norah was the younger daughter, tall for a woman, slim built, extremely handsome and my father's favourite, no doubt as a child spoiled by all the boys. She would speak about others but not of herself, had great affection for my mother, had no time for brother Jim and like my mother got on with Bill but thought he knew it all. She married Fred Cardwell who worked on the railway, a very gentle, humorous and considerate man; his sudden death was a great shock to Auntie Norah. They had no children, a subject never discussed but she had suffered with TB as a child. So Norah was left a widow and a cripple. She had suffered terribly from arthritis in the hips for some time and had rarely been out of the house for years, being unable to walk except with two sticks. When seen at Wrightington

Hospital by the renowned Doctor Charnley she insisted that her position demanded that both hips were replaced simultaneously, never done before, but Charnley agreed and it was successfully achieved mainly through Auntie Norah's 'guts'. When she got home she had a rope fixed on the stairs, and each evening she dragged herself upstairs to sleep rather than downstairs and in weeks was walking unaided. If she had one fault it was her uncompromising belief in her Catholic faith. There were no grey areas with her. She was a staunch believer in a United Ireland and supported the ideals of the IRA, refusing to listen to certain truths that I knew. In this way she was a bigot, but aren't they the same, on both sides? She had an inkling of what my job entailed and was upset when Chris went to Ireland on his first tour with the Scots Guards. Apart from all this she was a nice person, somewhat demanding because of her disability but she obtained some satisfaction from life in her last years. I always visited her if I was home and when I returned to Preston even more frequently, but I never knew her as I should have done. Maybe family background would have been more complete, so it's a pity. She died peacefully in Lytham Hospital after a short illness. Jean and I had been with her a couple of days earlier so she was not alone and she had good neighbours who were close till the end. So the last of a family died.

Jim (son of Jim Howard). At the time of writing Jim still lives in Longton, a widower for the second time. Now in his eighties he looks years younger. He is an extremely nice chap who makes me feel a villain because he appears to have no vices. Although we have only met infrequently over the years, we get along fine and have always thought of the few things we have in common; honesty, forthrightness and an inclination to be self opinionated or, said another way, self confident. Jim is a non smoker and drinker and has never had children by either wife, unlike his father and the family. We could get along in small doses but I think by character we are poles apart.

My Mother

Mary Alice Howard (née Smith). The little I know of her parents tells me nothing of her mother's background but that her father was a shopkeeper in Fylde Road, Preston but also something of a part time professional entertainer. I believe he died at a relatively early age. There was an elder son, William, who was killed in France during World War I while serving in the Army Service Corps; his name appears on the Memorial in St Walburge's Church in Preston. I can remember him being described as a 'very bonny lad' with a lovely nature; my middle brother was named after him. I can picture my mother once explaining to me how on her wedding night in 1917 she would not allow my father to enter the bed and he spent the night prowling the floor trying to explain to my mother what married life was all about. He was six years older than mother and she was twenty-four, so he was older, wiser and much travelled. The scene I can imagine, knowing her, and she recalled it with a humorous and tender smile on her face. Despite his frustration my Dad was a gentle man. A sad but lovely tale to tell: virtue and humour meant something to people really in love in those days, a pity it doesn't apply in some respects today.

Within a year her first child was born, John, and two more followed at four year intervals, William (Billy) and myself. Tragically for her Billy died when he was six years old and in 1933 I think Mother required a hysterectomy. After my father's death she was terribly distraught, plus the fact that the family income decreased from £5.0s.0d. per week (a princely sum in 1935) to 26/- per week. So for some years my mother worked as a cleaner and shed bitter tears as she scrubbed; she was a very emotional person. For the three years between 1935 and 1938 I was taken on visits from one friend to another and watched the constant tears fall as friends and relatives grieved about happy times shared with my father. My mother's closest friend since childhood was Maggie Barratt who married a very steadfast but extremely dour Company Sergeant Major of the North Lancs who saw service throughout World War I in France; his name was Hugh Bell. They lived in Wellington Street and during my father's fatal illness I lived with them because I was off school owing to measles. For three years after father's death they were both very kind to us all. In 1938 it was decided that both families should move to adjacent houses in Stanley Grove, Penwortham (we had No 90 and the Bells 88); this was done and both families settled in the new environment very satisfactorily.

The war came and went and when Jean and I left for Kent my mother decided to return to Preston and nearer our John's house in Ashton. So in 1953/54 she bought a small house at No 32 Priory Street, now demolished, near St Walburge's Church, almost back to her childhood environment. She enjoyed the close friendship of several individuals who all had a passion for dancing which as a young girl my mother had had quite a talent for. So from wartime until about 1958 my mother enjoyed her once, sometimes twice, a week sessions of Old Time dancing.

Unfortunately bronchitis and asthma caught up with her and she suffered terribly in her remaining years though maintaining a brave face in company. It tired her heart and sadly she died on 2nd January 1962; she was sixty nine years of age. John and I identified her at the mortuary. She looked tired but peaceful. Mother and I had our grave disagreements when

I decided to transfer to Kent, understandably on both sides. However the problem was soon resolved when Chris was born some months later and we remained close until she died. She was a very tender, loving and emotional person, devoted to her religion but not a bigot. She had been endowed with beauty, humour and over protectiveness. If she had faults it was that she was rather naive, gullible and expected more of her children that she was really entitled to. So much for a brief family background.

At this juncture I must include some words about my son Christopher Anthony. I must confess that as a baby he was no trouble at all, no sleepless nights, and as he grew up always encouraged to be an outdoors child, especially in my company with walks and sports. He started school at Windsor, then we moved to Frimley Green, Chatham, Towyn in Mid Wales, and Minden in Germany. At no time was I ever aware that he hated his educational environment at primary level.

When I was faced with the possibility of a posting to Warsaw, Jean and I, after serious consideration and with Chris's agreement, made arrangements for him to become a Boarder at St Joseph's College, Blackpool in order to ensure that my frequent postings would not affect his continual higher education. It is never an easy decision to make; personally I would have chosen one of two other schools but this was close to relatives and friends in the Preston area, and that swayed our decision.

His first term was not a raving success, and some harsh words were spoken by me when he returned to Germany for his first term holiday. Initially he had found it difficult to adjust from being top dog at his Minden School to a little puppy in this school and many of his fellow students had graduated from preparatory classes and were academically more advanced. In later years he regretted that his lack of effort precluded his streaming into the sciences in those early years.

When I left for Borneo and Jean resided at Ansdell, near Blackpool, Chris became a weekly boarder. Academically he remained just above average, but he thoroughly enjoyed his sports, the highlight being the ricochet of a javelin into his leg. At the age of fourteen he made his solo run to join us in Hong Kong. Although we had made provision for a UK escort by friends, he was growing up fast.

At sixteen, having achieved his five 'O' Levels, St Joseph's closed the boarding section, but by this time we had found another school who accepted boarders, in anticipation that my next posting could be Southern England or the continent. St John's College, Southsea, near Portsmouth, was a distinct change from the rather rigid teaching of the Christian Brothers to the more laid back academics of the De la Salle Brothers.

Within six months Chris was the prefect of his boarding house, playing Rugby for Hampshire under 19s, and thoroughly enjoying his academic life. As I recall he extended for another year with finally three 'A' Levels and six 'O's.

By this time I was now working in London and Jean and I encouraged him towards a University; he was accepted at Reading. However he spoke with a College 'old boy' who was in the profession he intended to enter and was somewhat disillusioned by comments 'from the horse's mouth'. So without any prompting from me he went through the process and was accepted for Sandhurst, having achieved an outstanding Officer Selective Board according to the Commandant of Sandhurst who was formerly my Brigadier in BAOR.

Again in his initial training he found difficulty at the beginning to accept that he, as all his squad colleagues, were the lowest of underdogs within the system which had been tried and tested for years. A high degree of humour and stoicism was necessary until more newcomers arrived, then it changed. Once again 'Daddy' had to paint the picture. As a former staff member of an Officer Cadet School I knew what the transition was like from school to manhood. He left Sandhurst with a very good report but did not show any exceptional talents.

He had opted for and had been accepted for the Intelligence Corps to follow in my footsteps, and for his two year infantry attachment I had arranged for him to join the 1st Battalion Scots Guards to have the rough edges smoothed off him, and it was not going to be easy, especially from a fiscal point of view, which was explained to him in detail. An early tour in Northern Ireland and a further eighteen months in BAOR was to form a first class basis for his career as an officer. In fact in later years I was told by Chris's CO at that time, Lt. Colonel 'Dicky' Mayfield DSO, that he had written to me (letter never received) advocating that I should persuade Chris to remain in the Scots Guards because of his excellent tour in Ulster and subsequently in BAOR.

When Chris left 1 SG he became a Training Officer at the Intelligence Corps Depot, Ashford, then as the Officer Commanding a Section in Hannover and it was here that he discovered that his future in the Corps was not going to be as expected. He realised that he had talented people to do the work and that he was there to direct and supervise, and that is not always easy to accept. The possibility of an Inter Service Transfer to the Royal Marines was not accepted, but he was accepted into the Queen's Lancashire Regiment in which his grandfather and an uncle had served.

Chris settled back into infantry life as if he had never left it; his tour with the Scots Guards had been a good apprenticeship. He was well respected in the Regiment especially with his soldiers. He had the great honour to carry the Regimental Colour on the occasion of the Queen's visit to Preston celebrating her Silver Jubilee of Accession in 1977. He had a couple of Ulster tours while serving in UK, and found himself a wife, Sally, whom he met when serving in Cyprus. He had a G3 staff appointment at HQ 1st Division in Verden, later joining his Battalion at Paderborn as Company Commander of 'C' Company. When the Battalion arrived in Belfast in 1987 Chris commanded almost half the Battalion at Great Howard Street Mill. It was his revised patrolling system and 'hands on' command, plus the first class expertise of his soldiers that resulted in a record award of decorations for the Regiment, which included an MBE for himself; we were very proud parents. The tour in BAOR ended, Chris was appointed an Instructor at the School of Infantry, Warminster. His duties concerned the Company Commanders' Courses which frequently involved him assuming the role of a Commanding Officer in charge of infantry tanks and artillery. He thoroughly enjoyed these responsibilities.

Not wishing to return to the Battalion at the end of this tour, he was offered and accepted to remain at Warminster as a G2 on the staff of the Director of Infantry, a job in which he found great and unexpected pleasure. Over the years he had become interested in climbing, and became a member of the Army Mountaineering Club. His personal pinnacle of success was the organization and training of a large group of inexperienced NCOs and soldiers for a challenging climbing expedition in the Italian Alps, a magnificent achievement with no casualties.

In the position he was in, Chris read the options for change well from a personal point of view and decided, albeit reluctantly, to leave the Army. I must confess my opinion was not totally in agreement with his decision, having experienced the problems confronting a mature person seeking employment in the alien civilian environment. Military personnel of all ranks have a host of attributes they can offer to present day civilian life, but unfortunately those without military background are usually rather reluctant to absorb these talents into their organizations. They prefer qualifications on paper and that in itself is a very shallow attitude. The Armed Services in general usually whittle out the 'deadlegs' as soon as the faults appear; some do escape the net but not often.

During release leave and afterwards, Chris began his search for employment, and found the experience of applications and interviews quite absorbing with just a little apprehension. Sally was still working as a teacher but had given mandatory notice in case they had to leave. I, in a modest way, also initiated some introductions with more to come if necessary. Then, following a successful interview he and the family moved

to an old farmhouse in Melbourne, Derbyshire and within eighteen
months he was the Security and Terminal Manager of East Midlands
Airport. They are happy with a busy and absorbing job, a settled family
life, Sally teaching and the children James and Philippa fully involved in
school and extra mural activities.

It is difficult to attempt to recall with accuracy specific incidents that
happened over fifty years ago. I just recall that the small two-up two-down
terraced house at 109 Wellington Street, Preston was a very clean and
extremely happy household, I never heard my parents have an angry word.
My father, although a very dour-looking man, was full of humour. I can
remember visits over the Christmas period to Uncle Bill's house in Ward
Street, Lostock Hall where everyone seemed to sleep on mattresses on the
floor; it was great fun. Christmas Day at our house was quite a hoot. John
and I were lucky, no shortage of presents although not like today; drink
and food was plentiful, relatives and friends packed the tiny house. My
father spent many hours in the weeks before Christmas writing a number
of topical sketches in which certain guests took part; this homemade
humour was hilarious. My most vivid memory was the arrest of my father
by Aunt Norah, the fastening of the handcuffs on each other and the
realization that my Dad did not have the appropriate key. He had been
delivering a most humorous but seditious sermon from the pulpit (clothes
maiden) dressed as one of our local priestly characters in a huge nightshirt
with two pillows. Aunt Norah was rather loosely dressed in my father's
police uniform with her underwear appearing in the most unexpected
places. The whole household accompanied the two down the street to the
local 'nick' in Water Lane, then after release, or was it before? into the
Wheatsheaf pub next door. That was talked about for years.

Uncle Bill and Auntie Win then moved to Cheviot Street, and about
this time Uncle Bill nearly died with a burst duodenal ulcer. I remember
my father staying overnight with him for quite some time until he
recovered.

In March of 1935 I contracted German measles and my father was
suddenly taken ill with a stomach problem. I was sent to stay with Maggie
and Hughie Bell with their sons John and Hughie who also lived in
Wellington Street. On the Saturday afternoon of 20th March I was rather
clumsily told by Uncle Bill (much to the anger of Hughie Bell) that my
father was dead and had been buried the previous day. It seemed like the
end of the world to me and I must confess it took many years before I
could accept it. Being close to my mother I shared her grief more than
anyone else, which probably accounts for the distress that I feel at funerals,

not necessarily mourning the dead but showing sympathy for the bereaved. The blame for the tragedy was placed on our own Doctor O'Kane, a handsome soft-spoken Irishman. His diagnosis was wrong, but in those days nothing was pushed. I only recall O'Kane when he removed my tonsils and adenoids on the kitchen table in Wellington Street (some surgery, ah!) and when he patched up the middle finger of my right hand when a half brick split it open.

My father being a talented musician and lover of good music had decided I should take up the piano and be taught by Agnes Singleton, the daughter of some close friends. Agnes was an extremely strict teacher and lessons started in spring when the nights were getting lighter. It was the wrong time for me. By the summer, much to my parents' disappointment, I refused to attend any more lessons and I've regretted it ever since: no fool like a young fool.

The highlight of the year was our annual holiday which we spent at Blackpool in a boarding house in St Chad's Road near South Pier and we stayed for a month, almost unheard of in those days. The holiday started the third week of July, the next week my mother's cousin Lucy who lived in Manchester stayed with us, and then in the second week of August my father took his week's holiday and brought us home. He of course visited us on his days off during the other three weeks. We met the same people in the boarding house each year and it was like a prolonged social event, in the house, on the beach or round the amusements. We all took part; people those days derived a great deal of pleasure in making their own amusement. It was simple and uncomplicated and at times very funny. After Dad's death my mother had difficulty facing the other guests and money was very scarce so only a week was taken with cousin Lucy (whose holiday my father had subsidised) and after three years, holidays in Blackpool stopped for me.

Hughie Bell was a painter and decorator and in 1938 was working in Stanley Grove, Penwortham on a new estate being built by a local man named Gabbott who lived nearby in a huge detached house on Liverpool Road. He was greatly impressed by the standard of the houses and took an option on two adjacent houses, No's 88 and 90, and then proceeded to persuade Maggie and my mother to move out there. Our John was not over enthusiastic, but having failed his Civil Service exam (he had sat it while my father was dying) he had started work at Leyland Motors, so it would be somewhat nearer. He was also courting a girl from Fulwood and was acquiring some notoriety in the Preston and District Cricket League playing for St Walburge's, so he had mixed feelings. I was horrified: what about school? All my mates? I was taken up to see the new house and to my eleven-year-old mind it was a new world. To the rear of the houses was a huge field (prairie) and a wood (Sherwood Forest) a pond (Lake Huron) and a stream (Zambezi). I'd never seen anything quite like this. Occasional sunny afternoons spent paddling in Cottam Brook near Haslam Park and playing on flat green grass would be nothing in comparison to this, I was full of it, so excited, and yet I did not want to lose my 'gang'.

But leave we did and began to settle in the house and meet the neighbours and other children, most of whom were girls or boys too young or too old. The nearest boy of our age (Hughie was eighteen months older than I) was Bill Charnley, who had an elder brother Frank and a horror of a young sister named Jean who always tried to follow us in the woods. 'I MARRIED HER.' In the early days both families concentrated on laying a lawn near the house, making concrete paths parallel to each hedge, and laying out the remainder of the garden which lay sunken from the lawn. It was hard work that summer but with the help of the Lonsdales (Harry and Minnie) our next door neighbours both our gardens had paths, lawns were growing and things were taking shape. In between times we played. Our imaginations ran riot, Hughie's in particular. In the early years it was all games, Cowboys and Indians, Robin Hood and so on, broken only by the construction of a series of steps to give easy access for our parents to the wood and a huge dam over which they could walk, that lasted for years. We fished the pond and made rafts; in winter, we even dared to skate on it. The stream was a watery racetrack. I lost count of the wet trousers, shirts and socks as in my excitement I incurred the wrath of my mother, as we all did.

As we got older, high trees became a challenge to climb, the stream in various parts was a frightening leap into space and sports like cricket and football became fashionable. Bill being bigger and older than me tended to lead and bully me to a certain extent. At football he used to hand me off like a wing three quarter and very unceremoniously used to put me on the seat of my trousers when going in the tackle; I was barely five foot and Bill was huge.

Shortly after our arrival in Stanley Grove our local newsagent, Mr Desmond, a one armed gentleman, asked my mother if she would allow me to deliver the daily papers five days a week; he would also sell me a lady's cycle for ten shillings, that would assist my own mobility and help to carry what was on occasions a very heavy load. For this work I would receive the princely sum of 2/6. Some months later I also acquired a *Lancashire Evening Post* round for five days, and for this I received 1/6. My morning round was conveniently between Penwortham Police Station and Howick and I could finish it at home; the evening round was in the area of Hill Road in Penwortham. When you consider that our total income was

Brother John and I, 1929.

26/- composed of Widows Pension 10/- and Police Contributory Pension 16/- (and we were better off than most) this extra income was most welcome.

In schooltime my daily routine was up at 6.00a.m., begin delivery by 6.30a.m., finish by 8.00a.m., breakfast, bus to school at St Walburge's. (My mother said the roads were too dangerous!) Home, collect cycle, evening round, then home for evening meal. In school holidays and Saturday mornings I also helped to deliver milk for a local farmer named Arnold Parry. The Parry brothers delivered milk by horse and cart, or two old decrepit saloon cars. I received a daily fee of 2*d.* or 3*d.* With Arnold his deliveries were to say the least haphazard: several 'calling shops', 'lonely ladies' he would glibly remark, plus several pubs. The smell in that old Ford was awful and he didn't smell much better.

All the cash was given to my mother, apart from some sweets. I had no incentive to save; there were no such things as Coke, pop records, pizzas or trendy clothes. My weekly 'spends' bought very little, neither was it looked for by teenagers in those days. Our lives were very narrow, but quite content. It was only when you reached 5th or 6th Form status or commenced employment that you broadened your outlook.

Our idyllic existence was somewhat shattered when war was declared in 1939. Our John was already in the Army. In July 1939 the first of the '21's' were called up for a period of training, and he was at Arrowe Park near Birkenhead when war was declared. He was partially trained and didn't return to 'Civvy Street' until 1946. His initial posting was to an Anti-Aircraft Battery of the Royal Artillery stationed near Dunfermline on the Firth of Forth. This battery was credited with the shooting down of the first German bomber over the UK. On promotion he later joined a mixed Battery in NE England near Redcar. He refused a commission but got himself married before embarking for India in 1942 to instruct the native soldiery in the complexity of Anti-Aircraft gunnery. As the war in Burma started to swing towards victory John left the Royal Artillery and transferred to the Royal Signals and joined the Chindit Force that was airlifted to 'Broadway' in the heart of Burma.

On the day the Germans marched into Poland I was taken by Uncle Bill, a rare treat this, to a cinema in Preston to see the epic 'All Quiet on the Western Front'. My Uncle Bill had great experience of wars, and this film was written and produced to show humanity the futility of war. I little realized that the carnage that I would see on film would be dwarfed by the loss of over twenty million lives in the war that Britain was about to enter. A few weeks earlier I remember reading the graphic description of the loss in Liverpool Bay of HM Submarine *Thetis*; it was an horrific accident that really touched the hearts of the nation.

In 1940 I was still attending St Walburge's School; I refused to go to the Catholic College even after passing the exams. Having watched my brother struggle, I was fearful of homework, i.e. Greek, French and Latin. The summer brought Dunkirk and Howick House (now the Blind Home) which lay just across the stream at the rear of our house, became a military establishment holding roughly a company of infantry from all sorts of regiments back from Dunkirk. Their role was to resist attack by Parachute Troops. They seem to spend more time hanging round 'my lake' drinking jugs of tea provided by the housewives of Stanley Grove. Then they left and Howick House was left to the LDV/Home Guard.

I was fourteen years of age in September 1940 and Uncle Bill and my mother decided I should start an apprenticeship in a good trade at Leyland Motors and I was persuaded that the electrical trade was ideal and for this I was accepted. It was normal practice that every apprentice should initially become a teaboy in a machine shop and help out on the inspection bench then after a few weeks he would gradually be introduced to the various stages of his chosen trade. One day per week was set aside until the age of seventeen years to attend Leyland Motors Day Continuation School, where you were taught Maths, English, Technical Drawing and PT (by Bill Elkington, a protegé of Uncle Bill's). When I walked into 3B Machine Shop at Leyland I was terrified; to a young kid straight from school the change of environment is drastic, the noise, smell and all adults; I was speechless. That morning I was treated with great kindness by everyone but I was so confused. When I met Uncle Bill as arranged on the cricket pitch at lunchtime, I was close to tears and didn't want to go back. It had all been a terrible shock and I don't suppose I was the first. Uncle Bill was a little more understanding on this occasion and he lessened my fears and told me where he worked and that I could come and talk any time I was able. After that day I never looked back. I enjoyed school and later attended Harris Technical College, Preston, three nights a week until I joined the Army.

Leyland Motors had two bomb attacks and I watched and identified the aircraft that made the second attack. I was luckily nowhere near the scene of the raid. From the electrical production set-up in North Works I was transferred to the tank factory at Farington (BX) still on production, inserting minor electrical items. All my adult workmates on the electrical side were professed Communists and wore the Red Star badge. It was by these people that I was persuaded to join the Electrical Trades Union. Meetings appeared to be more of a political nature and I was disheartened. In late 1941 I was moved to the Farington maintenance and installation squad; by now I was working seven days a week and overtime. I revelled in the job from a practical point of view though I must confess the theoretical side of electrical engineering was a struggle, plus the fact that I had an overwhelming urge to become eighteen and a soldier. Another apprentice, Jack Smith (now deceased), and I had two electricians, both from Blackburn; Jack Milton and mine was Jimmy Duerden; we couldn't have had better tutors.

When I wanted to smoke Jimmy forced me to smoke a pipeful of 'twist' till I was sick. If at lunchtime I wanted a drink he would allow me half a pint. When I was inattentive, careless, or very often mouthy and cheeky, he would almost knock me off my feet with a cuff on my head, and did it hurt! He frequently reminded me of my manners to adults and in many ways, especially in discipline, became a proxy father. Jimmy Duerden was one hell of a man. He gave me confidence to carry, erect, and work on double ladders, also on tower extensions; he taught me how to walk along crane rails, girders, planks and work from the height of 60 foot or so above foundries, machine shops and production line. Nothing frightened me, and I enjoyed the admiration of the workers watching from below. Mind you, I had one or two narrow escapes and Jimmy made sure I was brought down to earth with a fist under my nose. I learnt and I was grateful.

Although I was busy working I was also a runner for the ARP (Air Raid Precautions) in the Stanley Grove/Carlton Drive area of Penwortham and as soon as I was able I joined the Home Guard. I was also a member of Trinity Youth Club in Preston and a gang of boys and girls all from Penwortham used to attend the Club, and go to the pictures together till eventually the war claimed us all except one. Those were changing years from 1941 to 1944: the early war losses, then increasing confidence, struggle for rations, worry about loved ones, arrival of the Yanks, then it was time for me to go. So much happened in those years yet in reality it wasn't very significant. I was just growing up.

First Bill Charnley left for the 17/21st Lancers in 1941/42 and in 1943 Hughie Bell entered the Navy. In 1944 although in a Reserved Occupation I refused exemption and with the help of a Regular Army CSM I joined the Army on a regular engagement. My mother was never to know about this; she would not have been pleased. Bill C. served in North Africa, Italy and Greece and Hughie did a couple of runs to Murmansk, Russia. It's difficult to say why I was so keen to get into the war while so many tried to evade it and many succeeded. I should therefore accept the fact that from my family background I was born to be a soldier. My four years at Leyland Motors were good for me, especially the last two because with the help of Jimmy Duerden and obviously others, I, like most of my contemporaries, learned a lot about growing up and the strange thing was that girls did not figure very prominently during that period. I was extremely ill-informed owing to the fact that I lived with a very loving but over-protective mother, who certainly didn't spoil me, but neither did she talk to me as an emerging adult.

I was once put very much on the 'defensive' by the attractions of a sixteen-year-old girl from Leyland who worked in the office. We were both the same age and she had been 'going out' with a fellow apprentice older than I. Stories would be related about his 'successes' with her and I was not sure what all this meant. The girl was short in stature, with a nice figure and endowed with a large bosom, and when she walked through the shop men stopped work, cat-called and whistled and she loved it. The association ceased and much to my surprise she began to stop and talk to my boss and me and at his suggestion I made a date, my first. We agreed that we would meet at Hurst Grange, a small park in Penwortham, which meant that she had to cycle five miles from her home; in retrospect I thought this was rather forceful but amusing. We sat on the grass near some bushes while several children played some distance away but watching. For the next two hours or so till it began to get dark she teased me outrageously. I had my first feeling of the 'manly urge' unrequited, and this lasted the whole time, I was in agony and I didn't know what to do; it was no doubt being offered and I was clueless. We never dated again because she went back to her former boyfriend and within a few months she had become pregnant, left work, and married the lad. Was I innocent and didn't I have an escape!

The gang of boys and girls I associated with was a strange arrangement. The three girls had so-called boyfriends in the Forces. We all liked the girls a lot, so singly and sometimes in pairs we would ensure that the girls got home safely from the Club or Pictures. One would get a brief kiss or two and that was it, all very proper, and it certainly didn't appear to bring on terrible sexual frustrations. I think we enjoyed our all-male sessions in the back room of Bond's chip shop on Liverpool Road more than a preoccupation about the opposite sex. Fish and chips in preference, must be something in that.

Scots Guards 1944-46 Caterham-Pirbright-Wales

So in October 1944, as the original Virgin Soldier, dressed, as I had to be, in Home Guard battledress and greatcoat and wearing my father's old North Lancs regimental cap badge, I caught the train for London and the Guards barracks at Caterham leaving behind a very tearful mother. As I recall at that age I was not very emotional; my craving for adventure and a new life overcame the love I had for my mother. I had never been away from home before and to arrive in London, around rush hour, in the blackout, to find my way across wartime London for a train to East Croydon then on to Caterham was quite exciting and very mystifying. 'How do I get to Caterham Barracks please?' I asked a railwayman at Caterham, and he, looking at me with some pity, with a voice full of comfort and compassion said, 'See that bus, get on that and ask to be put off at the Barrack Gate, and . . . Good Luck, mate.' He knew more than I did of what was to come as did most of the local residents; they had heard tales and were somewhat sympathetic.

As I left the bus I stood for a moment to get used to the darkness. A faint glow indicated the entrance to the Guards Depot to my right. Facing me and running to my left was an enormous wall which protected the adjacent lunatic asylum. In later weeks I often wondered if I had entered the wrong gate. My first impression was that I had arrived at a dark and dismal seventeenth century prison, and my spirits sank. The depot entrance was of cold grey stone, depressing even in sunshine, thick and looking like castle battlements, I first saw a rigid greatcoated figure standing properly at ease with a fixed bayonet; he was as motionless as the sentry box behind him. I cautiously stepped between the gate posts and nervously looked around.

'Yes!' the word was uttered out of the darkness like a bullet from a rifle. I still couldn't see the author. A figure suddenly materialized in front of me, all cap and greatcoat with two stripes on his arm.

'Sure you've come in the right gate, lad?'

I didn't appreciate his humour; the asylum was the next gate along. I started to utter an explanation.

'Get in that door and stand to attention.'

I knocked on the door and a voice bade me enter; the warmth of the room was bliss. My rigid and ridiculous apology for a military figure at once became the object of attention from a sergeant of the Scots Guards who was seated behind a table.

'Come here, papers!'

I was obviously expected. One or two members of the Guard gazed at me with pity and curiosity; they had been here all of ten weeks, quite old soldiers.

'Runner!' screamed the Sergeant, and a figure hauled itself out of a near room.

'Reception room and get a move on!'

The figure was out of the door and disappearing in the darkness as with suitcase I ran after him, greatcoat flapping, arms flailing, heels digging into the tarmac. This recruit went off like a rocket and I had to run to keep up. As the darkness hid us from the Guardroom my escort slowed down, asked questions, whispered words of encouragement and kept up this ridiculous arm swinging. We arrived at the reception block having passed several other larger and grimmer looking edifices and I could hear a cacophony of voices coming from within in the darkness. It was all very off putting.

I was deposited into the tender hands of my first Trained Soldier, who is usually a person of many years service. He was joined by a corporal and we shared a supper of bread, jam and tea. I was shown a bed and made it ready for sleep only to be joined by two recruits to the Irish Guards, both from Liverpool and Borstal, with a sense of humour that was infectious. They were long haired and scruffy looking and full of amusing stories. My first night away from home was certainly not full of remorse and tears; on the contrary, I was tired and slept soundly. The early morning was shattered by bugles and I could hear the faint sounds of the bagpipes. The Depot suddenly sprang into action and the relative peace was rudely interrupted by shouts and screams; doors slammed and there was the sound of studs on concrete and lights could be seen through the blackout. This activity percolated from depot barracks to camp, from Grenadier to Mick; the production line of recruit training was beginning to wind up with immaculate efficiency.

We were instructed how to find the cookhouse, given a mug, knife, fork and spoon and stepped outside in the darkness. Bodies appeared to be everywhere but all heading in the same direction. Some were even being marched. We enjoyed a leisurely breakfast, whilst all around us recruits gobbled food voraciously and flew out of the door in five minutes flat. We left the cookhouse and it was becoming light. Two buckets stood outside the door, one for tea slops, the other for cleaning utensils; on the top of this latter was a slimy greasy scum and the water was getting cold. We were casually sauntering along the road when a figure with a long stick and a red sash confronted us. He was rather angry, and his verbal tirade lasted for about a minute. He heaped abuse on us: our appearance and casual attitude were not permitted in this establishment. He never repeated the same words twice and he was never lost for words to use. His final instruction was that we should crawl back into our holes and pointed to the reception room. Quick as a flash one of my Scouse companions said, 'If you hadn't stopped us we'd have been in by now.' This person with the stick had a flaming grenade in his cap and for a moment he was lost for words. He demanded and received the name and intended regiment my quick-witted companion intended to join and chased us into our temporary haven.

Later that day we were joined by Peter Moseley, a Londoner from Tooting also for the Scots Guards, and the following day by a Glaswegian named Brown who had also enjoyed the delights of Borstal; we were all regular soldiers. On the Friday we were escorted by the Trained Soldier to draw our kit, see the medical and dental officers and receive inoculations and vaccination, then came the highlight of the morning: just before lunch we were marched to the barber's shop. This small brick building was presided over by a rather large sergeant in the Grenadiers (surely they must have had the monopoly in this place) with two or three other assistants, and their production rate was first class, I don't think any recruit sat in the chairs longer than three minutes, maximum four.

'Who's first?' the sergeant enquired, to show he was not afraid of

Grenadiers and the man with the stick episode, our mouthy Scouse friend, swaggered over to the chair.

'Not too much off the sides and can you keep the back straight across,' he quipped, as he was rather proud of his thick, untidy Boston-style haircut.

The unsmiling sergeant's answer to this was to place the electric shears at the bottom of the victim's long side-boards and go up towards heaven keeping close to the skull. With his unoccupied left hand he grasped the boy's hair low at the back of the skull, brought it forward and over the forehead and with a deft movement with the shears just cleared a passage above the skull from front to rear. The expression on Scouse's face was one of incredible astonishment and personal horror, but he didn't utter another word. He was made to look more respectable but was he shorn, and he looked a different person – also somewhat younger. This rather chastened character sat and watched while the remainder of us were operated on, and when we returned to the reception room we all fell about laughing. Our torment however was only beginning. Incidentally, for his confrontation with the Grenadier sergeant, Scouse received three fatigues as soon as he joined his company, and weeks later when we were about to leave Caterham, Scouse and his friend had enjoyed Confined to Barracks, Extra Drills, Close Arrest and were thoroughly enjoying themselves. A sense of humour helped in a place like Caterham.

On the Friday Peter, Brown and I were taken to Roberts Block as part of 'K' Company. Peter and I chose adjacent beds in one room of twelve and Brown chose the other room. We were glad, he was a most obnoxious individual and somewhat of a bully. He and I had a confrontation after the second week and then he kept out of my way. He was never well liked. The other bed spaces were beginning to fill up with conscripts and all Scotsmen. We soon became friends apart from one lad named Black who was initially inclined to be podgy and sleek; he was well spoken and came from a good family background. For six weeks or so Black never directly spoke to Peter and me until the evening when we happened to be on our own in the barrack room when he confessed that before leaving home his parents, both Scottish Presbyterians, had told him he was going to enter an ungodly land inhabited by 'Sassenachs' who were not to be spoken to or associated with because they would taint him and he believed them. Unfortunately, out of twenty odd men in our Squad Peter and I, both Englishmen, were the only persons he admired because of our attitude to military life and because we were the most friendly and helpful. His unblinding faith in his parents was shattered.

Our beds consisted of three planks that rested on two low trestles. Our Trained Soldier who had about eighteen years service was an Englishman.

He showed us how to lay out, for pressing purposes, one best battledress, one suit of denims, one shirt, vest, pants, socks and one greatcoat. These items had to be watered nightly (did they grow?!) and slept on; no irons were available. In addition, the second best battledress had to be slept on for the daily drill parades; believe me, we even managed to sleep on this pile, mainly because we were always so dead tired.

Over that weekend we met our two chief 'gaffers'. First was our squad instructor, Sergeant Peter Bell, a tall, slim, sharp featured individual whose appearance can only be described as immaculate. His drill and instruction in general shared the same accolade. He was a man of few words but he drove us mercilessly in everything we did; we only really appreciated him when it was all over. It has always amazed me how successful the Brigade of Guards is when it chooses and retains its instructors at the Guards Depot and Sandhurst. Very few can ever be classified as failures as rubbish is discarded very quickly. Apart from the obvious attributes, an instructor needs to be a first class example as a guardsman and of his Regiment and this standard has to be ruthlessly maintained. Ideally he also needs to motivate and extract team spirit, ensure loyalty and impartiality, with strict discipline, verbosity and a healthy slice of wit and humour. Peter Bell had all of this.

Sergeant Joe Hughes was our superintendent sergeant. He also carried a long stick (pacestick) and wore a red sash. He had had a long war in Africa and Italy and as a prisoner of war so this job was somewhat of a 'doddle' to him. Joe was my RSM (regimental sergeant major) when I rejoined the Scots Guards 1st Battalion in 1956. He was later commissioned and I met him when Chris was attending officer selection at Westbury; his job was to supervise a given number of squads and keep them up to standard and suggest various forms of physical punishment if squads did not perform well.

Sergeant Hughes visited each room and threatened terrible violence if the room was not scrubbed out regularly and cleanliness maintained always. Sergeant Bell only spoke to the Trained Soldier, us he ignored. But he made up for this on Monday. Day one, we either ran or marched at terrifying speeds through Barracks, Camp or on the Square (known as Fox Square). We marched the speed and gait of my escort from the main Guardroom that memorable night six months before or was it only six nights? Those early days are so difficult to describe. The atmosphere was almost penal, Reveille was at 6.30a.m., first parade at 8.00a.m., and there was an average of five Drill, two PT and two Weapon Training periods each day plus other things spread out so that you were continually changing from battledress to denims to PT kit, all the time maintaining the cleanliness and neatness of your room and kit which was laid out on your bed in immaculate order and maintained throughout the day. Training ceased about 1645 hours and a mad dash was made to the Cookhouse for 5p.m. and tea. Following this the more subtle torture began; the room to be scrubbed out including ablutions and passages, all kit to be blancoed and polished having been used or not, items to be mended, boots to be spit and polished; although Army Orders stated dubbin should be used we just used polish. From just after 5p.m. to 9.30p.m. we were also harangued by either Sergeant or the Trained Soldier our Squad Office Officer about Regimental History. It was a very full day. Obviously it eased off slightly after a month but the pressure was still there as we found out later.

We always felt continually hungry. In the Cookhouse each table of twelve was personally supervised by a Trained Soldier who sat at the top. As you entered an NCO showed you where to sit and the bottom two men had to collect the food. The TS apportioned the food equally to each plate. Should there be an excess, because the TS was always conservative in his allocation, only the lucky ones sitting next to the TS received an increase. Oliver Twist had nothing on the plaintive cries of the bottom of the table unfortunates who frantically waved their plates towards the TS to no avail; they had to be satisfied with some fatty meat, two potatoes and a great heap of cabbage. The NAAFI and the Salvation Army made a bomb each night as every recruit was so hungry. I frequently dashed out at night, stuck a dozen halfpenny buns in my denim jacket, and ate the lot whilst finishing my polishing.

After the first month you began to feel the benefit of the constant hard training. You woke up after a deep dreamless sleep feeling full of abounding energy for the day's hard graft facing you. Our PT Instructor was a former Army heavyweight boxing champion and he did his best to kill us off but only managed to give us more muscle, an expanding chest, larger lungs and an enormous appetite. I never thought my body could take such punishment. After four weeks we passed off the Square in front of the Depot Adjutant, having proved that we dressed properly and cleanly, marched correctly, and were, importantly, able to salute officers. We were then told we could leave Barracks.

This however was not easy. First a recruit had to inform his TS that he wished to leave Barracks; if he approved he placed you on a list that was sent to the Guardroom by the first recruit to leave, which was following the TS's inspection of you before you arrived at the Guardroom. En route to the Guardroom hidden hazards lurked in the shape of NCOs, Drill Sergeants, CSMs and even the dreaded RSM whose quarter was near the Guardroom. On arrival at this holy building your chances of survival were halved. Those who survived the ravages of the initial inspection by the Sergeant dived gratefully for the safety of a passing bus to sample the delights of nearby Croydon, normally the YMCA for food, then the pictures, or a pint if money was available; some even tried a dance if they had the energy to dance, or the 'other'. The unfortunates who had incurred the wrath of the Sergeant or Corporal or Barrack Guard frequently spent all Saturday afternoon attempting to breach those insurmountable objects of terror who prowled the vicinity of the Guardroom. They were also gifted with second sight, they knew if you had been talking, not swinging your arms, laughing or looking around en route to the Guardroom. Even though they could only see for fifty yards, their perception was frightening. To some odd individuals the hurdle was too great and they never walked out; some make soldiers and others don't.

Every male group has its Lothario. Ours was called Jarvis. He had met this girl at a dance and had seen her several times, so just before Christmas Alec Campbell and I were introduced to the girl in Croydon and she asked the three of us to visit her house on Christmas Day. We accepted. Our Christmas dinner in Barracks was enormous and we were stuffed, but on our arrival at the girl's house some four hours later another dinner was waiting for us, our plates heaped with meat and vegetables. We ate it all but what a struggle. The family made us very welcome, and the girl's sister who was married to a Canadian serving in France seemed to pay a lot of attention to all of us young lads. She was very attractive and we were flattered. When it came to playing games, especially Postmans Knock, I frequently found myself waiting in the hallway with the married one who almost devoured me with her kisses. I was shocked by this unseemly and outrageous behaviour by a married woman especially as her husband was over in France. Alec also said that she behaved the same with him and he didn't think it was right but like me he enjoyed it all the same.

On a Wednesday night a fortnight later, Jarvis was told his girlfriend was at the gate and that he could take her and her companion to the NAAFI. Ten minutes later he was back again and asking for me: the married one was with her sister and wanted to see me, and I was eventually persuaded to go. Curiosity aroused the whole squad and singly or in groups they came to say hello and inspect the merchandise – they were all impressed. Taking her back to the Guardroom I was coerced to dally in one of the Drill Sheds (for wet weather) and I was never as close to being raped as that night. Only time and my reluctance to get involved with another man's wife prevented this; she smothered me and I didn't know what to do. She never came back, what a disappointment I must have been; she needed love and I wouldn't give it. I was the Virgin Soldier!

In the Squad I was left hand man of the front rank and next to me was what is known as a blank file, with only one person, not three, in the file. This character was a complete social misfit who spoke to no one but read the Bible in his spare moments, and he had difficulty marching in step. Peter Bell was patient but eventually I was ordered, on pain of being placed in Close Arrest, that I should not alter my step at any price and that I should kick this person round the ankles until he got into step or fell on the roadside or the square. He fell down, out, was thrown back in, but eventually he learnt. I didn't enjoy that. We were a smart squad and our inspection by the Second in Command was cancelled. Some thought it was because we were so good, but at nine weeks we were cock-a-hoop and our attitude became casual. At 8a.m. on the Saturday morning we had started to march off from the Block when Peter Bell halted us. He told us we had been warned about our attitude by several instructors so he would have none of this. In a space between a Barrack Block and some toilets, in total no more than 40 yards by 30 yards, he chased us at 180 paces to the minute and alternated this with rifle drill for $3^1/_2$ hours non stop. Most of them went through the motions. Peter and I, keen as mustard, kept it up, but even Peter began to tire near the end. We were dismissed without a word; I couldn't walk up the stairs to our room for five minutes: my legs had seized up and I was shattered. From Saturday lunchtime until Sunday teatime we continuously scrubbed out our rooms, and blancoed and polished all our kit until we were sick of it. On Monday afternoon on the tiny Roberts Square we were going through the normal five minute 'chasing' to warm us up, when that small percentage just gave up so the 'chasing' continued. Then one man fainted. We began to march over him and were halted. 'Do not alter your step, march on then,' came the order. Off we went again, down went another casualty, 'Halt!' and a member of the Squad was doubled away under close arrest for stepping over the body. A few minutes later another body was despatched to the 'jail'. The parade then ended and the casualties carted off to the doctor. By the evening the 'missing' men had returned healthy and unharmed and the lesson had been learned the hard way. We were their ideal recruits and did well to the time we left.

Our Weapons Training Instructor was Sergeant Golightly, a huge man who loved weapons and his job, which included Bayonet Fighting, Gas, and First Aid. A rifle looked like a toy in his hands and he was an expert shot. This was also something that I enjoyed and I won the Guards Depot Empire Medal for .22 shooting at recruit level, Sgt. G liked me for this; however at Bayonet Fighting everyone suffered and he literally drove us into the ground on the soggy, churned up Bayonet Field. One or two lads actually cried as they sank to their knees in the mud. One lad whose name I forget actually turned on Golightly with his bayonet and charged the few yards to him. In a flash Golightly had the rifle off him and he was sat in the mud, tears rolling down his face. He was never even charged. On the Square, in the Gym or back on the Bayonet Field if you did not make the effort and do your best the tormentors with stripes on their arms could very easily reduce you to tears, to the verge of collapse, or stick you in 'jail'. The latter was to be avoided. Punishment on top of punishment could result in 'Back Squadding' which meant an ever longer stay in that hell hole called Caterham.

When we had passed out and Recruit Training was completed our attitudes changed, Caterham had been rough but fun. We even talked to our Instructors who were actually human and we thought they were the best in the Depot. It was an experience most people could well do without, but boy, were we proud that we had actually achieved it. We were now bound for the Scots Guards Training Battalion at Pirbright, Surrey, where it was tough, interesting and a different atmosphere.

Before leaving Caterham we had the unfortunate position to be in the middle of the route of the V1 bombs that Hitler released by the hundreds and directed to London. Guardsman would not panic, no evasive action should be taken until the V1 engine actually stopped, and then under orders would you be allowed to run like hell. It was a weird feeling when you couldn't watch but you could hear them almost continuously overhead some days. As the train carried us into deepest Surrey it hardly seemed as if it was only fourteen weeks since I had arrived at those Barrack Gates, a callow youth, not very fit, and here I was a Guardsman, chest bulging, fit as a fiddle and looking every inch a soldier. My Dad would have been pleased in certain respects! I made my sad goodbyes to Peter Bell, he'd done a good job, and after a few hours at Pirbright seven days leave.

On return, training commenced in earnest, the pace never slackened but somehow life was easier. Drill was infrequent, Weapon Training and Field craft more interesting and continuous, and PT was extremely tough, nearly always outdoors irrespective of the weather. We had an Assault Course about a mile long and there was none in the Army to beat it; it's quite good these days too. Then calamity, I went sick with severe 'flu which turned to congestion of the lungs and it was six weeks before I could recommence training. I struggled to attain my previous fitness and the PT tests had me gasping, especially the two-mile run in full kit which had to be completed in ten minutes. I was literally on the seconds. Yet in the twenty-five mile march, the last five miles being done mainly on the double, I did fine, surprising myself. I carried the Bren gun initially for five miles then damn me it came back to me for the last two miles. On arrival back at Pirbright you attempted to cross the canal over a very sagging rope; invariably the majority fell in and had to do it again. Then the full length of the Assault Course was attempted. This course was probably the largest and the best in wartime England and it was hard when we used to play on it in our own time, but following a long and forced march it was rough and the training NCO and PT staff were tormenting animals if you failed an obstacle. By this time no one wanted to fail. As you came off the course muddy, wet and sweaty, you were given ten rounds to fire; failure to obtain a satisfactory score resulted in another stretch of the course. Now on completion of all this the bedraggled warriors were marched down to the square, given a couple of minutes 'chasing' to loosen the muscles (which was always expected), and then our drill had to be immaculate. It was amazing, everyone reacted in a predictable manner; we wanted to prove we could do it and we certainly didn't want to spend any longer time on the square. It was during this time at Pirbright that I volunteered for the Guards SAS Unit that was due to be formed for service in the Far East, but this of course never materialized owing to the dropping of the atomic bombs on Japan.

The eight weeks at Pirbright were followed by a fortnight at the Scots Guards own Battle School in North Wales at a place called Llandurog on the north side of a former coastal command airfield. The small collection of Nissen huts was situated along the sand dunes across from the coast of Anglesey. The staff at the school, a mixture of officers and NCO instructors and some administrative personnel, were commanded by a Major Bland MC. There was also a Demonstration Platoon of about forty men who daily showed the trainees how particular field training or tactics should be carried out. Live ammunition was used at all times and safety regulations were not always adhered to by this Platoon, although the trainees were not allowed to get carried away. Once again if you didn't do it right first time you would do it again with blanks and then again with live ammunition. The weather or terrain was usually diabolical, so believe me, at the end of a fortnight the trainees were extremely fit. The last couple of days were without sleep; you did a hike across Snowdon fully laden with ammunition, mortar bombs and food, then after a night dig-in the trainees were given a taste of battlefield conditions. Three-inch, two-inch mortars dropped high explosive close by and Bren and a Vickers machine gun poured thousands of live rounds on fixed lines as close to the top of the trenches as possible. Patrols were sent out and patrols attacked. It was non stop and at the end you felt that the Regiment had done as much as possible in just less than six months to prepare a Guardsman for combat. On our return to Pirbright, the following fortnight dealt with Patrols, mainly Night Patrols, and preparation for departure to the Battalion to which you had been posted.

I never returned to Pirbright with the squad; I shall never know why. I was told to take a week's leave and return to Wales as my presence was required as a member of the Demo Platoon. The war in Germany had ended, the SAS job was in the balance, I was barely $18^1/2$ years of age, and was a Marksman with all weapons, so I had mixed feelings about my future as a soldier brave. After all what had I joined for? – only to satisfy my craving for active service: ah, the innocence of youth!

Those months in Wales were tough but instructive. I learned a lot about the Army and myself. I thought I was physically fit until at the end of one demonstration when we had to climb into the 'enemy' position under close live fire, then run up the steep side of a mountain because the position was then hit with live mortar shells. I can remember Jimmy Love, my Section Commander, hitting me with his Sten gun to force my aching legs up that mountain to escape the shrapnel and the fins. I soon became used to running and climbing over various mountains in North Wales. Our officer used to climb a mountain just for fun after a Demonstration or march us fifteen miles or so back to camp just to keep us in trim and march us into the freezing sea if the Demo had not been up to scratch. Several other things happened to me as well: I was promoted, and saw my bedmate accidentally shoot himself and die the following day. This was followed by another tragedy, this time with explosives when Sergeant Frazer was killed, Lt. Bevan was injured and lost a leg, and others suffered minor injuries. I don't think an explanation for the tragedy was ever discussed.

I was so confident in my use of guns that when I had to fire for effect on my own colleagues either running or lying down I could fire within inches of them. This ensured reality. It had happened to me and I was capable of copying the best. I also volunteered to blow up the unexploded bombs that occasionally occurred after a demonstration. The dodgy part was finding them, which the lads didn't like doing. I quickly learned to be cool and calm when dealing with explosives. In my shooting or with the demolition kit I was never reckless; I don't think I could have borne the guilt had I killed or injured a comrade.

In one particular demonstration on South Snowdon called 'Japanese Bunker' it was my job to crawl under fire through a mud patch full of barbed wire and place a 'Bangalore Torpedo'. I made it up myself out of two mortar or PIAT cases, packed with AMATOL (High Explosive). At the same time three Bren guns and a Fire Section at 50 yards range covered my movement. Ricochets flew everywhere. I would then ignite the fuse, do an extremely quick backward crawl for ten yards, and cover my ears for the explosion followed by the surge of bodies as they leapt over my prostrate body in the mud. It looked tremendously spectacular but the Instructors from the Commando Training School at Llanberis were horrified when they watched it, totally disregarding all War Office Safety Regulations. They were convinced we were mad.

The Platoon Commander for most of my time in Wales was Lt. John Ramsey. About 6 feet 5 inches tall, he was extremely fit and every inch a gentleman. He was related to our present Queen, although like me he was a Roman Catholic. We always went to Mass together. He later was an outstanding Company Commander with the 2nd Battalion in Malaya from 1948-51. I saw him at the presentation of Colours ceremony in Edinburgh in 1951 and when I saw him next in 1968 he was a priest at St Cuthbert's Church in Edinburgh. I wonder if he ever made Bishop.

So another important period of my life closed down when it was decided that the type of harsh training that was carried out in Wales was not really necessary for peace time soldiering. The use of live ammunition had to be curtailed, and as a Platoon we wrongly thought that we were a class apart, being so far away from normal Regimental life. So in small parties the Platoon was broken up and posted far and wide.

Jimmy Love and I were the last two members to leave. He and I spent a happy few days with Jimmy's girl friend and her parents who owned the Albert Inn in Caernarvon before we took our deserter back to Pirbright. Pen-y-groes is a small Snowdonian village built on a crossroads and we were always greeted fondly when we passed through in our transport. A Scotsman was the licensee of a pub on the crossroads and we would call in for drinks when we did night patrols. In our few days leave, Jim and I were asked to play in a vital cup match for the village against nearby rivals. Our friend in the pub as a farewell gesture must have given us nearly half a bottle of Scotch apiece during our lunchtime 'session'. The first half was an unmitigated disaster for both of us, balls and players were coming at us in 'threes', most people knew where we had been and were somewhat amused but worried. However in the second half we tore the opposition to bits; we were both superbly fit and almost won the game ourselves. Jim eventually married his Carrie, and is a builder in Bangor with a lovely family. I last saw him in 1983 and we had a wonderful time remembering the times and friends from that period of our lives.

So ended my time in Wales and the return to the Guards Training Battalion in Surrey.

CHAPTER 2

Palestine

When Z1 Company was finally disbanded we returned to the Guards Training Battalion at Pirbright as men branded 'wild', 'savages', 'animals'. We then wondered about our next posting. I became a Courier carrying classified mail from Pirbright to certain Military HQs in London and return. It was a cushy number and I had finished by lunchtime. Travelling around Central London in wartime on a bicycle was easy. I wouldn't like to do it now.

At Pirbright I met up again with a Preston lad I had met several times on leave, Cliff Hickson, a tall, thick set lad who had been serving time with the 2nd Battalion in Germany. He was a very pleasant 'nutter'. He explained to me that he had applied to join the Palestine Police but had failed the interview. When asked his reasons for wishing to join the police his answer was 'to kill Jews'; he had obviously been refused. The advertisements for this Colonial Police Force, that I had not seen before, stated that you received £20.0s.0d. per month 'all found', a princely sum at that time, an interesting job in the sun, swimming, boats, camels etc; it looked like the answer to my prayers. My application for the Guards SAS (Special Air Service) Regiment that was being formed for service in the Far East had been held in obeyance when the war in Europe ended, and hostilities in that area could soon end. This of course happened, so I opted to join the Palestine Police.

Following a successful interview at Crown Agents in Millbank I was hurried off to Harley Street for a medical and by June I had been discharged on special reserve, had leave and was on board the *Arundel Castle* at Southampton. The vessel had been a wartime troopship and the 2nd Class compartment was still below the standard of peacetime. The dining area consisted of long tables and forms but we had small cabins accommodating eight persons. The ship was bound for Singapore and carried as 1st Class passengers former planters, colonial officials and so on, and the wives and families of some of the individuals who had been prisoners of war, or wives about to join husbands for the first time in both the Middle and the Far East. The Palestine Police contingent was made up of recruits and a large number who had been on their first UK leave. There were a few shipboard romances, as I recall, and several tearful farewells at Port Said when we left the ship. Apart from the first night and day at sea the voyage was perfect. The food was fantastic, considering what we had had to suffer during the war. I couldn't face kippers for breakfast that first morning in the Bay of Biscay but after that it was a gentle Mediterranean cruise and it helped to acclimatize the recruits.

The journey from Port Said to Kantara and then to Gaza was stifling and very uncomfortable, but from Gaza to Haifa it was a little more bearable. We entered Haifa railway station in the late evening and had our first real 'smell' of the Middle East. We climbed into 3-tonners for the journey to Jenin, where our basic training would begin. The contrast we discovered on that first ride along the lower road in Haifa, that I was later to know so well, was so typical of the country. The new buildings full of well lit shops and bars with European people in evidence changed rapidly as we entered eastern Haifa where all the passers by were Arabs. The buildings appeared drab, a hotch potch of odd designs, ill lit, mysterious, with a resident aroma particular only to Arab communities. A feeling of excitement and apprehension crept over me. I was here and it was all about to happen, it took time but it certainly did.

The Mandate for governing Palestine was under fire and the authorities and police so soon after the war ended were confronted by a terrorist situation instigated in various ways by three organizations whose aims included the establishment of a Jewish homeland in Palestine and unrestricted immigration amongst other issues.

Haganah (The Hebrew word for Defence): This organization was founded in 1920 and it immediately superseded all other Jewish organizations formed to protect settlers against attacks by Arabs. It was active in the riots of 1929, which were followed by seven years of comparative calm, but when the Arabs objected and began armed insurgency, the Mandatory Government authorised the formation of a quasi military Jewish force called the Supernumerary Police under the Command of the Palestine Police. Several thousand Haganah members volunteered for the force, which was legal, officially trained and issued with arms, but in reality took its orders from the Haganah. This organization was declared illegal and yet was trained and helped by Capt. Orde Wingate of Chindit fame to form small Commando Units or Night Squads as they were known, in order to show aggression to the belligerent Arabs. Among the original members were Yitshak Rabin, the late Moshe Dyan, and Yigal Allon. Dyan of course later became famous as an Israeli military and government leader. In 1939

when the Arabs had been subdued the British became concerned about the
real existence of an organized military force operating under the direction
of the Jewish Agency. The British arrested and jailed personnel when
training was located, but it could not be controlled.

During the 1939-45 war a truce was made and Haganah members
actively assisted the British in Lebanon and Syria and certain individuals
parachuted in Europe and the Balkans. It was estimated that by 1945 the
strength of the Haganah was approximately 40,000, and they were reported
to have hidden some 10,000 rifles, 4,000 revolvers, 500 SMGs and 125
LMGs.

Menachen Begin admits that the Haganah 'joined' the 1ZL in the
struggle against the British, and that can be interpreted in its widest sense
in respect of terrorism. So they were not virgin white.

Haganah Palmach (Plugot Machatz or Shock Platoons): In 1941 after the
operations by the Haganah in Lebanon and Syria the two units involved
under command of Dyan and Allon became the nucleus of a new striking
force financed by the British through the Jewish Agency. It was known as
Palmach. Permanently mobilised, it was trained for a while by the British
when commanded by Yitzhak Sadeh. When the British refused to sponsor
Palmach they trained themselves to a very high degree with great emphasis
on sabotage. They operated against the British after the war, concentrating
on the entry of illegal immigrants and it spearheaded Jewish military action
in 1948.

The Palmach was a Kibbutz army. Few of its members came from towns
or cities. Those in charge had political leanings to the extreme left and this
was the subject of great strife with the Jewish Agency and the Haganah of
which it was an integral part, but this never appeared to cause any breach
of discipline, although even after independence the members still wished
to remain a separate military entity (a Corps d'Elite). Personally there
appeared to be very little difference in the aims and objectives of either the
Palmach or the 1ZL, especially in respect of the Left Wing inclinations.
Ben Gurion eventually disbanded them to prevent further discourse, and
this displeased the Left Wing Labour circles under whose auspices the
Palmach had functioned. It was estimated that in 1945 Palmach strength
was approximately 1600; by 1948 I would think it would be nearer 4,000
and well trained.

Irgun Tzvai Levmi (National Military Organization): In addition to the
Haganah (and the Palmach) there were two other Jewish underground
bodies which opposed British Policy in Palestine and both were offshoots

of the New Zionist (or Revisionist) Organization that was founded before the war by Zeer Jabotinsky. It was his form of protest because the orthodox Zionists hesitated in defining their aims in the establishment of a Jewish State.

Jabotinsky fought for the British in World War I and by all reports was a flamboyant character. He was imprisoned by the British in 1920 for organizing Jewish self defence in Jerusalem against Arab rioters. In the thirties Jabotinsky was extremely vocal in his call for European Jews to emigrate to Palestine and his organization's military arm, the Irgun Tzvai Levmi, was prepared to use force to achieve that goal.

During the 1939-45 war, action against the British was suspended and their Commander David Raziel was killed in 1941 while on a mission for the British near Habbaniya in Iraq.

In 1945, under its new leader Menachen Begin, the Irgun maintained its political objectives as the recreation of a Jewish State within its historical boundaries on both sides of the River Jordan. (Begin maintained these objectives even in 1981 hence the problem of the West Bank.) The Haganah carried out an investigation on this organization in 1944 on behalf of the Palestine Police; its powers affected many people. At the end of the war they re-commenced their terror campaign against the British and were successful, mainly because as any urban guerilla organization they had local support either from fear, intimidation or sympathy and the element of audacity and surprise of hit and run raids or assassinations. They had many brave and dedicated soldiers.

Even in June/July 1948 after official Partition, when internally the Arabs presented no threat, the Stern Gang and 1ZL were not suggestive to Israeli discipline. The Irgun brought in the *Atalena* at Kfar Vitkin, 23 miles north of Tel Aviv against the terms of the United Nations. The ship was loaded with arms and ammunition for the Irgun (not yet disbanded) and this was despite a mutual agreement between Jews and Arabs to suspend importation of arms. The Irgun were asked by official forces, now the Israeli Army, to cease unloading but they refused and killed two members of the official forces before honourable terms were agreed.

Stern Gang (FF1): In 1939 some members of Irgun completely rejected any form of co-operation and help to the British, and formed a new group which they called Lohmei Herut Israel (Fighters for the Freedom of Israel) or LEHI. This group was known to the Palestine Police as the Stern Gang and was originally led by Avraham Stern who was killed by members of the Palestine Police in 1942 when evading arrest. To his ardent supporters he became a martyr and a myth.

Lehi's members were extremists whose ideals ranged in outlook from orthodox religion to pro-Communism and my personal view is mainly to the latter. They were vicious and without feeling to anyone opposing their views even Jews. Moshe Dayan, although he did not agree with their policies, was the person who intervened at one stage and made contact with them, because he considered Lehi members to be daring and courageous fighters, whose talents and energies could have been directed to better and more effective duties for Israel if only joint action could be achieved. In my humble opinion there was more knowledge about and co-operation between the Jewish Agency and these organizations than has ever been admitted.

Although they probably maintained a certain independence to perform their terrorist activities they could have been arrested or eliminated if the Jewish Agency had co-operated with the Police.

We were a mixed crowd in our intake, about twenty in all. All of us had travelled out on the *Arundel Castle* so we were not complete strangers to each other. I think without exception we were all ex-Servicemen, but no RAF. The accommodation was basic for training squads of approximately twenty men: huts, ablutions, dining hall, a Square and a 'Spinney's' Club. Spinney, whoever he was, seemed to have the franchise for all English Clubs and bars in the Middle East, quite a businessman.

There was the usual collection of senior officers in the Police Depot and the lower ranks were supervised by a Head Constable (a new rank to me), somewhat equivalent to a Regimental Sergeant Major. Basic Police Law was taught by inspectors; their Bible was known as the Criminal Code Ordinance. Based on normal British Law it was simplified for easier application and supplemented by Acts passed by Government and the British High Commission. Drill, Weapons Training etc. was taught by sergeants (all fairly recent arrivals). In fact the Law was the only new thing for the majority of us, and we only struggled through this in the afternoons when it was very hard to keep awake and interested. Jenin lies midway between Haifa and Nablus and is also fairly close to Nazareth and the Sea of Galilee. The Depot was adjacent to the Jenin Taggart (a Police fort), approximately half a mile from the town of Jenin.

Taggarts had been built throughout Palestine, varying in size dependant on geographical location and function. The buildings were strategically sited and were a symbol of Colonial authority. During our time at Jenin most of us found time to visit the nearby places of interest but time was short. We swam in Galilee, visited the Ruins of Capurnaum, ate in Tiberias and drank alongside the shrine at Nazareth. I recall the very tiny Catholic

Chapel in Jenin which only measured approximately eighteen by fourteen feet; the total congregation (excepting policemen) was probably not more than twenty. I found this strange considering it was basically a total Moslem community in the Jenin area.

Training over, we anxiously awaited our postings. Palestine was administratively controlled at local level by six District Commissioners. The Police also had six identical Police Districts: Jerusalem, Haifa, Jaffa, Gaza, Samaria and Galilee; these Districts were commanded by a Superintendent. The Districts were sub-divided into Urban and Rural areas each commanded by a DSP (Deputy Superintendent of Police). Each area had its own stores and administrative back-up. District workshops controlled the vehicle maintenance and repairs when local stations could not cope.

Six of us were posted to Haifa District, two of us to Rural. My station was Athlit, the first of three stations along the main Haifa–Tel Aviv/Jaffa Road, approximately ten miles south of Haifa. It was sited adjacent to the main road and was about two miles from the main railway line and Mediterranean Coast. At this point on either side of the main road was a quarry and prison camp. Between the police station and the village of Athlit, through which the railway line ran, was situated the Illegal Immigrant Camp for Jewish refugees. The Royal Ulster Rifles guarded this camp, followed later by the Irish Guards. When illegal immigrants were seized they were initially transported to camps in Cyprus, then by regulated quota to Athlit and then released in the care of the Jewish Agency for rehabilitation.

There were about three small Jewish villages within our station jurisdiction, and their population farmed the strip of land between the coastal road and the sea, a fertile area stretching from the police station to our boundary with Zichron Yarkov police area, our neighbours further south. The existing station personnel were as follows: Norman Carswell, Station Officer; he had his wife on station but we saw little of her. He himself was a pleasant bloke, a little inclined to be too serious, but on the occasions he joined the boys he was good company. Vic Duckett, Station Sergeant, was a mountain of a man, ex Coldstreamer, former bodyguard to the Mayor of Jaffa, and an excellent shot. Like Carswell, a good policeman with the right attitude for the job, they had both completed eleven or twelve years of service. 'Basher' Bates, the Mounted Constable, ex Hussars, was an excellent horseman of the old school. Joe Keeton, Garage Foreman, was another large man, excellent at his job with a nice sense of humour. Paddy Malone, Driver, had his wife on station, was very aggressive in drink. The wireless operator, whose name I can't remember, was ex RAF, a nice chap but not the social type. Jack Sowden, Investigations Branch, was

Wadi Rushmiya, Haifa, taken from the 'White House'. Known to HOP as 'Death Valley'.

a very lean ex soldier, good chap for a Yorkshireman, and there was Ernie Barlow, another ex soldier 'tyke' who left us to join the man Farran (a wartime SAS hero) and his 'G' Squad?! Finally there was Don (Danny) Peil, who today remains a close friend, a Cumbrian of high humour and competency. Don and I forged a friendship then that lasted during our days in Palestine, continued for four years till 1952, and resumed on my return to Lancashire in 1973: a wonderful person to have around.

With Inspector Soubbi Toukan and Cpl. Rashid, who had their families on station, plus about a dozen mounted and uniformed Arab constables, that was Athlit Police Station. In addition we had a military searchlight crew from the Royal Artillery; during the hours of darkness at odd but frequent intervals they swept the surrounding countryside for signs of terrorist movement. We were a station thought likely to suffer an attack. The crew and their duties helped to keep our temporary constables awake and alert on guard duty which was some comfort. The sergeant in charge came from Preston and had been a shop assistant at Linguard's, the well known gents outfitters in Fishergate.

I was introduced to the area by night and day patrols on foot and mobile. My police training was continued by the weekly visits of a training inspector and also language training in Arabic. We were helped enormously by the Arab policemen who understood some English. I learned a lot but I was never a linguist, though Don and Jack Sowden were very good.

Life until early December 1946 was fairly routine with some thefts and housebreakings, frequent injurious assaults by firearms or sharp instruments, and a murder of wife by husband. This crime and most of the assaults occurred in Tireh, the largest Arab village in Palestine and the most troublesome. They hated the Jews intensely and on principle; the British they tolerated, having a certain respect for the British as individuals but very little for their Laws and restrictions. They spirited away a Churchill tank out of 3 Base Workshop (Reme) during the final stages, and the army would not take the risk to get it back; there would have been one hell of a battle.

I had volunteered for a wireless operator's course at Jenin, in preparation for the arrival of new patrol cars (civilian type) as a supplement to the GMC armoured cars used throughout the country in the larger urban areas. The fortnight's course was interesting but it was something of a dream idea; soft skinned vehicles in the current situation were not going to solve the police and military problem that subsequently occurred. I successfully completed the course and shortly after I arrived back, District asked for two volunteers to attend a Bomb Disposal Course in Jerusalem. I don't know how many fools applied but I was one of the Twelve Apostles that found themselves rather hurriedly in Jerusalem. For our tutor we had a highly experienced Sapper Major. His opening words to the twelve of us as we sat in the classroom in the Police Depot at Mount Scopus were as follows:

'Gentlemen. I have seen Bomb Disposal service in France, the African campaign, Sicily, Italy, France and Germany and now here. I am wise and experienced, but here I haven't a bloody clue.'

It was like a sentence of death; what the hell had we done to ourselves? In a lighter vein he told us not to worry, he would teach us the basics, and if we were ever confronted in the future by a device that we were unhappy about, we should leave it *in situ* and blow it. Very much the easy way out in those days. He went on to explain that the majority of the bomb makers had learned their craft in Eastern Europe, mainly in the Jewish ghettoes of Warsaw etc., where they had the absolute minimum of materials, and no two devices were the same. The means of ignition varied from the crude to the ingenious; tin cans, buckets, parcels. We covered the standard methods and he told us of some of the devices he had managed to disarm and others he had studied and blown. If we learned one thing it was a very healthy respect for the ingenuity of our adversary. With due respect to our teacher in the time available, we left Jerusalem with a lot of facts, sparsely trained and very apprehensive. I was due to face the reality of the bomb disposal man far sooner than I ever anticipated.

I arrived back in Athlit after lunch to be told I was Station Security Officer that night, a duty performed only by the British Constables approximately every ten days. It necessitated remaining fully dressed in the recreation room and visiting the sentries periodically during the night. After the evening meal we decided to have a social evening. The party that had gone down to the post office at Athlit for the daily mail run brought back some beer so we all settled down to play darts or cards and have a pleasant evening. Vic Duckett was a former *News of the World* darts finalist and all sorts of tricks were tried to beat this excellent darts player. It was also the first time I was introduced to that well known drink called arak, similar to Pernod. A plain looking liquid like water, it had a strong aniseed flavour and it turned a milky white when water was added. It was also very potent. The finest arak was produced in a monastery in the Lebanon called something like Zachlouwi. Don and I sampled this stuff much later at Haifa Police HQ, what a disaster.

At about 1130 the party broke up. I visited the sentries and then reclined in a chair. Shortly after midnight the Arab constable on duty at the Station desk knocked and burst in the room shouting, 'Mr Howard there's a bomb at the JLC [Jail Labour Camp].' From what I could gather the telephone message from the JLC had said that the bomb had been thrown from a passing truck and was now lying just off the road near the perimeter wire. This seemed to be odd behaviour to plant a bomb, but all the prisoners were Arabs and it could be attempted murder or a prison break, who knows.

I ran upstairs and told Carswell, seized my official equipment (a long rope!), my tommy gun and magazines and headed in the darkness for the JLC. I didn't realize until I started running just how much I was 'under the influence'; we had consumed a fair amount, and my progress was certainly not in a straight line. I passed the prison sentries crouching down behind their sandbags and suddenly there it was. I came to a halt some twenty yards away and I was suddenly stone cold sober. In the poor light of the perimeter illumination, lying on the edge of the tarmac road was a metal container measuring approximately 21ins. x 15ins. x 10ins. I looked around in desperation for someone who could give me some indication of the circumstances, but despite shouts I was on my own. To be honest, I needed the sound of another English voice.

I placed the gun, ammo and rope on the roadside and with the help of a torch of weak illumination I inspected the object. It was made of steel and resembled an ammunition box, it had no obvious identification marks and the lid remained in position held by two metal clips; it was all very odd. Then salvation: from the direction of Tel Aviv came the sound of a fast moving vehicle, probably military as there were restrictions on civilian vehicle movement at night. I managed to stop the vehicle, a Para jeep containing four soldiers, and explained that I had a suspect bomb in the road; could they help by giving me some light from their headlamps. With the speed of light the vehicle was in reverse and on its way back towards Tel Aviv, leaving me open-mouthed and rather disillusioned about 'Les braves Paras'. My only solution, arrived at later, was that the four blokes were on a joy ride, and wanted no involvement.

My problem was still on the road. I took a chance and in the dark I placed it in an upright position, checked for exterior wires, unclipped the lid and opened it gently, checking for further wires and hoping there was no pressure switch. Nothing went bang. Now for the contents, which turned out to be twenty-seven East European hand grenades in 3 x 9 pack containers. Dry mouthed and sweating slightly from the problem of extracting the three containers from the box in the dark, I sat on the roadside and waited, thanking God for my deliverance in alcoholic remorse. We later ascertained that the box had fallen or been thrown from a small pickup truck when it took the bend in the road. The four occupants slowed down the truck then accelerated despite calls to stop; the answer was obvious: they were terrorists and what a chance they were taking carrying that stuff with restrictions in force on a civilian vehicles after dark.

Christmas came and went and was enjoyable in a Colonial fashion. An attack of dysentery also came and went, thankfully. I think I spent about forty-eight hours fastened to the toilet seat; it took days for the marks to leave my backside, certainly an experience.

By early 1947 personnel had changed drastically: Ernie Barlow left to join G Squad; Bates left for home being replaced by a young chap called Hallows; Joe Keeton left on leave and was replaced. I became the owner of a wire haired terrier called Peter, who was the son of Gyp, Duckett's bitch, and we also had two new constables. Both were escapers from military service, one a metallurgist aged twenty-one years, a really obnoxious individual; the other was a very well educated, immature, eighteen-year-old, the direct descendant of a famous author. I think enough said; they were impossible.

Hallows gave me my first introduction to horse riding which I enjoyed. There was a spare horse in the stable which had belonged to a B/Sgt who was on leave so it badly needed exercise and attention. My experiences on patrol in the hills, and when we took all the horses bareback to the beach at Athlit for a swim were really quite funny, but too long to describe. I think I could have made a 'cowboy'; I enjoyed it.

Lots of other things happening too around that time, including Duckett and Keeton's excursion into 'big business': the flogging of army marquees to Arab tribesmen. These tents, due for destruction when a military unit left, were dumped at the station for disposal. The subsequent hilarious nights out at the Eldorado night club in Hadar Hacamel with D and K, 'Cleopatra' and her dances, and our efforts to see the rehearsals. The Howard/Duckett episodes at Zichron Yakhov with the aggressive Jewish nocturnal wanderer and the Sunday shooting competition with either police teams and the Paras at Bat Galim and many other incidents were all very amusing. Incidentally, we worked in between.

Then back we went to the Police School in Jerusalem for the full Police course. I suppose I was fortunate as the course was the first for some time owing to the emergency and to be chosen was probably an indication that my seniors were looking to my future. I enjoyed the course which consisted of Law, Drill, Weapon Training, First Aid and PT. I could concentrate on the Law as all the other subjects were second nature to me, so I did rather well. When the general situation became tense the course was divided and placed on alternate 24-hour standby and we did several interesting operations (Cordon and Searches), including one at Mea Shearim Quarter with the Argylls, and one with the Irish Guards at Gival Shaul near Jerusalem on the Tel Aviv Road. These two particular jobs were only partially successful but the organization was first class and I was very impressed. The only amusing incident was at Mea Shearim, where Sgt. McDonald, (Ex Scots Guards, our PT, Unarmed Combat and Pistol Instructor), and I were allocated a particular building to search. We roused the occupant of the small flat, a female, who eventually opened the door to us. Considering the length of time she took coming to the door, she was either a very heavy sleeper or something was amiss. The door opened and there she stood, a plump but very attractive Jewess in her early twenties, the cotton robe she wore revealing that it was the only thing she had on. When questioned by McD. in Hebrew and English, her attitude changed from being provocative to being very obstructive and belligerent; our cat had claws. When I started the actual search she then made a veiled offer of sex to McDonald; her reasons were obvious. I found a couple of rounds of ammo, some military uniform, and military identification papers. When told to get dressed for further questioning, she acted as if she was participating in a Whitehall farce. We couldn't leave her alone and it was a small bedroom. I felt embarrassed at the start, Mac was unperturbed, the girl's English improved at once and her hidden comic ability came to the fore. It was very funny. I often wondered what happened to that girl.

Mac's choice of me for a partner stemmed from an unarmed combat incident in training in the early stages. Picking on me as an ex Jock I had to pinion his arms to his sides from behind, emphasizing 'in deadly earnest'. For him everything went wrong. He was threshing around in my arms unable to perform, then he got mad. We fell to the ground with the Squad silently surrounding us from prying official eyes. Due to a kick or a grasp at some extremity, we broke, with him on top going for my throat. I went for the eyes and applied the scissors. While he still could breathe he gasped if I'd had enough he most certainly had. I agreed and released him, he took it well and we all had a good laugh. The lads were good; they did not tarnish Mac's excellent record by derogatory remarks and what could have been a nasty incident enhanced both our reputations in different ways.

One frightening experience occurred when Taffy Maynard and I went to a cinema one night in Jaffa Road. At the end of the show we decided to have a walk around before returning to Mount Scopus. We were both armed and with the late evening crowd we strolled up Jaffa Road and turned left into King George V Avenue. Immediately on the left was a basement café/bar that had had two grenades thrown in by terrorists resulting in a couple of dozen Argylls being killed and injured. The avenue was a broad thoroughfare with lots of shops and cafés with a fair number of people about. We hadn't walked fifty yards along the avenue when like magic the whole of our side of the pavement was miraculously clear of people. I didn't fluff for a few moments, then we paused for a second. I looked back: not a soul within a hundred yards. Across the road some people in cafés and on the pavement gave us undue attention. It looked as if we had been set up; street assassination of policemen was not unusual. The feeling was terrible. It was obvious from our attitude, the pause and glances around, hands grasping pistols under coats, that we were alert. Inwardly our legs and feet were of lead, that feeling up and down your spine (not romantic), and a sickening feeling in our stomach stayed with us as we painfully walked to the junction with Ben Yehuda Street. Nothing happened, no cars passed, no footsteps hurried behind us, no bullets, no grenades. We could see that Ben Yehuda Street appeared normal and instinctively both of us turned round. King George V Avenue at a distance behind us was back to normal. We turned into Ben Yehuda Street, not the safest of thoroughfares. Some time later two British policemen were shot there in the back of the head, in crowded conditions, and died quietly, without help, their bodies abused. Hurriedly we reached Jaffa Road and in a safer area, got a taxi to Scopus and bed. A rather frightening incident. The course over, we all returned to our respective stations, in my case to crash my Arabic for the colloquial examination and my Police Law for the promotion examinations. I passed them both, the Police Law with some credit and with the advantage of the course, the language side with some difficulty. I was short of good tuition, especially with the grammar. I would never be a good linguist but in this case I was determined I would improve in time, though it never really worked out that way.

We had a new arrival, transferred from the Clearance Camp down the road, having briefly met him before. Apparently he was found in possession of an unauthorized pistol, disciplined and sent to us. He was distinctly odd, an ex soldier who had been badly shell shocked as an eighteen-year-old in 1944. I met him again in Minden in 1964 where he was a L/Cpl clerk in the RMP unit. He said he remembered neither me nor persons I mentioned. I think he wanted to forget all about the P.P. Due to his stupidity this person saved my life.

Don Peil had opted for a transfer to Rural Stores in Haifa Police HQ, so the new garage foreman and I joined the wireless operator in the small room. It was about midnight when our bedroom door was flung open. Peter (my dog) almost dragged my bed to the door to attack the Arab constable standing there. He told us a bomb had been planted in Athlit Railway Station and the staff threatened by several armed men. Within three minutes the garage foreman and I were dressed and the armoured personnel carrier was ticking over. Insp. Toukan, then Cpl. Rashid, joined us but we had to wait. Regulations stated that a driver plus four persons had to be present on a vehicle to attend an incident. The absent body was our odd new constable. We were fuming with impatience as any chance of a contact with the terrorists was fading; also a sensible look at the planted device was risky the longer it remained *in situ*. Well over ten minutes after we had assembled, this clown strolled down. He was properly dressed, shirt, shorts, hosetops, puttees, boots, as if he was ready for the drill square. He then had to be sent back for his rifle! So some quarter of an hour after the message we left the station. I asked Soubbi Toukan if we could avoid the normal road to the village; I thought they might stay and stage an ambush for our obvious arrival. Soubbi swung us off the road over rough ground then through vineyards and orange trees; it was slow going but safer. Showing no lights we stopped at the junction with the normal road which overlooked the café/post office and the railway station. As if it had been laid on, the station disintegrated before our eyes, completely flattened. In the subsequent busy moments that followed I didn't think about it, but as someone worked out, if it hadn't have been for the antics of our 'odd' friend, at the time of the explosion I would have been sitting on top of it! End of story, moral! God works in many diverse ways.

Duckett and I went to shoot near Acre. We both did well, especially me so we were both in good spirits as we unloaded kit at Police HQ, Haifa.

'Nebby' Samuels, the Rural Divisional Inspector, strolled up and said, 'Congratulations, Howard, you've just been made up Sergeant.'

I instinctively said, 'That's bloody stupid, I've only been here a year.'

Nebby all officious: 'If Mr Campbell [our DSP] thinks you are capable that's it, keep your mouth shut.'

Inwardly I was delighted, but I was right; although qualified in language and law I was woefully short of three or four years of experience and there is no substitute for that, a point I've always maintained. In later years I saw it happen so frequently when a rash and inexperienced judgement was made and then the voice of experience was heard from the the the back. If the advice was not always acted on immediately it did make them pause and think; usually it was accepted later, slightly modified, to save face.

The incident that sorted out my subsequent posting happened a few days later. Haifa Police Headquarters, the District administration, and the post office shared a six-storied complex of buildings in the form of a square with a small building in the centre. The buildings faced the main entrance to Haifa Port and were impressively situated in Kingsway, the main lower road in the town. Owing to a previous bombing where the terrorists had successfully penetrated the HQ and blown up the centre building causing many casualties, a four foot high fence of strand and dunnet wire surrounded the HQ and encroached on to Kingsway, reducing traffic to one lane to the south and west.

A few moments after 6 o'clock one morning, a British constable (actually he came from Lytham) was leaving on patrol from Central police station which was at the front of Police HQ at Kingsway, when he saw a truck being driven slowly towards him (down the wrong side of the street) alongside the wire. From a channel iron dual ramp constructed behind the vehicles cab, a large oil drum fitted with two military tyres was released. It moved down the ramp which curved to a level position at the height of the wire, cleared it and bounced ominously towards the main building. Later it was calculated that nearly half a ton of explosives was in the drum. In blissful ignorance and not even thinking about a breach of the law the constable yelled at the driver that he had lost his load. The driver ignored him! Exasperated, he turned to the drum and to his horror saw smoke coming from what was obviously a fuse. He ran the few yards to the entrance of Central police station and gave a hurried alarm, ran outside again past the bomb and was about to turn the corner when the bomb exploded. He was sensibly blowing his whistle at the time to give a general alert and the blast blew him off his feet high in the air. His contact with the ground only produced some bruising; however the blast blew his whistle down his throat and also many of his teeth, there was an internal stomach injury as well. I also think it also affected his head because I met him early in 1949 at a dance in the Public Hall in Preston, and although he had had a drink he talked in a rather disoriented manner. I later learned that he fell foul of the law on drinking charges, then he married and that failed; later he was again involved in some way with the police. It was all rather sad: not a bright lad but he had courage.

Four policemen were killed and many others injured, some seriously. Among the serious ones was the relative of the famous author, who had left Athlit to become a records clerk in CID. His bedroom overlooked Kingsway through a very large window. CD, lying naked, covered only by a sheet, was almost directly above the bomb; he took most of the glass in his body. When the rescue party reached him, his internal organs were hanging out as a result of one huge sliver of glass. No one gave him any chance of survival, but two days later I was talking to him in hospital. He had somewhere in the region of 130 stitches in his body and resembled the Chinese torture of a thousand cuts. Some of the injuries measuring three to four inches were held only by one, possibly two stitches. He looked amazingly well considering, and six weeks after was convalescing with King Abdullah of Transjordan, owing to his father's influence as an executive of the Iranian Petroleum Company. Although I once met his mother, who lived in a delightful little cottage on the A20 near Ashford, I never saw him again. He became a successful international journalist for a well known paper. He is now a clergyman with a parish in south-east England.

Following this disaster I was posted to Police HQ to reinforce the general security unit for the HQ. My colleague was a chap from Liverpool called Thompson, a nice chap who later died tragically in New York Harbour. We tightened up security procedures 'closing the stable door' somewhat, and after about a month when things were settled, Sgt. 'Paddy' Sayers, ex Irish Guards, who was in charge of the Haifa Operational Patrols (HOP), asked for my transfer and this was done.

At this particular time the Moslem Brotherhood began to give the police additional problems which they could well do without; we had enough with the Stern Gang, IZL and Haganah. The Brotherhood decided that its Moslem congregation were becoming too Westernized, corrupted and debauched and unless an Arab was a professed Christian they would now be compelled, by force if necessary, to strictly conform to the faith.

I can only speak of incidents in the Haifa Urban area in which I was involved, although there were countless throughout the Division and the country as a whole. The Brotherhood initially started their campaign against the brothels, the majority of which were situated in mixed areas, a few in total Arab areas, and one particular one, 'The American Flats', in a Jewish area. This last was staffed by Arab and Greek girls. They were given an ultimatum: 'cease your activities or else'; this was generally ignored until the 'boys' arrived. By threat of death, deeds of violence and the burning of establishments, they closed many brothels while others continued to trade. Frequently we and the fire brigade were called to the scene only to talk to bruised and tearful 'Madam and girls' who apart from cursing the Brotherhood said nothing. I responded to a 999 call early one evening concerning the 'Flats' and on arrival found three other mobiles outside plus foot patrols. All the girls were hanging provocatively out of their windows cheering the policemen and shouting lewd comments to them, with the policemen replying accordingly. It resembled a scene from a French farce and was quite amusing on the whole. Who could blame the policemen for being protective? Some of them were obviously valued customers. I don't think I was popular when I chased all but one car away. They could show their gratitude outside working hours.

A chap I knew who worked in Investigations at Central Police Station was living 'over the brush' with a rather attractive bar girl and they shared a small flat just off Jaffa Road. One morning he entered the flat for his usual cup of coffee and was seized by two Arabs who put a gun in his ribs, took him to a car, blindfolded him and drove off. On arrival at a house he found his girlfriend had also been abducted, because she refused to change her job and stop being with a Christian. The police were eventually informed of the disappearance and reason for the PC's abduction and his possible death at the hands of these fanatics. Negotiations were commenced by senior officers and the District Commissioner. Meanwhile off-duty PCs volunteered for mobile patrol of the Moslem areas and unofficial groups of PCs in civvies took to the streets on foot, all of us feeling very angry. Thankfully it was sorted out. Rather than lose her, the PC decided to change to the Moslem faith and marry the girl. He was returned to HQ under open arrest for his own safety. It took twelve days to sort out the preliminaries and during that time the Brotherhood had assassination squads outside HQ in case there was a move to get him out of the country, and we couldn't even touch them. After the marriage they were sent to Gaza and I believe they were some of the first to be evacuated.

It was just before this time when I met a rather attractive Jewish girl who lived in a tiny box like room in Kingsway. We had several cups of coffee together in a nearby café and one afternoon I took her to see 'The Jolson Story'. It was following this that I went to the CID to check her out. Coincidentally, the CID bloke said he had taken her out twice and then found she was deeply involved in Haganah; he advised an early exit. She had constantly stated her horror at the various atrocities carried out by the Stern and 1ZL, and to confirm her hatred said she would take me to a café where many 1ZL supporters and possibly active members gathered to socialize. I couldn't pass up the chance that her offer was genuine. I met her that same night well on my guard, pistol carried between the pages of the *Palestine Post.* In the taxi on our way to the top of Mount Carmel she reached over and touched the pistol on my knee saying, 'Give it to me, I'll put it in my bag, it's so obvious.' It was said and done so quickly and I couldn't make a fuss in a taxi; anything could have happened. I sat there feeling most apprehensive and thinking I was walking into the lions' den. Leaving the taxi we walked through the darkness to a dim, lightly wooded area where tables and chairs were scattered, and some forty yards from the café, which had an open air dance area. To the sound of lively Jewish and American pop records some twenty Jewish couples were living it up. As the waiter approached I was told to keep my mouth closed. We had received no more than curious glances from the older people near us but I was still worried. The waiter came to attention in front of me, bowed slightly and said, 'Good Evening, Sir, what can I get you to drink?' Quick as a flash the girl gave our order in Hebrew and the waiter retired, I nearly fell off the chair in silent laughter, it was so ludicrous. The girl was plainly annoyed at me and a little worried. When the waiter returned, a short conversation in Hebrew followed; the text was not disclosed but she was worried. We left shortly after. I never saw her again; she left her job and her room, and I was convinced at the time that she was the perfect eyes and ears for the Haganah or even possibly the 1ZL outside the Police HQ. She worked opposite in a café and knew many policemen; she also spoke excellent English when she wished and never disclosed her family background.

There was an incident that happened on Christmas Eve 1947 of which I am not particularly proud but it does tend to show an example of mind over matter. At this time I shared a room with a Scots lad, a Sergeant on Port Control. We had our evening meal together in the Mess but any thoughts of celebrating were dashed as the Police authorities placed a 100 per cent 'Stand To' on all ranks which meant confined to billets, although Roman Catholics were allowed out in fours to attend Midnight Mass, and I wanted to go. My Scots colleague suggested we have a drink in the room. He had received quite a few bottles from merchants in the port as Christmas gifts, but he stated categorically that any bottle was mine except the whisky, that was for his Hogmanay.

I was given a bottle of 5 Star Martell and, armed with glass and ginger ale, lay on my bed and read. We occasionally exchanged words but for an hour and a half rested, until a noise in the corridor followed by a knock admitted four of his constables. He gave them all the drink of their choice then they in turn asked us to their accommodation for a reciprocal drink. I glanced at my bottle; to my astonishment there was approximately one inch of brandy remaining, and I felt fine. In the crowded confines of the B/C's room I sipped uninterestedly at a glass of beer, but after half an hour I made my excuses that I was going to Church. It was only a few minutes after eight o'clock.

In uniform and armed with pistol I approached the main gate and as I said Church I was not stopped. I walked the fifty or sixty yards along Kingsway and turned left into Bank Street. Suddenly I became aware of shooting. At the junction of Bank Street and Jaffa Road, one of our armoured cars was stationary and the Commander (it was Tom Cook) was firing the occasional round in the direction of Stanton Street. Outside the Ritz Hotel I could see several bodies lying on the pavement and road (they were evidently Paras who were drunk and some had been shot by the Arab sniper). I asked Tom what it was all about. All he said was, 'What the bloody hell are you doing wandering around on your own?' I told him I was going to church and he told me to push off from there. They then dashed off towards Stanton Street.

As if by magic I found myself in church. The congregation were just about to kneel down and I was standing but my slowness to conform did not excite any curiosity from others nearby, so the Mass continued. I glanced at my left sleeve and observed a small L-shaped tear. My right hand crept to my holster for reassurance, Yes, the pistol was still there. To my relief no one was paying me any particular attention, so I had not been a nuisance to anyone. I attended Communion like most of the congregation and finally the Mass was ended with Christmas blessing on us all.

All I could think of was, where had I been for four hours? and what the hell had I been doing? Tom Cook had said the town was going daft that night, with sporadic sniping all over the place so what had I been doing? A cold sweat crept over me. At the rear of the church, servicemen and policemen were offered tea, coffee and cakes by English and Christian Arab ladies among whom was Victoria, the elderly and talented policewoman from Headquarters. She quietly came up and gave me a cup of black coffee. I explained my predicament. She laughed and said that I had already been in the church when she arrived and she presumed I had had a drink but that was all.

Unobserved I quickly checked my pistol. Every round had been fired, I was horrified. Where the hell had I been and who had I been firing at? My uniform was clean and tidy apart from the slight tear which could have been caught on barbed wire and there was plenty of that about. It was a mystery but was I worried! I later checked the patrol log in the Operators Room: nothing adverse in there. I spoke to the car crews next morning: nothing known or seen, I checked the several cafés usually patronised by policemen in the general area and I hadn't been seen on Christmas Eve.

So where had I walked to, who had I shot at, and why wasn't I aware of it all? I certainly had not intended to drink so excessively and certainly did not appreciate the strength and potency of the brandy, it never happened again. I was a lucky man.

But I just had to go to Midnight Mass.

I can't recall precisely the reasons that started this particular fracas but there had been some shootings of Arabs by Jewish snipers in the general area of Iraq Street and when on patrol we had come across a dying Arab lying on the pavement having been hit by several bullets. I got him on the car behind the turret and stood outside to hold him on, then we set off down Iraq Street heading for the Hospital at Bat Galim. Then we hit this riotous mob of several hundreds which grew later to thousands. The whole of the fairly wide thoroughfare was almost instantaneously full of incensed and angry Arabs. We were surrounded and slowly tried to make our way through. God it was frightening. If you have never been on your own under those circumstances I don't advocate it. I think it was only because the crowd thought I was comforting the casualty (who was obviously dead) and the fact that an English speaking Arab having been given the brief details jumped on the car and by gesticulations and shouts, that we got through this terrifying crowd. Their feelings were such that one wrong move by us or an adverse comment from the crowd and the mob would have torn us to pieces.

I was standing near the HOP car park one lovely sunny morning waiting for a car to come in. Sgts. Jacobs and Haubner and two other CID blokes walked past and asked if I was coming to the café for a coffee. I had to refuse. Five minutes later Haubner was dead and another wounded as they sat at a table in the front of the café. A Jewish gunman carrying a violin case had entered the side entrance to the café, stepped on to the balcony overlooking the tables, removed an automatic weapon from the case and opened fire at the table. The victim was obviously Haubner who was Jewish Affairs, but the more the merrier. In the confusion that followed, the gunman packed his case, walked out of the café unchallenged (obviously) and was never caught. Mrs Haubner worked as a clerk in CID; she suffered a terrible shock. I escorted the funeral procession two days later and shots were even fired at the cortège. I met Mrs Haubner in 1974 at the PPOCA dinner in Liverpool; we spoke at some length and she enjoyed meeting someone who was actually there at the time. She was a most charming and courageous lady, who had hardly changed in appearance after all those years.

Sporadic shooting was an everyday occurrence in most of the large towns but in lower Haifa Arab and Jew had intermingled in many areas over the years and the job of detection was difficult. Both communities in clearly defined small ghettos had designated houses as check points, sentry boxes, observation posts: call them what you will, arms, though not always evident were obviously within. To maintain the *status quo* and afford each community a certain amount of protective licence we left these posts alone unless they became aggressive. One morning eight shots were fired at a particular corner on Kingsway directly opposite Police HQ. It apparently happened over a period of an hour but was never reported. The eighth shot claimed a casualty which was not serious and the victim was a Jew. A puff of smoke indicated the firer's position: an Arab observation post further down Kingsway. Even as the casualty was being removed and telephone messages made to the local Arab Commander to stop the shooting a further shot was fired. The three police cars in the vicinity were ordered to open fire on the house. Like a scene from a Western, this time we were the Indians, the three cars followed each other at intervals. Both guns were firing at the house, when level with the house the firing stopped and the car dashed back along the other side of Kingsway, crossed over and repeated the process. Five minutes of this and hundreds of rounds later, with dust and smoke rising from the house, the three cars stood outside Police HQ as if to wait for applause from the watching mixed population and some policemen. The relative silence was shattered by two deliberate well aimed shots which hit the identical piece of masonry, scattering the watching crowd. One felt like applauding the cheek and courage of the unknown sniper. It was decided not to send the police in on foot. The Army would eliminate the menace as negotiations by telephone had proved fruitless.

Send for the Guards! On this occasion the Grenadier Guards. Within minutes, a 15 cwt truck arrived while several soldiers took up covering fire position. A Corporal stood to attention, his PIAT No 1, with weapon, and the No 2 carrying the ammunition. (The PIAT was a heavy, cumbersome but effective World War II platoon anti tank weapon.) Being an ex Guardsman, I am biased and one can only admire unexplained epics of mad, stupid disciplined acts of courage, and I witnessed one that day. When you consider that in that area of Kingsway were probably untold weapons (and our sniper) waiting to be used, this party of three Guardsmen supervised by a young officer behaved as if Kingsway was the front of

Wellington Barracks. With PIAT on back and bomb carriers in either hand No's 1 x 2 stepped off on the orders of the Corporal with precision and style 'à la Guards'. The officer, as normal, sauntered behind; the Guardsmen carried no personal weapons, the officer did not remove his pistol. Approximately a hundred yards from the house the party halted and in a flurry of foot drill and loud words of command under the noses of 'the enemy' the party faced its front, removed weapons etc., took up a prone firing position in the middle of a four lane carriageway, loaded, fired and the house disintegrated. They returned the weapons to their persons, stood at ease and amid the smoke and noise came to attention, turned and marched off. I must admit I was smiling and felt so proud. Not one shot was fired in retaliation and these Coldstreamers behaved with typical Guards aplomb, an isolated but significant incident. I think the Arabs were a little mesmerized by the 'bull'. As the army vehicle and its occupants drove away and the watching crowds and police began to disperse, a single shot was fired. The bullet struck the identical piece of masonry as the others! There appeared to be an invisible shrug of inevitability or acceptance from everyone around and life went on.

Within an hour of this incident I was taking my customary walk round the general area of Police Headquarters. I was in a narrow side street approaching Kingsway when I heard yells, screams and vehicles braking followed by several shots. As I ran into Kingsway people were running in all directions. All traffic appeared to have stopped. A Jewish gentleman hurrying by said that an Arab had thrown a grenade at a bus but it had not exploded.

Heading in the direction of a stationary bus I passed the entrance to the Old Business Centre. In one of the narrow streets I saw a body in the gutter being kicked by a large group of Jews. I yelled and dashed towards the group. I have never seen people vanish so quickly into various shop doorways and alleys. Leaning nonchalantly against his doorway a Jewish shopkeeper quite casually informed me that the body was that of the Arab youth who had thrown the grenade at the bus. With a cigarette dangling from his lower lip, this character had uninterestedly watched another human being be kicked to death in front of him, I would find that hard to accept.

I had never seen a body kicked to death and it was obvious that the youth was dead. His arms, legs and body were like jelly, quite indescribable and obviously the work of a mob. His body was uncontrollable as I found to my horror and discomfort when I tried to place the body on the floor of the HOP wireless van which eventually arrived on the scene and took the body to the mortuary.

Prior to the van's arrival, as I bent over the body I heard an English voice abusing the silent onlookers. Turning, I saw a young Traffic B/C who was verging on the hysterical. He was gesticulating and accusing everyone of murder. He had apparently witnessed the youth running from Kingsway into the Business Centre and being surrounded. It was some time before he could get to the scene and the outcome had obviously unnerved him. His rantings stopped when two shots were fired at us. The street cleared and I dashed to a doorway, pistol out, eyes searching the roofs and windows. To my annoyance the B/C almost climbed on my back. In anger I threw him in the roadway, ordering him to watch from a doorway on the other side. With comic patience, verbal abuse and guidance we slowly paced the empty street inviting another go. Nothing happened; our gunman had left. I got rid of the B/C and told him to submit a report to Central Police Station.

I was almost physically sick when unaided I had to drag this remnant of a human being into the van. Handling a corpse at any time is an unpleasant task. As time passed violence was continually thrust at you, and sadly for those who experienced it, we accepted it as the 'norm', in cold blood without feeling. We are strange creatures.

Haifa Operational Patrols, if I remember correctly, had approximately fifteen GMC armoured cars for patrolling the urban areas. These light vehicles were crewed by a driver, a wireless operator and a Commander and the last was not necessarily the senior (by service). Mechanically they were quite reliable and our drivers took a personal interest in their vehicles. A military '19' set in each car linked with a 'Master' in the HOP Control Room, formed the communication net. All Control operators were WT (Morse) trained and there were a number of WT operators among the car crews. Each vehicle had a Bren gun under the control of the operator. It faced the front and had limited effectiveness; sometimes cars had to move to enable the operator to fire his weapon. The Commander also had a Bren gun and he had a mobile turret with a cover which gave him an all-round field of fire. Cars normally carried twenty-four Bren magazines, 30 rounds per magazine; these were counted, loaded and unloaded at the beginning and end of patrol, and every Commander was accountable for his ammunition. Needless to say, ammunition was 'saved' especially after an action and should the occasional round be expended at a sniper or whatever but not reported over the radio, it was just replaced from the 'store' before the HQ count was made, thus avoiding awkward questions, such as the shooting of a Rabbi near Hertzl Street, Haifa.

The idea to form an Escort Section of four (4) Morris recce cars was very sound. It kept the cars who were detailed for town patrol from being diverted for various escort duties which were becoming more frequent. In between relieving various Commanders on patrol I was also on rota for the Officer I/C Control Room which was a very interesting job; we worked in conjunction with the CID duty officer (Sgt. Jacobs) next door. I was detailed to take over the Escort Section and given an office next door to HOP Admin. Office (Sgt. Linguard). The job was all right but lacked the action. I can remember my apprehension and horror when, reporting to Haifa Airport for a Barclays Bank escort, I was informed that £5,000,000 in used notes was involved. I personally sat on £2,500,000; the remainder was divided with the other two cars. I think I was more concerned about my other two crews in case they decided to do a gallop for the Lebanese border.

It soon became obvious that the requirements for escort vehicles fluctuated and that we were not fully employed. It was then decided that we should be based at the Carmelite Convent in Eastern Haifa (the busiest area for trouble). There we could patrol the area and perform escort duty when required. The ex convent was used as a police billet for MT personnel and Eastern police station and was situated between the Wadi Rushmiya Road and Lower Haifa Road leading to the renowned area of Wadi Rushmiyah. The building was completely surrounded by Arab dwellings but higher up the hill Jews were in occupation and as you examined the area Jew and Arab were in varied commanding positions on both sides of the Wadi; sniping and pitched gun battles frequently occurred. The Army

A Jewish casualty near the Arab area of Dock Road, Haifa.

sat, in Company strength, in the big 'White House' which overlooked the whole area, and was situated at one end of Hertzl Street (the main Jewish thoroughfare). There was a corresponding house at the other end which dominated a predominant Christian Arab area.

Returning to our new area, no Jewish transport could use the lower road through the mainly Arab area, so to reach the main Jewish area they had to use the Wadi Rushmiyah Road above our billet. The road was a gradual climb between Arab houses and flats at the roadside, entering the entrance to the Wadi where the road climbed steeply in the shape of a reversed figure S. It was a nightmare for Jewish drivers of any vehicles but mainly buses. It was also the scene where I put the first notches on my gun.

The stupidity of military personnel, especially officers, is often the source of many stories and jokes and I should know after my lifetime. The following incidents, though months apart, all concern Para officers who generally speaking are the salt of the earth, but they are sometimes guilty of stupid behaviour emanating from their peculiar type of training. I'm sure they think that the red beret will give them automatic immunity.

I was lying on my bed in the Carmelite billet one Sunday lunchtime; one of the cars was on patrol and there was some shooting. I was called to my bloke's bedroom and on the flat roof opposite you could see from the chimney the tell-tale puff of smoke from a sniper's weapon. In miscellaneous forms of dress we took a car out, and as we approached the area on the Wadi Rushmiyah Road above our billet we saw several Paras lying in the gutters on both sides of the road, doing nothing positive. A jeep was standing in the road with a rather irate red faced Major, pistol in hand, standing alongside. He was so annoyed, and ignoring the shooting going on around him. Apparently he had driven down the road in a lordly state alongside his foot patrol when someone, Jew or Arab, had fired at him, the shot striking the seat between his legs. He was more concerned about what might have happened if the bullet had been a couple of inches higher and had removed his private parts, and so indignant that someone had nearly removed his 'wedding kit' that when I told him where at least one sniper was it didn't seem to register. I put four magazines rapid into the sniper's brick and plaster position on the rooftop and it fell apart. We left the Paras to get on with it and I went back to bed; it was my day off.

In the No Man's Land between Iraq Street and Hashomer Street an Arab was using a heavy calibre weapon. It made a distinctive sound. This particular area consisted of patches of open ground and deserted houses. Each side patrolled and sniped. We were more concerned if they had got hold of an old Boys Anti Tank rifle which could have been disastrous for us in our 'tin cans'. Even in daylight we could not find any evidence (from the comparative safety of our cars) that this type of weapon was the culprit, so we nicknamed it the 'Elephant Gun'. In the darkness early one evening we entered the Jewish street which formed their 'border', switched off our lights, and up ahead we saw a vehicle, unmistakably an ambulance. It was surrounded by figures. It was a military vehicle and the persons were Paras; a groaning soldier with a shattered foot was being carried up to the ambulance by his comrades. A Para officer obviously in charge was issuing dire threats of vengeance against the Arabs in general. I asked him what he was supposed to be doing patrolling from a Jewish area into a No Man's Land in darkness. I also told him to appreciate the Arab reaction if they saw movement in the dark approaching their positions. He was still not convinced and said that his Company Commander had agreed with some high ranking Jews that he would protect their area. Someone possibly lost a foot for his sectarian bias. I won't repeat what I said to the officer but I was not very polite and my report was also in the same vein. Needless to say they never patrolled the area again. Despite our frequent patrols in this area when we sat there in total darkness inviting some action, we never located our 'Elephant Gun'; maybe he ran out of ammunition. I shall later recount how the Jews exacted retribution for the Arab aggression in this area.

It was approaching dusk one evening about 9 o'clock when we were told to pick up a convoy of buses and cars from the Jewish area east of Wadi Rushmiya and escort it through the danger road to the main Jewish area in Hadar Carmel. When we reached the area the driver and passengers seemed cheerful enough, but I thought the joviality was a little forced. To my amazement, down the road strolled a Para officer, in uniform, unarmed, with his arms round a pair of very attractive Jewish girls. Knowing that troops and sometimes ourselves had to travel in groups of four, I rather bluntly asked the officer, 'what the bloody hell are you doing here?' He explained, looking rather shamefaced, that he was the Catering Officer from Peninsular Barracks, Bat Galim, and that he was returning from a social engagement! and would I allow him to travel with me? I was speechless. This bloke was a fool; the Jews disliked the Paras after the search of Tel Aviv to such an extent that even when the situation was quiet, you would never see Paras in a Jewish area for their own safety. I refused to let him travel inside the car on principle. I gave him my pistol, wished him the best of luck and the convoy started off. Not one incident occurred, it was like a funeral procession; even so it was a very white-faced officer who politely thanked me and handed me back my pistol. In all honesty I don't think when he left us he looked quite the Gay Lothario.

Although biased as an ex soldier, I generally found the military efficient, but I think they suffered from post-war lethargy and were left with a percentage of below average officers at all levels, and experienced other ranks who had to be forced in a corner before they showed their proficiency. When they were geared up and on the job they behaved like true professionals but away from operational duty, they partied, boozed, womanized and were generally lax and this is where Begin's 1ZL and other terrorist organizations caught the troops with their pants down on more than one occasion. It also applied to a lesser extent to the Palestine Police but they were generally aware of local feeling, and their instinct for self preservation was more evident.

It was a very bright but winter's day, 30th December. We had started at 7a.m. and the sun as usual shone in a clear blue sky. It had been a busy morning and there had been various shooting incidents but we were not involved in any of them. About 10 o'clock we had a call to pick up a sniper's victim but I can't remember the details. I put the body on the back of 672 and drove to the hospital. The body was placed in the mortuary alongside the coffin containing our HOP driver who had been shot in the back, when into the mortuary walked the B/C's Jewish girlfriend, who was in fact a prostitute (a rather attractive one). She tended to drink heavily and also took drugs. When she very tearfully walked into the mortuary carrying a lavish wreath it struck me as rather ironic, knowing the trade she was in. A moment later she left rather hurriedly leaving the wreath on the floor. She was violently sick when two Arab porters brought in a body, the victim of a shooting incident, which was awash with its own blood in the stretcher, not a pretty sight, I admit. Less than three months later she was married to another B/C and on her way to England. I was covering the evacuation of dependents in Haifa port when she embarked on the landing craft en route to the larger ship. She sat near the bridge showing a lot of her attractive legs and smiling happily she gave a deliberate 'Harvey Smith' sign to the policemen commenting on the quayside, as prolonged gunfire came from the depths of Haifa town. That girl knew what she was doing.

Returning to that morning: I left the hospital to face a number of ambulances arriving and several groups of angry and riotous Arabs. I was summoned to the car hurriedly, as we were wanted at the Iranian Petroleum Company refinery on the Acre Road. Jewish terrorists had thrown a bomb at a queue of Arab workmen waiting for a bus outside the refinery, who were mainly from a Druze village on the outskirts of Haifa. These were the victims just arriving and their relatives had arrived before the bodies. The Druze Arabs were particularly anti Jewish and not very well inclined towards the British either. Leaving the hospital problem to someone else we arrived at the refinery to find the gates locked, a small angry crowd outside and within a crowd of approximately two hundred Arab workmen being kept quiet by a sole, very brave, British Security Officer and one or two officers from the nearest police station. He was armed, but on his own he had fought with his bare fists, on a narrow pedestrian bridge, the angry crowd outside, physically throwing several into the stream. We entered the gate unmolested. The Arab workers were waiting for buses to take them home as the refinery was being evacuated. Under the threat of our guns we made them sit down and most of them complied. From the heroic, white faced security officer we got a brief resumé of the events since the bomb outrage. Our gang of squatting Arabs had apparently gone berserk following the explosion, and in marauding gangs they had raced around the refinery, attacking and killing every Jew they could find. The Jews that survived the attacks were now locked and barricaded in the main office block protected by British security officers, British police and some temporary constables. The situation was very tense and if they had rushed us, we might have inflicted some casualties but we would have been overwhelmed. Keeping the engine running and swinging the turret and gun around rather menacingly we held on for about half an hour until a platoon of Paras arrived, from Acre I believe.

They deployed around the entrance and my crew and I felt much better and applied our safety catches. Then for some inexplicable reason the officer sent a number of his men into the group of workers who were now all standing. Within a few minutes a young Para came to the front of the crowd without his weapon. Panic! It could have been wholesale slaughter had a shot been fired. You may find it hard to believe but even following the arrival of the buses and careful systematic searching of every person the No 5 rifle was never found.

Leaving the crowd to embus I toured the refinery and at one point found a group of rather nervous and apprehensive British soldiers of a searchlight crew, under the command of my old Prestonian sergeant from Athlit. They had not been attacked but had wisely stayed at their post, unaware of what had actually happened. The sergeant and some of his lads later came down to the gate to assist.

A 15 cwt police truck then arrived with more men, from the Police Station at Kiryat Haim, and the task of recovering the victims was started. If my memory serves me right, 52 bodies were eventually loaded on three 3-ton vehicles without tops. Most of the bodies were naked and had been abused. They had suffered death in many ways, thrown into and from cooling towers, impaled to the ground with 6ft. crowbars, kicked, stabbed, strangled or bludgeoned. One unfortunate running from a gang had attempted to escape through barbed wire into a nearby Transjordan

Frontier Force Camp or was it Arab Legion? As the barbs held his clothing he was hacked to death by his enemies on both sides of the wire. Very tired and feeling sick, not only from hunger but from what we had seen, we escorted our grim convoy to the Hadassah Hospital on Mount Carmel. It began to rain very heavily as we started to climb towards the hospital, and there was a large crowd of tearful, waiting, distraught relatives and friends waiting on the hill as we pulled up.

The rain poured down washing the prostrate bodies and the gutter ran red with Jewish blood. It was pitiful to watch the cries and agony of the bereaved. Yet as I waited there for disposal instructions I couldn't help feeling that this was God's method of realization to the Jews. I think four Arabs were killed and many injured by the bomb, but many innocent Jews died as a result of their own terrorist outrage. Today some Jews must often think was it really all worth while, or did Menachen Begin remember these little incidents which initiated retribution? I wonder who made the decision not to carry out an immediate investigation at the scene. We allowed the perpetrators of 52 deaths to go home, and the attack on the Arab bus queue was never fully investigated to my knowledge. All in all 4 Arabs dead, 12 injured, 52 Jews dead, several injured, almost a form of poetic justice. Incidents like this were so commonplace in Haifa, but not of such magnitude that it was dangerous to walk around in plain clothes to carry out an investigation. One must presume that if the situation was such that a normal investigation would be almost impossible to conduct owing to adverse conditions the matter was shelved until conditions were more normal. Not a very satisfactory situation for any police force to be under but these were unusual and difficult times and much was left to the man on the spot and his judgement.

I suppose a sad but somewhat amusing incident told to me happened at Central Police Station Haifa some hours following the bombing incident. Through the shattered portals of CPS Haifa stepped our elderly *fellah*; the normally immaculate Inquiry Office still had a haze of dust in the air, plaster hung from or had fallen from the wall, the floor was dirty. Files, books and papers were not in their normally regimented places, voices were high and policemen were tired. Our rather humble *fellah* stood alongside the desk, seemingly unwilling to add his problems to the chaos that abounded. When he finally gained attention, a member of the 'I' staff was brought forward to attend to him. He then proceeded to admit that he had murdered his wife in a fit of temper and that he wished to be placed in custody and charged. We British certainly educated our natives well. How they respected our Colonial Law and behaved like thorough scholars and gentlemen. Ah, that it should happen today!

For reasons best known to the B/C 'I' concerned, the Arab was told to go and wait outside which he did for *three days* till eventually he was processed. It is hard to imagine a situation like that: to walk into a police station, confess to the most heinous of crimes, be told to wait *outside* and do so for three days despite various attempts to obtain recognition in this period. In all fairness, taking into account the bombing and the language problem, it is still an amazing story and shows a strange side of the Arab makeup. I wonder if the story was correct.

One afternoon as we drove slowly along Hertzl Street the sound of firing was heard coming from the direction of Wadi Rushmiya. Although not heavy the shooting was continuous. We drew up adjacent to the 'White House' and from our position we commenced to survey the area of the approach road through the Wadi and the surrounding buildings. To our left some twenty yards away stood a tank, probably a Cromwell. Almost immediately the tank reversed then proceeded forward down the hill. When it reached more level ground it began firing at various buildings identified as firing positions by either side; only the machine guns were used. When this sustained fire ceased the tank turned round and slowly climbed back to its position near the 'White House'. A deathly hush fell on the area.

Some minutes later the noise of a vehicle was heard approaching the Wadi and a heavily armoured bus came into view. With its protective armour the bus was almost twice its weight and a screeching second gear was all it could manage. One wondered what the feelings were of the driver and his passengers: the driver and his obvious responsibility, and his frightened and apprehensive passengers as they lay together on the floor of the vehicle praying that they would make the sanctuary of the 'White House' and the Jewish area.

As the vehicle approached all hell broke loose. Bullets hit and ricocheted on both sides of the vehicle. The Arabs were attempting to hit the tyres of the bus and disable it. We'd had difficulty on an earlier day extracting passengers from a stationary bus, some of the HOP lads exposing themselves to sniper fire during the transfer. This time Jewish luck prevailed and the bus struggled and waddled its way up the steepest slope to safety amid cheers from watching Jews and the Coldstream Guards.

Immediately I ordered my driver to go down the hill. I had seen several windows where weapons had been fired from. We had turned the bend on to more level ground when suddenly from behind the cover of rocks to my left sprang an Arab armed with a rifle. Initially he gave the impression that he was about to open fire on our vehicle, but he began to run quickly along the rocky slope of the Wadi towards the Arab houses. Owing to the number of gunmen of both sides in the general area and our slow progress I was wary and very tense with my finger on the trigger. In a second I had picked up the gunman, aimed off and brought him down in the first burst. As he struggled to find his feet a longer burst of fire from me hit him in his midriff and he died immediately. I then took on the positions that I had seen fire coming from. It was always a chance that the sniper was still at the location and you might hit him with a ricochet. A couple of magazines were expended; we turned round and in a deathly silence returned to our previous position by the 'White House'. The 'run' up Wadi Rushmiya over the months became quite a saga. At the junction of the Wadi road and the port road a motley selection of Jewish vehicles gathered each day: armoured buses, goods vehicles with armoured cabs, taxis and private cars assembled with drivers discussing the daily merits or otherwise of this mad, dangerous thousand yards of highway. The occasional vehicle attempted a solo run or if sufficient vehicles were willing and the HOP car was available a convoy would collect and be escorted along the route with the HOP car acting as a sheepdog. No one day was like the other.

Some days after the previously described episode we again stopped by the 'White House'. It was early evening and we had finished our evening meal. A few minutes had passed when we heard the sound of an approaching vehicle; shots were fired and a goods vehicle came into view. Rounds ricocheted off the armoured cab and as the vehicle approached the first steep bend the right hand front tyre was hit and collapsed. You could hear the groans of the groups of Jewish spectators who gathered to observe the daily runs to the Jewish area. It was a lifeline that had to be kept open.

The indicative signs of smoke from a group of houses to my left showed clearly where Arab gunmen had their position. From a gap in the nearby houses two men emerged carrying rifles and gesticulating. By this time I had the gap covered by my weapon. With waves the two men brought out a further half a dozen armed men and they began to dash across the gap. I opened fire and all of them fell and none arose; no one came to their assistance. There was a silence for some ten minutes then we moved off down the Wadi, past the waiting Jewish vehicles, turning left eventually to join Iraq Street which lay immediately below the area where the gunmen had been shot.

We slowly drove to the end of Iraq Street and returned to the collection of Jewish vehicles, informing the drivers of what had happened to the previous vehicle and suggesting that they followed me either now or after I had checked the road again. No one accepted the offer so we moved off.

It's an eerie feeling travelling along at 5m.p.h., finger on the trigger, waiting for someone to try and blow your exposed head off your shoulders.

Tenseness is hardly the correct word to use. Don't ask me why people should behave so stupidly, they should have seen us coming, but suddenly from the houses on our right half a dozen men carrying rifles ran across the road a hundred yards or so in front of us. To quote the common expression used by authors, I was like a coiled spring. Quickly aiming off yet again, I squeezed the trigger and they all fell, sprawled and still on the left hand pavement. Jack Robinson, my wireless operator and former Coldstream Guardsman, became very upset and accused me of indiscriminate shooting. I think it must have been the continuous tension we were all under. As we drew level with the bodies and he saw the weapons, he apologized profusely. We continued our agonizing crawl until once again we reached the 'White House'. That was thirty minutes I was not likely to forget in a hurry.

The situation was quite unbelievable and although incidents like the above did not happen every day we were kept fairly busy. I think that the reason I was attacked in the Iraq Street bombing was because I was recognised from the incidents previously described. A resemblance of police work continued, but the local population in urban Haifa appeared to be concerned in other things. HOP lost two B/Cs about this time; one left his vehicle to chase a suspect and was shot in the back, the other when moving under fire was hit in the head through a gap in his driving visor, an unusual fatality which was almost repeated at Mishmar Haemek.

One Sunday lunchtime Sgt. Joe Jacobs, the CID Duty Officer, and I decided to have a walk to Carmel Avenue to a hotel mainly frequented by officers of the services. Having quaffed a few glasses we were joined in conversation by a gentleman who was a Lt. Colonel in the TJFF (Transjordan Frontier Force), an extremely likeable chap with no edge. He informed us he had an appointment with a lady at 5.00p.m.; could we suggest a suitable establishment where we could all satisfy our thirsts (Joe enjoyed his ale!). We walked through the town, on the way picking up one of my blokes who was leaving the Blue Bar (a dive) and he was under the weather. Cox was ex RAF and a very able and competent Wireless operator in Morse and RT (Radio Telephone). The son of a Detective Sergeant in the Met., he was not of great stature and sported a moustache which never resembled Flying Officer Kite, rather an untidy resemblance to an effort of a later rebel leader. He should have been a radio or TV commentator. This chap frequently used to transmit without a trace of emotion, when he was actually shooting at snipers and the vehicle was being hit by bullets. Quite a character.

The four of us entered the Café — which was in Bank Street. L shaped, this café boasted a huge glass window onto the street on the foot of the L. The rear of the cafe faced a brothel.

We ordered beers at a table close to the bar and settled down to an hour or so of stimulating conversation. After ten minutes or so I had the gut feeling that only comes to you when you are used to living on your nerves and are intelligent enough to react to it. I looked around, to the front and side of us: not a customer. I turned round, and sitting against the rear wall were two soldiers of the RAOC, quite unconcerned. I turned to Jake (Jacobs) sitting next to me and one look at his serious face told me he knew. Apparently he saw a Jewish male moving from one table to another and although his Hebrew was limited he thought that customers were being told to leave the café. Quietly I slipped over to the two soldiers and explained the position and that we would welcome their support in case shooting started. Within thirty seconds they had picked up their berets and rifles and were out of the door and down Bank Street like dogs from a trap. Initially I was annoyed at their actions but on reflection, if you are not trained for a situation like that it's only natural, I suppose, that you walk away from it. Like people who walk away from accidents because they can't stand the sight of blood, but when the situation is forced on to them and they have no alternative they behave equally as well and often very heroically.

Returning to our own plight, the telephone behind the bar was out of order (deliberate?). We tried, so we decided to sit it out. To walk out into the street would have been an assasin's dream. The only conclusions for our selection as victims were (1) Jake looked like another Detective Sergeant who was on Jewish Affairs, both facially and in build; he was a known target, so it could be a case of mistaken identity but we couldn't very well explain. (2) I had been involved in many incidents and might have shot someone who had not been reported and might have been of some importance. (3) It was known that this particular café was a rendezvous for 1ZL terrorists either locally based or passing through, so it was possible that a meeting could have been arranged and all they wanted was to get us out of the area. It was later suggested that the upper rooms were used to provide temporary 'safe houses' for persons who had to be safeguarded and moved frequently.

The minutes dragged by and conversation was forced but very humorous (cheers for the Brits). We couldn't see the barman who appeared to be squatting on something resembling a child's stool, as close to the floor as possible. To prise him away from this position required a loud voice and some persuasion and his speed when his head and shoulders were exposed was phenomenal, he was so obviously aware that something was in the wind and was scared for even his own safety if bullets were flying. The café remained empty; the pavement outside, normally very busy with pedestrians, was practically deserted, although across the street movement appeared normal.

The Colonel, who was unarmed, watched the two small windows high on the rear wall while we three held our pistols on our knees, drinking with our left hands, not usual but still effective. The drink was really affecting Cox, so when 5.30p.m. arrived and customers suddenly began to enter we arrived at the conclusion that all was back to normal. Cox staggered off to assume his duty in the Control Room at HOP, and the Colonel, mopping his forehead, expressed his gratitude with a wry smile and hurried off to his late date. I hope she waited. His life in the desert was usually boring, with no female company, so between us (if she waited) we probably gave him a few hours that he would remember.

Friend Cox returned at 6.15, cleaned and smarter, having been relieved from duty by Paddy Sayers who ensured he was disciplined and fined. Apparently Cox reported on time for duty in good order, in an air of euphoria from his alcoholic excesses. He then opened up his tour of duty by calling up all the cars on patrol correctly, but having ascertained all was well he put his feet up on the table and started a hilarious ten minutes of radio conversation and singing with everyone out on mobile patrol. It was crude, extremely witty and certainly not in accordance with PP radio procedures. Unfortunately for 'Gunner' Cox, Paddy Sayers, who was working late, sneaked down the corridor and overheard about half a minute of Cox's music hall, and with the graciousness of an Irish Guards RSM had Cox flying out of the Control Room and down the corridor like Concorde. Following his baser instincts he retraced his steps back to Bank Street and the welcoming arms of his friends. I will not disclose the final count of what we drank on that day, it was outrageous, but the situation had such an effect on me that I was not drunk and neither was Jake. On many occasions since that day should anything ever happen, domestic or otherwise, when I have had a drink my reactions are predictable: almost immediate sobriety and an alert mind. The medical profession may have a word for it, though some would no doubt discount it; could it be experience and training or is it the body's metabolism? Whatever it is I'm glad I've got it; it has done well by me.

DSP Bill Sharman (ex Royal Marine Major), who commanded HOP, sent for me one morning and told me he had a very delicate and possibly dangerous job for us to do. The American Vice Consul had to leave the country presumably with certain papers. Two attempts to leave the country from Jerusalem had been prevented by the actions of Arabs who watched the Consul and had attacked the official car. The reason for these intimidating incidents was because of the American support for partition of Palestine in the United Nations. Feelings were running high and a fatal incident could spark off worldwide repercussions; the Arabs were extremely anti American.

The official car had managed to leave the Consul and via the Jewish areas take the road to Tel Aviv and then to Haifa. Most of the journey was through Jewish populated regions and now he was sitting in a hotel in Carmel Avenue hoping we could take him safely to the Lebanese frontier post at Ras en Naqura (now Rosh Hamikra).

A Morris recce patrol car was detailed as an additional escort, the Commander's name I forget, and I had one of the GMC turreted armoured cars driven by a former member of REME who had served in Italy and who apparently pre war had some connection with a racing car team as a mechanic. His name was B/C — and he had a scar close to one of his eyes. Owing to his mechanical knowhow he could state his car could do 75m.p.h. on a straight road. I was soon to have this clarified.

Before picking up the American, B/C — stopped at the Blue Bar and came out with a bottle of cognac, on the chit via the proprietor (a known Haganah chief). The fire extinguisher between him and the wireless operator was removed and the cognac inserted. He made the excuse that if we really hit trouble, as was anticipated, we might as well die happy. I hoped that he was just being a potential drunken pessimist; surely nothing that serious could happen. When I gave the Vice Consul the alternative of travelling in my car – uncomfortable but safer – he declined graciously: 'it would not really be on if I did that.' He also refused to remove a larger than life Star and Stripes pennant from the bonnet and to add to all this both front doors of the car carried large Embassy insignias. What with the size of the car as well, you couldn't have advertised the situation better.

Off we went, with me in the lead followed by the Consul and the Morris recce, whom I ordered to keep a fair distance away but not allow anyone to come between them. We had no problems travelling through the Arab area of Haifa. We had never allowed either side to erect a complete road block although unofficially if they were unhappy about a vehicle they would stop it, and guns would appear like magic and to disappear likewise. We turned left on to the rather straight road to Acre. After several miles there were three Jewish colonies situated astride the road. To my consternation we were suddenly confronted, without any warning, by an enormous crater in the road. This had been caused by an alert and suspicious Jewish sentry who had opened fire on a huge American built truck driven by Arabs. The truck was full of explosives and ammunitions, one of his lucky shots did the trick and the lot went up. I think an effort had been made to fill up the crater, but as I recall the depth was approximately 2-3 feet. I knew of course this incident had happened but outside Haifa Urban area. I should have anticipated a problem but I forgot. As we left the area of these colonies, armed women were completing work on their protective ring of barbed wire.

We passed through the outskirts of Acre gratefully without incident and although the remainder of the journey to the border was mainly through Arab areas we were only shot at a couple of times and they were wildly inaccurate and I didn't have to fire. On arrival at Ras en Naqura I entered the Custom Post to report in and on leaving was confronted by a thankful, smiling and still nervous Consul. We were joined at the front of the car by B/C — and his cognac. The Consul grabbed the bottle, swigged generously, coughed and spluttered (it was not one of Benny's best) but his smile and back slapping in North American style said how grateful he was, and so he went his official way into the fleshpots of the Lebanon.

I told the Morris recce to carry on back to Haifa: as we were faster we would soon catch them up. That was just an excuse for the three of us to attack the cognac. We started the return journey and reached Acre with no problems and B/C — asked if he could push the car on this nice stretch of road from Acre to Haifa and see if he could reach his estimated 75m.p.h.

He did and maintained it, and it was only when I noticed our other car in front and the woman erecting the barbed wire that I yelled, 'The bloody hole!' Our Wireless Operator had asked if he could use the Commander's turret on the way back; he had not been in the general area before, so I sat in front next to the driver. I have never seen a racing change down done as quickly and efficiently as B/C — did but it was no use, we must have hit the hole at 45/50m.p.h. According to the Commander of the Morris recce car who had just negotiated the 'hole' with great caution, we literally dropped into the 'hole' and came out like a huge metal frog, reaching a height of four to six feet above the ground. Luckily we landed on the road again and just bounced for what seemed an eternity. I don't know how B/C — maintained his control but he did, considering our respective heads were beating a tattoo on the partially protected roof. The unfortunate Wireless Operator as we hit the bottom of the 'hole' started to leave the turret like a rocket from Cape Canaveral. The turret was narrow and the butt of the Bren gun was fortunately above his web belt. As he was forced forward and upwards the butt prevented his inevitable departure from the turret for pastures new, by catching his belt, and as we hit the road again he collapsed in a heap on the floor of the car, frightened and bruised with a daft grin on his face. He thought it was great fun. B/C — and I were too speechless for words; we realized what could have happened if we had turned over.

The Arab equivalent of Hertzl Street (the main Jewish thoroughfare) in Haifa was called Iraq Street. It ran almost parallel to Hertzl Street and if my memory serves me right it started at its junction with Stanton Street, which was to the rear of Police Headquarters, and ran all the way through the town's Arab area till it met the lower road near the junction of the Wadi Rushmiya Road.

Unfortunately, because of the geographical position, the Arabs were overlooked and tactically dominated by the Jews and the following stories are linked with this particular street. The first story starts about 8 o'clock one mid week evening. It was one of those nights in the Middle East which can only be described as perfect. We had enjoyed a late evening meal, the town for once had been quiet all day and to drive around with doors open with a clear sky, myriads of stars and a lovely moon was most pleasant, quite romantic and idyllic.

We were stationary at the junction of Stanton Street and Bank Street when a military 3-tonner belonging to the Arab Legion turned into Stanton Street and 150 yards along the road it stopped. The 25-30 Arab Legionnaires, properly dressed and fully armed, disembarked quickly and disappeared into the night. I was very curious and drove towards the stationary vehicle which was deserted. To our combined knowledge we knew of no brothels in this particular area and there were no cafés either; where the devil had they gone? Some twenty minutes later we were parked in Hertzl Street. Traffic was busy and the pavements were full of evening crowds, and the three of us were being most verbal about the female talent that passed us by. They didn't enjoy being admired by British policemen; they usually never smiled and turned their heads away.

Suddenly the radio opened up, requesting us to investigate reports of shooting in the Wadi Nis Nas area which was just below Hertzl Street and where the Arab Legionnaires had vanished. The answer appeared to be obvious, but for what particular reasons we never found out. The road down from Hertzl Street was narrow and suddenly turned right; on the right hand side were houses and small blocks of flats while on the left hand side on the bend and beyond was a wide open space which looked down over Wadi Nis Nas and the mass of jumbled yet picturesque flat-topped houses built so haphazardly on the slopes of the Wadi and populated by a mixture of Moslem and Christian Arabs. We stopped on the bend and switched the engine off. This was the time when the nerves jangled and the mouth became dry; your head and probably shoulders were visible to any decent sniper and being stationary never helped. Every police car Commander, probably without exception, had experienced this situation in an urban environment, as you could not transmit a comprehensive on-the-ground report hiding behind a closed turret (I've no doubt some did). Everything was quiet, exceptionally so, which was suspicious. Further along this narrow street the houses began again leading to a crossroads, where a few weeks earlier Tom Cooke, one of our car Commanders, had been temporarily blinded by a phosphorus grenade thrown by Jews from one of the nearby houses when Tom had gone to investigate reports of shooting. This was border country between urban communities and very difficult to prevent incidents. As you drove slowly down the middle you became a sitting target for any hothead on either side, especially as houses and balconies were much higher than you, and this situation made you feel extremely naked and nervous.

The silence lasted five minutes or more. I noticed a motor cycle parked against a doorway where the houses started again and someone was trying unsuccessfully to drag it to safety. It was no doubt used by the Jews as a means of communication. Suddenly all hell broke loose from the Arab quarter down in the Wadi. I could see the flash of weapons as they were fired and heavier shooting was coming further along towards the crossroads. I could not identify where the shooting was coming from from the Jewish side and they were no doubt aware I was there. Although it was dark I began to locate firing positions occupied by the Arabs and commenced firing on them all and I also effectively immobilised the motor cycle with a well aimed burst (this was for Tom Cooke). Most of our magazines were filled 3 and 1 (tracer) to aid locating snipers, but the magazine I used was wholly ball ammunition and unfortunately the machine didn't catch fire.

We should have finished at 10p.m. but said we would stay on as other incidents were occupying the cars on the night shift. We remained in the same positions, only firing on both sides when a position was carefully identified. It was approaching 11.30p.m. when I became aware that the top of my Bren gun, the vehicle, my forearms and, when I removed it, my blue cap, were all covered in white dust. I turned round to look at the balcony of the Jewish house behind me and in retrospect did a very foolish act, I switched on the turret spotlight. I counted *23 bullet holes* roughly in a circle of approximately 20" immediately above my head. At the time all I did was utter a mouthful of invective and move the car a few feet. It was only days after the incident and when I had looked at the area in detail during daylight, that I fully realized that God was on my side that night.

How many casualties I inflicted on the Arab Legionnaires if any, was never determined although unofficially we had reports of many bodies (alive or dead?) taken out of town and not to hospital, which was common practice especially with the Arabs. What saved my life was a number of flat-roofed Arab houses which had been built below the bend of the road. A line drawn from the edge of these houses to the balcony must have missed my head by inches. Twenty-three holes were seen, and God knows how many bullets hit the edge of the roofs as the Arabs tried to gauge the correct killing position in the dark. As a good soldier I should have moved my position; as a good policeman, keeping good observation and remaining stationary saved my life.

When I was commanding the Escort Section from Police HQ I had an office opposite the Operations Room and Clark Linguard had the Administrative Office adjacent to me. The correct date yet again escapes me but I think it was late 1947. The work in HQ building on this morning was continuing as normal when without warning the huge building was shaken by a tremendous explosion. On our side of the corridor the offices were quite large, probably fifteen or sixteen feet square. I used to sit at my desk facing the two large windows with my back to the corridor. My first impression after the bang was a snowstorm hurtling across the room towards me. Plaster dropped, a table collapsed, files fell, miscellaneous papers fluttered and I hit the wall with a crash, ending up on the floor. I ran into the corridor. The Ops Room appeared OK, then Clark emerged from his office suffering a nasty gash on top of his head. The two female CID Clerks, Mrs Haubner, and a Scots lady, rushed up to fuss Clark which caused him embarrassment, while he was trying to tell them to look at me because we appeared to be the only immediate casualties. My head and face were covered in blood from a dozen or so small, superficial cuts caused by the 'snowstorm' which of course was shattered glass, none of which required stitching. Clark, who sat under a window, had just been hit with a large piece of glass. Our respective windows seemed to be in time with the blast from a Jewish bomb which severely damaged some Arab houses in the adjacent business centre or it could have been a token gesture against Police HQ as it was close to the perimeter wire. If that building is still standing it must surely have its fair share of battle scars.

CHAPTER 3

Iraq Street Bombing

This particular incident is rather significant to me in several ways as the story will show. I cannot recall the exact date and I forget the names of many of the individuals involved, but it must have been early in 1948, on a weekday, and the time approximately 6p.m. with the light fading. The four HOP cars out on patrol were commanded by myself, Johnny O'Neill, Tommy Cooke and one other. The last at the time was standing down for meal break and I think Johnny was on his way to eat when the 999 call was made and all three of us were directed to Iraq Street where an explosion had taken place and many casualties reported.

As previously described, Iraq Street was frequently the scene of many incidents. Its position lay parallel to and in between the main Jewish thoroughfare, Hertzl Street, and the lower road ran through Haifa Town adjacent to the port which was predominantly Arab. As Haifa was built mainly on the lower slopes of Mount Carmel, all Arab areas at that time were dominated by higher ground which was populated by the Jews. As the trouble developed an unofficial Arab-Jewish battleline was established between the two communities. The ends were fluid but the centre ran along the area between Iraq Street and Hertzl Street, with formerly joint-owned Jewish and Arab houses now lying unoccupied and forming a 'No Man's Land' where a deadly game of murder was frequently played by both sides. HOP presence often cooled things down but more often than not we were 'piggy in the middle'.

We all came to Iraq Street from the west: Tommy Cooke first, followed shortly after by Johnny, then myself. A military 3-ton Bedford truck showing Parachute Regiment Insignia had pulled up outside a three or four storey block of flats and shops on the south side of Iraq Street nearest the Jewish line. A party of 'soldiers' (four or five strong) had left the vehicle, turned right down a narrow alleyway and disappeared into 'No Mans Land' and were never seen again. Within a minute or so the truck had disintegrated and so had most of the block of flats. (The Jews claimed the flats were used for sniping, or could be used.) The next vehicle to come along Iraq Street was a jeep containing four genuine paras. Within seconds they had been stopped, ordered from their vehicle at gunpoint, disarmed and taken to a nearby house. To top all this the Jewish snipers started to add their misery to the terrible chaos near the demolished building. The feelings of the Arabs could only be described as horror stricken and lusting for revenge. Almost immediately every male seemed to produce a weapon and as the casualties were brought from the tragic scene the anger was mounting.

When Tommy Cooke arrived he was told about the four Paras held prisoner and that they were likely to be shot out of hand, as the perpetrators were in similar dress. Tommy's driver, an Irishman named Malone, who spoke good Arabic, left the vehicle unarmed to try and negotiate for the four Paras. Under the circumstances at the time it was an extremely brave thing to do but he at least prevented their assassination, though he never received any recognition. On my arrival I was told where Paddy had gone but at the time was more concerned in getting the locals to remove barrels from the road, used when necessary to implement a road block, and the debris from the explosion so that the ambulances could run in and turn around with greater efficiency. In front of me I think Tommy and Johnny were trying to locate and quieten the snipers and fired several rounds. I was trying to organize and hopefully ignore the snipers' bullets which occasionally made everyone duck, in between trying to clear the street. The first ambulance arrived and I was watching it to make sure it could leave without problems. I decided we should reverse to afford more room and turned to face the rear, away from the Bren gun. It is hard to describe in sequence how I behaved in thought and action in the short time that followed. As I turned I was aware of a figure crouched by the turret, who was quickly joined by four or five others.

Two things happened almost simultaneously. The man now facing me pointed a revolver straight between my eyes and on my right I had a quick glimpse of a person holding a 36 grenade. I don't care what books, doctors or people say but until you are faced with a situation as described no one knows how they will react. Most men or boys conjure up in their minds deeds of valour in which they emerge as the hero, with damsel in distress, but cold reality is so different, and usually you don't have much time to think about what will happen if you fail. If a person could sensibly stop and think and weigh up all the 'pros' and 'cons' there would be very few heroes walking the streets.

The Bomb Disposal man, the unarmed policemen trying to talk to and disarm an armed and dangerous person: this is cold courage. These people who walk into danger fully in the knowledge of the danger involved, in my

humble opinion deserve the highest accolades for bravery. People who react
by instinct, instantaneously and possibly without thought of the results or
repercussions of their actions, are usually described as stupid, rash,
impetuous, courageous or merciless. When on very rare occasions I have
been drawn into a discussion about heroics I find it very difficult to describe
why a person behaves in a particular way when faced by circumstances.

In the position I found myself in it seemed a very private matter. There
I was standing in the turret, arms outside the vehicle, the Bren gun facing
the other way, cocked with safety catch on. My Smith and Wesson pistol
was strapped to my side 'cowboy' fashion and the two constables sitting in
their seats behind the observation slits were completely unaware of what
was happening above. In what order I thought it I don't know, I was *annoyed*
and *indignant* at these Arabs for their actions because we had come to help.
Secondly, when I looked down the barrel of that pistol it appeared to be
like the 15" guns of HMS *Hood* and I didn't want to die: call it *self
preservation*. Finally, when I saw that grenade about to be deposited in the
vehicle my thoughts went to my two companions who wouldn't have stood
a chance from the blast and I might have lost my legs or more: call it
thought for the life of others and a drop more self preservation.

A Jewish victim of the massacre at the IPC oil refinery, Haifa.

Pulling my right arm back I hit the man with the pistol straight between the eyes and he somersaulted backwards off the car. Keeping the momentum going I backhanded the one on my right who held the grenade; he also had had a pistol in his hand as he fell off the car. Then I panicked, two down but how many to go? I knew there had been bodies all round the turret; which one would fire that fatal round? Then I thought, what the hell, in for a penny in for a pound and hit a third armed man on my left in the chest and he fell off. At the same time I heard two or three loud reports above my head, and three other armed Arabs leapt off the car like a flash. Fifty yards away Tommy Cooke gave a thumbs up and a wave from behind his smoking Bren gun. Luckily he saw that I was in some sort of trouble and fired the warning shots and was I grateful. Tommy Cooke suffered temporary blindness when the Jews threw a phosphorous bomb on top of his car near where I had the trouble with the Arab Legion. At the end of the Mandate Tommy went to Malaya and was killed out there. He was a good and conscientious copper. I probably owed him my life because surely one of these remaining Arabs would have pulled the trigger on me.

It was by now obvious that feelings against any non Arab were high and that our help was not required, so we withdrew. Paddy Malone, white faced and nervous, had returned just before my spot of trouble. He had at least persuaded the Arabs not to shoot the four Paras out of hand but to check out officially their identity; at one stage Paddy was in line to be No. 5. We then ate and finished our patrol. Later on, over a quiet drink in the canteen, we all tried to work out why mine was the car singled out to be attacked, and came to the conclusion that the car number had been taken several days earlier when in the three incidents in Wadi Rushmiya I had inflicted so many casualties on the Arabs. Needless to say I never let them get so close again.

CHAPTER 4

Good Friday 1948, Jaba

At this stage, apart from the knowledge that the partition of Palestine was to take place on 15th May, we of the lower echelon had no idea of the finer points of the evacuation. It was therefore with some interest the day before Good Friday that I was ordered to take two cars to Police HQ in Jerusalem on Good Friday escorting a 3-tonner which would have on board the driver, my old mate from Athlit days, Don Peil, and the Head Constable (Stores). I think they had a few small items to take to HQ but the most important reason for the journey was the large consignment of arms and ammunition and other attractive items to be brought back to Haifa. My other HOP escort car was commanded by Johnny O'Neill.

Before leaving Haifa we checked on the general situation throughout the country. It was a Christian religious festival and a public holiday and one side or the other might have tried to provoke trouble. All was quiet, so we decided to travel through the predominantly Arab areas of Jenin and Nablus. It was not an area well endowed with a strong military or police mobile presence, and it would be safer while we were without our intended cargo. If matters remained quiet we would probably take the coast road back; although the Jewish presence was greater, there was more military activity on that route and help more readily available. The decision not to inform units of our possible passage was for security reasons.

The trip to Jerusalem was pleasant. It was a bright day, not too hot, and the long journey made a change from the almost tedious but dangerous patrols round the narrow streets of Haifa. It struck us as strange to see Arabs in Jenin, Nablus and Jerusalem walking about quite openly with rifles. Even some of the road blocks we drove through (no stopping for us!) had Bren guns displayed in strategic positions. No one dared do that in Haifa; we would have shot them on sight. Obviously the person in charge had made a decision to allow this, but we were rather nervous at first; in fact I was cocked, finger on the trigger and safety catch off at one stage.

Police HQ Jerusalem, on arrival, appeared to be normal with no outward sign of the forthcoming evacuation. We British only appear to develop a frenzy some hours before the balloon goes up which I suppose has its good points: people just incur ulcers in the weeks and months before, organizing the preparations; the weak develop blood pressure or have heart attacks at the relevant time or get shot.

While the Head Constable, Don, the other B/C and the driver were busy we managed to grab a sandwich and a bottle of beer in the canteen and when we were all fed and watered and the truck safely packed, we left Jerusalem. It was about 2p.m. and the decision was made to take the coast road. The Head Constable, not used to the problems of shooting etc., was not happy about the route back and stated that Don could sit in the front of the 3-tonner and he would travel at my feet in the armoured car. An uncomfortable ride but he was obviously happier. He was a person who was almost always at loggerheads with HOP, a difficult man to negotiate with for normal stores, but with ammunition he could only be described as 'a bit of a bastard'. In the early days when the shooting really started, car commanders would only get the odd round off at a sniper or running figure and when on return to HQ you were a couple of rounds deficient (all ammunition for each car was counted at the beginning and end of a patrol), he insisted on a detailed explanation and written report as to why you had expended the ammunition. It was not as you might expect, to obviate legal problems that might ensue if you had hit anyone, but to justify the losses on his master inventory.

This prompted crews who had been involved in a justifiable exchange of fire, on return to HQ to remove a number of rounds from magazines and claim expenditure. Therefore every crew almost without exception had a small private store of ammunition which could replace the occasional round you didn't want to account for. I digress now, but when a car Commander in Haifa early in his patrol interrupted a fire fight between Jews and Arabs, he saw a number of Jews, all armed, on a roof top overlooking the Arabs in the Wadi Rushmiyah area. He fired a burst at the Jews and thought he had hit one, but he didn't report using his gun. The Jews left the roof when the person was shot and the firing stopped, which was indicative. The car commander had reported he was in the vicinity of the shooting and he left shortly after. Within hours the Jews had reported the death of a senior rabbi and claimed he had been shot by one of our cars. When a check was carried out, the Bren gun was perfectly clean and all ammunition correct. The matter, strangely enough, was never ardently pursued by the Jews, no doubt because they couldn't justify the reason for the rabbi being on the roof and tests would no doubt have revealed he had been firing a weapon (like the predominance of priests at the barricades on Bloody Sunday!?). The end justified the means.

However back to our journey to Haifa. We left the heights of Jerusalem with Johnny O'Neill in front, and I brought up the rear. Down the hill to Latrum, where many terrorist and other detainees were held in the Detention Camp. Then along the flat uninteresting plain towards the coast, passing Lydda (now Lod) Airport, Ramle then in a more northerly direction towards Haifa. It was so quiet that you became nervous; very few people were evident and traffic on the road was minimal. We felt better when we passed Hadera Police Station knowing we were back in Haifa District. Although our Head Constable had kept up a continuous flow of conversation to calm his nerves he must have felt damned uncomfortable sitting crosslegged on the steel of the car in between my outstretched legs and feet.

We had passed Zichron Yarkhov Police Station and just entered my old area looked after by Athlit Police Station when Johnny called on the air, 'Something funny in front.' When we had entered Haifa District we had switched our sets over to the correct channel and established contact, but made no further calls; also, one of our two wireless operators was an WT man (Morse) so we felt happier if we hit trouble. We slowed down, and could see ahead a large Jewish truck with an armoured cab, standing slightly at an angle, its tail end adequately blocking the road for the other trucks following behind; altogether twenty or more vehicles were standing nose to tail. As Johnny pulled alongside the armoured cab he shouted to the driver whom he could see through the narrow slit. The man did not reply, he was dead. Johnny saw the bullet hole in the man's temple and told me. The shooting was extraordinary, the slit was only 2-2^1/2 inches in depth and the driver had not even fallen over. We presumed he must have been almost stationary when he died or possibly a tyre was burst.

Johnny slowly passed the vehicle to find out details and get the traffic on the move. My wireless operator wanted to see the body and try and remove it from the vehicle. He opened his door and was leaning across to open the cab when the first shot hit our car. The direction in which we were travelling placed the hills on our right, on to flat ground, the road, then some three miles of flat ground to the coast. Some three or four hundred yards to our right beneath the hills was a small Arab village, I think it was called Jaba. I swung the turret round releasing the safety catch on the Bren. Standing in the turret I did not see much to shoot at but bullets were hitting the car and I could hear the very loud 'crack' and 'thump' above my head. Then I saw the tell-tale puffs of smoke from two houses, one in particular, and he was the one who was too close for my liking. From below me I could feel the frantic threshings of our beloved Head Constable and his verbal pleas for information on what was going on. Then I opened up on the houses in single shots and short bursts, not hurrying but keeping their fire down. From below me came the agonised cry of 'Keep firing, keep firing. Never mind about the bloody ammunition, have as much as you want, just keep shooting.' He emphasised this by keeping up a non stop stream of Bren magazines into the turret. In his eagerness for self preservation he hit me a couple of times in the nether regions and at that time I didn't know who to worry about more, the perpetrators of the ambush or the character below me who could inflict some permanent damage to my marriage potential. Looking back later that night we had a damned good laugh; our hated enemy in the cause of self preservation had suddenly changed. Life was more precious at the sharp end than his ammunition stocks. (He never bothered us again, he daren't, we might have said more.)

After about fifteen or twenty minutes, shooting at us stopped. Johnny who had been up ahead sorting things out and hadn't got in on the shooting because he couldn't see the houses, got the traffic moving. We got out of the way to let them pass and Haifa control told us to leave because Athlit were on their way and our cargo was too valuable to risk. It was strange that this particular incident was the only major one throughout the country that day, yet I doubt if it was laid on specially for us. Some years later I met Vic Duckett, the Station Sergeant from Athlit, my old shooting partner who gave me a sound rollicking, indicating the mess I had left him with. In his follow-up investigation he was told that a European was the main sniper who had probably killed the driver. In the shooting that followed he had not been hit but had escaped. But I had killed eight people including a woman and a donkey, who were all found in the houses; obviously they were not innocent bystanders. No weapons were found but empty cartridge cases were picked up in several houses, not only the ones with the bodies. From a religious point of view it was sad that it had to happen on the last Good Friday under British rule in this 'The Holy Land'.

CHAPTER 5

The Battle for Mishmar Ha'emek
and HOP Involvement, 1948

When Partition was authorized by the United Nations a particular area was nicknamed 'The Triangle', a strategic land mass centred on Mount Ephraim with its points on the 'cities' of Nablus, Lulkarn and Jenin. This was within the area allocated to the Palestinian Arabs and is now commonly referred to as the West Bank.

The Jewish settlement of Mishmar Ha'emek is situated on the south side of the Haifa-Jenin road in the foothills of Mount Ephraim. It was probably one of the largest kibbutzim in Palestine at that time. Its inhabitants strongly supported the Haganwah, and subsequent information reveals it was used as a training school/area. Arab villages, long established, effectively surrounded this strategically situated settlement.

Fawzi El Kaukji was a Lebanese by birth, and had served with distinction in the Ottoman Army; he also had a doubtful history and involvement in espionage in many causes. During World War Two he was reportedly in Berlin as he was a great admirer of the Germans. He was the holder of the Iron Cross! What for? Kaukji was appointed to lead the Arab resistance in Palestine, which was much to the chagrin of his great rival Mufti Haj Amin.

The force commanded by Kaukji was known as the Arab Liberation Army (ALA) and was formed by regular army volunteers from Lebanon, Syria, Iraq, Egypt and Jordan (the Arab Legion and the Transjordan Frontier Force). Reports vary on the reported strength of this force, from 1,500-2,200 approximately supported by some mortars and a battery of 6 x 76mm guns. Having assembled his men, Kaukji crossed the Plain of Esdraelon and dispersed his troops on the reverse slope of a ridge facing Mishmar Ha'emek. Kaukji had decided to capture this strategic Jewish stronghold for two reasons. The most important was that its capture would form an ALA Base which would effectively seal the only route the Jews had between Tel Aviv and Haifa as the coast road was closed. Secondly he would have been the first Arab Commander to have won a battle against the Jewish enemy and this would have enhanced his personal reputation. He did neither.

By 3rd April the guns supplied by the Syrian Army were in position and his men in good heart, so on 4th April Mishmar Ha'emek was attacked. The ensuing battle for possession of the settlement and the surrounding area lasted for over a week, the Arabs at one stage reaching the perimeter of the settlement and usually controlling the area by day because of the use of artillery, but the Jewish defenders recapturing their losses during the night. The only British involvement before HOP were in the area was the intervention of a 3rd Hussars officer followed by his CO, who organized a truce on the 5th, which didn't last, but gave the Jews a chance to safely evacuate the women and children, and some wounded. Some reinforcements also arrived at this time and they were probably the better trained and equipped Palmach, and men of the Carmeli Brigade. When Yitzhak Sadeh who commanded the Jewish forces left Mishmar on the 18th he claimed a creditable victory, having given the Arabs a thrashing, despite being outgunned 8-1 and the Arabs 3-1 ascendancy in manpower. He had to report that his men were exhausted. *Some Jewish historians claim that if Mishmar Ha'emek had fallen at this stage, the Jewish state might never have survived!*

No doubt following a report made by the two army officers the powers that be obviously decided that the Police should carry out a reconnaissance of the area and verify if it was still safe to use the Haifa-Jenin road from Haifa to the Lajun crossroads in order to facilitate the continued evacuation of those members of the military, civil administration and Police who still remained in areas of Eastern Galilee and other places, and required a road route to Haifa port.

The final home of the Haifa Operational Patrols (HOP) was situated in the Haifa Trade School, a group of buildings in the north-east outskirts of the town adjacent to the airport. There were some other members of the Palestine Police rear party at this location and only a skeleton staff, including the HOP Radio Control Room, occupied the former Police HQ building in Kingsway.

It was possibly on the 7th or 8th April at 1300 hours when I and three other HOP cars commenced our estimated 9 hour shift until 2200 hours. We all had our designated area and it was recognised practice that we always visited our more 'sensitive' areas first, making our presence felt and 'showing the flag', despite what was happening in other parts of the country. In Haifa no one openly carried arms. It was mainly HOP who applied this rule. If anyone was seen to carry arms, Jew or Arab, HOP would open fire without question; the circumstances at this time dictated that self preservation was of prime importance as was the rule of law. Road blocks were not allowed, but vehicles or materials were always in evidence at local strategic points and we knew that weapons were close to hand but out of sight. The *status quo* was maintained.

I had visited my more sensitive area of Wadi Rushmiya, Iraq Street, Stanton Street and the area between Hertzl Street and the Christian Arab area of Wadi Nis Nas, the three other cars reported quiet areas and we were all settling down to a hopefully quiet shift. Jimmy James in the Control Room told me to report to the Main Gate of HQ and meet one of our Morris recce cars which would have an Inspector on board. He was apparently a former member of CID Jerusalem spending his remaining days with the Rear Party. He informed me quite briefly that we were to patrol the Haifa-Jenin Road as far as Lajun and report road conditions. If he knew any further information he certainly didn't impart it to me. We all knew that skirmishing between Jews and Arabs was fairly widespread but we had no conception of the extent of it or the forces involved, I certainly did not know that the ALA was involved in this area.

When we left the outskirts of Haifa we passed a strangely quiet Druze village, then Yagur, the Jewish settlement where in 1946 the Army had discovered wonderfully concealed underground storerooms of arms and ammunition and very hostile settlers. Then as we came close to the end of Haifa District we passed Jalami Police Station all without incident, but I felt the atmosphere was strange, unnaturally so, and just a general gut feeling that something was about to go 'pop' and so it did.

The first signs of trouble were seen just before we reached Mishmar Ha'emek. The road had been blown up taking out four positions, two on either side facing each other. They had been roughly filled in, no doubt to allow vehicles to evacuate the women and children. As we drove on with me in the lead, we noticed dead cattle lying on their backs, legs erect in a grotesque charade, and mortar or shell craters were evident in the now empty fields. The settlement appeared deserted, many buildings were damaged, the scars of bullets and shrapnel were obvious. I began to feel extremely apprehensive. Opposite the settlement on our left was a long fir copse running east with an adjacent narrow track. (See sketch.)

As we passed the copse we found the road blown in an identical manner as before but the holes had not been filled in. This obstruction could be avoided by using the road verge and we did this, and while negotiating the problem we heard an explosion. Looking west towards Mount Ephraim was a village some two miles away, situated on top of a lonely but prominent hill. It was probably an Arab village. The mortar bomb had landed some

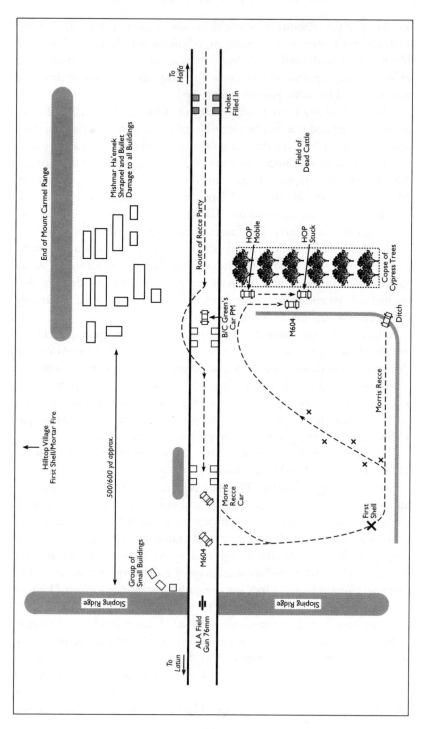

80

200 yards below the houses and within a minute a correction had been made and six or seven bombs followed in rapid succession in the centre of the village, obliterating the houses in smoke and dust. It was extremely accurate fire.

The road ahead of us began to ascend a ridge of high ground. Over this ridge the road dropped down to the flat plain and so to the crossroads at Lajun. Adjacent to the road near the top of the ridge on our side was a collection of houses. As we moved along the road we found it had been blown again and this time owing to high earth banks on both sides we could not circumvent the obstruction. I left my car and began to unscrew the two sand trays which were fastened to the side of my vehicle (sand trays were six foot lengths of channelled steel that could be laid on soft sand to facilitate the passage of a vehicle. We used them as a bridge to cross the blown gaps of road). We passed over first and while my driver and operator helped the other car across and replaced the trays, I watched the road ahead.

To my astonishment, where the road disappeared over the ridge an artillery weapon appeared, being manhandled by a group of khaki clad figures, I swung my gun round and yelled a warning of what I had seen. In seconds it had disappeared again and everyone was back inside their vehicles. At first glance, I thought it could have been a 25-pounder, facts would later say it was a 76mm.

'I'll go and see what it is,' shouted I.

'Bloody well stay there,' shouted the Inspector.

It would have been my intention to charge the ridge, take on the gun crew and anything else that was in range; we could have always run like hell if we had taken on more than we could handle. The Inspector was adamant, we had not to move. He was fifty yards behind us, and both wireless operators were unsuccessfully attempting to contact Haifa and report the incident, but we had no luck. I then heard the familiar crack and thump of bullets overhead and they were close; several hit the car below my head, and these were accompanied by two mortar bombs which fell in front and on the right side of the car which shook us somewhat. They were too bloody close for comfort. I told the driver, I think his name was Bell, to go forward about twenty yards for two reasons, the main one being that the persons firing at us could identify the Union Jacks on our wireless aerials and stop, and secondly that I would be in a slightly better firing position and that the ground to my left although deeply ploughed was accessible and would allow us to leave the road. To all intent and purposes we were cut off and couldn't leave the cars to renegotiate the blown sections of road.

As the persons continued to fire at us I had to retaliate and for some time had a sustained fire fight with the persons on the ridge and in the houses. Little did I know that the odds were about 1,500-1, in effect the Arab Liberation Army. I expended about nine or ten magazines in bursts and single shots and suddenly there was silence.

'Come on, let's go,' yelled I to the Inspector.

They had not fired as their gun was on a fixed mounting. We had a minor disagreement as we conversed at a distance. I could not help my younger instinct and my background of Scots Guards training; I wanted to get in and sort them out. The Inspector was much older than I, probably a married man with much to lose; he probably did not have a military background or my youthful dash and exuberance (or stupidity)! He was senior so we compromised; we would leave the road and head east following the slope of the ridge across the ploughed field, then we would turn north and head for the track which ran alongside the fir copse.

We had safely travelled over half a mile in four-wheel drive managing only about 5m.p.h. owing to ground conditions when we were faced with a ditch across our front. The Inspector told us to wait while he turned north and headed for the end of the copse. While attempting to cross the ditch his driver took it at the wrong angle and nose first went into the waterway and couldn't get out.

Seeing their predicament the Inspector asked us over the radio if we could get ourselves in a position to tow him out. Bell and I left our car and decided that the ditch was negotiable with sand trays, and as we turned to retrace our steps I heard the unmistakable whine of an incoming shell. I yelled at Bell and threw myself onto the upturned earth; the shell exploded a few yards away and I was covered in dirt and dust. As I glanced towards my companion I could see his half suspended figure and I thought, 'Good God, they've got him.' I thought he'd been slow in reacting and had been hit and I started to crawl towards him, but to my amazement he was off like a rocket. He covered the ground between us and our car in record time and I followed. When we were inside our 'metal box' and he was dusting himself down he said he was so scared that immediately he heard the bang he got up and ran like hell. He grinned when he said he preferred to die in his car and I think he meant it. He little knew in the following two hours how close he was to achieving that end.

We started on the long, slow drive back to the main road. Having got our range the ALA dropped a shell on us about every twenty seconds. Miraculously they fell all around us, but the car was covered with soil. Before the road we turned right, surmounted the ditch which was shallow at this point, crossed it, and after a few worried seconds kept the vehicle upright and started east along the track to rescue our fellow officers. We had travelled about two hundred yards when without warning the right hand side of the track collapsed, our vehicle sank up to its axles and we lay at an angle. My operator's gun would be ineffectual and mine could only be used towards the ALA with difficulty. Bell got out, looked at the problem and stated his intention to walk to the other car when a familiar noise followed by an explosion changed his mind and he scrambled back in his seat.

Until help arrived the Arabs put over at least forty plus shells at us, a completely stationary target. We were helpless. The nearest fell some 5 yards away; it was quite unbelievable. That was one miracle, the other happened after ten minutes. Since we had arrived in the vicinity of Mishmar Ha'emek, radio communication with Control at Police HQ had been impossible; HOP had organized a temporary Control set to take over when Police HQ was finally evacuated, but it had not been tested or used. Paddy Sayers, our operational boss, had decided to play with the equipment. Fate decreed that he picked the right time to hear our frantic call for assistance. He notified Jimmy James of our location then spoke to us again when my operator told him of the situation and that we were under continuous shell fire. Paddy's 'You what!': the assertion of policemen being shelled was beyond Paddy's comprehension and he queried the message. The operator placed the handset with the pressel switch depressed outside his door and the ALA dutifully responded and dropped a shell ten yards away. Paddy was convinced and promised all help immediately. We were not sure how long we could maintain radio contact as our engine wouldn't start and we couldn't charge the batteries. The Arabs by now also brought in sporadic machine gun and rifle fire to harass us and I found great difficulty in replying accurately and at such a distance, so at the moment repairs to the vehicle under shell and small arms fire was definitely not on.

Paddy was as good as his word. The three cars on Haifa Town Patrol were sent to get us out. I can only recall with certainty that Dodger Green drove one of those cars, no doubt with Jeff Howarth as his Commander. As they drove along the lower road in Eastern Haifa at 60m.p.h., lights on, horns blaring, they came across a huge American open top car that refused to clear off the road. Sprawled on the back seat was a well endowed Arab in dark glasses, enjoying a cigarette, no doubt telling his driver, 'Sod em, don't move.' Dodger came alongside, turned his wheel and shunted him off the road.

From receiving the message to reaching Mishmar Ha'emek it took all three cars under ten minutes to reach us; that meant an average speed of

65-70m.p.h., which through a town, on those roads, and in a 5-ton armoured car was excellent driving by any standard.

On their arrival at our location I told two cars to remain on the road and the third to tow me out. This car had overtaken me by some ten yards and was about to reverse in a towing position when the track collapsed on his side and despite great efforts he could not move either. The shelling was less frequent and it would have been idiotic to have attempted another tow and risk another car. Paddy Sayers was informed and promised more substantial help probably from the Army. We needed heavy recovery and until then we would stay with the vehicles. The sun was falling and dusk followed by darkness would no doubt bring additional problems.

I do not recall seeing the Inspector at any time during this period, so I decided that if an attack on us appeared imminent the radio sets in the three trapped cars should be destroyed; the Bren guns and ammunition were more than sufficient for our own protection. Of the two free cars one would remain mobile on the track while Dodger Green would stay on the main road. If the situation demanded it these two cars could evacuate us all until we could return to recover the vehicles. We would just have to play the waiting game and see if the Arabs renewed their aggressiveness, or the Jews decided to flex their muscles.

It would be tedious to attempt to describe the humour that manifests itself in times of crisis. For instance, was it possible to spend an adequate penny in between the shell bursts? – points to be lost if anyone dampened their trousers. All three of us smoked: total fags (seven), each cigarette shared by equal inhalations. None of us had eaten since breakfast: total edible food, several segments of chocolate, part of a stale roll, one bottle of mineral water, and part of a bottle of flat beer. The sharing of the 'goodies' and the humour shown throughout was a tribute to the British in adversity, and the Palestine Police at its best, because in all honesty we hadn't a clue as to the situation we were faced with. We could only remain extremely vigilant and pray that help was on its way. When darkness was upon us Dodger Green's car reported that the hills overlooking Mishmar Ha'emek appeared to be alive with human movements, but no firing. We couldn't dig in but only listen and hope; we would have little chance if they got close.

The shelling had stopped when darkness fell and it was probably fair to assume that by now both sides were aware who we were (if they didn't know at the start), but five armoured cars were a very attractive prize for either protagonist and each might have fancied their chances with us, although we knew the Arabs were not particularly keen on night fighting. The night was getting colder. We were hungry, thirsty and apprehensive as we cradled our Bren guns, watched and listened, and kept our voices low as the jokes and repartee flitted between the crouched figures round our two cars. We kept in touch with our comrades some hundred yards in the recce car.

It was approximately 1a.m. the following morning when we heard a heavy rumbling sound and Dodger reported the arrival of a Sherman tank recovery vehicle from the 3rd Hussars at Ramat David. The sergeant in charge told us that they had been hit by some sort of shell during their journey to us along the Haifa road. In less than ten minutes he had successfully extracted all three of us from our unfortunate resting places. We quickly ascertained that none of us had sustained any serious damage apart from our bullet and shrapnel scars and in convoy made our grateful way back to the Trade School. Our two original cars had been at Mishmar Ha'emek for almost twelve hours. How we managed to escape without casualties is something I will never understand because M604P, was, for most of the time a sitting duck. It had been quite a day. It took over thirty years to find out what was happening around us on that day, and fortuitous that I happened to read several books by Jewish historians who certainly mentioned nothing of this incident. One did indicate that had this battle been lost it could have been the key to the State of Israel! The Syrian guns were reportedly removed to the Jerusalem area on the 9th April following an Israeli air attack. We surely must have blunted the Arab ammunition supply with the number of shells they aimed at my car in retaliation.

Not being sure of dates: was I the last member of the British Armed Forces to be engaged in open warfare with regular members of the Syrian and Iraqi armies? And were HOP the last British recipients of Arab action in Palestine? It is all interesting conjecture: I only wish I could recall the names of all HOP members on that day. On our return, Paddy Sayers decreed that I would never take out another HOP vehicle on patrol, I had an instinct for trouble and it was best if I was confined to home. Therefore to prevent further casualties I was 'pensioned off'. I was twenty-two years of age.

Since I began to compile my notes in 1988, I have contacted Jon Kimche, the well known Jewish author who wrote a definitive book on the lead up to independence. He stated to me over the telephone that he flew in to Mishmar Ha'emek with Yitzhak Sadeh, who was the leader of the Haganah, by light aircraft. Sadeh was to command this vital operation and at the time Kimche told me he was a Reuters correspondent in the Middle East based in Jerusalem. What on earth did Sadeh want him for at MH? Was it historical PR and what if the battle had been lost?

In Kimche's book *Both Sides of the Hill* and many others by Jewish authors, has there ever been any reference to the PP involvement? I have contacted several Israeli senior Army officers in Jerusalem requesting information, verification and an admission that we were involved at this crucial time. Replies have been received claiming that no records are available so therefore they were unable to help. A letter to Kaukji's lifelong friend and Dr Amin Ruwayha's son, who is the author of *Terrorism and Hostage Taking in the Middle East* to his address in Paris requesting information was not even answered. It's almost as though both sides wish to forget because true facts and history would cause embarrassment.

At the time the Jews had two vital problems, the first being the ALA's advance to the coast in order to sever the Jewish population in two, the halves to be systematically destroyed bringing to an end the proposed Jewish state of Israel. 'THE OBVIOUS MILITARY SOLUTION.' This had to be stopped.

The other problem was the relief of Jerusalem, surrounded by Arab forces. This was subsequently achieved by the construction of a road from the area of Latrun. Mishmar Ha'emek was given priority. So why the necessity to refuse any disclosure of the facts?

CHAPTER 6

Approaching the End – July 1948

Life at the Trade School was quite enjoyable; we had comfortable accommodation, the food was good and we had a small Sergeants Mess. Our nearest military neighbours were Kings Company, 1st Grenadier Guards. What a size they were, none under six feet tall and several six foot six and over. They shared any social activity we had, and we all got on well.

Several of us members of HOP used to walk across the sand dunes to the beach on Haifa Bay and enjoy bathing in the nude, with not a soul in sight. It was most relaxing, although we were all armed, and one of us stood guard while the others swam.

HOP were still responsible for Town Patrol and although we had at the school all the GMC patrol vehicles from Jerusalem, Tel Aviv and Jaffa standing in the car park they were not used by the PP Rear Party which consisted of some four hundred plus volunteers. Later on it was discovered that nearly all the wireless sets had mysteriously 'disappeared'. I had a very shrewd idea who had been responsible and made himself, and no doubt others, a few bob. The Haganah were no doubt very grateful. It was wrong but a person's morals under circumstances at the time could be undermined and many policemen and soldiers can only examine their own consciences.

Some ten days after Mishmar Ha'emek, probably 20th April, we received orders to cease town patrol and the balloon went up. Although it has been said that ultimatums were given to the Arabs by the Jews that they should evacuate the port forthwith, the Arabs, no doubt believing in the sanctity of the UN Partition Agreement which left Haifa as a neutral port and the area to remain mixed if desired but under Arab Control, refused to believe that the British would allow the Jews to take over by force. How disillusioned they were and what loss of life they suffered. Following their success at Mishmar, the Carmeli and Golani Brigades, plus the Palmach, massed in the Jewish area of Haifa and without warning attacked the Arab areas. I am still under the opinion that the whole operation had the authority and tacit approval of the GOC, Generals McMillan and General Stockwell. Owing to the fact that in Haifa the two communities were not wholly segregated we had a lot of trouble, but neither side openly carried arms and we kept the town reasonably quiet. I have no doubt that General Stockwell, in order to facilitate an orderly withdrawal with only one side in charge, allowed the Jews to attack. Tactically I suppose it had merit but with the circumstances in Haifa at the time plus the numbers of police and army concentrated in the port area, the town would have remained quiet. As a result of this disgusting agreement and possibly other incentives several soldiers and policemen were unnecessarily shot. These casualties were suffered when troops and police left the safety of their confined areas, in this case the port area, in order to rescue the frightened and hysterical women and children and many old people who were attempting to flee from the guns of the avenging Haganah, Palmach, 1ZL or any other organization who might have been involved. The Jews slaughtered without exception any man, woman or child that they encountered, hence the panic to get out. The Arabs remembered Deir Yassin. The soldiers and police could not stand by and watch the innocent being killed, and many of them behaved very bravely and rescued scores of terrified Arabs who could not understand why the British just stood back and allowed the Arab population to be slaughtered. In all honesty I think the majority of the Police and the Army felt the same. To emphasise this point some 200 of the 450 Palestine Police volunteers for the Rear Party resigned forthwith and were evacuated home, thoroughly disgusted with the decision which had forced their hand. I and the ones who remained wholeheartedly shared their feelings and understood their sympathies, but we had volunteered to see a job through to the end and this is what we did.

The battle for Haifa raged for three days. From the Trade School we could see evidence of the battle and the noise of war was continuous. We felt awful and very frustrated, as we wanted to get into the action and restore the *status quo*.

After all, we had all worked so hard to maintain a fragile peace in Haifa and to see it all thrown away for expediency was a bitter pill to swallow. I was told that when the battle ceased the senior Police Officer of Haifa District, Superintendent 'Paddy' Meehan, had a brief ride through the affected areas. He contacted local Jewish officials, the Haganah etc., and at a meeting stated that he had been outranked when the decision was made to cease normal police patrolling, but after what he had seen the military could get stuffed. He gave the Jews a time limit in which to move the dead bodies, clean up the debris in the streets, restore power and water and try and bring the town back to normality. Looting would not be tolerated. If this wasn't complied with he would turn out the Palestine Police armoured cars in force and shoot every Jew on sight carrying arms. He was not polite.

It was also stated that normal police patrolling would be resumed and there had better not be any police casualties. Apparently within minutes 3-ton wagons started to appear and things happened. I have only read Jewish versions of the battle of Haifa; only one refers to an offer made to the Arabs that they should evacuate the town, but why should they and was everybody told? I don't think either side issued a casualty list and I'm sure the number of Arabs killed would never be disclosed because it was a massacre. The Arabs were certainly not prepared for a battle and they felt safe because the British were in control. How wrong they were. British politicians and the British Army chiefs in particular deserve no accolades for their cowardly and disgraceful conduct at this particular period of time.

Mobile patrols were routine and uneventful. The Jews didn't really need us at this point, but the gesture had to be made. We kept fairly well to ourselves and just occasionally went into town. All our favourite night clubs or bars were inhabited by male and female members of Palmach or the Haganah, sun bronzed, happy and carefree all getting slightly drunk. Most were armed and this was embarrassing. As we were armed and in uniform they knew we were mainly HOP and what Meehan's threat had been, so they put them out of sight. They wanted to buy us drinks and socialize but we were very wary, and the women in particular if they spoke English continually spoke of their success in the battle. It was pointless to argue; we just listened. They had achieved what they wanted, now let's all be friends; it left a nasty taste.

Then the American Marines of the United Nations Force arrived to restore and maintain the agreed terms of Partition. Whenever a Palestine policeman entered a bar where American Marines were sitting they left immediately. In the street they avoided you like the plague, in shops too, it was so strange. The mystery was solved after a few days, when three policemen walked into a bar toilet to find a Marine on his own. The bloke was terrified, he apologised, backed off and was stopped from leaving by one of the policemen, who asked him the reason for this attitude. The Americans enjoy being brainwashed, and to a man they had been told to keep away from us at all costs. We were the equivalent of the Gestapo, trained killers who would shoot at the slightest provocation, etc., etc. After a chat and a drink no further misunderstandings were in evidence and for the short time remaining we all got on extremely well.

With the exception of ten HOP armoured cars and a few 3-ton and 15-cwt vehicles all police transport had been delivered to a military pound near Bat Galim. On the morning before we were due to leave Paddy Sayers told me I would be taking old '604' on its last journey. As we were about to leave he quietly told me something had been fixed: the cars, without weapons, were being sold to the Jews and eventually we would be given a cut. We arrived at Bat Galim and to the obvious consternation of certain personnel a Para Major jumped on the leading vehicle and off we went. As we approached the Wadi opposite my old police station at Athlit we all saw this collection of Jews, some with bulging briefcases, standing by the end of the Wadi, obviously expecting us to pull up in convoy and the exchange to take place. There were open-mouthed looks of astonishment on their faces as we passed them and took the road up the Wadi. At a given point we stopped and each vehicle was pushed over the edge of a deep cliff. It was sad to lose a vehicle like that and although I and others were several hundred pounds lighter we all felt that justice had been done although the lads didn't know about the arrangements until we were on board ship. I did not hear one of them moan about the vehicles being destroyed. This was one instance when the power of money did not prevail.

The end was also not without humour and some frustration. We climbed aboard the trucks to take us to the port and drove slowly down the drive of eucalyptus trees leaving our last billet in Palestine. At the gate stood a ragtag assortment of Haganah! In some sort of line and standing at the present they looked awful. It was a nice gesture and probably meant well. This was the start of the Israeli Army. I was probably the most vocal in our party, being one of the few sergeants and also an ex Scots Guards NCO. From the truck I criticized their line, dress, stance and arms drill in Drill Sergeant's style. Another ex Coldstream, Jim Hagarty (now in Australia) who was also our barber, helped out and everybody had a laugh. Even the Jews without exception had faces wreathed in smiles, taking all the ribald comments in good order. I suppose this was the best way to leave.

We moved on to the 'Z' Craft which transported us to the troop ship *Empress of Australia*. Although we had civilian status and were entitled to Second Class accommodation, we understood it would be different on board a troopship but certainly not what we were given. All two hundred of us, irrespective of rank, were quickly shepherded down steps, passageways and gangways. To our disgust we were shown a large area below the forward hold, which had bunk beds, hammocks, with some tables and benches and a quick count revealed there were not enough bed spaces for our party unless people slept on the tables or deck. The officer said he had his orders and this was the Palestine Police accommodation. Like one man the exodus started, some still carrying their baggage. Our senior officer on board, a Chief Inspector whose name I forget, shouted for the 'Z' craft to remain until negotiations had finished. The OC troops solved his problems: he ordered the vessel to leave and we were on board like it or lump it. Talks between the seniors achieved nothing. There were incidents of a physical nature between MP's/troops and PP. Things were becoming ugly when out of the blue the Americans gave us a free floor show which temporarily cooled matters down.

Anchored in Haifa Harbour was an American Navy support or logistic ship which I believe had brought the Marines to Palestine as part of the United Nations Force. It had weighed anchor and was moving parallel to the main quay when someone noticed it was not turning seawards.

Then some half a dozen sailors who were up forward suddenly started moving frantically towards the stern. We were all strangely quiet as the drama unfolded before us. We could hear bells ringing and shouts on board but the ship ploughed majestically on towards the oil jetty, veering not an inch. Some fifty yards or so from the jetty the anchors were dropped but it was a futile effort; ship and jetty met with a resounding crash and the ship appeared to bounce back in the water for a few moments. There was a hush, nothing seemed to be happening on board, then suddenly the anchors were raised and the ship reversed, turned to port and slowly limped out of the port to loud cheers and jeers from our ship and no doubt people ashore. All we could see was a huge hole some distance above the water line, which had no doubt been considered safe. To the US Navy an embarrassing disaster and no doubt some bruised bodies and reputations, but to us it gave a breathing space. The OC troops allowed Superintendent Meehan and a senior Mandate official on board and certain concessions were obtained. Owing to the intense heat an airshaft would be dropped into our area to help reduce the temperature, we would be moved to other accommodation after calls at Cyprus and Malta, we could sleep on the 1st Class Promenade deck, discipline ourselves and give *limited* fatigues to the ship's routine. A veiled antagonism remained throughout the voyage between the ship's staff and PP and violence nearly erupted again when we wanted to give an impromptu concert for all on board and wished to move the piano on to the aft deck. OC troops said no, so having suffered four days of insufferable restrictions to normal life on board to 2nd class passengers and civilians, a party of the lads went to the officers' lounge who gladly said 'take ours' and came and watched the concert with the various ladies on board who enjoyed First Class passage.

If my memory serves me right it was a great concert, with 'Scouse' Hanlon and I singing duets and solos and a host of other volunteers. The PP morale soared accordingly. At the end it was noticed that the OC troops was applauding enthusiastically from the top deck with the other officers. Do I remember correctly or did I shout for silence, salute and ask for permission to dismiss the parade, tongue in cheek of course. The piano was returned undamaged with thanks and as a result we seemed to be treated with a little more respect. Representations were made on arrival at Liverpool; what the final outcome was we never found out. Our baggage was very thoroughly searched at Liverpool, but we had been warned and a number of us paid surreptitious visits to the side of the vessel and disposed of our private firearms. I did hear that one bloke was seen disposing of a Tommy gun; what the hell he wanted that for I don't know.

Paddy Sayers, Clark Linguard, George Stewart and I were met by Sgt. Tommy Thompson, a Haifa HQ Security bloke who lived in Liverpool. He had been home quite a few weeks. We all stayed the night at his parents' home at Huyton, then down to a pub, drinks, supper, and many tales later we fell asleep in various parts of the house. All the bedrooms were occupied. We were home.

Some weeks later, with the band of the Grenadier Guards at our head, the last few hundred members of the Palestine Police marched proudly out of Wellington Barracks towards the rear of Buckingham Palace. We even received a smile and a cheerful wave from Princess Margaret who was standing at a window at the side of the Palace. There on the back lawn the King inspected our lines and talked to many. I think his final words were: 'You can look back on a job well done.' It was something of an understatement.

The Palestine Police Force was an elite, although circumstances dictated a change towards the end with an emphasis on the gun rather than the Criminal Code Ordinance, and selection of recruits not as thorough as in normal times. Of course there was some corruption but it was minimal. The Force had its cowards but it had a lot more heroes. Looking back, one remembers loyalty, dedication, professionalism and a wonderful comrade-ship that will ever be hard to match and which is still shown in the Palestine Police Old Comrades Association. Time will eventually catch up even on the PPOCA; there will not be many members left in fifteen years time.

So ended a very significant period of my life. I had become a very mature person, I had travelled thousands of miles by sea, seen strange lands, held responsibility way above my age bracket, endured horror and violence, seen death many times and was also responsible for many. I learned to drink like a man and hold it, play darts like a *News of the World* champion, and shoot like Annie Oakley. It was a shock to learn I could converse in a foreign language after a fashion, and pass educational and police law exams by applying myself to study. I also matured in many other ways which are not always appreciated at the time but I remembered quiet tears when a friend was killed on patrol in the streets. A man I was, brimming over with confidence, probably too cocky by half, but all that was part of growing up.

In London we had been asked to consider joining the Malaya Police Force, which was expanding owing to yet again a problem with the Communists. The matter was broached with my mother who was aghast. I had been away from home for over four years, my brother John 6¹/₂ years, and was now married; she said surely I could remain at home. I had a great affection for my mother and felt obliged to stay. Since my father died in 1935 and until 1944, my mother and I were very close; she had had several proposals of marriage but never felt that any man was as good as my father, and thought we felt the same way. So if I had gone to Malaya I might have been killed or injured, knowing my penchant for locating trouble. On the other hand I have might have risen to greater heights and become a leading figure in Colonial policing like several other ex PP. God obviously directed otherwise and my future life formed a different pattern. I am not sorry that it continued on its stated course otherwise my memories would not have been written.

CHAPTER 7

Police 1948-56 – Preston and Kent

My eight years spent with the UK Police Service in Preston Borough Police and Kent County Constabulary in many respects were wasted, which was a great pity because I think if the police system at that time had been fair, I and many thousands of disgruntled policemen could have made ourselves a very successful career.

Let's start at the beginning. The Chief Constable of Preston in 1946, Mr H. Garth, and his predecessor had always stated their willingness to help my mother in any way as she was a police widow. When my brother John after $6^1/2$ years war service and a perfect record attempted to join Preston Borough Police he was refused because he was a quarter inch under the five foot nine so called height limit, although I knew of several pre-war and post war officers who were slightly under: a lot depended on who you knew. John served on the Birmingham City Force until enforced separation from his wife and family forced him to resign. When I came back from Palestine I wanted to continue in the Colonial Service and join the Malayan Police; former members of the Palestine Police had been asked to consider joining this expanding force because of the advent of problems with the Chinese Communist Terrorists. Several contemporaries of mine were killed, and many transferred successfully to other Colonial forces and Government jobs to promotion and great success. Paddy Sayers, my senior Sergeant in HOP, became an Assistant Commissioner in Malaya. My mother was extremely successful however in persuading me that I should remain in the UK and look after her; she was only fifty-five years of age at the time and every inch a woman but she made me feel guilty contemplating leaving her alone again as she had had a worrying time between 1939-48 until John and I were both back home and there were other problems too.

I had never been particularly keen on parts of Lancashire that I had seen, they always appeared to be drab and dismal so I did not relish working in these conditions so I opted for Preston Borough Police which in retrospect was the wrong choice. Not only was the Force restrictive towards personnel but the internal intrigue was so close to a Mafia type organization, that it was only when the Borough Force was amalgamated with the County several years later that many qualified individuals on the Borough were promoted to high rank. Before amalgamation two individuals moved away from Preston because due to circumstances they suddenly found themselves promoted as a result of an increase in establishment and a death. They were in a position to apply for jobs in other forces. After a number of moves Ronnie Gregory and Donald Roy became Chief Constable and Assistant Chief Constable respectively of the West Yorkshire Force; both had been talented Detective Constables in Preston. Fortune smiled on them or something did, as I think within seven years both had moved from Constable to Deputy Chief Constable and Detective Superintendent respectively.

In many respects the small Borough forces were failures because they were riddled with intrigue or in conjunction with Chief Constables' peccadillos. One exception in the North-West was Wigan Borough where a Catholic monopoly had power for promotion. Local Watch Committees also wielded some influence: if your face fitted your competence as a policeman was insignificant. Intrigue and influence with the necessary Police Committees held the key to success.

I was accepted by the Borough and started the Course at the Police Training Centre at Bruche, near Warrington. Since my return from Palestine I had met Jean Charnley, Bill's sister, and we had been seeing quite a lot of each other, so I always had company on my weekends away from Bruche. I also found time in between studies to drop her a line during the week. Bruche however was busy and interesting; if we were not studying we were practising for our swimming proficiency medals and time passed very quickly. Suddenly it was time to start our initial period of an introductory month on night duty.

After two years on probation and satisfactory reports you were officially accepted as a Constable and it was customary to return you to the School for a Refresher Course or other Training School. This was essential to clarify any anomalies you had experienced in this period of your service; it was terribly important to the future of every Constable. Our Chief Constable refused to allow this or take steps to give us local instruction. As a result many officers became discontented, feeling that the future was bleak and they had no incentive to strive for higher rank. This attitude to a limited degree contributed to a terrible scandal in the Force which did not help morale and should have resulted in the removal of the Chief Constable forthwith but he held tremendous influence in the town.

One Constable was given twelve months imprisonment for warehouse breaking and larceny, an Inspector, a Sergeant and two Constables were summarily dismissed; others were asked to resign but refused; others were suspected of crime but the facts could not be proved; about a dozen in all were involved. It was suspected that this group over a period of time had been entering premises on night duty with keys left in the safe custody of the police and removing cash or goods. It was a worrying time for many people including myself because the Inspector and Sergeant were in charge of my shift and so were many of the suspects, who knew what the jailed man had said when he was questioned, and who he could have innocently involved or left under suspicion. My fears were removed when, on a police trip, Ronnie Gregory (who had been in charge of the investigation) put my mind at rest and opened it with other information.

Apart from work my favourite preoccupation was sport. I was instrumental in starting the Preston Borough Police football team in 1949 and was elected Captain. We won the Thursday League in 1950, 1951 and 1952 and also were Cup winners against Preston Postal in 1952 when we played before *10,000* people on Preston North End's ground at Deepdale. I scored the opening goal, Postal equalized, and PC Bert Jackson won the match for us in extra time. Owing to another little piece of intrigue I was relieved of the captaincy ten days before this match. The manner in which this was done upset me but I was transferring shortly and I took it all philosophically, getting a lot of support and sympathy from the 'straight ones' on the force. The other enjoyable sport was cricket, which apart from two or three exceptions included a lot of the football team. All the playing was done in our own time; we all enjoyed the sport but we had greater fun on the social side. Transport was carried out by a Chorley Coach firm. The driver insisted he should undertake all trips for the Borough Police, and had special notices made for the front and rear of his coach on who his passengers were. We used to stop at various pubs on the way back from matches and we would entertain the locals with songs etc. It was hilarious and often we were asked to return. It all helped to escape from the restrictive tediousness of the job. They were happy days for me and for others who are still around at the time of writing; they too recall the fun with great affection.

To be totally critical of a Borough Force would be unfair. There were certain aspects of 'Borough bobbying' which were good and to the public's benefit. Within three to four years, having served on all three Divisions, a Constable knew every villain by sight and a lot of other information too. Frequently on nights each beat had a Constable until 2a.m. so the town was extremely well policed when villains were around. Actually, during four years' service, about eighteen months or so on nights I only had one break in on my beats and that was over a wall. Conversely, during daylight hours we spent more time directing traffic than patrolling a beat, and speaking to members of the public was classed as 'gossiping' which was a very inward looking outlook towards police work. I could recall many instances of incidents involving humour, fright, violence, intrigue and crimes stolen by CID personnel from uniform PCs; it all contributed to a feeling of utter frustration of job prospects for the next twenty odd years and as my marriage to Jean was in the offing I approached 1952 with thoughts of a move or even leaving the force and taking a Tetley pub which I had been offered.

We married in February 1952 and settled in with my mother in Stanley Grove, where we had said we would take care of the day to day running of the house, food, electricity and so on. You can imagine my chagrin when my mother confronted me with a three figure bill for road charges and she thought it was my duty as she intended to leave the house to me eventually, although nothing was in writing. I hadn't fifty pounds to my name in any case. As the house was still in my mother's name and she stated she would pay the rates I didn't feel I had any commitment towards the house in any way; she could always change her mind. When she began to involve Jean in her anger, we both had long discussions and decided to transfer down south very reluctantly, away from both sets of parents. I fancied the City of London or Metropolitan force but Jean was not keen on living in the London area so we agreed on the Kent Constabulary. The preliminaries were soon sorted out and in May 1952 I reported to Hythe on the south coast near to Folkestone. Jean had moved home and had a suspicion she could be pregnant which was later confirmed. I had been found 'digs' with a lovely old couple in Dymchurch Road, Hythe. My main moan was the repetitiveness of the food, the old girl was no cook, but I was very comfortable. In a matter of weeks I had found a suitable top storey flat at 26 Seabrook Road opposite the Catholic Church and Jean joined me, to really start our married life together.

At this stage I must place on record my comments concerning the influence of Freemasonry within the Police Force. Much has been written about it in the past and no doubt more will follow. On my arrival in Kent a family friend on the Isle of Sheppey and a very senior Mason, made me an offer of membership, knowing full well I was a practising RC, and told me he could guarantee a successful Police career for me. Dear old Ted Ashton, a PC at Hythe, also tried persuasion but no way would I join. Another friend at Hythe tried to encourage me to join the Catholic society of 'Catenians', not a secret society but religiously inclined. Membership was almost totally well established, influential professional men, I refused this too.

I take the strong view that when you join a society, group or club you must abide totally to 'the rules', and there is no way in this world that I would enjoy exerting any influence or help towards a fellow member who was not a genuine friend, who commanded my respect, and deservedly needed help. I could never pull out the stops, just because 'he's one of us'.

I don't believe it necessary for any person who believes in the Ten Commandments and loves his neighbour to join a so called charitable and philanthropic society and contribute a great deal of money, in order to do good deeds. This can be done within the Church of your choice or any public society.

By choice I shun Buffs, Knights, Rotary and Round Table; from Lodges to poky rooms all of these associations mentioned contain a percentage of members who are genuinely honest and well meaning, but more whose only reason for joining is 'What can this association do for me?' *not* 'What worthwhile contribution can I make to my association?' and that is when the first threads of corruption begin to manifest themselves. People join for totally the wrong reasons and I find that sad.

If I could produce legislation I would forbid membership of these 'associations' to all Police Officers under the rank of Assistant Chief Constable. I would also include the Fire Service and the Civil Service under the grade of Senior Executive Officer. Why do people of obvious talent consider it necessary to have a Masonic/Catenian crutch; are they frightened of more competent competition in the stakes they are striving for or is it a 100 per cent insurance policy? It does not appear to be so evident in the Armed Forces, but no doubt it is there. I was once told of a Captain, a very senior Mason, who was confronted one evening with his recently joined Brigadier; similarly this also happened in the Police Force – how embarrassing for all concerned. How could you possibly maintain discipline?

To those who join and succeed on personal merit may your God go with you. I prefer to have done it my way, then I know it is all my own work and from this I have derived great satisfaction, egotistical but honest.

The Inspector in charge of Hythe sub Division was Inspector Stickings. Not only was he a good policeman but he was a gentleman too. Life was very placid in comparison to Preston. One instance was an order to visit the local Mackeson's Brewery several times a night, not only to visit the Bonded Warehouses and ensure the watchman was safe, but also drink a special jug of ale that was left each night for the Constable. The Brewery didn't like it if it was not drunk. It was also possible to get more!! I also played for the Divisional football team with a fellow Hythe policeman called Rex Gilham, who played for Folkestone in the Southern League on

Saturdays. This lead to me playing for Hythe Town in the local Amateur League and eventually we qualified to meet Erith and Belvedere in the sixth round proper of the Kent Amateur Cup. Erith was one of the top amateur clubs in the country; they had two England internationals, and three budding candidates in their very talented side. On a day when a thaw was in progress and playing on their ground we were beaten 6-2, four of their goals coming from the left winger when our goalkeeper couldn't move for the mud round his ankles. I don't suppose we would have beaten them in better conditions but the margin would not have been so great. Even their supporters stated this. My personal satisfaction was that I had kept England's No 2 Centre forward Vic Parris in my pocket for the whole match. In his frustration to score he turned to me and asked me to 'Go away' or something similar. Although we were well beaten, in the Erith clubhouse we were well praised, so the experience was worth it.

I had forgot to mention that shortly after my arrival in Kent I was offered a trial for the Force's County side but I did not impress. I was most uncomfortable and my boots hurt playing on an iron hard pitch which I was not used to. There were two England Police internationals in the side I played for. I played out of my normal position and I failed. Three years later I played at outside right for the County and also practised against Gillingham FC. I did not play again following an incident when the Gillingham captain tried to climb up my back; he was knocked unconscious and had a broken nose when he met my head.

Christopher Anthony Howard, weight 9lbs 8ozs, was born on the 24th February 1953 at Willesborough Hospital near Ashford; they were both well. On the afternoon of the 23rd Jean and I had gone to the cinema in Hythe, and the first picture was about a woman, heavily pregnant, whose name was Howard, who entered hospital only to lose the baby in the operating theatre. This did not make Jean very happy when things started to happen the following day. I was on 6p.m.-2a.m. evenings. Inspector Stickings told me to stay close to home. In the end I had to order the ambulance and force Jean from the flat. In those days there was no opportunity to stay for the birth so I left a very apprehensive wife, still protesting that the baby was not due, and I went back to work. At 2.30a.m. there was still no news so I went to bed. At 9.30a.m. when I rang from the call box opposite the flat I was a father; they were both fine and I was delighted. When Jean left hospital her mother joined us at the flat for a couple of weeks which was a great help although rather cramped. We never had any sleepless nights; maybe it was the sea air. Chris was an ideal baby.

Spring arrived and the tragedy of the east coast floods involved the north coast of Kent, but although I was detailed for flood duty at Herne

Bay I was not required. In actual fact we were extremely close to a flood problem in the area of Hythe and Dymchurch.

The next main event was the Coronation of Queen Elizabeth II and I was selected for the three-day duty in London. Our Kent detachment was accommodated under canvas on Hyde Park and our area of duty was on the east side of East Carriage Row which is situated between Marble Arch and Hyde Park Corner. Every Police Force in the country sent representatives, usually their tallest, most impressive and be-medalled, as a large percentage were ex servicemen. Although on the day it was a tedious and tiring duty, it was a day to remember as most ceremonials are and I was privileged to be chosen.

On the day prior to the Coronation Ronnie Gregory and I met again and had a few hours in a pub owned by a friend. Ronnie was a Detective Constable at that time in Preston, and later became Chief Constable of West Yorkshire. In the evening of the Coronation I was in the company of 'Taffy' Dwyer, a PC from Preston and an ex Welsh Guardsman. Together we located Johnny O'Neill and his family in a pub in Bermondsey; Johnny was ex Palestine Police and Irish Guards. The ensuing party was quite monumental. The tables were awash with bottles of beer and I can't remember having to pay anything for the food or drink. Within the pub was the Borough Irish Pipe Band; John's father was the Drum Major. The evening ended in fine style at approximately 2a.m. with the Pipe Band led by John's father and flanked by three ex Guardsmen marching and playing through the near deserted streets from Bermondsey to the Elephant and Castle. It had been quite a day and one I would not have missed. I enjoyed meeting old friends and it was an experience to deal with the British public on such a celebration; it demonstrated their patience, orderliness, understanding and more importantly good humour on public occasions.

The one aspect of police work that I had not experienced at Preston was acting as Coroner's Officer with Sudden Deaths, and also attending Post Mortems. My first Sudden Death was a lady who had died in bed, who had a history of cerebral problems, and was also badly burned, no doubt due to the electric blanket being switched on after her demise. When I attended the mortuary at Folkestone I was confronted by the Senior Pathologist for South East England whose name I forget. He stated that we had never met before so I explained where I had come from.

'Ah, so you have never attended a PM before,' he said, rubbing his hands.

'No,' says I.

'Good, I have a bit of time, let's begin,' he said, and for the next hour or so I was treated, if that's the right word, to a lesson in the make up and functions of the human body particularly the female one. A PM is not for the squeamish but once I had overcome the initial revulsion of the first incision and that odious smell I was quite captivated, he made it all so interesting. I just wish I could have retained all the information that he imparted in that hour or more that I spent with him. The many others that followed were mainly routine and quick. They are never a pleasant experience but a very necessary one.

The PM I was pleased to miss occurred when I was in Ashford CID and the whole case was quite an eyeopener for all concerned. George Hutchins was one of the English police football internationals I wrote about earlier and he was a Detective Constable at Ashford; we both played in the Divisional Football Team and I worked as his partner in CID. We were dealing with a burglary at a large house in Kennington when George was called away to attend to a complaint from a householder in Willesborough. The lady in question had rented her front room to a young lady (Miss D) some months before and without warning about three weeks ago the young lady had left leaving behind a large trunk. The lady of the house stated there was a terrible smell emanating from the trunk; was she allowed to break it open? George did it for her, and inside were the bodies of two small babies wrapped in a plastic mac. I joined George and removed the bodies to the mortuary. It was not pleasant as they had obviously been dead some time. We made initial enquiries then I had to leave to continue on the burglary enquiry.

When I returned to the Station I checked with our telephone operator about information I required from the Metropolitan Police and also engaged in conversation with a very pleasant young lady who was sitting in the exchange. When I entered the CID I was told that the person responsible for the deaths of the two children had been found and arrested. I asked where she was being held and they told me she was in the Telephone Exchange downstairs; she had been found in Dover. I was amazed. I could not believe the person I spoke to for so long could be responsible for the deaths of those poor innocents but more was to come and poor George was the person who had to attend this rather gruesome PM. If my memory serves me right the PM assessed the ages of the bodies as approximately twenty and ten months respectively; this was corroborated by Miss D.

Initial police enquiries had revealed the conviction of Miss D at Ashford several years earlier when she worked in a Government Department. She was the subject of comment from associates about her weight increase over the last four months which she laughed about. One morning she stated she felt unwell and went to the toilet; on her return some time later she stated her intention to return home which she did, saying she would be back the following day. Some time later that day a female colleague entered a toilet and to her horror found the body of a newly born child lying head first and dead in the toilet bowl. Miss D was eventually charged with infanticide and jailed. She admitted that she had visited a pub near the TA Camp at Shorncliffe near Folkestone the previous year and had had intercourse with several TA Soldiers over a long period of time and subsequently became pregnant. She could not offer a satisfactory explanation for her actions concerning the baby. The two bodies in the trunk were from her last two pregnancies for which she had acquired a sense of parental responsibility and wanted to keep them near her. In between her conviction and the latest 'find' she stated that there were three to five other bodies disposed of in various places which she couldn't specify but all had been conceived during her annual 'holiday' or 'visitation' to the area of Shorncliffe Camp or its environment.

To return to Hythe. It is a beautiful little town and its weather must be considered some of the best enjoyed on the south coast so it was with some disappointment in certain aspects that I was offered a police house and a move to Ashford some twelve miles up the A20. The house was No 13 Birling Road opposite the Energen Factory. It was three bedroomed and had a garden, not an ideal property but we were delighted. The decorations were somewhat bizarre owing to the previous occupant but we later changed this. We also borrowed some £200, interest free, from the Police Fund, to us an enormous amount, in order to furnish the house, and we settled in most satisfactorily with our neighbours. Ashford was a busy market town and it had a considerable traffic problem in the summer months but life was never hectic, just routine with the odd accident or drunk thrown in.

We had our share of visitors. My mother had come to her senses and agreed to make the long journey, also Jean's father and mother, Uncle Bill, John, Marie and the children and others. The following year Jean lost twins with a miscarriage which took us by surprise as she was so fit; apparently her womb, no doubt weakened by carrying a heavy baby like Chris, just could not carry two. It was all very sad and disappointing especially for Jean as she always wanted a large family, and further pregnancies could be doubtful.

I used to spend a lot of time with Chris watching the new Ashford bypass being built which quite fascinated him; the bulldozers and scrapers held his interest for hours. We also acquired a black Labrador named Bruce, but unfortunately he broke a leg and had to be put down. He was chasing a cat that approached the pram and was hit by a passing wagon. I was also involved in sport: as a member of the Divisional Life Saving Team we came second in the South of England competition involving twenty-one teams. It was hard work but enjoyable. As it was summer I also played for the Divisional Cricket Team, made more enjoyable because we sometimes played civilian teams from the surrounding villages which was a day out for the families. During the winter months football was 'king', played on Wednesdays in the Divisional Police League. On Saturdays augmented by three civilians we played as the Ashford Casuals and were very successful winning the Premier Division for three seasons and a junior Cup Final. In the Police League we were in alternate seasons Winners and Runners Up in Divisional football and cricket plus the life saving effort which in those seasons produced nine trophies.

On arrival at Ashford I had of course amassed five years service and was earmarked for a fifth year Refresher Course at Police Headquarters at Maidstone. I have never felt so inadequate, my colleagues could leave me standing on Police Law. I was hopeless in comparison and this was mainly due to the failure of Preston Borough to send us on the two-year Refresher Course. In addition some Divisions had former instructors from Police Schools who volunteered to coach personnel in Police Law. I finished the Course, though not with a great difference in the number of marks, nevertheless a very disappointing second from bottom. Some months later I passed the Inspectors' Educational exam, but failed the Sergeants' exam in Police Law. I failed to achieve an average of 60 per cent although mine was 59 per cent; it just showed that my background knowledge of the five

Kent County Constabulary, Ashford, 1954.

subjects was lacking. It needed more coaching and more time spent on reading; I suppose one can blame home, garden, sport etc., but I still think the classroom is the correct place to learn law in the early stages.

However things were not improving at work. I seemed to need more activity, a change. My application for permanence into CID came to nothing, also Traffic Section, Dog Section, and a short tour in Cyprus were refused and I seriously considered our future. My Superintendent admitted that he had shelved all my applications for transfer because he did not want to lose my services as a sportsman and he later apologised. I even contemplated a move to the Hong Kong Police but I was about a year over the age limit and they were not prepared to make an exception even though I was a former Colonial Police Officer. All the probabilities of promotion or transfer were looked into very closely. The prospects were not encouraging at that time and many others like me wondered about the future. Maybe it was me, I needed more to do, to get really involved, that's why the CID held my fascination and I had been well recommended but my chances receded as more men came on the list for selection. Many selected gave it up after a few months. The hours, dedication, and other aspects of the job just did not suit them, good 'Jacks' are born not made.

It was not an easy decision to make and Jean was not keen but I was returning to Army life where I felt I could at least progress on my own ability, where Freemasonry was not so evident and it certainly had power in Kent as in Preston. I would never have been a 'legal eagle' as a policeman, but having got over the first hurdle and with incentive I think I would have made a good 'bobby'. Quite a lot of the attributes of a senior police officer showed up when I was involved in Intelligence work but who knows? Should I have gone to Malaya, stayed at Preston, later to Lancashire Constabulary, or taken my chance in Kent County?

The decision was made. I was resigning. Jean and Chris moved back to Preston and her parents, and I was bound for the Guards Depot. I felt sad really because I could have made a success of a police career, but I, like many thousands of others, became disillusioned with the job and some of the people within it. The police service will never be perfect; they can only strive to achieve perfection but certain anomalies should be removed and more emphasis made on ability, personality and dedication of individuals before consideration to higher rank. In later years I was privileged to know many very senior police officers of sound reputation (some of them were possibly Freemasons) but all were scathing of a system that allowed a fair percentage of incompetent individuals to attain senior rank. During my last night of duty in Kent County Constabulary I finally hit the jackpot.

I commenced my last duty at 10p.m., taking the view 'just one more and that's the last', and anticipating nothing out of the ordinary as I started to patrol my given beat for the night in Ashford town centre. Sergeant T was an old policeman close to retirement whom I had slowly grown to dislike; he was generally surly, incommunicative, unhelpful and in certain aspects of police work, incompetent. I had witnessed this at first hand, but as the sergeants rotated he was tolerated by the PCs. About 11p.m. I received a message via the telephone kiosk to apprehend a Ford Prefect, colour white, and a given registration number. It was believed to be heading towards Ashford along the A20 from Folkestone. The occupants had been involved in a serious warehouse breaking and larceny. I waited for over an hour at the top of the hill in Ashford but no vehicle arrived so I slowly made my way back to the centre to contact the Station. I could hear a car approaching me from behind and as it passed I noticed it was white, it was the latest model Ford Prefect and very distinctive, the number tallied, and the two occupants were obviously agitated and looking behind at me, so I ignored them. When the car was out of sight I dashed off to the Station only 100 yards away. I yelled to PC Lou Chapman the information and to tell Maidstone HQ.

Sergeant T was unimpressed. He finished off his writing, slowly dressed himself, and even more slowly walked into the yard and the police van, in which we set off in mad pursuit doing 30m.p.h. along the deserted A20 heading for Charing some six miles away. The car radio was 'duff'; I couldn't even raise Maidstone HQ. As we were passing the Swan Hotel at Charing I yelled for Sergeant T to stop, as I could see a new model white Prefect parked outside the hotel.

'You go and check it out and I'll drive up the road and see if the radio will work,' and off he went like the clappers.

I reached the empty car and the number was the wanted vehicle that had passed me in Ashford; the rear of the car was full of cartons of cigarettes, as was the boot. As I reached the top of the steps near the entrance two men appeared, one of average height and build, the other as tall as I but several stone heavier. I instinctively knew that this couple were the criminals involved, but I had to box clever, I was alone with no help immediately available and was likely to get hurt if they decided to make a run for it. The big chap was the danger man so I moved close to him, keeping my right hand free. He was the driver and if anyone had to be thumped it was him.

'Good evening, gentlemen; I presume that is your car standing there without lights.'

'That's right; what's wrong with that? We're not on a road.'

'I agree. What are you doing here at this time?'

'We wanted a bed for the night, but they're full.'

'Where have you travelled from?'

'Folkestone'.

'Can I see your driving licence please.' The big man handed it over.

'Which way did you travel from Folkestone?'

'To Canterbury and then here.'

'And you stayed on that road the whole time?'

'Yes, sure.'

It was now crunch time, I'd memorised the man's name and address on the licence and his insurance, but I dropped the licence in my pocket just in case. I was ready to hit him if he made a dash.

'Mr — you are a liar. You have just driven from Dover along the A20 and I personally saw you in Ashford a short time ago, your car is also full of stolen fags.' They both looked at one another and I thought this is it and on my last night too. My right arm drew back and exactly at that moment the Area Traffic car flew into the hotel car park, spilling out two PCs. The two criminals looked at each other, gave a rueful grin and rather resignedly walked slowly down the steps. Then the 'Lone Ranger' arrived in the shape of Sergeant T. 'I managed to sort the matter out and get you help!' he exclaimed. One of the Traffic PCs drove the Prefect back to Ashford and we took the two men in the van where they appeared to be rather agitated, moving about a lot.

After ascertaining certain particulars from the men they were placed in separate cells and the 'booty' was brought in to be counted. Then came the head of Dover CID, a Chief Inspector, with entourage.

'This is great!' he cried. 'The two most wanted blokes in the county, nailed with the goods, this will clear a lot of stuff up. Who arrested them?'

'He did,' said a Traffic PC, pointing to me.

'Son you have no idea how much this will do for you in the job,' said the Chief Inspector.

'I doubt it, in about six hours time I'll be handing in my uniform,' giving him a rueful grin.

'I'm really sorry about that,' and he meant it.

A search of the car only revealed the stolen items; the Chief Inspector needed proof of the actual break in. A few minutes later I asked him to come with me. I lifted up the rear seat of the police van and there lay a selection of screwdrivers and chisels covered in brick and mortar dust and fingerprints. The job was tied up, so I went back on the beat, being told to report in at 5.45a.m. which I did. Sergeant T then presented me with his statement for me to countersign. I was quite astonished. The statement was outlined in such a way that Sergeant T would get the credit and I would just corroborate. It was vague and a good defence counsel could have torn it to pieces. By this time I couldn't care less. I signed and walked out in disgust. At 9a.m. I was back at the Station handing all my kit in for forwarding to Maidstone.

George Hutchins tapped me on the shoulder and said, 'The DI [Detective Inspector] wants to see you.'

DI Hall came from the Manchester area and was a good 'jack'; you worked hard under him, but he was fair. All the office sat around and listened. Mr Hall looked at me and waved the papers in his hand.

'I've just read the report on last night's job and I've never read so much cock in all my life, I've known Sergeant T for many, many years; he is not capable of doing the things he implies in this statement, it's all lies and you have signed it, why?'

'Because he disgusts me, and I just wanted to get out of his way; he left me and I could have had my head caved in with those chisels.'

'You had better tell me what really happened.'

So I did just that.

With the DS at my side and George Hutchins writing it down, a comprehensive statement was compiled to leave no doubt of the true events leading to the capture of these two dangerous characters and so that a jury would have no doubt either. Some time later the men appeared at Dover Sessions. I gave my evidence. Sergeant T was not called; he didn't even acknowledge me. Hopefully he felt embarrassed. He also shook hands the right way. The two men received heavy sentences and with that my Police service ceased on a high note.

So Kent came to an end but not quite. Within two months I was back again at Lydd, and five years later to Chatham and Gravesend. Kent is a lovely county now facing the ravages of more urbanization with the advent of the Channel Tunnel which is so sad, and dear old Ashford became the home of the Intelligence Corps.

CHAPTER 8

May 1956 – Lydd ISG

The removal of our furniture, handing over the house and so on, was trauma enough following the departure of Jean and Chris to Preston. I must confess my mind was full of doubts at this time and I was experiencing some apprehension about my decision. Family life disrupted, a sad and worried wife, house and furniture gone and the start of a new career facing me; the success or failure of this totally down to me.

I stayed a couple of nights with neighbours and reported eventually to the Guards Depot, Caterham, Surrey and found my way to 'K' Company. Reporting to CSM Croucher he immediately said, 'Major Phillipson, the Officer Commanding, wishes to see you: how do you know him?' and I recalled that at the end of the war, at the Battle School in Wales, Major P was a frequent visitor from the Training Battalion and he attended each demonstration, taking many photographs. One particular morning Major P had been extremely lucky not to be killed by me, when in his anxiety to take a particular shot he stood up close to a wall from which I was firing my Bren gun. His head suddenly appeared in front of the gun barrel; fortunately I was changing the magazine. Not immediately realizing who the head belonged to, I came out with a mouthful of invective, not very complimentary, I can assure you. Major P apologised and told me to carry on; nothing further was mentioned. So I wondered why the OC specifically wished to see me.

When Major P saw me he very kindly offered me a very warm welcome back to the Regiment and wished me well for the future. The squad I was posted to had completed seven weeks of training and all of the members were eighteen years of age and very fit. I was quite choked when I returned from the Stores with all my kit; most of it was taken away by individual room mates, boots were burnt and highly polished, kit was blancoed and polished, buttons sewn on; it was very satisfying. I had been accepted as 'the elder statesman'. As an extraordinary incident I was issued with a set of four brushes all stamped with the number 2703567; this was the number

I had been given in 1944 and the brushes had been handed in when I left the Regiment in 1946.

I experienced some difficulty in the initial stages completing long runs but after a fortnight, three miles without stopping was not unusual. Within days I was marching the Squad around Barracks and generally taking over the duties of Trained Soldier (a mature soldier allocated to each Guards Depot Training Squad).

Major P was an eccentric but with a dynamic personality. He insisted that every Scots Guards recruit could swim before he left the Depot, because of his personal experience at Salerno in World War 2. He was also an ardent cricket fan, so I was co-opted in the 'K' Company team, and also made Captain of the Recruit Team, and that year we won the Recruit Competition.

After Recruit Training was completed I was able to make a personal assessment of the training standards. Understandably there was a twelve-year gap and a difference between wartime and peacetime. I found that discipline was harsher in 1944, over training, and there had been a greater sense of urgency and efficiency for obvious reasons. The current standard of training was excellent, but it lacked that slight degree of necessity that wartime training demanded. I think the Falklands War showed that Scots Guards Training was of an extremely high standard.

A few days leave followed Caterham, and I reported to the Training Battalion at Pirbright on the Monday. By lunchtime I had two stripes on my arm, assisting with training recruits. On Friday I was in Lee Metford Camp at Lydd, Kent with the 1st Battalion Scots Guards and despite my quiet objections, the RSM and Adjutant ordered me to join the Regimental Police. I settled in quite quickly to Battalion life; the three rifle Companies were under strength at the time so a relative quiet period ensued, but not for long.

Within a few weeks I found myself temporarily in charge of the Police. Britain was faced with the closure of the Suez Canal, partial mobilization was ordered and organized chaos commenced. The Gymnasium was designated as a Reception and Stores area and over a period of 2/3 days, approximately two hundred Reservists were recalled from various parts of the country, some specialist senior ranks were sent on brief Refresher Courses and a very comprehensive training programme was commenced. 'B' Company was almost totally reformed by Reservists; all the other Companies were reinforced to full strength, which included two squads from Pirbright. My comrades from Caterham were among the newcomers. I was sent on Commanding Officers' Orders, promoted to Lance Sergeant and posted to Left Flank Company. Capt. Prior was the

Company Commander, a tall, slim and very efficient officer. The CSM was a Harry Norton, a recently promoted warrant officer; he was a dour Dundee man, enthusiastic, a former efficient Army boxer but lacking in humour.

As I reported to the CSM he immediately said that I would be taking over 'In Waiting' duties. I stated that I had never undertaken these duties before, but he answered that now would be a good time to learn providing I survived the RSM etc. He appeared to be taking a fiendish delight in my predicament which he had obviously given some thought to. I later appreciated that being thrown to the lions with my lack of experience made me grasp the nettle and I learned quickly. In the Guards each Company has a Sergeant and Corporal in Waiting, a duty they normally perform for one week: to summarise they assist the CSM in the efficient running of the Company.

They are awakened half an hour before Reveille, properly dressed and carrying the 'In Waiting Book'. The Company personnel are raised then chased off for breakfast. Next would be Adjutant's Orders at 0800 hours and the Marching In of personnel, the same routine for Company Orders, then Commanding Officer Orders. Depending on location attendance is necessary at Guard Mountings, inspection of the Company lines and accommodation, and generally ensuring that personnel attended wherever they were ordered. This included the detailing of personnel for Battalion and Company punishment and fatigues parade. At approximately 4p.m. all In Waiting NCOs were summoned to the RSM's Office where he gave out the Orders from Battalion Headquarters to each Company, which had to be repeated verbatim to avoid any mistakes. The final official duty was Tattoo at 10p.m. but it was usually midnight before bed was available: a good eighteen-hour day.

In the days and weeks that passed, the Battalion trained long and hard in personal fitness, skill at arms and tactics. We were part of 3 Division who made up the Strategic Reserve, although we were temporarily restricted by lack of 3-ton transport. Local buses were employed to transport personnel to the nearby training areas. Fortunately we had excellent range facilities and for the weeks that followed rarely was a range vacant, Battalion marksmanship was at an all time high and ammunition did not appear to present any restriction in expenditure. Although we lost our Advance Party for several weeks – they reached Malta, then returned – it was probably a good job that we were not forced into the role of active service. It was later ascertained that the dockers at Barry had managed to carry out sufficient theft, damage and vandalism to our vehicles and equipment to have rendered the Battalion ineffective had we been rushed into action, even to emptying our emergency water jerricans, and that I find inexcusable. A disgraceful action by the few.

As the temperature of the Suez crisis gradually receded, the Reservists were sent home with grateful thanks, and a depleted Battalion commenced a reorganized training cycle. Left Flank moved their accommodation to allow the Pipes and Drums to occupy the 'Spider' accommodation and we moved into brick built accommodation near the gym. One of the first aspects of our new training cycle was Assault Landing training which was to be carried out at the School of Amphibious Warfare at Poole, Dorset under instruction from the Royal Marine Commandos. Without going into great detail, we all found this type of training extremely interesting and quite a change from the normal infantry. Our food and accommodation were first class and the weather warm and sunny. The climax of the training was a Company assault landing on a beach adjacent to a small holiday camp.

On the outskirts of the camp which overlooked the beach were situated at intervals large refuse bins. We were told that the Major General commanding the Royal Marines would be a VIP onlooker, and that our participation should be first class. Indeed everything went perfectly, and our rapid advance was text book stuff. As 10 Platoon scaled the high ground among the explosions and defensive fire I was confronted by a refuse bin belonging to the nearby holiday camp so I deposited a Thunderflash within and retired. To my horror, along a cliff top road a large black car bearing pennant made a slow appearance. It was the Major General RM! Agonizingly it approached the 'primed' dustbin. It couldn't have been timed better: as the car drew level, the bin disintegrated. The driver's reaction was swift and effective and the vehicle disappeared in a cloud of dust. 10 Platoon watched in astonishment and tears of laughter as above the cloud of dirt, sand and smoke at a height of some 20 ft., a straightened, oblong shaped length of galvanised tin slowly floated to the ground like a discarded autumn leaf. Mr Hubbard Ford, my Platoon Officer, was highly amused but forecast a public flogging on board ship for my sins! Capt. England RM (he had a brother serving in the Regiment) was our instructor and he carried out the de-brief on the exercise. He told us the exercise had been extremely well done, and had impressed the Major General, who expressed his reservations on his inadvertent involvement in the proceedings, saying that the person responsible showed initiative but should pay for the replacement of the destroyed item. I was formally charged, the charge was dismissed and the damage paid from Company Funds.

Altogether everyone in Left Flank thoroughly enjoyed this different training. We learned a lot and it was good to work closely with our Royal Marine colleagues.

By now we were aware that our next posting would be to Public Duties at Windsor and certain items of clothing and equipment were issued. I was also better prepared by this time. I had successfully attended a Cadre Course on Drill and Duties, followed by a Small Arms Course at Hythe. Briefly, in the initial stages of the Hythe course I had been a complete disaster. All members of the course were experienced NCO Instructors, but some weapons and items I had never seen or used. The Course Instructor took me on one side to discuss my obvious lack of background. He was given details of my return to the Army, and as a result when each of the Students Teaching Practices (TPs) was announced I was the student nominated. Our Instructor was certainly giving me 'stick' and my knowledge and confidence grew as the weeks progressed. In the initial stages my experienced student colleagues were obtaining 'A' Grades for TPs while I was lucky to attain a miserable 'C' minus. Our final exam was crucial and everyone was quite nervous; to some extent futures depended on Course Results. We all worked like hell for each other, as perfect timing was essential. Some of the lads made unexplainable mistakes, I made none and my timing was down to the last second. When the exam results were announced I had obtained a 'B+' and the remainder 'C's, quite a shock for all concerned but I was delighted. End of Course results gave our syndicate of eight a total of 4 'C's and 3 'B's. I was given a 'C' plus and an apology that I would have had a 'B' if it were not for my terrible start, over which I had had no control. Initially I had felt very inadequate, but this was overcome by hard work and long hours, and it certainly paid off.

CHAPTER 9

Battalion Training – Bodney North, Norfolk, 1957

If my memory serves me well, in mid March 1957 the Battalion plus a Battalion of Coldstream Guards reported to the Norfolk Training Area for intensive unit training for six weeks. Following this, Left Flank would spend eight weeks administering a Camp for three Territorial Army Armoured Camp units each performing their fourteen day Annual Camp.

The Norfolk Training Area, now used for more specialized training, is quite large and was capable of limited Brigade movement. For our six weeks we enjoyed idyllic weather and all aspects of training were covered which everyone appeared to enjoy. Little vehicular movement came through the camp and the area swarmed with pheasants plus other wild life; different wild life could be enjoyed at the weekend in the lovely city of Norwich when transport was provided for those interested. I think I made two visits wandering round the shops, visiting the cinema and later a pub. One of our former officers, from a very staunch Roman Catholic family, lived nearby and offered the services of a small family chapel for Mass.

Lt. Hopkinson, the Assistant Adjutant, was in charge of the party, and his briefing and map reading were excellent, We entered the extensive forestry area around Brandon and travelled along fire breaks and other minor tracks before we eventually stopped. Into the forest we plunged, down an almost undiscernable path and after approximately fifty yards entered a clearing where stood a small chapel hardly larger than the average household garage. Although I never verified it, I presumed the building was situated as such, owing to the Restoration, which was not uncommon in those years of anti Roman Catholicism purges. In 1959 I found another, rather more decorative, building, which as a family chapel was demolished brick by brick, re-assembled and hidden within the confines of the main building, adjacent to the main road between Worcester and Hereford, at that time utilized as a home and laundry for 'wayward' Catholic girls.

Battalion training concluded with a three-day exercise which included aircraft. Our Seniors were well pleased and a well trained, happy and healthy Battalion prepared to return to Lydd. Left Flank less a few individuals travelled a few miles down the road to our tented camp that was surrounded by forestry which owing to the perfect weather was tinder dry, constituting an extremely worrying fire hazard, and I was detailed to be the Fire Officer, plus other administrative duties. The Company personnel were also to be available to the TA units to assist in their training, mainly acting as mobile 'enemy'. In our last involvement an accident occurred which could have resulted in a TA driver nearly losing his sight, when his vehicle commander stupidly picked up an active Thunderflash, and dropped it in front of his armoured car. It exploded in front of the driver's aperture; he suffered facial burns and both eyes were sealed. We eventually removed him to hospital and some four days later he resumed light duties. We were fortunate during our eight weeks of residence that because of adequate briefings and the alertness of my fire piquet we had no fire incidents. We were fed extremely well and the Company was praised for helpfulness and efficiency. A very enjoyable summer.

If I had to recall a particular, tragi-comical incident, I must explain that our catering was civilianized and supervised by the London District Catering Adviser, a Warrant Officer in the Army Catering Corps. He was an enormous figure of a man, short in stature and weighing twenty odd stone. He became quite friendly with some of the civilian staff and of an evening they would drive to some nearby pub for a drink.

Towards the end of the Camp, a colleague and I obtained a lift to a pub called the Roebuck. Darkness was falling and as we walked into the pub car park we saw a van with the rear doors open and we recognised the van as one belonging to one of the civilian cooks. When we reached the van, protruding from the open doors was a pair of very stiff legs. 'Murder,' we thought. To inspect the body we pulled the rigid flesh out of the van and unaided it stood up in a semi-perpendicular position. It still breathed but what it emitted would have floored a regiment. He was stiff with booze. Placing him carefully back in the van we entered the pub.

The sole occupants of the bar were the Warrant Officer, ACC and one of the civilian cooks, who was having great difficulty in maintaining an upright position. We ascertained that the body in the van was that of a member of the Cookhouse staff, and the Warrant Officer, who maintained a correct military posture, gave us a very slow and dignified explanation of what had happened over two days. His companion was incapable of speech and could only nod.

It transpired that the previous day, as the conclusion of a successful Camp approached, the 'Three Musketeers' started a binge around midday, and in the early evening found themselves in the Roebuck when in a fit of joint bravado they decided to sample each bottle on the three-tier spirit shelf behind the bar. They had made some progress when the evening's jollifications ceased. Today's expedition was a resumption of this ridiculous alcoholic test which could have resulted in death or serious illness, plus the added problem of a driving accident. If any humour came out of this incident, it was the situation of the body in the van and the antics and alcoholic conversation of the remaining persons in the bar.

As Sergeant in Waiting, I had just marched in the last of my Company's (LF) Miscreants, and I cannot vouch for the authenticity of my story but I do know the two persons were on parade behind my Company.

L/Sgt. 'Stinky' Miller, 'C' Company, was a good soldier, but frequently failed to adhere to discipline and protocol and as a result in the promotion stakes he was up and down like the proverbial fiddler's elbow. He and a fellow JNCO of 'C' Comp., of similar ilk, were about to be 'reduced'. Once again, quite a regular occurrence, over the previous few months.

Owing to the absence of both D/Sgts., CSM Douglas of 'C' Company was acting, and as I left orders, the hatless A/D/Sgt brought his own two JNCOs to attention, gave Quick March and flew into orders at 90m.p.h. Miller and his companion did not move, but doffing their forage caps to their right hand they broke into the song of 'Here we are again, happy as can be' and with delicate footwork that would not have disgraced Wayne Sleep they 'fishtailed' into Orders facing the CO's table. (Fishtailing is an intricate exchange of dance footwork.) They replaced forage caps, saluted smartly, turned left and doubled away to the nearby Guardroom.

Apparently the scene in the Orderly Room was difficult to describe. The three officers were undergoing severe convulsions attempting to suppress their laughter. The RSM (for once) was completely speechless throughout, he could have been in the first throes of a coronary, and CSM Douglas just prayed for deliverance and a transfer to 2SG. Although a nuisance in many ways, these characters made the Regiment. Would it be worth a separate chapter with a resumé of the many outrageous antics (inclusive of officers!) of individuals? They certainly keep the Battalions ticking over and usually they turn out to be extremely good soldiers.

The next main event Left Flank were involved in whilst still at Lydd occurred when I was summoned to the Company Office and Major 'Spandau' Denham (he had a slight stutter) informed me that I would be issued with a new suit of 1958 combat clothing and a set of equipment. Having fully dressed myself he would inspect me and if satisfied he would issue 10 Platoon with the clothing and equipment, and I would ensure they all knew how to wear and assemble it. The next week I would take a small Section out into one of the nearby Training areas and the group of us would live in two-man tents and eat off twenty-four hour man packs for approximately seven days.

We fired our new weapon, the 7.62mm self loading rifle, on the range, much to the interest of many of the Battalion who wished to use it and discover its peculiarities. Apart from the kick after the round was discharged I found that the folding backsight had constantly hit me on the right eyebrow and in fact had caused a small laceration. This was cured when I was issued with a weapon with a long butt.

Our exercise under canvas was quite successful. We marched and patrolled, day and night, the art of field cooking was experienced by everyone, and we were impressed with the clothing. The weather generally was extremely warm and sunny but we did endure some heavy rain and the clothing dried very quickly indeed. On our return we were told that we would take part in a Battalion exercise on Salisbury Plain. We were to be air lifted from a nearby RAF Station to RAF Colerne, near Bath and we would march the 30-odd miles to our position on the Plain. Again we were the subject of curiosity from both military and civil eyes and at the end of this exercise the general consensus of opinion from the men of 10 Platoon was very favourable in respect of the clothing and the equipment.

The last days at Lydd were hectic. After the exercise all the new clothing and equipment was cleaned and stored away for the Winter Trials in January 1958. We also prepared ourselves in drill and equipment for our advent into Public Duties. On the whole Lydd was not a popular posting; it was isolated and without amenities so everyone was pleased to be returning to an urban situation.

I thought I'd seen the last of Lydd but some fourteen years later I found myself adjacent to the Old Left Flank accommodation running a linguistic exercise for our own and Dutch interrogators, I found it rather nostalgic to walk round the old area again, and even took our Dutch friends in a tiny pub I used to visit, where they made us most welcome. So Lydd ended and the Advance Party began the journey to Windsor.

CHAPTER 10

Windsor 1957-8

This particular period of my Military Service was to afford me my initial experience of Public Duties as they are referred to in the Household Division. The Atholl grey greatcoats and blue serge trousers had already been issued at Lydd in preparation for the winter period. The more sensible majority of personnel wetted, soaped and slept on these items rather than use an iron; some who used the latter scorched the clothing and suffered a rather hefty bill. I was fortunate to have a figure to suit the greatcoat without alteration. It fitted perfectly and the creases were razor sharp. My boots shone like mirrors, the white leather belt and brasses can only be described as perfection, but the *objet d'art* of all my equipment was my rifle. It was worthy of Sotheby's, and after all the range work and exercises over the previous eighteen months I stripped it down to the bare wood, applied glass paper, copious amounts of Kiwi and spit, and when it gleamed I decided not to apply varnish which would have spoiled the effect. Not only was it a very functional item, but it drew gasps of admiration from those less fortunate. As I was to learn, an inspecting officer would take one look at this immaculate weapon and he was sold on the remainder of my appearance; the reputation was established at the beginning, and I rarely received more than a cursory glance. My crowning glory, the dreaded bearskin, was a good one of perfect shape and I groomed it with more dedication than a female star. I now considered myself ready.

At Lydd, Left Flank had been detailed for the Advance Party and to mount the first Guards, having taken over from the Grenadiers, the honour of the first Guard fell to Sgt. Bunyan and myself. So at Lydd we practised the form-up in Barracks, and the handing and taking over of the Guards at the Castle. The Adjutant and the RSM appeared to be satisfied with our performance.

Our journey from Lydd to Windsor was without incident and we soon settled in to our accommodation. By tradition at 6a.m. the following morning we were rudely awakened in our rooms by the Corps of Drums of the Grenadiers playing 'Long Reveille' with great enthusiasm. The noise was tremendous, and the ribald comments and threats equally noisy. In battle conditions the Scots and Grenadiers fight like hell for one another going back to Waterloo and beyond; during peacetime in pubs and on the playing field there is a healthy antagonism between the Scots and English Guardsmen, which is really no bad thing. So during our first day in Barracks we prepared for the first duty.

It had been decided that the Assistant Adjutant, one Capt. Hopkinson, a disciplinary martinet, would be the first officer of the Castle Guard, ably assisted? by Sgt. Bunyan and L/Sgt. Howard. The Guard, forewarned, was immaculately turned out and the drill was perfect, ably supervised by 'Little Spud' D/Sgt. Thompson.

Led by Pipe Major Roe's superb Pipe Band, the Guard drew the admiration of the many citizens of the Borough of Windsor as they marched to the Castle and removed all traces of Sassenach occupation.

After lunch and following the posting of the 2p.m. sentries Capt. H decided that he and Sgts. Bunyan and Howard would familiarise themselves and form a joint patrol. The first sentry was visited outside the nearby Gate and as the Patrol approached the first Gate affording access to the Main Drive, a Castle Police Officer in plain clothes kept the Pedestrian Gate open and locked it behind us. This incident begat subsequent events.

It was normal procedure that when Patrols went out the NCO carried the key that opened the three Gates the Patrol must pass through. The NCO would carry it in a suitable pocket or the cuff of his Atholl Grey greatcoat.

The Patrol halted at the rather sheltered Gate which gave access to Castle grounds, and the sentry at the top of the Long Walk.

There was a pregnant pause, then a sharp cry: 'Well, open the Gate, Sgt. Bunyan.'

Another pause, 'A havena got it, Sir.'

Heated comments followed and a quick discussion followed even more quickly. While Howard kept discreet 'obbo', the others quickly divested themselves of bearskin, greatcoat and rifle and negotiated the spiked railings of the Gate. When the Patrol was safely over and properly dressed one of the Guardsmen was heard to say, 'The next Gate willna be sae f... easy,' and how right he was.

We reached the sentry on the ramparts overlooking the Park and Smiths Lawn and arrived eventually at the third Gate, also spiked and built into a wall. The gap between the spikes and the overhanging wall was barely two feet. However, by now suitably trained in the art of 'strip' and the expertise of passing kit that would not have disgraced a Scottish rugby XV, we emerged, breathing heavily and so wary of discovery, at the top of Chapel Walk.

At least three of us could escape blame and quietly laughed hysterically as we approached the haven of the Guardroom. I never heard what transpired between Capt. H and Sgt. B. I do not recall the latter being charged, but at least the honour of the Regiment was saved. 'Necessity is the Mother of Invention.'

When the remainder of the Battalion arrived the duties were shared which made life more comfortable. I was given Christmas leave to see Jean and Chris at Preston but had to return in order to mount Guard on New Year's Day allowing the Scots personnel to enjoy Hogmanay on their native soil.

The warning came from the RSM and from those on high. Personnel mounting Castle Guard on New Year's Day should be extremely circumspect in their consumption of alcohol. Failure in turnout, drill or conduct would invoke the severest of punishment if the Battalion was disgraced.

So behaving as a well disciplined Englishman in a Scottish Regiment should, I took a liberal road and managed a few hours deep sleep. Without incident the Guard duly arrived at the Castle Guardroom watched with interest by a group of some thirty tourists and locals. The Officer and Sergeant left the scene as is their wont and the minutes passed.

I was standing on the right of the Guard when the hidden whisper came down the rank: 'Sarge, —'s going to pass out!' I glanced to my left to observe a rifle and bayonet making undue movements. Decision time. I came to attention, turned right and took up what could only be described as a near homosexual position behind the errant Guardsman.

As I breathed vicious whispered profanities into the neck of this Guardsman, he began to breathe deeply, and did antics on his toes that would not have disgraced a prima ballerina, enforced by right-handed digs in his kidney region by myself.

He then had the audacity to complain of a pain in his back and he groaned accordingly.

'You will have pain when I get you in the Guardroom,' I hissed, and glanced down. To my horror I had forgotten that my bayonet was fixed and that my final thump in the Guardsman's back had actually penetrated all his clothing and he was standing on his toes adequately impaled on the end of my rifle and bayonet. There was a quick withdrawal and the Guardsman sank to his heels.

'Don't be soft, do you feel all right now?'

'Yes Sarge,' he whispered, and I resumed my rightful position. My unofficial action was never known. I only dared whisper a rude mouthful to the Guardsman who gave me a grateful, rueful grin and probably never knew that he had been slightly injured.

What we do for the honour of the Regiment.

We had been told that the whole of January 1958 would be allocated to Left Flank for the two Platoons to carry out full Winter Trials on the new 1958 clothing and combat equipment, alternately Battledress or Combat Clothing. This would include route marches up to twenty miles, speed marches then dig in, Section Attacks, then all night in two-man tents, three days in slit trenches, and two crossings of the River Thames in flood. A very full but interesting month. Each training day every soldier completed a pro forma and stated his own particular comments on his daily experiences. Accompanying us on each day was a team of senior officers and NCOs as observers, and some from foreign armies. There were of course many amusing incidents far too numerous to remember or record, but one incident I recall quite vividly followed a late afternoon arrival on the former tank training area at Pirbright. We had speed marched from just outside Windsor on a very cold day. There was a light covering of snow on the ground and a hard frost was forecast for the night. Our test was just to sleep out in the open inside the new sleeping bags. It was to be non-tactical with just a prowling sentry.

We arrived quite breathless at Pirbright in the dark, selected our positions and in this respect I opted for a hole in the ground which I cleared for Mr Swallow, my officer, and myself. It was on the side of a small hill. The hot stew arrived plus the rum ration and I started to feed the men. Out of the thirty men involved only one accepted the rum; all the others being Scotsmen and preferring whisky, gave it to me. I filled my small mess tin with stew and a thick crust of bread, drank my 'tot' of rum from my cup then filled it with tea, and armed with my large mess tin filled with a pint of extremely strong Army rum, made my way to Mr Swallow and my place of rest. We ate and talked with our Section Commanders; the men found wood and some fires were allowed. Mr Swallow produced half a bottle of whisky which he passed round, and I demolished the rum.

About 10 o'clock we crawled into our bags and I fell into a dreamless sleep. I was rather surprised when at 6a.m. I woke up feeling extremely refreshed with no trace of a hangover but with a mouth like the bottom of a birdcage. I spoke to the sentry and asked if he had found it difficult finding his way round in the dark. He laughed and said, 'No, and your place was very clear.' When I asked why he pointed back to my hole and there suspended in the morning air was a distinctive white cloud.

'And you can smell that for quite a way,' he added. The cloud was of course my rum infected breath which had solidified somewhat and gave an obvious indication of my whereabouts. It was the source of great amusement and 'mickey taking' from the lads which subsided when I threatened to run them back to Windsor. Morale was extremely high and this was needed when the river crossings were attempted. Upstream from our crossing area was an island mid-stream, which divided the flooded river into fast and slow lanes and made the crossing very difficult to navigate. Eventually we were all wet. There were humorous moments but danger was always evident when the boats were uncontrollable owing to the fast flow of the river. We lost one automatic weapon when a boat overturned but this was subsequently recovered. When the trials were completed everyone agreed that it had all been worthwhile and interesting.

Two other matters occurred in conjunction with the trials which I was placed in charge of.

I was given another task that was slightly more complicated. I was given a sheaf of papers which contained the proposed Arms Drill for this new FN rifle and bayonet. As I recall I had approximately three days to personally peruse the papers, choose Guardsmen to form a Drill Squad, instruct them and myself in the new Drill up to Guards Standard, and present them to a special Committee chaired by General Whistler. We travelled down to Warminster on the third day having been closely monitored by the Adjutant and the Regimental Sergeant Major, both of whom had strangely left me alone to get on with it.

At Warminster the resident Demonstration Battalion was the Somerset Light Infantry. They had carried out the Summer Trials and their Arms Drill was also different. They were in a far more advantageous position than ourselves in every respect, but my lads were tremendous. Their marching and foot drill were excellent and I can only recall one minor error with a Guardsman with the Arms Drill. I had to give several close-up demonstrations, mainly with the fixing of bayonets. The Committee were also curious of its effect when wearing our bearskins. Fortunately we had, as was normal, practised on occasions wearing our bearskins. I think the Committee appreciated our shortage of time for preparation; we were warmly congratulated and I believe a letter was sent to our Commanding Officer to this effect.

On the way back to Windsor the lads caused a good deal of horror and humour to motorists by their antics in the rear of our truck. This had started the previous night in Warminster when we had gone out for a drink. We parked the truck on a small car park where nearby we found some bankrupt stock thrown out of a ladies' outfitters. Among these items were several ornate hat stands (excellent for bearskins!) and demonstration 'legs' for ladies' stockings. As we were about to leave the car park we had a debate with a rather over zealous young Police Constable which was sorted out with the Sergeant, but as we travelled along the main road A303 the following day, passing motorists and their passengers gave us undue attention of high amusement or obvious disgust, indicating the rear of the truck.

From the cab I could see two Guardsmen lying on the floor, each holding a pair of 'legs' over the tailboard; one other was performing various comical acts to motorists who came too close. Some were obviously offended, but the majority of the passing motoring public thought it was hilarious. I had to stop the truck and issue a reprimand (tongue in cheek), as I didn't want a blot on what had been a most successful episode!

A very unofficial but amusing episode occurred in the spring of 1958 when Mr Hubbard Ford who had been my Platoon Officer for a long time was invited to have dinner with the Queen and her family. Needless to say he was over the moon at this honour and so was his family, but when he spoke to me about it he expressed a certain degree of nervousness, though this was quietly dispelled. He later asked Sergeant Bell and myself, who were not on Guard with him, if we would join him later for a drink in the Officers' Room and we agreed. On the evening concerned we both had a drink in a pub outside the Castle and at about 10p.m. presented ourselves to HF. He was really elated. His dinner had been fantastic, the Queen and her family had made him completely at home, and the conversation had flowed. He was really on a high and delighted he had been chosen. He confessed to a slight over-indulgence with the demon drink, and brought out a bottle of whisky to celebrate. During this consumption we were joined by the Sergeant of the Guard who wished to know the time of Officer's Rounds. In the ensuing conversation HF said it had always been his ambition to experience being a normal Guardsman.

We three seniors said, 'And so you shall be.' It was decided that Bell would be the Drummer, the Sergeant would take the Officer's place, and HF and I would be the Guardsman escort. Bell and I were in civilian clothes, the appropriation of suitable items of clothing for HF and myself from the recumbent Guardsman was difficult but hilarious; the others had problems too. To give access to the outside world adjacent to the Guardroom was an archway manned by a Police Officer. This was secured when the public had no access by a large wooden double gate and a small pedestrian entrance. Our smart and motley crew were formed up and marched off, leaving by the small gate. The Police Officer obviously did not notice the civilian shoes and trousers of Bell and myself. Outside the double gate the first sentry even in the darkness expressed curiosity but was reassured. We passed through the two gates on the approach walk and halted at the sentry posts facing the Long Walk. The Guardsman sensibly queried us, recognised us all, smiled, and we marched on. The Queen has never had a smarter, more alert or high powered Officer's Rounds whilst in residence in Windsor. Our dress may have been somewhat unorthodox and bizarre but our tip-toed marching beneath her bedroom window was worthy of television: woe betide a potential intruder. Then the next sentries and back to the Guardroom. A wish granted, a very efficient Officer's Rounds, very alert sentries, although somewhat amused and confused seeing their seniors in unaccustomed roles. Efficiency was maintained; and to that was added a touch of humour.

The next three important Ceremonials were the Major General's Inspection, Trooping the Colour and Mounting from Horse Guards, and lastly the Garter Service at Windsor Castle.

The Major General's Inspection, especially on Household Division Battalions performing Public Duties, is mainly of an administrative nature. With the aid of his staff, the clerical work and books are checked, and accommodation is thoroughly inspected together with the stores. With the aid of the Regimental Band and Pipes the whole Battalion is formed up, inspected, and ends with a March Past. As Public Duty Battalions are normally resident in confined Barrack areas it is not possible to demonstrate field training; he will have observed this when the unit undergo their Annual Field Exercises in a designated Training Area. Normally the unit will attempt to demonstrate some aspect of military activity they have been involved in and which can be shown within the confines of a small Barrack area.

On our inspection day in 1958, attended also by the Duke of Gloucester, it was a scorcher. Lt. Col. Sam Rhodes, our Director of Music, had a northern sense of humour, and in the middle of the inspection had the Band play 'Steam Heat', a very popular piece of progressive music which brought smiles to soldiers and spectators alike. After lunch I had been tasked to lay on a demonstration of the new 1958 clothing and equipment. This was done very enthusiastically by a party of the lads from 10 Platoon and all our visitors showed great interest. The Battalion was given a first class report.

Trooping the Colour is the highlight of the ceremonial season in London, and in 1958 the Colour to be trooped was that of our Battalion. We would find the Escort and No 2 Guard, and I had been chosen as a member of the Escort, left hand man of the front rank; I was delighted. I also managed to obtain tickets for Jean and Chris for the day.

In Victoria Barracks the Barrack Square is very small and it is difficult to simulate Horse Guards Parade and practise the March Past in Slow and Quick Time. However it is done, prior to the Troop, Guard Mounting from Horse Guards and the rehearsals do help to eliminate any problems and it all seems to work in the end. Great emphasis is placed on physical fitness to obviate the disgrace of any soldier collapsing on parade. It is not always easy to maintain high physical standards on Public Duties, manpower is usually short and duties many, and off duty the temptations of London tend to reduce the standard of health, very often due to over-indulgence in alcohol and girls. Being stationed at Windsor necessitated travel to Wellington Barracks, and in unsatisfactory accommodation the 'tarting' up of uniform and equipment had to be carried out in very crowded conditions but pride and good humour overcame all the obvious difficulties. In 1948 the 1st Battalion Scots Guards were to have the privilege of Trooping their Colour for the first time in Tunic Order after World War II. Owing to an incorrect weather forecast it was cancelled, but the weather was perfect, so we all prayed for dry weather on this procession. Guard Mountings on the rehearsals were accomplished without too much adverse comment, and any huge 'howlers' were commented on and rectified. There are eyes everywhere: very little goes unnoticed.

So came the day. As I recall I spent the night in Barracks to wake up to 'Rain!' – not heavy but steady; we were very pessimistic. As we changed and cleaned our kit I would find it difficult to describe the atmosphere.

Mons Officer Cadet School 1959. CSM Bert Croucher and the author.

The usual ribald comments were missing; after all the hard work we were subdued. We were kept in suspense right up to the last moment for departure. 'Capes on!' We had hope, we formed up and with the Regimental and Pipe Band leading, we proudly marched up the Mall amid by now a light drizzle and cheering crowds. We swung into the Horse Guards approach road to the tune of 'Coronation Bells'; it's a real foot tapping march and very expressive. I was so choked and proud. It's hard to describe my inner feelings. Unless it is in your blood people cannot understand; my father would have been a very proud man on that day.

By 10.30 all troops were on parade and correctly formed up. We knew the decision would have to be taken before the arrival of the Royal Family's carriages, and then to everyone's utter joy the order came 'Off Capes!' The thousands of spectators cheered like mad and it spread down the Mall. Like magic, transport and soldiers arrived and within minutes, the atmosphere and picture of the parade had been transformed. It affected everyone especially the troops who seemed to say, 'we've had a reprieve so let's make it good,' and so they did, but when the Queen arrived the drizzle still persisted. It was during the Queen's inspection that the rain stopped, the weather improved and as a result the parade was a success. Plaudits came from all sides, the Escort was described as the best since the war, but irrespective of all comments, it was a great feeling to march at the head of the troops behind the Monarch and the Massed Bands, truly magnificent and something I will never forget.

We did not enjoy an anticlimax because being stationed at Windsor our next Ceremonial parade was the Garter Service. How well I remember it. The Scots Guards lined the route from the Queen's entrance through the Main Quadrangle before the Household Cavalry took over. It was a perfect day: a cloudless sky, brilliant sunshine and within that Quadrangle the temperature was in the 80s. In Home Service clothing we boiled, but no one fell out. It was worse for the Household Cavalry and they had one or two casualties. We were on parade for almost four hours. It's a hard slog in hot weather and a question of mind over matter.

Our next Ceremonial which involved most of the Trooping Escort plus some additions, was to Scotland in order to form a Guard of Honour to welcome the Queen and Royal Family to Scotland. This would take place at the docks at Leith, near Edinburgh. The State Colour would be taken and I was held personally responsible for its safety on the journey. We formed up opposite *Britannia*. I again was left hand man of the front rank, the weather was warm and as we waited standing properly At Ease we all began to feel somewhat uncomfortable. In fact one Guardsman (who had not been on the Trooping) fell backwards stiff as a board, hit the ground and resumed his position as if nothing had happened!

As I recall, Her Majesty was in the early stages of pregnancy, with Prince Andrew I think, and was definitely under par which we didn't learn about till later. When she finally appeared nearly an hour behind schedule she carried out the inspection with her normal discipline and aplomb. Her Majesty had expressed her concern about our uniforms after the Trooping, but had been assured that no damage had been done and that she could see for herself when the Escort provided the Guard of Honour on her arrival in Scotland. You can imagine my horror when she came to the end of the front rank and stopped, and with the thoroughness of an Adjutant her eyes started at the bearskin and slowly travelled down my red and blue frame. Slowly she walked behind and stopped again, then carried on. Knowing her reputation for not mincing words I was prepared for the worst, for incarceration in the Tower. However she was well pleased, we were congratulated. The following day she made a semi official visit to Falkland Palace where she called on Major Crichton Stuart, a family friend and former distinguished Regimental Officer. As her official car entered the street approaching the Castle I had to walk alongside Her Majesty until she entered the building where we had posted sentries in Home Service clothing.

That morning and subsequent days we visited various small towns and Glasgow, showing the flag and hopefully drawing some recruits. It was a busy, time-consuming period but generally enjoyed by all ranks. We were stationed at Penicuik some ten miles or so south of Edinburgh and I well remember the night before we returned to Windsor going into the city with two other sergeants, one a piper. We had several drinks, and met some other ex members, who decided to go to a dance hall. I declined and stayed with the others. The two didn't arrive at our agreed meeting place so I started to walk. Not one car stopped to give me a lift; I walked the whole way and was I tired. Needless to say the other two came home with the milk. Then back to Windsor again in time for various sporting activities and collecting a medal for the London District tug of war.

Major Denham received a visit from our 'Schoolie' who desired my attendance at the Army Education Centre in London. In order to obtain my 1st Class Army Certificate of Education ('O' level equivalent), a Drill Sergeant, the Pipe Major and several other Seniors were to attend including the CSM Harry Norton who objected, but was overruled. Harry and I had never been close in the eighteen months I had known him, but in London I helped him a lot and his attitude had changed. We had totally different views on military life, and I don't think he liked Catholics either, but he found he could trust me. I eventually passed the exam in five subjects, one a distinction, so I was qualified for promotion and eventually a possible Commission.

Attending the Course in London was a Staff Sergeant in the Intelligence Corps. We became friends, and he said that with my background why didn't I transfer to the Corps? The work sounded very interesting. It was in August or September some months prior to 1SG training for BAOR that the lack of quarters were mentioned, plus a certain lack of encouragement from the top to pursue more qualifications in my military career and these factors led me to become somewhat disillusioned so I applied to transfer to the Intelligence Corps. The CO wrongly refused to forward the application; he said I was biting the hand that fed me. Had I known better I had a genuine redress. Surprisingly some three weeks later I was promoted full Sergeant and posted to Mons Officer Cadet School where an unexpected vacancy had occurred.

So the twelve months at Windsor brought the family together again, achieved Educational qualifications, experience in Public Duties, and promotion. My gamble was beginning to pay off. So to Mons OCS.

Windsor and Mons OCS

The Battalion was informed that the quartering situation in Germany would have to be staggered, and that Jean and I would be in the second stage. This would mean that personnel who currently resided in hirings would have to move into the vacated accommodation in Victoria Barracks when the Advance Party left for Germany. Jean said that wild horses wouldn't drag her into that type of housing, and in a subsequent meeting with the Second in Command and the Superintendent Clerk she stated that she was not prepared to live in what she considered to be close to 'slum' accommodation. The long talk was conducted in a very amiable, quiet and sensible manner, which I was told rather shook the 2 I/C; this sort of talk usually consisted of anger, high voices and a lot of bad feeling. The matter was then left in obeyance, Jean having created a marked impression by her manner. Without warning I was marched in before the Commanding Officer and promoted to full Sergeant, which was not bad going: from Recruit to full Sergeant in just over two years.

Shortly after this promotion I was informed that I would not be posted with the Battalion to BAOR, as a vacancy had suddenly occurred at Mons Officer Cadet School and I would fill this position. The posting would take effect from October or November 1958. Next to Sandhurst this was a plum posting, many people thought it was more important than the Royal Military Academy. You had to produce an officer within four months, unlike the three years at the RMA which included a predominance of academic studies. I visited Mons to sort out various administrative details. Accommodation for the family was not available at this time but within days I was offered a former officers' hiring at 179 Frimley Green Road, Frimley Green. Although there were snags it was a comfortable bungalow within five miles of the School and I could travel by bicycle.

'A' Company, to which I was to be posted, was about to be re-staffed, with a new Company Commander, Major Gatehouse of (The Buffs) Royal West Kents. Harold Gatehouse was a Russian speaker, a very charming, competent and efficient officer. It was a pleasure to work with him for the next two years. The new Company Sergeant Major was Bert Croucher, who had been the CSM of 'K' Company at the Guards Depot, Caterham, on my re-joining, and had been most helpful to me in that rather difficult period of transition. He was a good instructor, smart and efficient, and a competent administrator. The Admin. Sergeant was an easy-going chap from a Yorkshire Regiment. He was close to retirement and had very little interest in matters military. We also had a private soldier who was the Company Clerk. Our course starting in November would be much larger than normal, approximately 150 Cadets, which necessitated having four Platoons instead of the usual three. The 'A' Coy Spider accommodation was adequate for only three Platoons so we had to take over an adjacent brick building for the additional Platoon.

I said my farewells to the Battalion, helped to pack our goods and subsequently returned to Mons, living as a single person in my bunk in the Spider. Within days we had moved in the bungalow, and so to work.

Mons Officer Cadet School was situated off Princes Avenue, Aldershot surrounded at that time by 33 (Para), Lt. Regt RA, the Army Catering School, an RASC Training Battalion, Depot Army Physical Training Corps, and the Para Depot. The Commandant was Colonel Fortesque, Coldstream Guards; his Adjutant was a Captain Tollemarche of the Coldstream Guards. The Regimental Sergeant Major Desmond Lynch, DCM, Irish Guards, was a dominating figure of a man who disliked Scots Guardsmen, and he was assisted by 2 Drill Sergeants from the Coldstream and Scots Guards. There were three wings. The Infantry wing consisted of 4 Companies, A-D, and a Basic Training Company which as its title implies gave Cadets the basics before they moved on to the two other specialized Wings of Armour and Artillery. Each month therefore necessitated a Commissioning Parade which justified the RSM's presence, ably assisted by the Royal Artillery Mounted Band who were stationed at Mons. This band was occasionally supplemented by other bands depending on the personality taking the Parade.

Thus started two years of extremely hard work, made enjoyable and informative by the personalities of staff and students. It was to me an unforgettable experience and helped me enormously in Regimental and Administrative matters which I would not have participated in had I remained with the Battalion.

Very briefly, Cadets at Mons started off as in most military training establishments with intensive physical and weapon training, Drill and Radio Skills. The Adjutant carried out a Company Inspection on the Drill Square at the end of a fortnight when all kit had to be of a high standard of cleanliness and appearance. Tactics then were introduced and officers responsibilities in respect of Leadership, Unit Administration, Man Management, Pay and Fiscal Duties, Mess Etiquette etc. It was an extremely comprehensive and time-filling programme. At the end of six weeks the first exam was taken. If they failed it was back to square one (Relegated) or possibly RTU (Returned to Unit). By this time certain personalities began to emerge as very obvious leaders, and character defects showed in the case of others. Relegation was initiated at eight weeks and rarely was this challenged. Another indication to a Cadet's background and character was a short autobiography each Cadet submitted within days of his arrival at Mons, so a Cadet was under reasonably close supervision from his Company instructors and others teaching more specialized subjects.

As the eighth week approached the first field exercise occurred, a three day Defence Exercise which confirmed certain opinions and gave certain opportunities to borderline cases. The next four weeks concentrated on short field exercises and tactical lectures building up to weeks 13 and 14 which were spent at Battle Camp in Sennybridge, near Brecon, South Wales. In the twelfth week the Company Commander appointed a Junior Under Officer for each Platoon, and from the ones appointed would emerge a Senior Under Officer who received a Stick of Honour.

The movement of 150 personnel by rail, road and private car to Sennybridge was accomplished without mishap and everyone was settled in and briefed for the work ahead. Sennybridge Camp lies some five miles west of Brecon and was manned by a permanent staff formed mainly from Welsh Regiments. The accommodation was basic but functional. This Battle Camp, as its name suggests, was to introduce Cadets to the use of live ammunition and the control of personnel under near battlefield conditions. Commencing with House Clearing, various exercises were introduced to test certain Cadets on their ability to control men. This also confirmed candidates for Relegation and possible RTU, and for others it enhanced a promotion or an above average report on Commissioning.

It was a fortnight of hard work for all concerned but especially for the Cadets.

Anti Ambush and Night Firing were also involved and the training culminated in a very arduous three-day exercise in which every aspect of Defence, Advance and Attack was involved. It physically drained all concerned and supervision of personnel under these conditions was of the utmost priority. Soldiers who are physically exhausted and unaccustomed to carrying live ammunition twenty-four hours a day are prone to make mistakes, so close supervision was essential. On one particular attack the OC had posted some Cadets with rifles and a machine gun supervised by myself, with the object of simulating enemy fire by aiming, within the safety zones, high above the soldiers' heads. When the Cadets commenced firing the LMG jammed. The Cadet involved was having difficulty in rectifying this so I moved him away, cleared the obstruction, and to save time and maintain effectiveness I 'fired' the attack home, aiming much closer than the Cadets would have done. The effect according to the Cadets was most realistic. The OC agreed with this practice and this became my job on many live firing exercises, that I personally fired closely over the heads of the soldiers involved in subsequent visits to Battle Camp.

It was generally accepted by the Cadets that although physically taxing and despite the extremes of the Welsh weather this part of their training was the most enjoyable and instructive. It was also a period of character building for the inexperienced Cadets and we watched very carefully the changes, if any, in the face of adversity. This was important when it came to the final assessment and my personal opinion was that this particular period gave the greatest indication of a potential officer's character.

A highlight to finish off a Cadet's training before Commissioning was the Drill Competition, officiated by the Adjutant, RSM and a Drill Sergeant; each Platoon was the responsibility of the CSM or Company Sergeant. Initially each Platoon was thoroughly inspected by this formidable trio, then followed a set procedure of foot and arms drill. In total each Platoon was under the microscope for approximately 45 minutes, which reflected a Cadet's competitive spirit, smartness and appearance, personal pride and also the hard work over a relatively short period that the Company Instructors had put into the training. There was a consensus of opinion that drill had no practicable place within the Army but I always found that soldiers responded to the challenge of a drill competition and even more so with potential officers.

It was accepted that under normal circumstances 'A' Company would take all the Brigade of Guards Cadets and it happened that each Platoon adopted a Regiment of the Brigade which helped the competitive spirit.

All in all Brigade Cadets did extremely well during my tour. Two were chosen as Senior Under Officers and several more achieved similar Under Officers status. Among the more notable personalities were Michael Heseltine MP, James Fox the actor, John Clavering MC who became Regimental Lt. Colonel of the Scots Guards, Robert Fellowes who married Princess Diana's sister and is currently the Queen's Private Secretary, the Honourable Archie Hamilton MP, Armed Forces Minister, and so many others, some of whom I have met since in their military or private occupation. All agreed that Mons was a very important period in their lives.

'A' Company also did rather well with its allocation of overseas Cadets. These came mainly from the West African states but occasionally we received an odd one from the Arab Emirates and the West Indies. We had a Junior Under Officer from Ghana who was excellent material, and on his return became ADC to President Nkrumah.

So Bert Croucher and I started our partnership together. It was most successful and I learnt a lot on the instructional side and the correct attitude towards Cadets. Within weeks I was more than confident and competent in my instruction duties which was very satisfying, because my introduction to RSM Lynch had not been helpful; he had made disparaging comments about my Regiment sending an instructor to an Officer Cadet establishment who had not been an Instructor at the Guards Depot. I couldn't use a pace stick therefore he thought I was not the right calibre. He threatened to return me to my Unit at the first sign of inefficiency which I thought was rather unfair until he had observed my capabilities. We never really saw eye to eye but more about that later.

As the weeks went by everything began to fall into place and things we had anticipated might go wrong did not do so. The Company Commander was more than pleased that everything was going so well. For whatever reasons Bert fell foul of the RSM on a couple of occasions and he gave him various duties to perform outside the Company, sending for him on the slightest whim, and this continued for the following months until he unfortunately fell sick on our return from our third Battle Camp and never returned to duty. I was promoted Company Sergeant Major until CSM England was posted in some five months later. From Recruit to CSM in under three years was not bad going.

Our first Company on the whole did extremely well in all aspects with no major horrors. Some were Relegated and we took some Relegatees from 'C' Company. Our Junior Under Officers were of a very high standard and eventually a Welsh Guards Cadet named Elliot was made SUO, but it must have been a difficult decision for Major Gatehouse to make. Prior to the Commissioning Parade the Cadets invited the OC and Platoon Commanders to dinner and laid on a most entertaining and hilarious cabaret. The Cadet mainly responsible for organizing this event was the former Producer of the Oxford Review, who later entered television. So having completed our first Company Course, from the OC down to our Company Clerk, we looked forward to the future with confidence.

The Commissioning Parades took place on Thursdays and by early Friday all the Administrative tasks were completed and we awaited the new intake of Cadets. The accommodation 'Spiders' lay slightly below the level of the surrounding road and it was forbidden for any vehicle to be given access to the area of the 'Spider'. As I approached the Company Lines prior to our Second Company I saw parked adjacent to the entrance door an immaculate white Jaguar car, and unloading suitcases from the boot was a tall, blond, handsome character in civilian trousers and shirt. He appeared older than the average Cadet.

'You!' I screamed at the miscreant from the roadway. The result was an electrifying motion to rigidity, dropping the suitcase on assuming the erect stance of attention.

'Who are you?' as I moved towards him.

'Heseltine, Sir.'

'Regiment?'

'Welsh Guards Sir.'

'That will be of no assistance to you here,' I screamed. Twitchings of the body could be seen; he was plainly nervous. 'Don't you realize that it's forbidden to bring vehicles into this area?'

A rather strangled, 'No Sir!' emitted from his rather tight mouth.

'Then move it on the roadway now!' With the speed of light he drove his car away.

In the first fortnight Cadets were expected to work late ensuring that all their personal kit was brought up to a very high standard. It was noticed that Heseltine appeared to be absent early in the evenings. When the OC and I made our weekly inspection not only was Heseltine's kit not up to standard but the layout was apparently rather hurriedly prepared. I threw the mattress, bedding and all the kit on to the floor; the OC smiled and reciprocated with another one. This action was carried out in most rooms and mentioned on Daily Orders that evening. As a result the following lunchtime I had a visitation from Heseltine. He was upset about the kit, so he was told in no uncertain terms the standard that was expected, and after some discussion he agreed and gave some reasons for his absences. He was made aware of all the various ramifications which he accepted and that matter was closed. However his next query took me aback.

'I believe a Senior Under Officer is appointed as the best Cadet and receives a Stick of Honour; what steps do you think I should take to achieve this?'

I sat him down and explained in some details what we, the Platoon Commanders and the OC, expected of anyone who could be considered for JUO and subsequently SUO. Any ambitions to this end was down to the individual Cadet. He left my bunk in a very thoughtful mood. The effect of our little chat was quite edifying. By the end of the fourth week, the whole performance of Heseltine had changed 100 per cent and staff were talking about him. After eight weeks and the Defence Exercise it was obvious that Heseltine had no serious challenger in No 1 Platoon for the position of JUO, which he eventually attained. There were however three other serious contenders for the position of SUO and all of them were severely tested in Wales. They all performed well and it must have been a difficult choice for the OC to make, but despite Heseltine's change of attitude, great determination to succeed and assimilation of matters military, another JUO from the Scots Guards named Madden was eventually appointed Senior Under Officer.

Soon after we had our little talk I took the trouble to read Heseltine's submitted autobiography and it was most enlightening. After perusal I then understood his reasons for wishing to attain No 1, and his desire to be top of the pile. His later dedication could only be described as outstanding. I only remember one other Cadet who asked me the same questions and showing the same dedication and ability achieved SUO on a later Course.

Junior Under Officer Michael Heseltine was commissioned in the Welsh Guards. Some months later he left the Regiment to become a candidate for Parliament, though on that occasion he failed. Some time later he was given the opportunity to contest a safer seat and he was successful. It is a well known fact that Michael Heseltine held two Cabinet appointments before he resigned and is still considered by many senior Conservatives to be in contention for the office of Prime Minister. He was my Guest at the Scots Guards Association Dinner some years ago and was his normal charming articulate self, diplomatic and tolerant when speaking with other guests who did not share his political views. My opinion had not changed over the years: he could be my leader at any time. I was privileged to help in the formation of his character and consider him to be a person of outstanding quality and acumen. He fully deserves all the accolades I tender.

During these early days at Mons I played rugby with the Cadets and was a member of the School's football and cricket teams, I can remember playing against well known professional footballers such as Alec Young of Everton, Plenderleith of Manchester City and others who were doing their National Service and stationed around the Aldershot area. Reputations do not mean a great deal in the Army and they were allowed no privileges on the playing fields, which, in many cases was no bad thing; it often prevented many 'prima donnas' from becoming big headed.

As in most training establishments, especially those involved with hundreds of trainees the occasional hiccup occurs within the Staff or the 'victims'. Fortunately at Mons in my time this rarely occurred and considering the miscellany of ranks, Regiments and civilians involved it all ran like a well oiled clock. I cannot recall any particular incident, humorous or otherwise, that occurred in our first Course. We were all so keen yet cautious that Staff mistakes were few and insignificant and the Cadets worked hard and gave no trouble. Personalities among the Cadets included Field Marshal Alexander's son Brian, who entered the Irish Guards, together with another Cadet whom I lost trace of. I think he recently came to notice when the Berlin Wall came down: Major General Corbett was British Commandant in Berlin and Major General commanding London District.

The second Course, as previously mentioned, had Heseltine as a member plus several others. One noticeable Cadet who remained in the Welsh Guards was the CO of that Battalion in the Falklands War, now Brigadier General Ricketts.

CHAPTER 11

Mons – Proposed Commission Candidate

At the School we had a Sergeant in the Durham Light Infantry who decided to apply for a Commission and was accepted. Prior to commencing his Course at Mons we had a long talk and as a result of this the School's Programme Officer, a Captain in the Royal Signals, asked me to visit him. Throughout the School all officers acted as the representative of their own Regiment or even additional ones; this particular officer was also the representative of the Intelligence Corps and the Royal Military Police. Having verified my background and qualifications he said I was eligible for acceptance in both Corps, but he considered I would have a better chance of acceptance of a vacancy in the RMP.

Within days, I arrived at the RMP Depot one afternoon and had a long interview with the Commandant and the Adjutant. It was made abundantly clear by both officers that I was more than welcome to join the Corps. At the present time however they could only guarantee a three-year tour, each additional year being conditional on vacancies being filled by Regular Commissioned Officers from Sandhurst. As I wished to embark on a full time career they suggested I should think about it for a few days. After due deliberation I refused the offer. Some four years later the role of the RMP in support of operational Brigades in BAOR was drastically changed and officers were in great demand. In retrospect maybe I made the wrong decision but I needed security and in all honesty I don't think I regretted my action.

CHAPTER 12

Mons – Ten-Mile Run

An interesting incident happened on a Saturday morning when the temperature was approximately 80°F. It had been decided by two of our Platoon Instructors, both Captains, that they would take the Company on their ten-mile forced march as part of their Physical Proficiency Tests; time allowed was two hours. As I was holding the Company on Parade, and no doubt with tongue in cheek, the two officers invited me to attend as well, and I could hardly refuse. The Cadets rather savoured this with loud cheers.

I was not unfit but I was not prepared for what was to come; the two officers obviously intended this physical interlude as a form of punishment and character assessment. No doubt this was why no member of the resident Army Physical Training Corps was asked to supervise. We started off at the double, but after two miles several Cadets started to fall back. I too began to struggle for my second wind and I was grateful; it gave me a chance to gain composure and 'chivvy' those falling back. After a further mile the Company were spread out with only the super fit keeping up to the two officers. 'Break into Quick Time' was called and eventually a resemblance of order was achieved, but the pace slackened, Capt. D asked me to go to the front and set the pace which I did, completely unaware of what eventually transpired behind me.

Two miles from Barracks, I was called back a few ranks to attend to a Cadet about to drop out. I took his pack and rifle while his two friends on either side forced him on. I also screamed encouragement for a final effort; this I received with eyes full of pleading and open hostility. Some two hundred yards before we entered Barracks I ordered the Cadets to slope Arms and the Company marched into Barracks in good order as if they were on the Square. It took an awful lot of guts and effort but they did well. The two officers brought in a few stragglers and with Capt. D's permission I dismissed the Company, many of whom were on the verge of collapse. One in particular was delirious but I brought him round a few minutes later. One Cadet who fell out on the road was taken to Hospital and I was told sixteen others finally made their way back.

On the Monday morning following the run I was approached by the senior APTC Warrant Officer and asked what had happened. I suggested he should speak to the officers concerned. He had apparently seen me bring the Company back and had later been informed of the hospitalizations and the late arrival of the sixteen others. He left me, mumbling about a punishment run, Court Martials etc. I heard nothing further of this. We did the ten miles in 1 hour 25 minutes, I never thought I could have managed it without some preparatory training but I did. It also indicated to Cadets that Instructional Staff could still undergo the physical aspects of military training.

CHAPTER 13

Promotion to CSM

We brought our third Company back from Battle Camp on the Friday and by Monday morning Bert Croucher had reported sick and never returned to duty at Mons OCS. I therefore took over as Company Sergeant Major and after the statutory period of time the promotion to Acting rank was granted and the increase in pay allowed.

By this time we had a new Admin. Sergeant. He was a Scotsman serving with the HLI (Highland Light Infantry), his name was McDonald and he was a very competent Regimental Boxer. 'Mac' was no doubt a good Platoon Sergeant but as an office administrator or Drill Instructor he was no help to me, and he did have a strong liking for the demon drink. The fortnight before Commissioning was therefore more than hectic for me, considering I had also a new Company Clerk who was not really 'a ball of fire'. However, all went extremely well and the Company Commander was well pleased as he received congratulations from his seniors, so that was one big hurdle overcome and I had cause to feel happy.

Almost without pausing for breath the next contingent of Cadets were arriving and I had a fortnight to get them up to scratch for the Adjutant's inspection. The object of this inspection was to ensure that items such as boots, anklets, belt and uniform were in good order not only for the standard of the School but also that they were presentable for the next Commissioning Parade a fortnight later. The Adjutant and RSM, as to be expected, made their comprehensive check and made comments which Major Gatehouse and I later checked; it was no better, no worse than our previous Companies, and the OC was quite pleased. An hour later I was ordered to the RSM's office. He marched me in front of the Adjutant who proceeded to warn me that he expected the high standard of 'A' Company to be maintained despite the fact that I was on my own, he did not expect the standard to drop; and with a slight smile he dismissed me.

The matter did not end there, I was back in front of the RSM, the two Drill Sergeants sat at my back and in this cosy environment I was told by the RSM that I was a disgrace, that my Company was dirty, scruffy and

138

not working hard enough and that it was my fault. He also asked why I was not spending my evenings with them in a supervisory capacity. All of this was untrue and I was getting angrier, especially when he said it was the worse Company of Officer Cadets he had ever inspected. When he asked me for an explanation I told him the Company Commander was more than satisfied. I pointed out that I had only recently acquired an Admin. Sergeant and Company Clerk and had been performing their duties, and my duties had kept me in Barracks until 9p.m. most nights. He then made a sarcastic comment that I should have informed him of my difficulties and he would have ensured that I had the help of one of his Drill Sergeants. I was so annoyed, and without thinking of the consequences I took a short pace forward, both hands came up to waist height in fists and I said, 'What did you want me to do, Sir, cry to you?' I then realized what I had done and I could hear the clanging of the cell door, and I slowly assumed the correct stance of attention.

Through lowered eyes I could see the RSM look up at me and with a changed voice and attitude he said, 'No, I wouldn't expect you to cry to me, one of my Drill Sergeants will assist you in any way he can.' I was then dismissed. Apart from one close visit on the Square I never enjoyed the assistance of either Drill Sergeant.

As a follow up to the incident described, when the time came for the Company Drill Competition I had four Platoons. It was normal for the CSM and myself to take alternate Platoons and here was one opportunity when I needed help but none was offered. At the relevant time of the Competition the larger percentage of the Company were Corps personnel. They were all aware of the difficult situation I was in, and they had made up their minds between themselves, and with the encouragement of their Junior Under Officers, that they were not going to let me down. They had heard about the RSM's attitude and I was not prepared for what eventually transpired.

All four Platoons were marched down to the Square and paraded for Inspection. This was done by the Adjutant, RSM and the Coldstream Drill Sergeant. They were immaculate and stood like Guardsmen. I marched three Platoons into the Drill Shed to see the Scots Guards Drill Sergeant standing in the background and thought that help would be on hand but nothing happened. Each Platoon then performed a predetermined set of Foot Drill movements followed by Rifle Drill; this whole procedure took approximately 45 minutes. On this occasion I was giving words of command for a continuous period of almost three and a half hours. I half expected my voice to break down but it didn't. I was so proud of my Company; they were absolutely magnificent, I could see every single Cadet giving 110 per cent of effort. Everything I had taught them on the Drill Square they did with great aplomb. It affected me and my voice never faltered.

You must consider that Drill Competitions of this nature had been carried out for many years at Eaton Hall, Cheshire and at Mons OCS for Short Service Commissioned Officers. At the conclusion of this particular Competition my winning Platoon broke the existing record by 8 points, the Runner Up by 2 points, the third Platoon had level points with the record and the fourth attained three points below. It was an extremely proud and elated Acting Company Sergeant Major who drew the Company 'Properly at Ease' and asked permission to march off. We marched off the Square and up the road to 'A' Company Lines as if we owned the world. I had some difficulty in expressing my thanks and admiration for all. I didn't know till later that all the Under Officers plus others had convened a meeting and decided that a special effort should be made to ensure that all my hard work had not been in vain, and how well they succeeded.

Approximately five months after I was promoted, Bill England arrived to take over as CSM. The handover was prolonged because of the Commissioning Parade and the commencement of a new intake, but Bill soon fell into the routine. Yet again RSM Lynch decided to get on his back and for several weeks Bill, who enjoyed a drink and a dabble on the horses, was made the object of the RSM's attention and I managed by quick talking to keep him out of trouble on more than one occasion.

CHAPTER 14

Unlawful Discharge – Battle Camp

An incident occurred on our fifth Battle Camp which almost involved me in a Court Martial. This matter concerned a Cadet who unlawfully discharged his weapon after it had been inspected by myself and cleaned. This was following a night firing exercise with live ammunition.

The circumstances are as follows. On a particular designated range and dependant on the light at the time of the year a night firing exercise was laid on with static and mobile targets, fixed and parachute flares and a verbal scenario adding to the realism. Platoons were rotated and a total was made when each of them completed their shots. Close supervision was carried out by the permanent staff (ourselves) of each section.

On this particular occasion when I returned to Camp to collect a Platoon I had the feeling that some Cadets had been drinking: a number were asleep and others were in high spirits. Later when the live firing was completed I approached this particular section I was supervising, giving them the order 'For inspection Port Arms', and with the aid of a torch, my eyes and my fingers I checked each weapon, that the working parts were cleared and eased forward, and that the accompanying magazine shown was empty. As I checked each Cadet he lowered his weapon and as it was dark he was allowed to relax and discuss the shoot. I had just checked the last man when I heard the sound of a weapon being discharged. I turned and saw the second Cadet I had checked now standing at the 'Port Arms' position looking with some disbelief at his smoking weapon. Another Cadet whose head was inches away from the muzzle was standing dazed and open mouthed. I will not attempt to repeat my words but a full magazine had been placed on the weapon and obviously the working parts operated and the trigger squeezed. Major Gatehouse was fuming and in his presence I formally charged the Cadet.

The following day the Cadet appeared on Orders and evidence submitted. He was remanded for higher authority when we returned to Mons. On the Monday morning following our return, I paraded with the Cadet and other witnesses on Commanding Officer's Orders. With no explanation from the RSM I was marched in and formerly charged with 'failing to carry out my duties'. Major Gatehouse and others were more than surprised especially as there was no evidence as yet that I had in any way been negligent; the OC had ascertained this in Wales. It all had the hallmark of the RSM interfering in a matter of which he had no knowledge of the detailed circumstances: I had been the supervising officer and therefore I was to blame.

No evidence was offered against me and there was a short embarrassing silence, then I was marched out, immediately returning with the Cadet. Major Gatehouse briefly outlined the circumstances on the Range until the time the shot was fired. My evidence was more detailed and precise. I could feel an intentness emanating from the RSM's gaze; he really wanted my scalp. I made no mistakes in my evidence.

When the Cadet gave his evidence he completely exonerated me. He could not offer an explanation as to why, having returned to the 'Order Arms' position from the 'Port Arms' with an empty rifle and magazine, he then removed the empty magazine, replaced it with a full one, cocked the weapon, and squeezed the trigger. He said he was probably tired after a full day's training; it was late at night and needed his sleep. After due deliberation he was found Guilty and Severely Reprimanded. He was allowed to be Commissioned because of his Course conduct and his unblemished record, supported by Major Gatehouse. He was fortunate that he wasn't facing a manslaughter charge. After he was dismissed I was marched in. No evidence was offered, and with a smile the Commandant ordered the charge be taken out. I could never understand the reason why I had to be charged until some evidence was forthcoming to show that I or others had been negligent in our supervision, and there the matter ended. I could only conclude that the RSM was being unnecessarily vindictive.

CHAPTER 15

HMS Plover

A brief break from routine was afforded me when a Sergeant from the RA Wing and I were chosen to report to the Royal Navy Depot at Portsmouth and board HMS *Plover*, a minelayer, for a seven-day cruise. I must confess I was not over enthusiastic about a sea trip; previous experiences had shown I was not a good sailor. My colleague and I joined ship and were made extremely welcome in the Petty Officers' Mess of which as I remember there were seven POs. The accommodation was restricted and you had to sleep in whatever space was available; table, bunk seats or even the deck.

We soon adapted ourselves to the routine and we were shown all aspects of the workings of the ship including its operational role which was all extremely interesting, but not an occupation I would enjoy as a career. We cruised down the English Channel and practised various emergency drills which kept us busy both day and night.

The social life of the Mess was very good and rather unique. A small group of men of varied personalities spending a lot of time together in a confined space necessitated a great deal of humour and tolerance. The Navy are used to this within their career at sea: a ship is a confined area and so are the various Messes on board. To operate in their role, the Army needs space and we found the environment somewhat claustrophobic and restrictive, but nevertheless very instructive and interesting, and it is a good thing that your colleagues from the other Services appreciate the role and conditions under which their opposite numbers have to work and therefore ensure support and co-operation. This of course does not always manifest itself but these exchanges are essential and welcome. I have good reasons to be grateful to my opposite numbers but not necessarily from the Royal Navy.

All in all it was a very enjoyable and instructive break from the strict training routine, but I'm afraid a career in the Royal Navy would not be my choice.

I must recall an amusing story which has more serious connotations and which I recalled before a group of ex Jocks when we were present at Hopetoun House near Edinburgh when HM the Queen presented new Colours to 2SG in August 1989. The object of the story was Bill England who had joined the group and who laughed long and loud when the story finished.

Bill had served with 1SG in Italy during the war, eventually leaving for civilian life where he worked for a Glasgow bookmaker. He was a tall, heavily built person with a loud Glaswegian accent; intelligent, forthright and humorous, he enjoyed a drink, was a very shrewd card player and followed the horses.

Within the job, Bill would be described as a good soldier but he was not the epitome of a Guards Sergeant Major. His build denied him this accolade. He was smart, an adequate instructor and administrator but somehow or other he also got on the wrong side of the RSM and yet again the knives were out. There were times when Bill didn't help matters owing to his own conduct; however with luck and some deviousness I managed to keep Bill out of serious trouble, not that I gave it much thought.

I had first met Bill at the Guards Depot when I re-joined and he was the CQMS (Company Quartermaster Sergeant) of 'K' Company. It was common knowledge that he was an ardent member of the Orange Lodge and in Glasgow they were extremely anti Catholic, so I had never given him any reason to comment. As time went on I was convinced that he was well aware of my religion but he still did not comment. Having negotiated him through all the initial pitfalls, especially with the RSM, we arrived at Battle Camp, with Bill anxious to do some socializing outside our spartan accommodation. A Cadet gave us a lift into Brecon, where we first visited the South Wales Borderers Depot Mess and then various pubs and it was in the bar of one of these, near to closing time, that Bill was demonstrating to an impressed licensee the mysteries of various card tricks. He had had more than sufficiency of beer and whisky but he was in full possession of his faculties.

When the licensee left us to call Last Orders, Bill turned to me, looked hard and long into my face and said, 'You know, Eric, in the whole of my Army service I have only ever trusted two people, one was [and he described a particular soldier of no consequence] and you,' and in a voice breaking with some emotion he added, 'And you're both f . . . g Catholics.'

Rather surprised at this statement, I said, 'What difference does that make?'

'Well, you know what I am, I don't understand why you have saved my neck so many times knowing this.'

I then attempted to explain to Bill that a person's religion or lack of it meant nothing to me, I judged a person by other means, he was a comrade in arms and it was my duty to treat him as a brother, not as a religious bigot and I expected him to relate to me accordingly. We continued to discuss this. Surprisingly I did most of the talking until the licensee requested our departure. Bill and I never had a cross word and worked together as a very successful team; we've met on several occasions since and our friendship remains the same. As a very intelligent person I hope Bill realizes that you cannot isolate Catholics as a breed apart because of their religious convictions. What a pity this can't be injected into the warring factions in Northern Ireland. Why do misguided parents and clergy continue to poison their children's minds? Sadly, Bill died of cancer in 1998.

The next humorous incident I wish to relate concerns two Brigade Cadets: Billy Guinness, Irish Guards, and Andrew Parsons, Scots Guards. Both persons were just about justifying further training and under the microscope from all instructors. Prior to the period at Battle Camp Major Gatehouse assembled the Company in the large Lecture Hall mainly to instruct on the tactics involved in 'The Advance to Contact' which would be used constantly in Wales. On the previous evening Billy and Andrew individually had driven to London to attend separate social functions which continued till the early hours of the following morning. Andrew returned to Mons safely and managed to have a few hours sleep; Billy however was involved in a road accident on a large roundabout west of London and his car was a write-off. Billy did not sustain any visible injury that required hospital attention, but he managed to return to Mons and obtain the minimum of sleep.

Having spoken for a couple of hours the OC sent the Company outside for a mid morning break and taking advantage of the warm sunshine Guinness and Parsons fell fast asleep on the ground adjacent to the Hall. When recalled, it was generally agreed by all the Cadets to leave them *in situ*. It was somewhat unfortunate that the OC on return outlined a problem and said, 'Now, what would you do, Parsons?' When the named Cadet did not stand up the OC, a little miffed at the lack of manners on Parsons behalf, said rather testily, 'Come on, Parsons, stand up.' There was still no movement and a pregnant pause. 'Parsons stand up!' Nothing moved.

A voice then said, 'Excuse me, Sir, I think you should look outside.'

'Why the hell should I?' came the immediate reply.

'I think you should, Sir.'

In a few determined strides the OC reached the door and angrily threw it open. Some twenty yards in front of him, in somnolent posture, lay the figures of two Cadets, their joint snores mixing sweetly with nearby bird song. Recognising them he called their names, to no avail, so he picked up a couple of small pebbles and threw them in the general direction of the recumbent bodies. Like most officers his aim was poor and he missed. By this time almost the whole Company had acquired a grandstand view at the door and windows but they did not yell encouragement. By this time the OC was most exasperated and looking round for a more substantial weapon he saw a reasonable portion of brick; seizing this he lobbed it like a grenade and this time his aim was perfect. It hit Billy Guinness on the point of the jaw. As Billy yelled in agony, Andrew awoke and sat up, but I was informed that without the help of a magician, Billy's body actually left the ground in a perpendicular motion for several inches before Billy sat up clutching his bleeding face. He was quickly removed to the nearby Medical Centre, where he was stitched up and sent to his bed.

I was sitting in the office when the OC returned and called me in. He was worried as he briefly recounted what had happened.

'Well done, Sir,' I laughingly remarked, 'That should keep him on his toes. I'll have a word with Parsons too.'

'I'm more worried if there is a complaint,' wailed the OC, his thoughts on facing a Court Martial for serious assault.

Billy was lying in a comatose state on his bed when I entered his room and after a short conversation it was evident that Billy was more concerned about being charged for his absence, possible relegation or even RTU. Painting this picture to him Billy stated that he did not blame the OC for his accident, all he wanted was to go to Wales, do well, and obtain his Commission, and of course this is what happened. He was fit to go to Wales and did quite well, subsequently he was Commissioned. Needless to say the OC was relieved but word had got around and there was a host of humorous comment. Billy's father had a car delivered to the Camp driven by the family butler the day after our arrival in Sennybridge so he was not inconvenienced too much, and in the long run I think the episode did him the power of good.

My period of service at Mons OCS was probably the highlight of my career with the Scots Guards, I had proved that within a relatively short time my instructional capabilities were of a high order; I could oversee 140 bodies and adequately administer them, including clothing and equipment.

I had learnt how to impose a high standard of discipline on the persons I was responsible for. In these particular circumstances, dealing with potential officers, the imposition had to be partnered with diplomacy and humour, and I think that most Warrant Officers and NCOs who have worked at Sandhurst or Mons would argue that apart from their particular expertise these two facets were of great importance.

The most satisfying aspect to be achieved at Mons was the fact that apart from a small percentage, the majority of Cadets were two-year National Servicemen and to reach the very high standard that was required, great credit was due to all the instructional staff. Although it was extremely hard work and the pace was somewhat hectic I personally derived great satisfaction in what was achieved. I presume it was almost a repetition of wartime when time was short but standards had to be as high as possible.

Overseas Cadets did pose a problem, at times. During my period we had trainees from various African states, the West Indies, the Arab Emirates and I think one Malaysian. I would say that approximately 70 per cent of the Cadets were satisfactory; some in fact carried on and completed the long course at Sandhurst. At holiday times we had a organization who arranged British families to sponsor and entertain Overseas Cadets who wished to participate in this particular scheme and quite a lot of them took advantage of this; others either had friends in this country or decided to remain independent.

A small percentage had language difficulties and really should never have been chosen for Officer Training, and our weather also affected others. I recall the terrible distress that was experienced by a very charming African Prince (tribal) who sustained a very heavy cold. On his return from Sick Parade I found him sobbing his heart out. He felt so sick he thought he was dying. He had never experienced anything quite like it, the coughing, sneezing, headache and snivelling was indicative he was about to meet his Maker and he needed some persuasion to assure him that it was only a temporary setback. It was unfortunate that the same Cadet when we attended Battle Camp at Sennybridge also suffered from a mild case of snow blindness but he quickly recovered. I remember the Chinese and Dyaks who saw the film 'Doctor Zhivago' found it difficult to comprehend the vast open spaces of snow or waving corn in the summer. One can understand how it could affect certain people. We had one particular success who attained JUO and this was well deserved; he was every inch a soldier and a gentleman.

It was also pleasing to observe how the Cadets from totally different social backgrounds worked and slept together, shared tasks, organized each other and finally worked together as a team in order to achieve the common objective. You could not find any greater contrast than the Brigade of Guard/Greenjackets and the Pioneer Corps/Royal Army Service Corps. Rarely did you find them mixing socially because their interests were different and finance also played a part, but within the military environments they all worked for each other which is how the Army works; every soldier needs each other.

Before I left Mons I received a letter from Regimental Headquarters which contained references to my excellent Annual Report and other comments from an unknown source. It stated that my conduct showed me to be an excellent representative for my Regiment. I was rather 'chuffed' about that; it's nice to know that your superior officers are aware of all your hard work and inform you so. Speaking to other Senior Ranks at a later stage, I discovered that this form of accolade was most unusual. Had I received more encouragement when I was posted to Gravesend I don't think I would have considered a transfer to the Intelligence Corps.

Personally I held very partisan views about my Regiment. I was extremely proud to be a member; my family held strong military connections over the years and to achieve the rank of Regimental Sergeant Major would have been a great honour. There were however certain feelings about Roman Catholics. Some officers had achieved Commanding Officer status and above, but I cannot recall, to my limited knowledge, that a Catholic RSM had ever been appointed, and I think that rather than become a frustrated and disgruntled soldier I weighed up the odds and regretfully decided to transfer after a period at Gravesend when I had rejoined the 1st Battalion again.

I must recall the attitude of a particular Cadet following my introduction of the Inter Platoon Boxing Competition. Some Cadets had made comments about the lack of a competition of this nature so I discussed the matter with the APTC (Army Physical Training Corps), a ring was available and I was left to generally organize the event as part of the Champion Platoon Competition.

As I recall we had the Honourable Archie Hamilton as a potential officer for the Coldstream Guards at eighteen years of age and recently a pupil at Eton. Archie could only be described as a 6'2" beanpole and extremely slim; he could not be classed as a well muscled athlete. I had little alternative when I chose the pugilists (volunteers or otherwise) but to put Archie in with a six-foot member of REME who played Rugby League. Archie paid me a visit expressing great apprehension about facing such a formidable adversary, who was known to be competitive and aggressive. I explained that neither of them had done any boxing but if he really felt hurt he should take the count. On the other hand he was likely to face aggression when he joined his Battalion and therefore as a matter of personal pride and that of his Regiment he should get into the ring and conduct himself accordingly. Initially I don't believe that I convinced him, and it was an extremely thoughtful Cadet who eventually left my bunk, no doubt thinking he was about to face a fate worse than death.

'Let battle commence!' On the afternoon in question we were treated to some extremely good bouts, one in particular would not have disgraced a professional match, then in great anticipation we all waited for the heavyweight bout which everyone considered would be a mere formality. In the opening seconds both men just made circles, neither offering any violence but in response to the cries of the spectators the REME Cadet began to strike Archie around the body with rather tentative blows which didn't hurt and he chased Archie round the ring, his opponent back pedalling furiously. Archie bounced off the ropes and his arms fell, whereupon he received a very painful right hander in the area of his left ear. As the REME chap stepped back to applause, Archie feeling pain and some indignity made a rather petulant stamp with his left foot. At the same time he threw a immaculate long straight left hand directly into the face of his opponent. This blow must have contained all the annoyance, pain and fright that Archie felt and his opponent staggered back a couple of paces. There was a short silence, then everyone roared their support. The effect was magical and Archie's confidence grew. From that moment till the end of the bout both Cadets fought well. The REME lad was more aggressive but his punches were wild; when they did connect and hurt Archie he retaliated promptly with a straight left and a swinging right which stopped his opponent in his tracks. This is how the fight continued right to the end. Both men, thoroughly exhausted, thankfully embraced each other when the final bell rang and the whole Company rightfully showed their appreciation of a gallant bout which as I recall was judged a draw. The general consensus of opinion was that the boxing had been a very informative assessment but only for a small percentage of personnel and as the Platoon Commanders changed, boxing was omitted from the Inter Platoon Competition.

I cannot accurately recall all the minor horrors, humorous or otherwise that took place during the Mons tour; the introduction of a Pace Stick Competition for all Instructors and the early morning practices was not a particularly welcomed innovation, but to be fair if you carry a pace stick you should be able to use it with some degree of expertise. When the decision was made to introduce the Self Loading Rifle for service with the Cadets, because I had demonstrated before the Whistler Committee I took a prominent part in the periods of instruction all Instructors had to attend. It was obvious that I had more experience of the weapon than the RSM and his two Drill Sergeants. Some of the Instructors had had limited practical use of the weapon with their Battalions but not the finer points of all the Arms Drill.

It was following the introduction of the weapon that I was stabbed in the hand by a Cadet with one of the new bayonets. It occurred during the final rehearsal for a Commissioning Parade. The RSM indicated a Cadet who was making a nonsense of returning his bayonet to the scabbard, I approached the Cadet from behind, told him what he should do and took hold of the scabbard, pushing it forward. Yet again the Cadet instinctively made an effort to insert the bayonet in the scabbard and instead he stabbed me in the fleshy part of my left hand between thumb and forefinger. With blood pouring from my hand I had to present myself in front of the Parade and with all due decorum ask the RSM for permission to attend the MI Room for treatment. As I approached him he gazed at me with some annoyance, and after my request was made he tersely said 'Why?' despite the obvious bloodied hand dripping on the Square. I had to explain and show him that I had been injured. I was told to leave. Subsequently the Doctor gave me an injection, and it was necessary to stitch it so the wound was bandaged and I returned to duty.

I suppose the next matter that I recall is a problem that recurs with some regularity at the moment of writing. We had returned from Battle Camp and I attended the dentist for a tooth extraction. I was also running a temperature and had a sore left eye, with all the symptoms of 'flu. Eventually I had to call the doctor who diagnosed 'flu and conjunctivitis. A few days later I returned to work still with a sore eye; the Medical Officer saw me, checked my eye, and sent me to the Cambridge Military Hospital in nearby Aldershot. A Colonel, Ophthalmic Surgeon, immediately operated for a large ulcer on the left eye, taking an hour and a half. At that time it was general procedure that ulcers were removed by burning off the offending infected area by careful and precise application of acid. As the patient I found the operation an uncomfortable experience as one had to lie perfectly still with a metal instrument inserted into the eye socket and the eye placed in an operating position for this very delicate procedure.

I was given the maximum injection of pethidine to numb the oncoming pain and placed in bed. Some time later I was in such intense pain that I actually tore the top sheet trying to stifle my agony. Leaving the bed I staggered towards the toilet only to be detained by Sister and two nurses who told me I could have no more pain killing injections, I had to grin and bear it. The following day I brought to the attention of the doctor that the left side of my throat was extremely sore and swollen. Over the next two days no fewer than four dental surgeons studied X-rays on my mouth and throat, and eventually, under sedation, I was taken to the operating theatre to allow the civilian surgeon to see me.

At that time I was unaware of the tremendous change that had taken place to my appearance, so much so, that as I stood there supported by two nurses, also waiting to see the Surgeon was Capt. Bowater, Scots Guards, at that time serving as 2IC of the Guards Parachute Company; we knew each other quite well and he just failed to recognise me. It rather shook me but I think I was beyond caring. When the surgeon saw me he looked at my eyes and nearly threw a fit until it was explained about my previous operation and the drugs that were still being used. He made a mark across my throat and said he would operate in an hour.

Following the operation and for whatever reasons I was given VIP treatment for the following week. I had visits at various times from all Seniors in the hospital and others, for reasons I was not aware of. Jean could visit at any time and Sister provided raw eggs, brandy or sherry as I couldn't eat in the normal way. I was also like a pin cushion, so much so that when a nurse approached my bed I automatically threw back the sheets and bared my backside. Quote of the day from a 'gay' male nurse: 'I like injecting you, Sergeant, you don't resist me!!' It was with some relief that I began to improve. I was told that my problem had been a serious infection of the sub mandibular gland and this had no doubt been infected through the wound following the tooth extraction. It was a most unusual case and had obviously caused a great deal of interest with the medical staff.

During my incarceration, as well as Jean and Chris, I had a constant stream of visitors and messages. Somehow former Cadets heard of my problem and made the journey to visit or leave messages. It was nice to know that so many cared about my welfare, and Jean had many offers of help. After release from hospital and a few days rest I returned to work feeling no adverse after effects and my eye had healed well, but since that time I have been susceptible to any virus infection which causes an ulcer to form on the eye, and until the treatment changed the ulcers were treated with acid, the last two carried out in Singapore when I was Casevac from Borneo and I had had cholera. Subsequently when I experienced the slightest discomfort in my eye I sought medical help and I have lost count of the many times I have needed this. In retrospect I suppose I have been lucky as the eye specialist at the Edinburgh Royal Infirmary told me in 1968 that within five years I would lose my eye.

It should be said how well Jean and I had settled in to the village life at Frimley Green. The bus service was quite efficient to Camberley and Aldershot and it was possible to travel to London from a nearby railway station. The bungalow was reasonably furnished and we received permission to carry out some decorating which made the interior somewhat brighter. Chris attended the local school a hundred yards up the road and the Catholic Church was in Frimley, approximately a mile away. We also increased our family by two. Our first acquisition was a beautiful seven-week-old Alsatian bitch puppy whom we named Rinny. After my arrival at Mons I had called to see a local Alsatian breeder, and she was very impressed with my handling of two of her animals. After my visit she rang me at work and told me she had two bitch pups which she had taken from an American Army Colonel who had brought his pregnant bitch over from Germany avoiding quarantine whilst at AAF Base at Blackbushe. Four pups had been born and at the time he and the dog left for the USA two pups had been sold and he gave the other two away to the breeder. The pedigree was quite outstanding: International Champions from Germany and the UK and the grandmother was a working sheepdog. It will always be my considered opinion that Rinny was by far the finest dog I have ever been in contact with. In the six years we had her she displayed an uncanny instinct in matters protective that are difficult to explain and though some of it was by my training, it all appeared to be second nature and she never gave us one moment of trouble. It was a sad day when I handed her over to a former Army Dog Handler before I left for Germany.

The second addition in later years caused Jean and me so much sorrow, despair, anger, embarrassment and many, many, hours of bitter tears that I find it extremely difficult to place it on record.

After prolonged assessment of current medical opinion and long discussions between Jean and me, we decided to take the first steps to adopt a female child. At this stage no relatives or friends were consulted. We obtained the assistance of the resident Roman Catholic Forces Padre and the initial formalities were begun. Subsequently interviews were carried out by the Catholic Adoption Society from Portsmouth and we were accepted as prospective suitable parents. We commenced our interest in January 1959 and by midsummer we had our second child whom we registered and baptised Carolyn Anne Howard.

Our reasons for considering adoption stemmed from two miscarriages that Jean suffered in 1954 at Ashford and in 1958 at Windsor; on both occasions she lost twins. It was therefore the advice by doctors that unless she was prepared to confine herself to bed for at least four months and possibly longer after conception, any hope she might have of carrying on a pregnancy would be doubtful. The fact that Chris had been such a large child and Jean was so small, probably damaged the womb making retention extremely difficult, and as we wished more children, adoption appeared to be the only sensible solution to avoid mutual disappointment and the possibility that a further miscarriage could have a detrimental mental effect on Jean.

In retrospect, and I speak personally, I don't think I would regret the twelve years that were uninterrupted by any trouble whatsoever, but since the problems commenced at Barking in 1972 the subsequent years for Jean and me were hell on earth until Carolyn was nineteen years of age. By this time she appeared to be a different person. A bedsit had been acquired in Ashton, it was reasonably decorated and furnished, she was in regular employment which she enjoyed. In all fairness, in any job she had, she always worked hard. Jean and I went on holiday in 1978 satisfied in our minds that Carolyn was happy and settled. On our return I visited her bedsit to take an item of furniture, a present and some clothing, I was informed that Carolyn had left a week earlier without leaving any message or forwarding address; sadly we have not seen her since.

All the excuses, lies and absences from home: these actions by Carolyn all boiled down to the fact that we were not her parents and therefore she rejected our parental authority; she had no love for us, and preferred and undertook actions that kept her away from our love and authority. Prior to leaving this area she told Jean she was ashamed of her conduct, that it was all contrived to hurt us and for this she was sorry but unrepentant. However I am convinced that another person became involved with whom she had formed a relationship, and if she considered that this person would be unacceptable to us she would revert to her previous behaviour and run away, unwilling to face criticism or reality. Call it a character weakness but over the troubled years immediately Carolyn was faced with a problem, she would never attempt a solution but behaved in a completely irrational manner inviting further trouble and this was a continuing saga during this period: one problem compounded another.

I would like to think that we were just unfortunate and that adoption is worthwhile; I suppose a small percentage of failure was to be accepted. Jean and I never thought that we would become a statistical failure. Considering all the love, affection, guidance and protection given to Carolyn we found it extremely difficult to accept why over six years she should behave in the manner she did. It is conjecture on my part but I would assume that as she matured the realization of her guilt and subsequent embarrassment was a personal worry. She had been accepted back into the bosom of her family and all relatives/friends. When confronted with the dilemma of whether these people would accept this doubtful relationship it was the straw that broke the camel's back, and she ran, reverting to past behaviour.

Even attempting to recall at this juncture the incidents over the six years would cover many pages and serve no purpose. It was an extremely sad episode of life which deserves to be forgotten but it never will be.

CHAPTER 16

1SG Gravesend – January 1961

As the time approached when my tour at Mons would be completed I was informed that I would be posted to 1SG who would be returning from BAOR to take up Public Duties in London, but would be stationed at Gravesend where limited accommodation was available for married families. Those families not afforded quarters were given accommodation on a Royal Navy estate at Walderslade, near Chatham; some others had private hirings in nearby Rochester and other areas. In December 1961 I visited Gravesend to attend to housing and administrative problems, also to renew acquaintances. Although somewhat isolated and lacking in amenities, the house was most satisfactory. The estate was clean and presentable, situated on high ground surrounded by open spaces and woodland.

After a few days leave and having settled in the house, Chris attending his school, I joined the Battalion, on a Monday morning before we were due to commence Public Duties on the following Tuesday. Personnel at Walderslade were picked up after 7a.m. by 3-ton truck and I attended Adjutant's Orders at 8a.m. I had been posted to Right Flank Company and spent some time acquainting myself with personnel and accommodation. Later I watched a Guard Mounting Rehearsal with a great deal of interest as I had never performed London Public Duties before. At 11a.m. I attended Commanding Officer Orders and was welcomed back, I was then told to attend the RSM's office.

Regimental Sergeant Major (Jolly) Rodger, in my estimation, was the epitome of a Scots Guards RSM. I had known him as a Drill Sergeant at Lydd and he always impressed me both as a soldier and as a person. When I entered his office the Drill Sergeants and all the Company Sergeant Majors were present, some of whom I knew, and I was well scrutinised. The RSM looked up at me and said, 'Tomorrow night certain members of the Royal Family will attend the Tower of London to watch the Ceremony of the Keys for the first time since before the War. This Battalion will perform that duty. It will be perfect, there will be no slip ups, you will be the Sergeant of the Guard, any questions?'

For a couple of seconds I struggled to reply, then I finally came out with, 'I have never done London Duties before and I'm not familiar with procedures.'

I might have known what the reply would be; he again looked at me and said, 'There's a rehearsal for the Tower at 2 o'clock, be there, and collect all the instructions for the Guard Mounting and Tower duties, also ask other Mess Members, now fall out.'

I was dismissed. On leaving I had the distinct impression that I was being observed with a mixture of interest and some sardonic smiles; this was to be quite a test. I discussed procedures with other Senior Ranks, watched the rehearsal, read the instructions, prepared my uniform and kit and with fingers crossed, prayers said, I hoped for the best. The Guard Mounting at Wellington Barracks was performed without a hitch, and I was quite confident when we arrived at the Tower; again the Handover was achieved without problems. I took over the Guardroom etc., and then hit the Jewel House alarm. Considering it was a first effort all the Guardsmen were at their designated posts in various orders of dress in 21 seconds (I later achieved 17 seconds). Later in the day after the public were cleared from the premises I took the participants in the Ceremony through the whole procedure and I felt much better about it all. In fact it all went extremely well, not one mistake, just one slight hiccup occurring with the first couple of notes of the Last Post, otherwise it was a perfect rendition in the cold January night. We were all roundly congratulated, none more relieved than I.

For the next five months or so with only three Bank of England Guards and maybe a dozen Tower Guards I spent every other day at Buckingham Palace. As Jean jocularly remarks on occasions, I spent more time living with the Queen than I did with her and the family. I must confess that I never lost my enthusiasm for the various Public Duties I performed over those few months and I hoped that my pride and attitude was infectious and that the NCOs and Guardsmen under my command worked as hard as I. Certainly I do not recall any monumental nonsense occurring but the following incidents are worthy of recollection.

I sat one Saturday evening with Roy Lyon, my Lance Sergeant, checking off the football results and I had eight of the nine draws. I suffered quiet hysteria but there were about six late kick offs. The atmosphere in Buckingham Palace Guardsroom on that evening was hard to describe. I would have to wait for the Sunday papers for the final results. When I returned home I literally fell on the paper only to find that a further four draws had been added to the nine and no claims were required! And that was the nearest I have ever been to financial security.

My first meeting with Lt. Wilmott (BT) Baronet occurred in 1958 at Windsor soon after he had been commissioned. I found him to be a pleasant but rather flippant character. Meeting him again some $3^1/2$ years later he had obviously matured but was still inclined to flippancy. On an early summer's day we were both on 'Buck House' Guard, the forecourt formalities were concluded and Mr Wilmott disappeared for his lunch at St James' Palace. On his return we had certain matters to attend to such as inspections, and then in the early evening he told me he was leaving for 'Jimmy's' and his dinner; he would return at about 11.30p.m. when the sentries would be visited. The evening passed without incident: life at 'Buck House' is usually quiet and without problems. At ten minutes to twelve I was beginning to wonder where my officer was. I walked on to the forecourt and looked down the Mall and in the far distance I observed this lone figure. Some minutes later the figure materialized into Lt. Wilmott. He was walking in an odd manner carrying his head at an angle which threw his bearskin at an obscure angle. 'He's drunk,' thought I, but this was not true. As he entered the Guardsroom door he carefully removed his bearskin and from underneath his headgear he carefully removed a full bottle of VAT 69 whisky, hence his ungainly gait. With a smile he invited me up to his flat. I said that I would first ensure the sentries were posted at midnight, but when this was done I joined him and we had a long chat. After about 15 minutes he said he would visit the sentries and then we could relax and have a drink. He reminded me that he was a senior shareholder of VAT 69 and the brew was obviously his favourite tipple.

With our escort we halted at the farthest sentry on the Forecourt and after a couple of procedural questions, the sentry, a rather dour West Highlander, was asked did he drink whisky.

'Aye Sir,' he replied.

'Would you not agree that VAT 69 is one of the best whiskies?'

'Think it's f . . . g rubbish, Sir.'

At this Lt. Wilmott berated the unfortunate Guardsman about his choice, and in raised tones extolled the virtues of his tipple and suggested the Guardsman improve his drinking habits. As Lt. Wilmott visited his other three sentries they all subscribed comments to the detriment of VAT 69 in very basic invective which positively infuriated the officer. After the first answer each Guardsman made no reply to the officer's comments, standing rigidly and stoically with eyes averted as the tirade was inflicted. When we returned to the Guardsroom Lt. Wilmott removed his bearskin, and with a smile and a twinkle in his eyes said, 'That should keep them awake for an hour or so.' We then retired to his flat, had a chat and a couple of drinks, then went to our respective beds.

Some years ago I read that this rather charming gentleman had been knocked down and killed in Edinburgh outside the Divorce Court when his divorce had been declared. I felt so sorry he had to lose his life in such a way. The actual date escapes me but it was published on Orders that for the next fortnight I would assist one of the Drill Sergeants and take a young NCOs' Cadre Course. The squad consisted of NCOs and some potential candidates, approximately fifteen in all. If I recall correctly my 'partner' was rarely seen during the Course. London Duties and other matters kept him busy so it was all down to me. It was almost like being back at Mons with more emphasis placed on individual participation. I quite enjoyed it and I think the Adjutant and BSM were satisfied with the end result.

The same Drill Sergeant could be rather vindictive towards Guardsmen whom he particularly disliked and derogatory remarks on the Drill Square could be raw to say the least. On this particular day he was taking a Guard Mounting rehearsal on the Square watched intently by members and supporters of the London Scottish Rugby Club who were either playing against or practising with the Battalion team. The Drill Sergeant, observing a very attentive audience, with much humorous and caustic comment, slayed the Guard and one Guardsman in particular. After some time, enough was enough; during the fixing of bayonets this Guardsman in anger threw down his bayonet, then his rifle, his bearskin followed and with a loud 'Keep your f . . . g Guard' he took himself off to the Guardroom and refused to return to the ranks. I was not told of the outcome but the image was somewhat tarnished.

My most embarrassing but humorous incident occurred on a late April Saturday morning. The weather was perfect, warm and clear for that time of the year. At Wembley Stadium that afternoon the Rugby League Cup Final was to take place and when I was awakened at 6a.m. the Corporal said, 'They're already waiting outside the railings.' To my surprise, bedecked with Club scarves stood about two hundred supporters, and as the morning progressed there must have been well over a thousand people or more on the footpath, Victoria Statue and other places. We were all highly amused.

The Corporal brought out the 10a.m. sentries and a hush fell on the assembled crowd, I inspected them and off they went. At 10.20a.m. with my escort I made my final inspection of the forecourt sentries to ensure that they understood the various procedures they had to adopt during the Changing of the Guard. There was a distinct quietening of the crowd as I marched across the forecourt to the farthest sentry. I reached inside his box and removed the board that contained the sentry's instructions emphasising with my hand what I wanted him to do. I replaced the board.

'Sarge, will you fix my bearskin, it's killing me.'

It was noticeable that the headgear was sitting at an angle. Anyone who has worn that particular item would know that if not sitting correctly on the head it can inflict terrible headaches or even fainting. Reaching up I seized the side of the bearskin, shook it violently, placed it in a position agreeable to the Guardsman and stepped back.

At the same time the assembled audience of happy supporters erupted with unrestrained anger. 'Leave him alone!' 'Bully, Gestapo!' and any other invective they would normally inflict on a non supportive referee. The Guardsman just smiled at me and as I marched across the front of the Palace booing and comments continued. At the next sentry comments like, 'Don't hit him too!' 'No wonder they won't join the Guards,' 'I'll report you,' etc. The noise continued until I disappeared inside the Guardroom when we all had a good laugh. Some minutes later I marched the remainder of the Guard and joined them up close to the railings. This involved a great deal of shouting, orders and generally 'chivvying' everyone about. I was recognised immediately and the comments began again, but were quickly silenced when the Band began to play and the new Guard began to march from nearby Wellington Barracks. All the ceremonial of the Changing of the Guard was completed and we as the Old Guard left the forecourt. I was close to the crowd on the pavement when I was verbally abused by three ladies. I remember comments like, 'I've a son in the Army,' 'Have you got children?' 'What would your mother say?' Within seconds it all stopped. Ah, for the innocence and ignorance of the spectators; if they only knew.

The next important matter for me before I applied for transfer was the ceremony to be held on Horse Guards Parade to commemorate the Duke of Gloucester for twenty-five years as Colonel of the Regiment. Both Battalions would be involved, plus members of the Guards Parachute Company, personnel under training at the Guards Depot and last but by no means least, Scots Guards Associations from Scotland and England.

I was nominated with another Sergeant to be Escort to the first Battalion's Colours which were to be carried as follows: Queens Colour, 2/Lt. The Lord Vestey; Regimental Colour, 2/Lt. P.R. Hill. Needless to say I was delighted. To leave my Regiment having performed this honour made me extremely proud. I have to admit that Royal occasions in particular brought out the best in me. Like most soldiers in the public eye I liked to swank and show off. Owing to a very busy period of duties I can only recall participating in two rehearsals for this event.

On the day, the weather was perfect, London looked at its best and the crowds lined the pavements and observed from Horse Guards Parade. The parade was a magnificent success. Even unbiased observers stated it was one of the finest parades they had witnessed. As expected the turnout was immaculate and the Foot and Rifle Drill were way above the normal high standard. It was an excellent tribute to a member of the Royal Family and an officer of the Regiment; he had over twenty-five years worked diligently for the Regiment, affording the strongest support when it was deemed necessary.

A special mention was given to the Scots Guard Association who despite their dress of civilian clothes were positively identified by the standard of their appearance and the 'swank' in their marching. It never fails to amaze me when attending functions of this nature that despite the length of time most members had been absent from Regimental duties, old habits of marching and dress remain of the very highest standard. Now a member myself, the old feeling of intense pride never fails to surface. In all honesty I was different to all my contemporaries: ten years as a civilian, and a Police Officer at that, gave me a totally different outlook on life and matters military. Since I joined I had proved I was an above average Instructor on Drill, Arms and Tactics, I had a Parade Ground voice that on a good day could be heard on Horse Guards from Buckingham Palace, my appearance and conduct could not be faulted and I could accept responsibility. My method of man management to achieve results was somewhat alien to most of my colleagues, but did it really matter as long as standards didn't drop and the right result obtained? I hope I was always considered a good Scots Guardsman.

My feelings towards the Regiment will never change. It formed part of an important and formative period of my life, an indelible facet of my character that will never be erased. My years as a serving Guardsman were drawing to an end.

CHAPTER 17

Gravesend and Maresfield 1961-2

Following the address of the Commanding Officer many of the more recent senior ranks began to look very seriously at their future in the Regiment. They looked around and could see that many above them in seniority would not advance much further; this would serve as a block. I did not wish to hide away in some obscure job that offered no challenge so my mind turned once again to a transfer to the Intelligence Corps.

My application for transfer was processed immediately, the CO commenting that he thought I had made a very wise choice and providing personal transport for the initial interview. The introductory talk at Maresfield was thorough and I was accepted on successful completion of Positive Vetting which is mandatory for the Corps and the SAS.

Several items had to be completed before the move: the Parade to honour the Duke of Gloucester's 25th Anniversary as Colonel of the Regiment; another visit to Horse Guards for Trooping the Colour; and a month's duty running the Mess and the less said about that the better. At that time those who knew all the circumstances within the Messes of both Battalions could only offer genuine sympathy and understanding.

I deemed it a great honour for my final Ceremonial participation to be among the Escort to the 1st Battalion's Colour Party for the Duke of Gloucester's Parade and what a marvellous day it was, stirring the blood, swank in your step, and great pride in your heart. When you feel like that surely that is the epitome of being a soldier, especially a Scots Guardsman.

With the formalities concluded I left the Battalion, but no Guardsman ever leaves his Regiment, it is in him till he dies. I left with reluctance and some regret, but in retrospect I think I made the right decision. During my service and outside it I would like to think I always upheld the finest traditions of my Regiment.

Now began a five month period that was both tedious and very interesting, I only say tedious because of the travelling difficulties encountered each weekend between Walderslade and Maresfield, the home of the Intelligence Centre. I would leave the Centre after work on the

Friday and by bus travel to Tunbridge Wells, change to a bus to Maidstone, then another bus to Chatham, finally another change to home, reversing the procedure on Sunday evening. I only missed seeing the family on one weekend when I was on duty.

The Centre at Maresfield was situated in a very pleasant area but as an open camp it was without protection, and accommodation was basic but adequate. What had to be protected was afforded maximum facilities but it would have been a dream to terrorist organizations in the present climate. All my contemporaries were some fifteen years younger than I but oddly enough we got on extremely well. In every group you find an idiot; we had one but he was dismissed shortly after I arrived. Despite their academic achievements I found no difficulty in absorbing the syllabus. I had the added bonus of my association with Senior Operators passing through the Centre who lived in the Mess during courses or on transfer; I learnt a lot this way.

During this time I met two officers who transferred to the Corps both of whom I had known at Mons. One, an ex RA Cadet, eventually became Lt. Col. Commanding Int. and Security Group (UK); more of the other, whom I shall call Lt. C, and who was ex 'A' Company, later. I played lots of sport, help to organize social functions in the Mess, finished the Course successfully and finally with great elation passed my driving test. With some sympathy the Corps looked around to find me a post in which I could retain my rank without financial loss and it was decided that my talents should be pointed at the Intelligence Corps Junior Leaders at a School in Wales, but before the vacancy was available in February 1962 I should work in the Joint Services Interrogation Unit and be a member of the Administration and Interrogation Team for a large Escape and Evasion Exercise to be held in Germany and this would take up most of January. 1962 did not start well as my mother died on 1st January and I had to make the sad journey to Preston. John and I made the formal identification, attended to all the various details and personal effects, then following the funeral at St Walburge's and the cemetery, she rested with my father. I had to leave John to finalize the odds and ends as I had to fly to Germany.

Mum died peacefully in bed but alone in the house, 32 Priory Street, now demolished. Over the years she had endured the problems of bronchitis and asthma; she spent hours in thought and prayer when she was without visitors, suffering long spells of loneliness when she was unable to dance and meet her friends, a pastime that she loved immensely. She was a person capable of great love and affection; naive and often misguided, but those who knew her well loved her dearly. Her heart became too tired and she slept in peace. I just hope my grand-daughter inherits some of her qualities. From the humble beginnings of a very virtuous mill girl, through the worries of death and well being of loved ones in two World Wars, the loss of a child then a husband, her life had not been easy. It was to be hoped she had found ultimate contentment. But I digress.

Our small Advance Party of a Major, WO, and Signalman, another WO and myself, with five tons of equipment, arrived under escort at RAF Butzweilehof on the outskirts of Cologne. We signed for a complete Accommodation Block and in the succeeding ten days or so turned it into a very workable Interrogation Centre. After discussion we presented the Station Commander and his staff with certain stores we required and these were delivered; we then blacked out the whole block which gave the Staff, but mainly the local German workers, something to excite their curiosity. Then we erected a twelve-foot high hessian screen and concealed entrance around part of the building and in the middle of this placed two large tents which we later 'bugged'. Having completed all the outdoor tasks (it was January) we quietly attended to all the other indoor items, and eventually the arrival of the main party.

Several amusing incidents occurred prior to and during the Exercise. On our first stroll into Cologne we met a former member of the Corps who was the overseas sales agent for Germany on behalf of Securicor. His sister in law, a German lady, later joined us for a drink in a Gasthaus. One of my companions brought back from the toilet a most extraordinary 'washable condom' with 'bits' so we all bought one, all different! Tom, the Signals chap, was 'Curly'; I was 'Spiky': we had a very humorous evening. The lady, who owned a restaurant near the Ringstrasse asked us to join her two days later, and on our arrival at the restaurant she had her boyfriend with her, an ex POW who hated the English. We had with us two bottles of whisky and some coffee for the lady. An hour or so later at the lady's flat, the boyfriend, who obviously had been drinking before we arrived, became quite obnoxious so I stated to my companions that I was leaving otherwise I would hit him, and I had no wish to upset our hostess. They agreed so we made our apologies and left; I'm sure she understood.

We stood in the deserted street of large blocks of flats with no taxis about, but we found a small Gasthaus with half a dozen souls inside.

'Drei Bier bitte,' Tom said.

'Good evening gentlemen, how nice to see the English again,' came the greeting from the owner.

It transpired that he had worked at the Ritz Hotel, London, for several years and thought the English were great. Hours later the owner, his customers and ourselves had had a most enjoyable evening fortified by a bottle and a half of whisky and many beers; what a lovely coincidence following an initial disappointment.

But the evening didn't finish there. We arrived by taxi at the main gate of 'Butz' only to be arrested by the RAF Police. They even brought out two dogs to look after us; they didn't know us and wanted an RAF Pass. It was a rather irate senior RAF Officer who verified our authority to be there. I suspect it was a put up job just to show we were 'strangers in an alien land'!

Then one night we left our hotel early before assuming duty and inadvertently entered a homosexual bar. All eyes were on us as we entered, and the couple of dozen incumbents were all paint and powdered: talk about 'backs against the wall lads'. The 'girls' soon lost interest in us; we were highly amused but could not understand the reason for the barbed wire that surrounded a door and a wooden partition. The barman explained that the door led to the toilet and if we wished to use it we signed for the key 'one at a time please'!

During the Exercise a party of rather hard Belgian SAS were brought in. They had heard about the Exercise and decided to 'run' unofficially. Reluctantly we had to throw them out. Then we had the most extraordinary Captain from the Parachute Regiment, another unofficial 'runner' but we kept him for his cheek. Remember this was late January; snow and frost abounded, and this character was in the 'bugged' tent handcuffed to a bed, dressed in nothing but his underpants. The 'listener' began to get suspicious by the lack of noise, and when the tent was checked, the Captain and the bed had disappeared. He was picked up by the Police running barefoot on the runway with the bed 'tucked underneath his arm' enjoying himself immensely: what a hard man, but he volunteered for SAS.

I had checked the long list of 'Runners' who were mainly aircrew, some foreign, but in among the other 'odds and sods' was Lt. C. At Mons six Royal Marine Cadets had joined us but only two could return to the Marines if successful, the remainder would be offered Army Commissions. Lt. C did well but was out of luck so he joined a County Regiment and went to Africa with the United Nations. I had met his charming mother and aunt at the Commissioning Parade and escorted them to their car.

During conversation with the 'Boss' I pointed out that Lt. C was well known to me and that of course he was the only Int. Corps 'runner'. When he was brought in he had suffered an injury to his leg but he elected to carry on and was doing extremely well when I was told to impart my knowledge of Lt. C to an American officer of mountainous proportions. He was huge, 6'3" tall, and 18 or 19 stone to boot, a beautiful sight. I gave him reasons for Lt. C not returning to the Marines, dates, personalities, his mother and auntie, the make of car, etc., and armed with this information he confronted Lt. C. Despite some instinctive facial contortions and looks of incredulity at the knowledge this stranger had about his private life, Lt. C said nothing. Less than an hour before he was due to finish our Medical Officer decided that as he was finding it difficult to stand, Lt. C should be taken out of the Exercise.

I had commenced to climb the staircase when above me I saw the slow descending figure of Lt. C dressed in underpants and vest clutching a large bundle of clothing and equipment. Halfway up we looked at each other. 'Good morning Sir,' I said brightly; there was no audible response, I turned left at the top and the silence was shattered by a high pitched, agonizing burst of invective.

'It was you, you bastard, it was you, Oh God.'

I closed the door of Reception and forgot about it; the sequel happened in Borneo years later.

CHAPTER 18

Wales 1962

On the completion of my induction Course and the exams, I was informed that it had been decided to post me to the Junior Leaders Unit at Towyn in Mid Wales and that a married quarter was available, but I would have to attend an interview with the Commanding Officer of the unit to ascertain if I was considered suitable to have close association with boys (Junior Soldiers)!

Subsequently I attended an interview at Towyn and was accepted. Married accommodation was available but would be in a temporary building for a short period before a house was available for occupation. After a few weeks we eventually moved into more agreeable accommodation on the Married Quarter estate. At the same time I purchased my first car, a grey Standard 8, which had a rather chequered few months before it became unfit to drive, but that comes later on.

Life with Junior Leaders during term time was quite hectic. I had a colleague, and between us we shared the instructing side of the basic Intelligence Course and on top of this we also had obligations for limited Drill Periods, Sport, Company Administration and an outdoor activity which in my case was Canoeing. I knew nothing of this sport but I soon learnt. During the winter we constructed and repaired the canoes, and in the summer we spent time on the nearby River Dysynni and the open sea of Cardigan Bay. I enjoyed the physical side of this sport but the winter months were rather boring.

Our social life was rather limited as Towyn is in an isolated area with very few leisure facilities. Public transport was almost non existent which was very restricting to Jean and the children. We had of course Rinny so a lot of our free time we spent walking the beach or in the nearby hills which we all enjoyed. It was a fairly placid existence but very time consuming, a seven-day week job, during term time. If I learnt anything during this period it was how to deal with teenagers and a great improvement in classroom instruction and presentation. I also had the misfortune to meet two Corps Officers whom I can only describe as pathetic. It was probably indicative that neither continued their career in the Corps. The remainder of the officers and NCOs were a mixture from various Regiments and Corps, some very good and a small percentage of nonentities who just wanted a quiet life.

A visit to Tonfanu by the Posting Officer in August 1962 rang alarm bells. The purpose of my job at this unit was to ensure if possible the retention of my rank, and that I would not suffer financially; a posting out, especially as I was not fully qualified, could reduce my rank. This officer was insistent that I needed to be in an Operational post. A short time after my interview I received my posting orders to 17 Intelligence Platoon, HQ 11 Infantry Brigade, who were stationed at Minden, West Germany. Jean was not dismayed but it was ascertained that married quarters would not be immediately available and that she would have to remain in Towyn until she was sent for. In fact after I had left for Germany certain senior personnel put her under severe and unnecessary pressure to vacate our house, and upset and reluctantly, Jean and the children finally left and moved back with her parents in Preston.

However in the November I reported to Maresfield, and sat and passed the A2 exam with flying colours. The senior officer in charge of the Board, a Major with MI8, acted a character part in the investigation phase. On completion he asked me about my background, and stated that I had made him feel most uncomfortable and even guilty during my questioning. I apologised and he laughed and told me not to worry as it was most refreshing to be confronted by someone who knew precisely how to conduct an interview and an investigation; he wished me well. I had not had the time to do much studying and I could afford to be pleased.

By December most of our packing had been completed, and vaccinations and inoculations had been undertaken by our local doctor, so the family could move within reason at short notice. It later transpired that our flat in Minden, owing to adverse weather conditions, could not be completed on time and the subsequent delay meant that it was early June before I could bring the family out.

There are only a few highlights to quote during our period in Wales. The first was my success in the Annual Shoot against other personnel who were mainly Infantry. I think I collected one Winner's and one Runner Up's medal. Another incident was our expedition with the Smith family to carry out Christmas shopping in Shrewsbury. On our return journey we had reached Machynlleth and were preparing to cross the River Dovey by the causeway which crossed the river estuary. What we didn't know was that the river was in flood. The Smiths, followed by ourselves, decided to follow a bus along the flooded road, I unfortunately had to brake and, immersed in water, the engine stalled. I had no option but to leave the car, and when I opened the door, having first removed shoes and socks, the water flooded the car. I then struggled and managed to push the car back to dry higher ground, and retrieving our shopping we made a dash for the nearby railway station and caught the last train for thirty-six hours!! Dusty Smith and I returned the following day, Sunday, and managed to start my car and drive it back. It could have been a disaster and our lives at risk, but fortunately circumstances dictated the engine stalling and the risk was eliminated. We often laugh about this incident but as our car was small and not particularly heavy the possibility that the force of water could have easily overturned us was very realistic and the result would have been fatal.

I would not say this period of my career was wasted. It was a period of adjustment and consolidation. The posting was accepted for all the best reasons but it was certainly not enhancing my career prospects and giving me the practical experience I needed.

We spent the Christmas and New Year at Jean's parents and on a foggy, frosty New Year's Day morning we set off to return to Wales and prepare for my move to Germany. As we drove along the A59 I stayed behind a large goods vehicle as the fog was quite thick. I was some 25 yards distance from the truck travelling at approximately 20m.p.h. As we approached the traffic lights at Ormskirk, the lorry showed its brake lights. I slowly applied mine which were ineffective on the icy road and we became wedged underneath the tail of the wagon. The driver emerged and apologised for his decision to brake quickly. While we were discussing ways of extracting my vehicle from under his tailboard, another car saw our lights, braked and uncontrollably skidded into the rear of my car. Chris and Carolyn were still inside and luckily were not injured. Damage to the rear of my car was minimal, but at the front the radiator was fractured.

Eventually we continued our journey; it was quite horrendous, interspersed with humour. Frequent stops to refill the radiator which issued huge clouds of steam which did not help observation especially in foggy conditions. Some thirty miles from home we inexplicitly ran out of petrol; obviously the tank was damaged. A friendly farmer who was passing offered us a gallon of petrol and eventually we arrived home.

The following morning I went to my local garage where I had left the car to be told it was a complete write off. All the tyres were down and every conceivable thing that could be wrong, was wrong. It was not understood how any vehicle in that condition could have moved from the accident, never mind be driven for over a hundred miles. God certainly looked after us that New Year's Day.

So that ended the Welsh saga. None of us were particularly sorry to leave, the sad thing was that we had to leave Rinny, but she would be in good hands with a Pioneer Corps Warrant Officer who had been a Dog Handler. The decision was difficult but the odds were that I would be posted further east after I left BAOR and that it would be unfair to the dog. So reluctantly we parted with her, in my view the most loyal, protective and intelligent dog I am ever likely to meet. I wish I could have replaced her.

CHAPTER 19

BAOR 1963-5

The day in January arrived when I made my tearful farewell to Jean and the children and hoped that it would not be too long before we were all together again as a family. At that time I was content to know that Jean was adequately housed until our alternative quarters in Minden had been completed. I did not appreciate that the Army, or the Major I/C Housing would hound my wife and make life so unbearable that she quit the house and went home to her parents; that officer or any others like him deserve no credit.

I arrived at Hannover Airport in the darkness of late afternoon to be met by two corporals from the unit, Mick Courage and Bill Ward. Our careers intermingled as the years passed; they were both very capable young soldiers. They had very kindly attempted to find me temporary accommodation in a village called Bad Eilsen, near the town of Buckeburg. The snow lay thick on the ground, the frost, crisp and fresh. Bad Eilsen was like a winter fairy tale but rather isolated; the flat I inspected was perfect but impracticable for a young family who did not speak the language. Regretfully I turned down the offer and in retrospect I was right.

The lads deposited me at the Mess and my room had been prepared by my next door neighbour Sergeant Bob B— who was the Brigade Intelligence Sergeant; we had met at Maresfield. Bob was a former medical student, a junior NCO in the Black Watch who later left the Army, joined the Police and was last heard of as a member of Special Branch. I unpacked and prepared for the following day, later joining Bob in the Mess. I was introduced to the two or three members who were round the bar and was given a bottle of Carlsberg lager. In the space of twenty minutes or so, as additional members arrived and were introduced I had five bottles in front of me. As each person came in he automatically ordered a round of drinks from the bar. In time you learned to avoid this pitfall, but as the new boy I behaved stupidly, finishing the beer and being persuaded by Bob to have a whisky instead. This of course was fatal: whisky came as a double and in no time they in their turn were lining up on the bar. When I had the courage to say 'enough' to the barman no one seemed offended. I had been accepted and I managed with difficulty to leave the bar with decorum and a wonderful feeling of pleasure. Of the dozen or more members I had met each one over the next three years became good friends; in fact with only one exception every member of that Mess was first class considering practically every facet of the Army was represented. Socially it was the most enjoyable Mess I was privileged to belong to, and Jean would support me in this. We all worked hard and were frequently away from home but everyone helped each other and this included officers too. It was a very happy Headquarters.

Our General was assisted by seven officers and their respective staff. There was also a Signal Squadron and a Provost Unit attached to the Headquarters. Sharing the Barracks was a REME Telecommunication Workshop who were Corps Troops. Our 'teeth' arm units were three infantry battalions and Armoured and Artillery Regiments. Knowing this basic information I presented myself to Lieutenant B, my new Officer Commanding, slightly dissipated but refreshed after breakfast and a hot bath. The OC was a pleasant, sophisticated person in his mid twenties, a talented musician, but rather laid back in his attitude to service life and his operational control of the unit. This was shown in the fact that within twenty months the case files had doubled and 90 per cent of this work was initiated by my small section. Delete three months at Maresfield and five months in Cyprus; it showed what could be achieved if personnel were inquisitive enough. Counter Intelligence work I found was fascinating, frequently routine, but if the right questions are asked in the routine work the interesting aspect follows. The Intelligence Corps demands a reasonable academic background but it cannot produce a person with a naturally suspicious and inquiring mind.

The next senior member of staff was Ssgt. R, a former member of Airborne Forces and an experienced Operator. He was married to a German woman and spoke the language fluently. He was a very competent person but I always felt that he spent too much time in the office and not enough on the ground: alas a fault throughout the Corps.

I eventually met the person I was to replace. We had met before and I was not impressed; he was a womanizer of repute, later left the Corps and was commissioned elsewhere. L/Cpl P was the junior, a pleasant lad who always needed urging.

Now down to work. To say I was scared would be wrong but, my God, I was apprehensive. I had three stripes on my arm and I had never worked in the field on Operational Intelligence, neither had I any experience of Counter Intelligence duties or the carrying out of a Security Survey, and the administration of the unit was a foreign body to me so that is where I started and began to understand the procedures. During the day with Cpl. C, units were visited and introductions made to unit Security Officers. I sat in on two surveys and made notes. In the evenings I read profusely in the office and in my room. I was determined as far as possible to know what I was talking about even though I lacked practical experience, and I also asked a lot of questions. In a relatively short space of time things began to fall into place; it was all worth the effort and long hours and I did not feel so inadequate. During this initial period I met the General and all the Headquarters Staff and I could not have been made more welcome by every individual. Then came the pleasant shock, I was to report to the Intelligence Centre at Maresfield for an upgrading course to A1 Operator beginning in mid February. The course would last eight weeks and would be followed by the A1 Trade Test, when Operators came from all worldwide postings to take the exams which lasted for three days.

Considering I had only been a member of the Corps for approximately twelve months this was a very unexpected achievement and not to be missed. On the other hand I was woefully inexperienced. I was going to be in the company of personnel who had the minimum of three or four years experience, so yet again I felt apprehensive. Those initial few weeks in Minden consisted of enormous cramming sessions but much more was to follow.

Before I left for UK I was introduced to and made several visits to a very valuable German Police contact named Fräulein Selenthin. This was an official arrangement of mutual benefit to both parties, although I must confess we derived the greater kudos as she rather liked Cpl. C and myself and helped us more than we were entitled to. Jean and I also became social friends. She was a very nice person although large and imposing. She had a great sense of humour, loved gin, and cried genuinely when I left Germany for Borneo. Quite a character.

I left a snowbound Germany for an equally snowbound UK and after settling in the Mess I met several senior NCOs also on the course. On the Monday morning the twenty or so corporals and Senior NCOs were introduced to our various civil and military instructors and the course began. The greatest difficulty in trade training was the ability to keep the bloody stove alight in your room, an art in itself. I thoroughly enjoyed the course, and after my evening meal I would read again the issued précis on the day's work plus my notes, go back over some of the previous work then read up on the next day's work. After a bath, two or three of us would gather in a room and chat, or we would go to the Mess for a pint. At weekends we rarely left the Centre apart from Mass on Sunday. I think I visited friends in Ashford on one occasion. So as we idled the time away we also studied, and for me this paid off but there were several interesting incidents worthy of note.

One of our civil instructors was a person of foreign extraction, experienced in routine intelligence and an author to boot. He was a very charming person and full of himself. During a particular CI (Counter Intelligence) lecture he made certain comments with which I and others disagreed, but as I fired most of the bullets, he was not pleased. I had to take an intermediate exam which counted towards the course assessment, but barely passed it which was marked by this particular instructor. Checking notes and précis, some of my answers were word for word, and I was awarded 4-5 marks out of 15; all in all we reckoned he had knocked me down 20-25 marks. Then following an investigation exercise I was brought before the Directing Staff to be admonished because of my conduct during the exercise run by this particular character. A civilian employed at the Centre volunteered to play a character part in the investigation; he only had to be reluctantly co-operative if the right questions were asked, as he had done on previous exercises. After his session with me he said he was frightened, confused, insulted, contemplated seeing his Doctor and was doubtful if he would ever take part again, it was too real for him. The military staff appeared amused by it all, our civilian friend made comments, but I answered all these satisfactorily and the matter was dropped.

The next incident with the Directing Staff (DS) occurred near the end of the course when the course was divided into four syndicates representing Counter Intelligence Units. Unknown to us all, we were to be presented with a factual espionage case involving military personnel that had occurred in the Düsseldorf area of West Germany. A Corporal and I were given the initial papers of this case. We were to choose the first person to interview, make some photographic comparisons if applicable, and formulate our line of questioning. I chose the first officer to be interviewed and the Corporal agreed, so we made an appointment via the DS; this was within half an hour of starting work at 8a.m. While I talked to the officer, the Corporal checked the photographs. He gave me a sign that the comparisons did not match, so I concluded the interview. Until approximately 3p.m. our syndicate chased all the other leads which I was convinced would get us nowhere. Then the Senior Instructor (a Major) who played the part of the Major I had originally interviewed demanded we return to see him; it was then proved that we had been given the wrong photographs!!

Some rather hurried questions were made by me, and the syndicate then interviewed another person, and the individual questioning botched it up. Before he left the room however the Corporal and I put to him some hurried questions. We got all the right answers just as the exercise finished and it transpired that we had actually solved the case. We analysed it later and worked it out that if everything had gone as we planned we could have solved the problem in approximately three hours. Apologies were tendered by the DS and did they have egg on their face. We were disappointed but certainly not disgraced. It's not often you get the opportunity of exercising your wits in a case that has been solved.

Now for the climax, the A1 Trade Test. Some forty-five persons took part from all parts of the world; some had been previous failures and all were desperate to pass to ensure rank and future promotion. For two days, almost sixteen hours, we manfully struggled through this jungle of intelligence and all its various facets. The third and final day consisted of an investigation of a Top Secret nature which we were allowed twelve hours to complete if I remember correctly. At 8a.m. we were presented with certain papers, and after perusal we had to submit a logical plan of action and applications could be submitted for persons we wished to interview. At 9a.m. I was on my way to interview a particular officer. In reality he was the Centre's Senior Instructor in Russian studies and Interrogation; he had a reputation for being difficult and awkward but had a brilliant brain (I met him later in Hong Kong). After fifteen minutes or so, when he could see I was getting close to the relevant answers, he theatrically flounced from his chair and headed towards the door, stating he could not waste any more time talking to me, he had better things to do and I should remember that he was an officer. His hand was on the door when I hit his desk with the flat of my hand and the room shook. He stood rigidly by the door. I then said, 'With all due respects, Sir, I have been specifically tasked for this investigation by a General who wishes a successful conclusion and any difficulties to be reported directly to him, so I suggest we finish our interview and then you may carry on.'

He was trying desperately not to smile but sat down, he answered all my questions and I got the answers I desired. I thanked him for his time; he was smiling broadly and said quietly, 'Well done.'

As I left the office feeling rather elated I saw across the corridor the name on the door of the person I knew I would have to interview next, so I knocked on the door and entered. The character appeared somewhat surprised as he had not received any warning. Not giving him time to think I started with my questions and credit to him, he answered without any evasiveness and ten minutes later I had all my answers and the case was solved. I returned to the main room and commenced to write my report.

At 11a.m. a voice behind me said, 'I thought you would have had this solved by now.'

It was the Senior Trade Testing Officer, the Major from MI8 who had congratulated me on the A2 exam. I told him I was completing my report; he then said, 'I thought you wouldn't let me down,' and walked away. At half past eleven, to the obvious astonishment of the forty or so people still sitting in the room, I handed my papers in and went back to the Mess for lunch. In the middle of the afternoon another senior NCO came into the Mess, stating he hadn't solved the problem but he had gone as far as he could and submitted his report. The others began to drift back after 6p.m. and as it transpired not one other person sitting the exam had been able to bring the matter to a successful conclusion.

It was with some trepidation that we all assembled the following morning. As each person was called the Major gave them the marks attained and congratulations where applicable; only abut 50 per cent had smiling faces. I was near the end. The Major smiled at me and said, 'I don't need to tell you how well you have done.'

My average on all five subjects was 94 per cent; for the investigation I was given 96 per cent, something never achieved before; I wonder if it has been since. The Major wished me every success for the future and I left the room feeling ten feet tall. It had all been worth the effort. As I passed the Course Office I felt like making a rude sign. In just over twelve months I had overcome what I would have considered the unsurmountable object. I was qualified and I reckoned I could cope with any situation that was thrown my way, and in the years to come I was faced with plenty.

CHAPTER 20

British Embassy, Warsaw

In 1963, after my return from Maresfield, I was ordered to report to the Ministry of Defence for an interview. I had earlier been asked if I was interested in a particular sphere of duty by senior NCOs of the Intelligence Corps under the umbrella of the Foreign Office in overseas countries. Having talked to Jean I replied in the affirmative.

Three other colleagues had also been selected for a short list and I had met two of them before. The proposed posting was to the capital of an important Iron Curtain country and following the initial information supplied at the interview I could visualize certain domestic problems that I would be faced with. My interview was quite searching and I obviously satisfied the officials, because on my return to Germany I was the one chosen, subject to acceptance of certain domestic issues. After due discussion with Jean, I decided that living conditions were not acceptable to us as a family and very reluctantly refused the posting. In retrospect it was probably for the best, as I would have missed so many things that did well for me and my future would have been so different but that is all part of life's great tapestry. The authorities later had second thoughts and they also decided that the domestic issues were unacceptable and readily agreed to my refusal. I don't think I ruffled any feathers. Subsequently I believe more adequate accommodation was produced for our personnel in Foreign Embassies.

Back in Germany work started in earnest. Even lacking in experience as I was when I first arrived I was not satisfied with the Security Surveys, especially on the Major Units. Existing reports gave no details or background, just the comment 'Satisfactory'. I made myself a rough proforma of the questions that should be asked in order that a more comprehensive report could be submitted to be helpful to all concerned. In 1965 when the big changeover was made and more money available, C1 Coy at HQ BAOR produced a more detailed proforma to work from. This was criticized, amended, added to and became a very worthwhile document. In fact, I produced one for acceptance in Hong Kong, and later in Scotland, nearly five years later! The wheels turn slowly.

My first involvement with the East Germans took place during a special Border Patrol of Intelligence Corps personnel only from Division and our Brigade. Each formation in BAOR had an area of border it was required to patrol and this was carried out at regular intervals by patrols furnished from the 'teeth' arm units. Each patrol was accompanied by a member of the British Frontier Service who was usually a former Serviceman, a fluent German linguist, a good liaison man who knew the border backwards. At this particular time there were two specific areas of interest. The first reported excavation in the area of a farmhouse close to the border wire where the work could not be observed from the normal tracks that the patrols used. The BFS man did not wish to be seen with us at this point, so Ssgt. R and I walked tentatively down the original track to the wire and the farmhouse. I then saw the circular wooden window on the gable end of the building open and a ciné camera start to operate, then there was silence as work ceased. At the wire we could still see nothing. The camera was then replaced by a machine gun pointed directly at us. Acting flippantly, we doffed our berets, bowed to the building and slowly walked away.

Not satisfied, I left Ssgt. R, and with Cpl. C plus camera we made our way through thick woodland, 'bellywise'. Although I got partly through the wire I was still unable to observe the work taking place. When we rejoined the rest, smoke bombs had been thrown in their direction to discourage further interest so we left rather than cause an incident. The following day we watched as the East Germans laid a new minefield. The actual border followed a small stream and no wire was actually visible at this spot. Here was a large party of men who could have literally walked or run across the border into West Germany. While Ssgt. R chatted up a local I was dropped off a quarter of a mile from the minefield and slowly walked along 'our' side of the stream watching the soldiers at their labours. Some of them were only fifty yards away from me. My peace was suddenly shattered when the grass parted some three yards away, a machine gun pointed at my midriff and three members of the dreaded East German border guards complete with red armbands showed themselves. The silence was broken by the ominous cocking of the weapon; not a word was said. My throat was somewhat dry by this time and as I sauntered nonchalantly away from them I had a queer feeling in my spine and a damp crotch! It did stir things up, work ceased and Border Guards appeared from various places. The ones with red armbands were specially selected. Border patrols could be fun on occasions!

Another job that we were all involved in was that, by request from 1(BR) Corps, we had to 'raid' a particular Signal Regiment and attempt to find out names of personnel, equipment, role of unit etc. For approximately six hours we talked to people, entered buildings, made ourselves suspicious, and generally tried to make a nuisance of ourselves. In fact I actually got into Regimental HQ, and the door of the Cypher Room was opened to me. It is not a nice thing to happen to a unit but providing the Commanding Officer, to whom the follow up report is sent personally, deals with it in a sensible way people don't get anti the Int. Corps and a lot of good can result. Scapegoats are not required, just an increase in security awareness.

Summer approached and the cricket season commenced, Brigade HQ team usually consisted of six officers and five others and was for three seasons successful and a joy to be with. Captain Yeomans, Royal Signals, one of our Staff Officers, was a very competent and enthusiastic 'skipper' who like us all thoroughly enjoyed his sport. Team spirit was great and it was a pleasure to participate. The team we never managed to beat was 2 Division Signal Regiment, captained by a young subaltern. The remainder of the team and a 2nd Eleven were all West Indian and what natural talent they had, great sportsmen.

In 1965 we even managed to reach the final of the BAOR Minor Units and were narrowly beaten in a very exciting match, when Howard's last minute strike of 23 brought us within a few runs of victory. All in all it was a very enjoyable period for my enjoyment in a sport that I loved.

I must relate a particular 'lost' weekend which occurred before Jean came out. On a Saturday evening we had a Mess dinner, formal, men only; the ladies were invited to join us after the speeches to make it a social event for all. To assist the bar, Sgt. B, my colleague, volunteered to set up and run a small exclusive bar at the end of the Snooker Room. By 9.30 dinner was over and as I had no wife with me I stayed with Bob until 10a.m. the following morning. Very few people patronized our little hideaway but the customers were selective; we had a wonderful time. I was quite astonished when Bob pointed out I was within an inch of my second bottle of whisky, as I felt great. I ate a good breakfast, washed and shaved and went to Mass. My OC gave me a lift to Church and was almost overwhelmed by my breath. I vaguely remember Mike Kelly demonstrating a parachute jump from a window of the Mess. However the best was yet to come. Fortified with a Carlsberg, I reported to the REME Workshop for a cricket match, where I proceeded to score 72 not out, smashing the windscreen of a staff car in the process. A very satisfactory afternoon to round off a 'disgraceful' weekend. I slept well that night.

Then the happy news. Our flat had finally been connected up following the hard winter. The decoration had been finished, furniture and crockery delivered, all it required was occupants. Mike Kelly, my close friend and neighbour in the Mess, was informed that we were to be neighbours in these excellent flats at the rear of the Cameronians' Barracks. Working together we sorted out and cleaned all the brand new items we had signed for, packed it all away in the respective cupboards, put the cleaner on and it was fit to walk in. I came home to UK and brought the family back. I had by now purchased an Opel Record shooting brake so we started off well. Jean and the kids were delighted with the flat and within days Margaret Kelly and the two children flew out and we have remained friends to this day. Mike was a REME storeman in the Telecommunication Unit and when the other two families joined us we had a nice community in our block.

Our social life was good, mainly concerned with Saturday evening functions plus sporting events, and we always endeavoured to visit places of interest which were within striking distance of Minden at the weekend.

General King was an ex Para, and very much a soldiers' general. He kept himself fit and believed that all soldiers, not just the infantry, should maintain a high standard of endurance, so he organized a Night March across country, approximately twenty-five miles by direct compass bearings and just over thirty miles if you wished to march by road. The march ended near the banks of the River Weser near Hameln, the final hurdle being a range of hills which tested the guts of each participant. The General insisted that every one took part and teams of ten were to be organized; it was an outstanding success and was won by a Royal Engineers team who ran most of the way by road. The General went out the first night, I went with the Brigade Major and considering the RQMS and I were the two oldest we did not let him down, in fact we chivvied the younger ones over the final stages. Major Pope was not an admirer of the Int. Corps but he looked at me in a different light after the march.

Within my area of responsibility was a particularly isolated installation which because of the contents, carried a high security classification. When I carried out my initial visit I was horrified by what I found and submitted a report immediately. I also spoke to the USO of a minor unit who sponsored and had administrative and other responsibilities for this compound and the personnel who guarded it.

Briefly, this location was protected by an eight-foot high chain link fence topped with strands of barbed wire and inside were a number of buildings which housed certain items. The Guard Force consisted of a number of the MSO (Mixed Service Organization), staffed completely by personnel of East European nationality, Poles, Yugoslavs, Hungarians etc., some of whom had been trained as Dog Handlers to work within the compound.

On the day of my visit the parent unit had informed the Guard Force of my pending arrival. As we drove up to the gate I noticed a gap between the gate and the ground through which a normal person could effect an entry with ease; I was not impressed. As I drove and walked around the location the Guard Dogs did not react, the security of some buildings was a disgrace, and I found on the door of one building the description and map reference of where the contents were to be located in the event of hostilities! This was the reason for my immediate report.

I checked with the Dog Training School at Senneglager and they informed me that on the last Efficiency Inspection the Dog Handlers were assessed as only reaching just over 30 per cent efficient and had been recommended for re-training. Some time later HQ BAOR allocated a substantial sum of money to enable various buildings to be brought up to the required standard. To briefly sum up, owing to this lack of interest and finance from HQ BAOR the parent unit 'caught the bug' and a serious lowering of security standards ensued because the unit had their normal operational training to perform, and their frustrated commitment to the Compound took a back seat.

The story continued. No doubt as a result of my initial report, it was decided to carry out an exercise authorized by HQ BAOR, in order to assess the efficiency of the rapid withdrawal of stores from this location to their potential wartime position. Knowledge of the exercise as expected was very tightly controlled and at *2.30a.m.* Cpl. C and I left Minden to surreptitiously supervise the location and the surrounding area. We passed the entrance to the Compound, and the time was approximately *3.30a.m.* as we turned left onto the one way circuit into open ground. To our astonishment we saw two cars parked either side of the narrow road each manned by a male driver conveniently reading a newspaper in the early morning light!. As we were wide awake and bushy tailed, we each took particulars of a car, and did not stop but continued to the main road, where we waited for about fifteen minutes then started on the one way circuit again. No other civilian vehicles were observed in the vicinity. We parked up to observe the entrance and the arrival of the military vehicles; we also watched the perimeter area on foot. At approximately *6a.m.* I decided to make one last sweep of the area. On reaching the open space the two vehicles had left so we made a further complete circuit and returned to Minden.

I contacted my next higher authority at Verden, also the G3 (Intelligence) at Brigade, then went to see my German contact in Hameln. They gave me certain information about the vehicles and owners, but adamantly refused certain information about one owner and suggested that I contact a higher West German Security Unit in Hannover. Once again I spoke to Verden and they agreed I should go to Hannover and make arrangements. We had to go through extremely elaborate precautions before gaining entrance; the incident was described to a Security person who left us, returning some twenty minutes later. He thanked us most profusely, stating the man was known to them, we had done well, gave no other information and literally rushed us out of the entrance. We had to smile at this brusque efficiency, but I suppose as a branch of the equivalent of MI5 the precautions were necessary.

As this incident faded into the background, information was obtained on yet another rather sinister aspect concerning this compound. Members of the MSO could live as normal German civilians, or in single accommodation provided by the British Forces; there was a rank structure but not a very elaborate one. Following the obtaining of my first item of information my enquiries took me to various locations in the BAOR area, also to the British Consul in Hamburg. Initially my enquiries concerned one member of the MSO whom we shall call S. Later other members of the MSO were involved in procedural omissions and this reflected on their seniors.

In Minden we had a former Polish Army Major whom we shall call M. He was responsible for a number of MSO at various locations not necessarily all in my area of responsibility. M was the most charming of persons. He had married a lovely German lady much younger than he, and they had a small male child on which M doted. As a Cavalry Officer M had fought the Russians and had been captured; later he fought the Germans and was also captured. He was a gentleman, extremely loyal to the British and linguistically competent in Russian, German and more importantly Serbo Croat.

When I found it necessary to interview S I had to obtain the services of Major M and to put him completely in the picture and to my amazement he confirmed that he also knew of certain items of my information but had not appreciated the security aspects.

S was a former Yugoslavian soldier, a prisoner of the Germans. At the end of World War Two he became a Displaced Person, living in a camp. Unable to return to his country he joined the MSO. He was a magnificent figure of a man, 6'6" tall, 17/18 stone in weight, quite a fearsome person to confront. He married a German lady who lived in the Hamburg area. He spent all his free time with his wife but when on duty he found it convenient to reside in the single accommodation. My information was that S had returned to Yugoslavia on more than one occasion, and furthermore he had been interrogated by the Security Police; in addition, he had not made formal application for the visits. As a casual resident in Hamburg he could obtain part time employment and therefore when he applied for a visa via the British Consul (he was still a British responsibility) he did not disclose he was employed as a member of MSO and more importantly, where!

I experienced some difficulty in arranging a firm time for an interview. I suspect that S was told that I was involved and became evasive. However he was given a direct order from Major M, and the interview commenced with an outburst by S in his native tongue towards me in particular. His potential for physical violence was very real; he was like a caged animal. Major M made a comment like a whiplash, and in seconds S had sunk in a chair and was weeping like a child, Major M then spoke to him, calmed him down, and S told his story.

S had made three visits over a two or three year period to his home village. On his second visit he was thoroughly interrogated and also contacted on his last visit. Although much general information was given he was adamant that he had not been tasked to become involved in any action of sabotage, espionage or subversion. I personally did not believe him. Although not a person of great intellect, in fact you would say he was 'thick', he would be capable, with intimidation by other MSO, to commit sabotage in the event of hostilities. With Major M's help we extracted much useful information. It also highlighted a breakdown in supervisory procedures of the MSO in general when many members had returned to countries of the Eastern Bloc without the knowledge of higher authority, including ourselves (Intelligence), when it would have been necessary to de-brief them, had permission to leave West Germany been granted. Leave to travel would not have been advocated as a rule, though no doubt consideration would have given in genuine circumstances if it could have been proved. An interesting series of events which involved operational commitments, it was hoped that the action taken closed at least one of the many stable doors left open in the security of BAOR.

CHAPTER 21

Cyprus

Christmas 1963 in West Germany was extremely cold but as a family we were extremely comfortable in our excellent flat surrounded by friends and parties. When the Exercise period ended about November the pace of work within BAOR tended to fall from the frantic to a normal existence; you could even converse to Staff Officers.

However in Cyprus in the weeks prior to Christmas tension had been building up between the Greek and Turkish communities, fairly widespread in the larger centres of habitation but a flash point in Nicosia. On 26th December 1963, 1 Glosters, 3 Green Jackets and the RAF Regiment, all resident units in British Bases, left in a hurry to keep the peace in the capital of Nicosia. They manned an area which was nominated as the 'Green Line' and was roughly the dividing line between the Greek and Turkish communities in the city. It no doubt prevented mass attacks against each other but did not prevent snipings etc. and there were casualties. The troops, as is normal to British soldiers, worked under the circumstances: 'You can only open fire if you are fired at first.' You have difficulty in firing back if you are dead or lying there with a hole in you, however.

Where or who was the enemy? Where were their arms dumps and hides? Who were the groups composed of? Were they in towns or forests? Who were the leaders? In fact there was no enemy. As the days passed incidents in Nicosia and elsewhere were reported, investigated and information grew, names and personalities appeared. It is difficult to understand how the British Government and the military in particular failed so lamentably to continue to gather information between 1958 and the end of 1963. Appreciating that Greek and Turk barely tolerated each other and that we had under our protection two of the most important NATO bases in the Near East, one would have thought that from MI6 and Army Intelligence the effort would have been continuous and effective. Counter Intelligence Company Cyprus is reported to have provided about 80 per cent of all information during those years, no doubt acquired from the safe confines of the towns that act as dormitories to the Sovereign Base areas, and their scope, though unofficial, should have been greater. Any Intelligence Officer worth his salt would have kicked official orders into touch and with reliable operators quietly set about establishing a network around the island bringing in information which could have been used to cross-check on possibly more *reliable* informants near the bases. There is no doubt in my mind, following events, that MI6 were quite confident they had the place sewn up. How wrong they were and Army Intelligence were left with egg on their face.

I have no wish to enter into the whys and wherefores of the Intelligence set-up in Cyprus, but to honestly outline my experiences in the five months or so that I was out there as a Field Operator is difficult because I cannot quote from reports I submitted. Suffice to say that it was a *six year* gap that had to be overcome about personalities, convictions, villages, *mukhtars* (headmen) and so on. In order to gauge local feeling it need not necessarily have been regular and extremely comprehensive information, but produced just sufficiently to justify greater effort if thought necessary. But Cyprus was a holiday base and the authorities, lulled into a false sense of security, had conveniently forgotten the horrors of the terrorist war against EOKA. Maybe they did hear whispers of trouble but certainly not emphasized enough to initiate contingency reinforcement plans. When this was done it can only be described as shambolic and this continued for weeks.

Let us briefly recapitulate:

The Republic Island of Cyprus

In August 1960, the island of Cyprus, with the exception of two small base areas which remained under the United Kingdom sovereignty, became the independent Republic of Cyprus. This solution to what had seemed an impossible problem was the result of an agreement reached between all the interested parties, namely the United Kingdom, Greece and Turkey, as well as the Greek and Turkish Cypriot communities on the island. It was hoped that this agreement would bring to an end the unhappy period of tension of their relations with one another. Until 1963 the island had been comparatively peaceful, but now the Greek President of Cyprus, Archbishop Makarios, announced his intention of going back on the agreements and this led to open conflict once more between the island's two main groups of people. The present situation was made dangerous by the fact that both Greece and Turkey had troops on the island to protect their own people and there was every likelihood that unless something could be done to keep both sides apart, they would reinforce these troops. This, in the long run, could lead to war between

Greece and Turkey, both of whom were bound by treaties to the countries of the Western Alliance.

Historical Background

Long before the Christian era Cyprus was colonised by Greeks and in due course, the Greek Orthodox Church was established among its Greek speaking inhabitants. In 1191, Richard Coeur de Lion, King of England, took possession of it during the Third Crusade, and used it as a military base. Later, in 1489, Cyprus was taken over by the Venetians. In 1571 it was conquered by the Turks and became part of the Turkish Empire.

On the outbreak of the First World War, Turkey sided with Germany and Austria and Britain annexed the island of Cyprus. Britain offered the island to Greece in return for military aid but Greece refused it. Cyprus then became a British Colony.

The Enosis Movement

During the occupation of the island by Turks, the members of the Greek Orthodox Church wanted freedom from the rule of the Turks who were Muslim. Their great desire was Union (Enosis) with Greece. The movement spread and continued to do so, after the island had been taken over by Britain. In 1931 there were widespread disturbances which led to the exile of ten Cypriots including two bishops. When the Second World War was over, the UK government put forward proposals for a new constitution for Cyprus but the Greek Cypriots refused to consider anything which did not provide for Enosis – Union with Greece. No amount of argument or offers of self government would change their minds.

In November 1954, the Greek Colonel Grivas returned to the island and began to organise the National Union of Cypriot Combatants (EOKA) in support of the movement for Enosis. There followed a violent period of murders of Turks, of Greeks and of British soldiers. EOKA, hunting in small bands under the leadership of Grivas, made frequent raids on Turks and British alike. Great tension grew up between the Greek and Turkish Cypriot communities. The Turks were firmly opposed to Enosis and a Turkish Cypriot organization emerged as a counterweight to EOKA. A State of Emergency was proclaimed and Archbishop Makarios, the then President, and three other prominent members of the Greek Orthodox Church in Cyprus were deported.

Many attempts to find a solution to this problem were made by the

British government. The Greeks wanted Enosis. The Turks decided that the island must be partitioned – one part should be given to them and the other to the Greeks, Britain had to safeguard her bases and installations in the island which were necessary to enable the UK to carry out her international obligations – above all those she had assumed towards Turkey, Iran (Persia) and Pakistan in CENTO. During all the discussions which followed the Governments of Greece and Turkey supported the stand of their respective people on the island.

Against a background of murder, arson, ambush and military operations the discussions went on. Eventually agreement was reached in a compromise. The main thing was that there would be no Enosis, that the island would be self governing, that the Turks would get a fair share in the government of the island and that Britain, Greece and Turkey would stand by to see that there was fair play.

In addition, Britain was to retain complete control of certain areas of the island for use as military bases which she could use to do her job in the Near and Middle East.

The agreement provided for a Greek Cypriot President and a Turkish Cypriot Vice-President. Archbishop Makarios was appointed to the first job and a Dr Kutchuk to the second.

The Island of Cyprus

The island of Cyprus occupies a key strategic position in the Eastern Mediterranean. It was under British control from 1878 until 1960 and its economic and social development has been such that today the people enjoy material benefits comparing very favourably with those in neighbouring countries. Some four fifths of the population speak Greek. The remainder are mainly Turkish in origin and speech.

The island of Cyprus lies in the Mediterranean, 240 miles north of Egypt, 60 miles west of Syria and 40 miles south of Turkey. In fact you can see the coast of Turkey from the north coast of Cyprus. The area of the island is 3,572 sq. mls. The north coast is bordered by a steep belt of mountains rising over 3,000 feet and in the south-west an extensive massif rises to 6,400 ft. These are the Troodos Mountains. Between these ranges lies a broad fertile plain. The climate, which is characterized by long warm and dry summers and mild, moist winters, is one of the healthiest in the world. The annual rainfall is slight, averaging about 15 inches in the lowlands and from 20 to 30 inches at higher altitudes. In some years there is a serious shortage of water.

The capital is Nicosia with a population of 40,000. It is an interesting old walled city which was fortified by the Venetians against the Turks. Part of the city, mainly the northern part around the Kyrenia Gate, is predominantly Turkish, and the remainder is Greek. During the previous emergency, the two areas were separated by barbed wire along what was locally known as the Mason-Dixon Line. The centre of the Greek section of the city is Metaxas Square and that of the Turkish section, Ataturk Square. Other large cities are Limassol and Larnaca, both on the south coast, and Famagusta on the east coast. In the north there is Kyrenia with its magnificent old castle and glorious bathing beaches.

The civilian population is about half a million. More than one fifth live in the six principal towns. About 50 per cent are Greek speaking and the Greek Orthodox Church has great influence among them. About 15 per cent are Muslims of Turkish origin, and the remainder includes Armenians and Maronites.

Agriculture is the basis of the economy of Cyprus, although it is not self supporting in foodstuffs. A wide variety of crops is grown including corn of various kinds, potatoes, green vegetables, cotton, tobacco, melons, oranges, lemons, grapefruit and many other fruits. Many grapes are grown, both in private gardens and in vineyards and much very good wine is made. Carobs, beanlike things which grow on trees, are important. They are exported for making cattle food. Asbestos is mined in the Troodos Mountains and copper is produced by an American owned company at Xeros. There are a number of small manufacturing industries, mostly catering for the home market. Manufactures for export include wines, buttons, false teeth and hand-made lace. Cyprus lace is world famous.

The sovereign base areas for British troops lie on the southern side of the island at Akrotiri and near Limassol and Episkopi, and at Xylotymbou between Famagusta and Larnaca. There is an RAF Station at Akrotiri and a civil airfield at Nicosia.

Cyprus is a beautiful island with the wonderful climate; a stay there is much to be enjoyed. During the emergency, however, it was difficult to enjoy it to the full. Not only was it necessary to go about armed but it was also necessary to keep a careful watch upon one's weapons. Cypriots appear to be fond of firearms and many were stolen from the possession of British troops who were careless and later used against them. The Cypriots are normally friendly people but in a situation like that, it was better to trust no one.

So dusting my memory: on an afternoon in January 1964, Bob B, the Operational Intelligence Sergeant for 11 Brigade, was warned by signal of an impending move to Cyprus. This was followed before close of play by another signal with the same instructions to 'Pat' Patrick who worked with me; both had served in Cyprus between 1954-8. At 6a.m. the following morning a grinning B got me out of bed and told me that I was taking his place but definite departure details were not known. I had to report in at 0800 hours but I would definitely be leaving Germany en route to UK. I was in a quandary. Things could change at a moment's notice, so I packed, told Jean that I was now on standby, kissed a tearful wife goodbye and kept my fingers crossed. My hopes were dashed. Confirmation arrived for our move and Pat and I caught a train at Minden en route for the Hook of Holland dressed in combat kit! Already on the train was our boss Capt. John Althorp from Hohne, and further down the line we picked up S, another senior operator. In addition a corporal, lance corporal and private joined us to make up the team, making seven in all, and all strangers apart from Pat and me.

The journey was tedious but at least we formed opinions of each other which helped in some ways in the weeks ahead. I think the most humorous part of the trip was the expressions and comments of the commuters on the Harwich to London train faced with three card-playing soldiers at 7a.m. with a bottle of whisky on the table. We had to make our own way across London and it was when we pulled up in our taxi opposite the Bank of England that I saw Robert Fellowes (now the Queen's Private Secretary) on his way to the office. Bob was a former Scots Guards Officer Cadet of mine. I lowered the window and in my loudest parade ground voice way above the traffic I called his name and remarks about his head, shoulders and the way he was carrying that bloody stupid umbrella. He halted rigidly looked across, recognized me and yelled 'Staff!' raised his bowler and walked off the pavement towards me straight in front of a luckily slow moving bus. We moved off and my last glimpse of Robert was a rather energetic kaleidoscope of arms, legs, bowler, brolly and briefcase, I don't think it hit him.

It was a shambles at Reading Station but eventually we arrived at Bulford Camp to be shown our accommodation in the Mess and informed that if we left for Cyprus we would be under the operational and administrative care of HQ Royal Artillery 3 Division. I don't know how they knew, probably via Capt. Althorp, but because of my infantry background I was made acting RSM responsible for training, and by seniority I was probably the most junior of all the SNCOs. Those few days were quite chaotic: clothing issue, documentation, inoculations and in between, the efforts to increase the military efficiency of Intelligence, Signals, RMP and RAOC in a mixture of route marches, PT, range firings, Anti Ambush drills etc. The advance party of the DAAQMG and his

WO 2 Chief Clerk left for Cyprus and 40 Int. Platoon as we were now called, sat there with no equipment to go to war with. For light relief the Royal Ulster Rifles, stationed nearby and just about to depart for Borneo, decided to burn down several of the huts in which they were billeted and 'Needles and Pins' by the Searchers was a record you couldn't escape from. The mother of S had a pub in Croydon so we three took ourselves off to my old 1944 stamping ground and enjoyed a most hilarious weekend. The highlight of this was on our return in the early hours of Sunday to the pub. Poor little Pat, slightly inebriated, received the amorous attention of the pub's rather large shaggy dog, which appeared to be a cross between an Irish wolfhound and an Old English sheepdog. That dog was canny, it ambushed us in every part of the pub we went, and as we were sharing the same double bed it was even worse. We would remove it downstairs and it would be trying to break into the bedroom minutes later. Pat and I were hysterical. For hospitality and humour it was a great weekend.

The following Saturday the lance corporal was detailed to finally collect our equipment; we would unpack on Monday and clean it up. Sunday afternoon was dull with rain in the air. I had an early tea and the gloom was oppressive outside, I felt very miserable and purposeless. Some comment made by a chap having a late meal made me prick my ears up, and S and I questioned him closer. Then I dashed to the window to look across the intervening ground, and found that lights were blazing from HQ RA 3 Division; they were on the move. S went to find the other three, while Pat and I went to HQ RA. They had known since before lunch. We received all the excuses imaginable, but why we had not made our appearance like the others didn't seem to strike them as odd. Our other three did not appear for some three hours but in the meantime we cleaned, unpacked and repacked, in two large wicker baskets, our filing cabinets, typewriters etc. These would be placed in a HQRA long based Land Rover for us, as we still had no transport. The other lads cleaned our weapons and in the early hours, packed and ready to move, we fell into an exhausted sleep. Then followed the trip to Brize Norton and the flight to Akrotiri, Cyprus where we alighted into darkness and the strange but pleasant smell of eucalyptus trees, burning wood and a much warmer climate.

We sat around in Movements for about three hours. We couldn't unload the plane and our kit, no food or drink was available; we just felt mounting frustration. Eventually word was given and it was mainly RMP and the Intelligence group who physically unloaded all the transport and stores from the Britannia. That was hard work but we wanted to assuage our frustration somehow. The Warrant Officer on the advance party took us by bus to our accommodation in the barracks at Episkopi. The lads were dropped off at a Barrack Block and we went to the Mess; Patrick and I sharing a room. I went to see that the other ranks were OK only to find that they had been given pillows and blankets, but no beds and mattresses. The Advance Party had been there a week; what the hell had they been doing? I was livid but there was very little I could do at that time of the night, but by God it was sorted out later, bloody incompetent sods. Typical Gunners, very rarely considered the other ranks.

After sleep and a breakfast we arrived at the area designated as HQ Western Region or HQ RA. Capt. Althorp was at a briefing so we organized our stores and weapons and waited. The Brigadier and entourage eventually turned up and gave us an introductory pep talk which meant very little as to the job we were to perform. Everyone else's job was straight forward but ours?! John Althorp told us that HQ RA and staff had been allocated a region of responsibility to the west of Lefka (a Turkish stronghold) and virtually along a line due south to the coast. HQ RA was operating officially as representatives of a United Nations Truce Force and as such were not allowed Intelligence backup; we would therefore be acting unofficially. The Western Region was to be divided in two, on a line running roughly west to east just north of Stroumbi and Polemi. S would take the south-west area based on Ktima/Paphos with some Glosters in support; I would take the north-west based at the Limni Mine just outside Polis with 9 Para Squadron Royal Engineers to keep me company. I had the corporal as my driver, S had the lance corporal. Pat and Private Campbell would collate, evaluate and disseminate all the up to date information we could dig up, and that was all he knew at this time. Apparently mine was the dodgiest area in the country apart from Nicosia. There had been abductions, shootings and murders in the area which was predominantly Greek and the Turks had suffered worst. All Turkish inhabitants of Polis had fled in fear from their houses, which were later pillaged, and currently were housed in a large Turkish school and two adjacent houses on the outskirts of Polis. Living conditions were very bad. They were short of food and water and being surrounded by Greeks were continually sniped at. The Paras who had only been there a few days did not guard the Turks, only patrolled the roads and streets, investigating and acting as conciliators in the event of trouble.

The miracle happened and a battered Land Rover was given to us. I asked Capt. Althorp for ammunition, grenades, first aid kit, beds and sleeping bags; also a briefing from the Counter Intelligence Company and several other items I thought would be necessary. The corporal and I, unarmed but with a full tank and a map, disappeared up the road to Polis to meet the Paras. I was not impressed by the villages we passed through.

They reminded me a lot of Palestine, ill planned and scruffy. Ktima was busy and the looks we got were hostile; the last six years had all been in vain. We passed the Turkish enclave at Polis but did not stop and eventually found our way to Limni Mines. The Squadron Commander was a typical first class Sapper officer. He and his men had taken the infantry role into their stride. He showed me round the base which mainly consisted of bungalows and several administration buildings. The corporal and I were to have a kitchen in a bungalow as our office and bedroom; the other two rooms held five of his Senior Ranks. Introductions over we drove back, only to find nothing I had requested had been obtained, we would just have to take a blanket roll. I told the corporal to find out about repairs and servicing and what system of collection we would need for our reports and I went scrounging.

My first call was on a RAF Sergeant at the Medical Centre. When I explained my predicament and the job I would be doing, he filled a cardboard box with all kinds of 'goodies' for minor ailments; he didn't argue but was understanding and most helpful. I then trailed down to the Ammunition Compound and poured out my tale of woe to a lance corporal in the RAOC who again was most helpful; he was not prepared to offer two grenades but gave me four smoke grenades in lieu. I could have had more but took 200 rounds of 9mm and 30 rounds of .38 in case John Althorp changed his mind and gave me the revolver. I could have had some 7.62mm SLR ammo but my chances of obtaining an SLR which would have been handy was unlikely. I now felt happier that I could tackle the job and look after myself. First thing the following morning was a visit to C1 Company where I spoke to Bob — who when I first transferred to Intelligence took me through the initial Counter Intelligence phase. In all honesty to Bob, the only item of interest and use was a name and this person had once worked for the Government. He was last heard of in the Polis area but his present whereabouts were unknown.

After tying up one or two loose ends the corporal and I left them all to get on with their trials and tribulations while we got into the war. On arrival at Polis we had a quick run around the town several times to orientate ourselves and decided to visit the police station to see how co-operative they were. Having dismissed all the Turks it was now run solely by Greeks and I had one or two questions to ask and several more to hide my real reason. The only one on duty who spoke reasonable English was the sergeant and as time went on I learned only too well this man's influence on the Greek population, and hatred for him by the Turks. He was of course involved with EOKA but was one of those who escaped the full notice of the Security Forces at that time.

He inadvertently told me where the Turkish contact was located, and told a very biased story in connection with the kidnapping and subsequent murder of three prominent local Turks which I knew was untrue, and as he conversed on various topics I just gained the impression that this person was an unprincipled liar and not a particularly good policeman. He was very curious about my presence in the area and I also told a very plausible but vague story. I didn't think much of it at the time but I had my beret in my hand and the sergeant did not read the badge. The following day when by accident or design our vehicle was stopped near Ayia Marina on the coast road by a mixture of goats and people, a male person came up to the vehicle, made some fatuous remark and apologised for the hold up. He looked hard at my corporal's badge and exclaimed, 'Ah Intelligence!' and to me that spelt trouble. As a result the following day our badges became RAOC and our cover story, plus our excuse for being in the area, could be explained even to the United Nations; in other words we 'almost' became legal.

We left the police station and sat in the vehicle for a while in the main street consuming a soft drink and some chocolate. That half an hour taught us a lot; the attitude of passers by, their looks, the spitting around the vehicle and from across the street told all; the Greeks were offering no welcome mat, they hated us. As we were about to leave I thought our luck had changed. A rather old distinguished looking Greek gentleman in his late seventies came up to the vehicle, raised his hat to us and in excellent English stated how nice it was to see British soldiers back again; he was so sorry that trouble had started but hoped it would soon be over. He offered cigarettes, talked of many things and answered several questions with great frankness. He was formerly a NAAFI canteen manager in Egypt during World War 2, also in the Canal Zone, and very pro-British. I thought to myself, here is a pot of gold, so I said I hoped we would see each other again and he agreed, adding maybe we could call at his house at a later date. Two days later we pulled up alongside him in the street and greeted him. Instantly he was petrified, eyes like saucers, head and eyes turning and looking all around. In what could only be described as a strangled whisper he pleaded, 'Please don't ever speak to me again, I cannot speak to you, I'm not allowed, do you understand, please understand.' The man was terrified; his eyes were pleading and apologetic but he had the smell of fear; he hurried away and we never saw him again. I hope they never harmed him.

He had said that he frequently argued with his contemporaries in the café, they were so anti British he felt he had to speak up for the organization he had served so well. Following our initial meeting and talk in front of many townspeople he was a marked man and no doubt the 'boys' had paid him a visit.

Back at Limni I called in at the HQ and introduced myself to the three Royal Signals NCOs who were maintaining the Rear Link communications direct to Episkopi. We discussed a non-de-plume for S and myself as the line could be monitored so I became Oaktree and S Crabapple. Intelligence, in military terminology, is referred to as Acorn, so I suggested we had something that derived from it. The Squadron Commander took me to one side and said he was rather disturbed about the way I would be wandering around the countryside with no communication; he expressed the view that our lives would be seriously in danger under present circumstances. Therefore, having talked it over with his Signal Sergeant the unit would supply and fit me a radio in my Land Rover. I was delighted: it would be a great help in every way but particularly if I hit trouble when I knew help would come, hopefully not too late.

That evening I lay on the floor and tried to work out what was needed and how I could get it. The General's initial requirement was general information on the region and what were likely to be the trouble spots. In two and a half days it was obvious that the Greeks had the initiative and in general 90 per cent support of the Greek population. They were militant and aggressive, had generally nullified the Turkish population by forcing them into enclaves thus reducing their resistance potential. In some areas problems did not occur, Greek and Turk lived amicably as they had done for years; in other areas trouble arose between communities because of threats and intimidation, and of course open hostility existed as a matter of habit in many urban conurbations of mixed habitation. So to ensure a constant flow of information I had to complete a lot of mileage, visit as many villages as possible and play one side off against the other. The main problem was that I wouldn't stand a chance if things went wrong. Approaching a village, every cart could be a potential road block and every village a possible castle or strong point (we had no information on the number of shotguns held), and possibly most frightening, every person over the age of sixteen years could be termed a 'soldier'. It was the Squadron Commander's brief that he assist the population in welfare, food, medical and other problems as a member of the UN Truce Force, so I decided that my cover story should enlarge on this. When I visited villages I was to be akin to the International Red Cross but not by name. I had a logical explanation for touring round the area but I wished I had an extra man and more adequate weapons.

It also made sense that all information should be graded F6 as it would be many weeks or months before the grading could be improved. Military

Intelligence had a method by letters and numbers which fairly sensibly gauged the accuracy and reliability of informants and information, and so the process started.

We set off the following morning to have a look around the Akamas forest area, with our radio installed and the Royal Signals corporal coming along to sort out any technicalities and as a break from his work. We covered the brief visit of President Makarios to Polis and got a couple of photographs of locals that were helpful, then continued north-westwards along the coast road which ended abruptly somewhere near Klisia. A large uncompleted building with a lovely view overlooking the sea below was empty and was situated at the beginning of a rough track which appeared to run round the edge of the nearby cliffs. This building was to have been a casino but lay idle and unused. The old man in Polis had mentioned this and also that nearby was one of the legendary bathing places of Aphrodite. I was curious so I took a walk and found the bathing place; I also found some spent cartridge cases and detonating wire; other items also pointed to illegality. The bathing place was quite attractive otherwise. My corporal and I walked down the track towards the sea and where the track turned left and headed north-west it was evident that a track had been literally hacked out of the cliff face (I believe members of TA Sapper units achieved this on annual camps). I hesitated but my corporal was most enthusiastic and wanted to drive along it. The map showed a track but I didn't anticipate having to drive along a cliff face hundreds of feet above the blue sea and no way to turn round.

I was outvoted and apprehensive, the radio wasn't functioning either. So we set off yet again with barely six inches from the cliff face to the vehicle. It seemed to take an age but eventually we approached an open area. We stopped, looked around, and as it appeared clear we drove on to the centre of this ideal little beach, backed by trees. What a beautiful isolated spot this was, especially for a training area. Yet again there were cartridge cases etc. as of course the military had been in the vicinity but had they fired here? Interesting but not conclusive. We had a good look around, then left. I said I would drive back as the corporal was not keen on a return drive; I think he began to feel nervous. That drive certainly did test your nerve but I was concentrating on not making contact with the cliff face. My corporal and the other lad suddenly realized that they were literally hanging over a sheer drop of hundreds of feet into the rocks and sea below. When we left the track the Signals lad was green and looked sick, my corporal was pale and rather quiet (a change for him). I wouldn't like to do it again.

We dropped the corporal off at the mine with the radio, while we took the road to Neokhoria to enter the forest from a different approach road.

This village was very hostile and no way could we encourage people to speak to us on community affairs; they certainly didn't like the idea when we disappeared towards the forest area. Again we drew a blank but it was such a vast place people could train anywhere. It was ideal for an ambush too. We reversed and the rear wheels were stuck in mud and tree roots, then the engine died and the hush was ominous. We both looked at each other and laughed; it was better than crying. The corporal sorted out the engine, finally got it in four wheel drive (it was faulty) and with me pushing at the back we extricated ourselves. It was decided then and there that unless something was definite, two mere mortals like ourselves were wasting our time in the forest.

That evening we visited the Turkish school. Here we had the whole of the Turkish community of Polis, several hundred persons in all, crowded into the confines of a small school. Water and food were in short supply and toilet and cooking facilities at a minimum, but they were bearing this hardship with fortitude, also thinking that matters could have been worse and many could have been killed if it were not for the presence of British troops in the area. I met the contact who was a most charming and helpful person. Although not the official local leader this man had an executive (military) function. His close associate whom I shall call H was much younger, better educated and full of Turkish charm, and it was he who organized and personally led the supply vehicles which brought in the meagre supplies. He also carried a Colt .45 automatic in his belt. Refreshments and brandy were produced and we got on fine. I promised what help I could, and took away names of people to contact in villages. I was assured that no Greek would speak to me and this was so. I was ignored or people just did not appear; it was very one-sided.

I met these two Turkish chaps most days, bringing them domestic items not readily available when the supply trucks went shopping. I arranged for medical facilities and occasional items they could not obtain, and the odd bottle of 'better booze'. This help redounded on me when they told me about the plight of a mother from a surrounding village who had taken her young child into the small hospital at Polis for a minor operation and then following surgery the staff threw out the mother although allowing visits, but refused to release the child until a domestic problem between the village and its Greek neighbours had been agreed in favour of the Greeks. That evening I paid a surprise visit to the hospital and spoke to the Senior Sister who understood English. The mother and baby were produced and some belongings. Satisfying myself from what the nurse said that the child was OK I placed them in my vehicle, much against the wishes of the nurse who said she had orders from a Mr Raftis that the baby had to be held.

This Raftis was not a medical person but a local personality! – more about him later. We drove away and returned mother and baby to their hillside village. The anger and fear of the hospital staff was most evident and vocal, but I was not prepared to do nothing in the face of obvious abduction and intimidation.

Within the next few days several things happened. The first was probably my initiation ceremony by the five Para Senior Ranks who shared the accommodation. On first arrival at the deserted mine they had obviously liberated some hooch from the bungalows, and this night was acceptance night. The six of us sat on the floor or camp beds with three bottles of whisky (the Army free fall champion was among us). They thought I was an intellectual bastard (their words) and wanted to drive me into the ground by booze. We had a great chat and only two of us stayed to the end. Another hurdle overcome.

Two days later 9 Para Squadron had left, just like that. They went along the coast to a base outside Lefka, the Turkish stronghold. They were replaced by a Battery of 26 Regt. Royal Artillery who until a few days before had been resident Regiment at the Artillery School, Shoeburyness in Essex. I have no doubt with Northern Ireland, Gunner Regiments are now better trained to assume an Infantry role, but 26 Regt. were a disaster. RHQ of 26 Regt. was based at Ktima. They also had radio links between Episkopi and Ktima and midway between Ktima and Polis with protective troops on the ground. The Gunners are justly proud of their own radio communications and insisted they were used, despite duplication with the Royal Signals. They agreed to keep the latter *in situ* because R Signals had an island wide network *and* were more reliable. The mind boggles.

When I met the Battery Commander (BC), a Major, we were poles apart in our thinking; it was obvious I was not welcome to his area and events proved me right. His Second in Command (BQ) was a direct contrast; helpful, understanding and more of a practical soldier. The less I say about certain senior ranks and other ranks the better. They were untidy in dress, and military efficiency and discipline was poor. To give one example of general apathy at one stage: we ran out of food for two or was it three days? Onions were the only edible item available to eat. Most days the corporal and I grabbed a piece of cheese, some bread, and a couple of cans of beer and that was our lunch up in the hills, but we wanted something more substantial when we came in late at night. The cooks looked after us but they couldn't cook what they didn't have.

It was a day or two after the Gunners had arrived when I again visited the nearby Turkish village of Magounda. We were drinking coffee and talking to some villagers when a very distressed and tearful woman told us her ten-year-old son had just been abducted from the fields where he had been grazing a large herd of goats. The goats were jointly owned with a Greek family friend who resided in the adjacent village of Kinousa. Three armed Greeks were holding both goats and boy in a field near the coast. We left immediately and minutes later skidded to a halt where the child was held. One Greek held his rifle towards the petrified kid who had tears pouring down his face while the other two adopted aggressive attitudes waving their rifles around. I told the corporal to cock his Sterling machine gun and watch the antics of the two on the side. I left the Land Rover and deliberately cocked my weapon, walked over to the kid, wiped his eyes said something sympathetic which he didn't understand and motioned him to the Rover. I said to the one nearest the kid, 'You're a big brave bastard threatening a child, try someone bigger.'

He said, 'We're only carrying out Mr Raftis's order.'

'Who's he?' I asked.

'He's in charge and will be here shortly,' was the reply.

Some minutes later an open Land Rover containing four men arrived in a cloud of dust. All wore dark trousers, shirts and black leather jackets, and everyone appeared armed. A small dapper person leapt out of the Rover and looked around. My Sterling never left his guts. So this was the renowned, Mr George 'Spirou' Raftis! To add to the theatricals Raftis had two guns strapped round his waist; it looked like a scene from 'Gunfight at the OK Corral' or 'The Godfather'. He immediately objected to my gun in his direction, but before an argument developed another cloud of dust announced the arrival of the BC who appeared to know my friend Raftis, who immediately claimed to the BC that I was threatening him.

I said that until all the Greek illegal weapons were put away I would keep one up the spout and that as this abduction and theft was instigated by Raftis he would be the first to drop if there was trouble. Raftis then claimed that the goats had been stolen and that the Greek gentleman had complained. I called him a liar and that he knew they were jointly owned and that nothing had changed even with the troubles. Eventually the BC agreed to take the Greek gentleman to the Turkish village to meet his friend; this happened and the friendship was maintained. The BC was not happy that I had stolen his thunder by being on the spot and sorting the matter out amicably, and he strongly objected to my attitude to nice Mr Raftis who was co-operating with him and his men. I said that terrorizing and abducting children was hardly co-operation, and that set the seal to our relationship.

George 'Spirou' Raftis was in his early thirties and was born in the village of Drousha outside Polis. He was an ardent member of EOKA and

George 'Spirou' Raftis, local Greek leader for Western Cyprus. Jailed in the 1950s for the EOKA killing of five British soldiers.

was eventually credited and later convicted of the killing of five British soldiers (two or three were Gunners) and was jailed. He was a talented man and apparently learned to pilot a plane. My information was that it was he who took delivery and flew back to Cyprus a plane that was a gift to President Makarios from the West German government. He moved in high circles and later I formed the opinion that he was probably the Greek Cypriot Military Commander for North-West Cyprus. I also obtained information that he had been to Moscow and received some training. That rather long drawn out incident placed George and me on a collision course.

So it came to pass that some ten days after my arrival in Cyprus, the *Cyprus Mail* stated that 'a top level British Intelligence agent was working in North West Cyprus'. Sounded like typical Raftis theatricals but they really put tabs on me; we were trailed, noted, hindered or watched constantly. In fact my corporal had to be backloaded to Episkopi mainly because he began to be short tempered if there was any hindrance, and almost got us into unnecessary trouble several times because of his untimely aggressiveness. It was this and the fact that he wished to speak Turkish that was at the root of his problems and when we visited a village or friends at the school he spent more time trying to improve his language limitations than acquiring information, making notes, or looking after my safety. The lance corporal who replaced him only lasted a couple of weeks; his only interest was driving and he was murder on Cypriot roads and tracks. Young

Campbell eventually joined me and was first class; he only made one boob but more of that later.

The corporal and I drove miles visiting and talking to all who would converse and information which in the first few days was but a trickle now began to be a flood. I was writing at least five foolscap sheets of info every night; we couldn't have a typewriter. I did however get the pistol; it was handy when I was talking and making notes and John Althorp had no use for it. I gathered info on anything that was relevant in the area. It was not for me to collate and evaluate, I was the 'Collector' and it was to be hoped that my intuition and curiosity kept us safe. The corporal and I once went out late one night to identify and locate the Greek positions surrounding the school: dangerous, but information was reciprocal.

Several days after the goat incident we were driving along the coast road when the sound of shooting was heard from the direction of the Turkish village of Yialia. We turned off to investigate and stopped on the track approximately midway between the attacking Greeks and defending Turks. The Turks would recognise me as I had visited the village once before, so I took a chance and walked in to the middle of the two sides, hoping to stop the shooting, and miraculously it stopped. I don't think it was solely my appearance as 'piggy in the middle' that stopped it, because they were still firing when I started to walk, but what I had not seen, but the Greeks had, was a small convoy of military vehicles and my friend the BC driving along the coast road. The Greeks retired, the Turks vanished and the BC said, 'Bloody hell, you again, how is it you always find the trouble first?' He checked about casualties, then drove off. I then stayed in Yialia some time; my intervention had paid off and we talked of many things.

It was suggested that more attention should be paid to the Forestry Station at Stavros as it was alleged illegal activity took place there. Its telephone line was used mainly for illegal communication with Ktima and Polis and they did not discuss trees, also that a fair amount of vehicular movement was seen during the hours of darkness, though this in itself was not unusual. The following day from the direction of Yialia we took a look at Stavros, which meant we approached it from the east. It was a natural high-sided valley with the road running downhill from the east, and halfway down we saw a substantial brick and stone building which obviously was a small telephone exchange no doubt permanently manned. Thinking we might get a drink we pulled up. The Greek inside was obviously taken aback to see two soldiers. We bought two bottles of pop, sat in the vehicle and nonchalantly looked around. On the south side there appeared to be a relatively new track leading nowhere, and to the north a side track seem to lead to a number of substantial bungalows or villas situated on the side of the high ground facing South. The person inside the building pleaded, 'No English.' No one else appeared so we slowly drove down the hill. On more level ground the valley opened up and more buildings were seen. These were not houses but more like barrack rooms, and outside were laid out long tables and forms all of wood. All these buildings were scattered but were extremely substantial. Not a soul was seen; it was deathly quiet and rather disturbing. I had the feeling of hidden eyes and a sudden shot. We decided more visits were needed.

Poor old S in Ktima was having problems; living with RHQ of 26 Regt. was not helpful and to try and keep them off his back he got involved. He seemed to spend more time at Episkopi and was making the fatal error of over grading the information he was obtaining, which was not a lot. Ktima was a mixed area and when the Greeks started a takeover bid, S, in the wrong belief that he was on to something really big, was persuasive enough to get an RAF helicopter to fly into Ktima, amid shot and shell, God Bless the RAF, to land on a house roof and evacuate at all costs this man so vital to British Intelligence. This was done without a hole in the bodywork. The chopper landed at Episkopi, the chap got his feet on the ground and legged it, never to be seen again. So S and others got egg on their faces. Ktima was Greek dominated and S was to all intents and purposes out of work and sadly disillusioned.

Meanwhile back at the ranch I had a visitor. He was a Major in the Tank Corps, and had been sent directly from the Ministry of Defence as a Military Intelligence Officer: I shall call him C although he was double barrelled. Normally an MIO is attached to Special Branch in formerly held territories but not this time. He apparently had been sent specifically to take over North-West Cyprus, God knows why. However he had briefed himself up, read what I was producing about the various incidents and decided that I should remain as I was; he would undertake a roaming commission for the whole of Western Cyprus and had informed MOD accordingly. I took him to a garage in Polis where they were building an armoured car on a lorry chassis, and C took photographs.

I felt I had a friend in C so I talked to him of certain matters which did not seem to be making much impression on 26 Regt. or Western Region and one was Stavros. He explained that the Government were particularly worried about the storage of arms and ammunition by the Greeks. It was suggested that for some time now Limossal had been used to unload illegal arms etc., and since the trouble started attempts to follow suspect convoys of vehicles had been foiled by well placed farm carts or lorries. Although different routes were taken they all appeared to be heading for the monastery at Kykko (Makarios's birthplace) and on into Paphos Forest in which lay Stavros.

C had some hours to spare; could I take him there? so I did. I had earlier been up west to east and had been followed for part of the way. This time I again went via Yialia and what a fright we got. We came slowly down the hill and pulled up at the brick building, I was about to leave the vehicle to get some pop when from out of nowhere appeared six of the twelve Apostles; they stood all round us about ten yards from the Land Rover. All had long dark hair, some moustachioed, dark and swarthy, dark shirts, trousers and shoes and black leather jackets: a replica of Raftis's bodyguard. It was like Hollywood; only bloody frightening.

'What do we do now,' asked C.

'Keep our — fingers crossed, have a fag,' says I.

So we passed eight or ten minutes smoking, making stupid inane remarks to each other and from the vehicle I offered our 'watchers' a piece of Cadburys Fruit and Nut which was greeted with complete indifference by our stony faced friends who never uttered a syllable but kept their hands inside their open coats. No arms were seen but they were there. With a loud, 'Well, let's away,' which visibly shook some of our friends I reached for the ignition key and gearstick and in five or six seconds was almost out of pistol range, out of imminent danger. I think C said, 'Jesus Christ, I don't know how you did that, we were lucky, I've never been so frightened in my life.' I told him he wasn't the only one with a sweaty crotch. He certainly believed in me, and we discussed my idea of setting up a surreptitious vehicle night watch at both ends of the valley. I had already picked the spots and methods, so on our return to Polis, C eventually persuaded the BC to provide tea and rations plus a six-man team guard for the following night for each of us.

The following afternoon, as we were about to leave, the Commanding Officer of 26 Regt. asked the BC what the twelve Gunners were waiting for. The BC explained the full implications of the job and the CO said cancel, and no more jobs for Intelligence; he was not having the lives of his soldiers endangered. I hoped to God he never reached the rank of General. It made you wonder why we wore a uniform and had a job to do.

This item has to be written in as a follow up to Stavros. After the CO of 26 Regt. refused to assist myself and MIO C in the confirmation of unusual vehicle movements, we thought the official involvement had died a death, despite all our appeals. My information was still coming in and obviously channelled into HQ Western Region (HQRA) and so to HQ 26 Regt. at Ktima. It would seem apparent that ours was not to be the glory, because

I was not told and I don't think John Althorp and C were told of what was contemplated.

Apparently one day, so I was informed, a force said to be two or three hundred men in trucks accompanied by Ferret armoured cars and armoured 'Pigs' invaded the Stavros valley from the west to carry out a 'Search and Find' mission. (I never found out if they adequately sealed off all the other routes out or the East end, otherwise it would have been all pointless, which of course it was) because a leading vehicle broke down in a spot where it couldn't be overtaken, and the whole convoy was stuck in questionable territory. Fair enough, the operation could have gone on, done solely by the men on foot, but 26 Regt. wanted armoured support and that was immobile at the end of the convoy. Reluctantly and with tail between legs an ignominious withdrawal was made. No one did much shouting about it, but what a shambles. If only the matter had been properly discussed, and that these people who normally do an excellent job in their own field would only admit to their limitations in the infantry role.

Day followed day and the work went on, I had bumped into Spirou on two or three occasions; he was always in this crumby open Land Rover. They looked like four redundant undertakers, all in black and armed to the teeth. On one occasion we met near his home. I was only having a mosey round and didn't expect to meet him but I smiled and waved, shouted, 'Good afternoon Georgie,' and drove on, knowing full well he couldn't turn round. The look he gave of curiosity and astonishment made my day. The other couple of occasions were in isolated places and we greeted him in exactly the same manner although out of his sight the corporal put his clog down.

When the incident of the abducted child in hospital occurred I had to return to pick up several items of the little girl's clothing. I had spoken to the Sister and told her I would collect. George was in the hospital when I arrived and he wanted to know why I had interfered in the situation. I threw the ball back to him and asked him if it had been a Greek girl under the same circumstances what would he have done? He made no reply. I then added that the military were not prepared to tolerate murder, abduction and intimidation from either side and he should understand that. He still remained quiet, then suddenly he put his arm round me, smiled, and asked me to come to his little house in Polis and have some supper the following night (he was not known to have a house in Polis), there would be plenty to eat and drink and we could have a long talk. I said I wasn't sure I would be back from an appointment I had, but I would ring the Police Station and leave a message if I could make it. I was told from up above that on no account should I meet him, especially in the hours of darkness. My life would not be worth a light.

This amusing yet pathetic incident happened on one of my rare visits to HQ Western Region. The Land Rover needed certain repairs and servicing and I had matters to discuss with John Althorp and C. As I walked into the 'Int. Cell', Pat as usual was hard at it and gave me his normal enthusiastic welcome. I was staying the night so we would have a long natter and he really looked forward to it. I must explain that Pat took on the role of an introvert out there, because his whole life revolved round his family, and now he was separated he would spend at least fourteen hours a day at his work, a very dedicated soldier in the set-up. From out of John Althorp's office stepped a figure; three bright and shining 'pips' adorned his shoulders, his uniform was immaculate and he looked like a twenty-two year-old male edition of the Virgin Mary, and just as handsome. A withering glance at my untidy 'warrior' figure drew the following appraisal: 'Ah you must be Howard, I'm Capt. — your new G3 (Int.); come in, I want to see you *now*.'

As Pat was explaining something important I acknowledged and waited for Pat to finish.

'I said *now*, Staff Patrick,' came the rude but authoritative voice from within.

The expression on Pat's face said it all, a mixture of horror, resignation, humour and inevitability, so I walked in.

The Virgin Mary stood in front of a map that covered the wall; he was equipped with a stick. I received acknowledgments from John Althorp to my left and MIO C in front of me; their heads were curiously low.

'Pay attention!' came the command and for some minutes I was subjected to the Virgin's assessment of the Intelligence and Operational commitment in Western Cyprus. After some two minutes of this and he was really getting warmed up, I glanced at C whose gaze was at his desk; his head in his hands and his body was shaking uncontrollably in silent laughter. I turned to my left and handsome John gazed at me through glazed but humorous eyes in a dog-like appeal for mercy and understanding. His hand was to his mouth and his teeth tightly fastened on his first finger to prevent the laughter contained within him.

'Well, what do you think of my assessment?'

'Frankly, Sir,' says I, 'It's all balls!'

There were no histrionics at my statement, only his colour changed.

'Why do you say that? It's all based on your personal reports.'

'Ah yes,' says I, 'but my reports are all F6, and to base information gathered, to issue summaries and make statements as you have done, requires known reliable information and some form of corroboration before an accurate assessment is made and nowhere do you have this. This is all surmise and should be known as such.'

'We told you so,' chorused John and C.

'I still think I'm right,' said the Virgin, and with an indignant rustle of skirts flounced out to join the comfort of his Gunner contemporaries who understood him.

'Where on earth did he emerge from?' I gasped.

It was explained that the Captain had been at a Boy's unit in UK as a 2nd Lieutenant, very recently given his 2nd pip to Lieutenant, and had suddenly been propelled into a senior role of a Grade 3 Staff Officer with no military background. It was ludicrous for someone actually to have to serve with a walking disaster area like him, and really it wasn't his fault wholly, but the idiots who sent him there. He made another great boob later, which was once described to me but I forget the details. Such are the problems of the man in the field who sees his work twisted around to suit the personal line of thought held by some senior, and how often did it happen to me in the years to come.

Looking at the general situation, a longer look around the north coast and north east area of my patch was indicated, mainly in the areas of Kokkina, Mosphileri and Mansoura. My information was that the Turks around this area were very militant and aggressive and had ties with the mainland. I had one or two names to play with from my newly acquired friends but I had to box clever; after the abductions in Polis in early January, this lot in Mansoura only knocked off a Greek bus with thirty-odd passengers and threatened to kill the lot if the victim was not returned. It was a Turk who negotiated the release of the Greeks, and he was later murdered, how he was repaid. So it was essential I was careful and played my cards close to my chest, and after two days I was more than convinced that here, around Mansoura and Lefka, would be the heart of Turkish resistance. Not only were they anti Greek but they were dedicated fighters, and what was more they had the weapons and ammunition to do it and were not afraid to take on the Greeks. They knew that if the Greeks made a move to remove the Turkish Cypriots they would have to start along this part of the island. All this information came in bits and pieces, an odd question in the brandy fumes, a confident answer and a retaining click in the brain. They were genuine people, grafters and were not about to be forced out. My report on this area stated that any outside help from the mainland would be here, the Turks could not afford to lose it, and that if they were being overwhelmed help would come in some way and that if any Turkish area in Cyprus was capable of resisting or attacking from, it would be here and that long range thinking should be based on this assumption.

In later months Turkish ships landed arms, ammo and food. Ten years later Turkish soldiers landed here, and the Turkish Air Force blasted the attacking Greeks out of existence. Many battles were fought between Greek and Turkish Cypriots in the surrounding area and the current truce line is not far from Kokkina. My assessments and predictions unfortunately were all correct in every detail. I suppose it was worth a pat on the back but there was a terrible price to pay in casualties.

Following the visits to the north-east of my area the MIO 'C' asked me would I be prepared to visit a particular Turkish village which was completely surrounded by hostile Greek villages, about seven in all. Although the Turks could maintain contact with other Turks it was solely on foot and across country. Access by road could be achieved from Ktima and S said that this was not possible, which was why he hadn't been. Alternatively it could be reached from my area but it meant passing through or past four Greek villages whose attitudes were unknown. I said I'd give it a whirl; I just wished I had a SLR and 36 grenades. The road out of Stavros running south-west to Ktima also passed close by and the Turks might have some information about the reported vehicular movement from Stavros; I should also find out anything on the personalities in the general area of Ktima.

I told the corporal it could be dodgy getting to this village and that the Land Rover should be in good order because if anything happened we wanted to get out fast, with no breakdowns. The roads between villages and in their confines were generally little more than extremely rough tracks and without busting springs you couldn't travel much above 5m.p.h. This was what I was worried about; we were sitting ducks. We left the main road and began the journey through the villages. It was eerie. I don't recall seeing one Greek civilian on the journey there and back, not even a dog. The villages were occupied because most houses had smoke from their chimneys, but to all intents and purposes the villages were dead, at least to us. My Sterling was cocked with the safety catch off. The track from the last Greek village to the Turkish village filled me with apprehension because it was obviously 'No Man's Land' and the ample bullet scars on the walls of Turkish houses didn't help my inner fear of a bullet in the back. Out of sight of the Greeks we entered the Turkish village and it was overflowing at the seams. It had been decided that a smaller nearby Turkish village was not well protected enough and manpower was not available so they evacuated it and made this village a veritable stronghold; the Greeks reciprocated by attacking whenever possible. When we arrived the reception was distinctly unfriendly as we were an unknown quantity, and our vehicle was surrounded by a hostile crowd of about a hundred men and youths. We stayed in the square; every house surrounding it was liberally daubed with slogans: 'TNT' (the illegal Turkish Underground Army) and many others. The corporal and I exchanged worried glances. We had nothing loose in the vehicle; I was already holding my weapon so reminded the corporal to take care of his.

Although I asked for the *mukhar* or school teacher no one appeared to make a move; it was odd and very disconcerting. Some minutes elapsed and then a group of men appeared. The youngest, a man in his late twenties, appeared to be the leader and the spokesman. He spoke excellent English and asked us to go for a coffee. I told the corporal to drive round to the café, park in front, then join us. The mention of my friends in Polis worked wonders and the smiles returned, the crowd started to disappear to their nefarious tasks and we carried on a long and very interesting talk. The general situation was thrashed out and the Greek antagonism itemised by incidents and so it went on. My newly found friend had held a Government post in a highly specialized field and when I mentioned Stavros and what I had heard and my worries, he confirmed the movement and offered help. He also showed me a distant telephone line: this was the line from Stavros, he claimed. He said if I got him the wire he would tap the line and monitor all calls for his and our benefit. Many other matters were discussed but the most important to me was the monitoring of the Stavros line and the vehicle movement, otherwise the village appeared to be self sufficient despite the circumstances. I could have offered many other avenues of help but I had to be mercenary and pay attention to factual rather than human matters. None the less we were not sorry to leave, everyone was tense.

It had all been very informative and much could be derived from it; only time would tell. We made a pretence of stopping in the squares of two of the Greek villages but no one was evident. This was done solely to eliminate any suggestion that it was only the Turks who were being visited. We were not sorry when we eventually reached the main road again and comparative safety.

Certain administrative jobs had to be done in Episkopi at the same time as I was informing the bosses of the wire tapping job; the initial reaction was mixed, which I found puzzling. We were as a Truce Force so inadequate and handicapped for methods of obtaining information that I would have thought they would have jumped at it. I suppose they were scared of the terms of the Truce Force and if found out this would have caused a great scandal in the United Nations. Even so we were illegal and operated with mild support, but with balls round our ankles. The following day I received a message telling me no way would the tap be permitted. I never returned to that village. A couple of weeks later the battle for control of Ktima began; as a result many died and more were injured. If we had been forewarned of this, many lives would have been saved by British Army intervention.

So in the mid afternoon we slowly chugged our way along the winding road between Ktima and Polis. The sun was bright and warm and all appeared at peace. We were in our area when the noise of shots were heard and it sounded ahead of us, so I cocked my Sterling and we drove slowly on. Coming over the brow of a ridge we saw an unusual sight. The shooting was coming from the high ground to our right, ahead of us on our left was a small collection of Turkish houses, and in the middle of the road, on his own, was a senior member of the Battery at Polis doing what could only be described as a ballet turn on the toe of one foot, a sort of mixture of Nureyev, a whirling Dervish and a deranged traffic policeman. I couldn't see any soldiers evident but as we stopped he dashed up to me and shouted, 'You ought to see what the bastards have done behind there,' pointing to a house. I walked round to find an elderly Turk had been shot several times in the head; he had fallen to the floor from the chair he had obviously been sitting in, possibly asleep, a very senseless murder. There was nothing I could do. The local Turks had gone off to trace the culprits to the Greek village of Steni. This had caused the shooting and the soldiers were trying to calm matters down. The senior was not helping by having hysterics. It all aroused the baser instincts of my corporal, who had not seen a dead body before. He walked round full of spirit, but he was close to vomiting and was extremely quiet for the remainder of the journey to Polis.

My corporal, like myself, was older than his contemporaries and I expected more help from him. He had this bug about the language and as a result he failed to gather information, and he was rather short tempered, almost getting into physical confrontation at Greek roadblocks which drew attention to us and risked our lives. Basically he was a good chap and a more than adequate driver, but he sadly lacked imagination in this sort of situation. The matter came to a head when we were on our way to the Stavros area. We quickly toured round Polis and picked up a mobile tail who followed us to the Greek village of Argaca then left us, satisfied that we were on our way to Stavros and he could inform them. As we slowly drove along the winding road I saw ahead two figures who were unaware that we were behind. One was the elderly road maintenance man whom we had seen before, the other younger man was armed with a rifle and a bandolier. The road went to our left in a wide sweep so we came up to them from round the bend, unheard, to within fifty yards of them. The young man turned round at the sound of the Rover, expecting to see a familiar forestry vehicle. When he saw who it was he unslung his rifle and leapt down an almost perpendicular slope to the bottom of a dried up stream bed full of low scrub.

I left the Rover before it stopped and followed the Greek, frightening myself to death as I didn't realize how steep it was. In a shower of loose rocks and dust I ended eventually in the stream bed. Nothing was moving. I was standing there like Wyatt Earp, legs apart, gasping for breath, pistol pointing in the general direction the Greek had gone. To my right was a high wooded feature, so if the bloke opened fire and missed I had a 50-50 chance. If he tried to go up the high ground, my corporal really shouldn't miss from his vantage point up above. To my astonishment as I glanced above the corporal wasn't even looking down at us; his attention was to his weapon and he was looking at it from all angles completely oblivious of the drama below. I was standing there, scared to make the wrong move and the armed bloke could have been five or forty feet from me levelling his rifle at my guts for all I knew. I dared not make the wrong move and I couldn't fire first. Another glance showed my companion vainly trying to cock his weapon and getting annoyed. I was more frustrated so I knelt down and yelled advice and some obscenities at him and at the same time the Greek moved. He must have realized my position; he could see my driver could not hurt him so he took off and I have never seen a person move up a steep slope like he did. Granted he was probably scared, but he excelled any goat and in seconds had disappeared from sight and out of range. I climbed out of the little ravine, snatched the Sterling from the corporal, *took the safety catch off safe*, cocked it and threw it back at him in disgust. That was the straw that broke the camel's back, and I strongly protested to John Althorp so a couple of days later he was replaced by the lance corporal who with S had left Ktima. The lance corporal lasted a fortnight; he wasn't interested in Intelligence, but he thought he was a great racing driver and proceeded to show me how it was done and I could do without that. He was eventually replaced by young Campbell, who was interested in just being involved; he was a good lad.

We went back to Yialia, and as time went by more people used to come and sit with us to talk and it was purely a chance remark I overheard which aroused my curiosity. I asked for amplification and clarification and it transpired that some three years earlier and for a time period of 12-18 months or even more, Greek waggons had used the Yialia road to transport ballast from the beach and take it to the Stavros area but they could not say what it was used for. I was excited but didn't show it. I patiently extracted the details about the frequencies of truck journeys, capacity, and so on, and found that the quantity moved *could have been* in excess of 20,000 tons! Where the hell had all that gone? Possibly some had been used as bases for the 'barrack' blocks or the bungalows or even roads but what had the remainder been used for?

The MIO C, John Althorp, and I talked it over, and I believe two separate Canberra flights were made and photos taken. The Photographic Interpreters (PI) said that nothing was evident. I presumed they flew over the right area but I later proved them wrong – but more as the story goes on.

It was about that time that an additional boss came into my life, a gentleman we shall call Major A. He worked from HQ Cyprus District and when appointed as G2 (Int) he asked for all field reports as well as unit Intreps (Intelligence Reports). Apparently my reports were the only ones that were regular, made sense, and were productive, from anywhere on the island. Especially when comments were made on Raftis, Mansoura and the wire tap, he wanted to see me personally. Security was tight, but I had been given a special pass available for any time. I was eventually taken to his office. He introduced himself and asked me how the devil I managed to get such a vast amount of information. I told him partly the truth, but admitted to buying the odd bottle of brandy to socialize at the school in Polis and other villages. He asked where I got the money from to pay for food and booze, and I said from my own pocket as 40 Int. Platoon had no fund. He immediately took two £5 notes from his desk and handed them over. A couple of weeks later he gave me a further £5 and that's all I got for five months of cultivating informants, so I still paid for most of it myself, a good civil servant!

He said he couldn't introduce me to the MI5 individual but another Major would like a word and this he did, briefing me on different aspects of the situation which were causing concern and the areas I should now try to concentrate on. I had another brief chat to Major A when he emphasised I should not be held back by boundaries, I was free to wander at will if it was worth it; just try and keep in touch from the base at Polis. As I left the office, a figure appeared from along the corridor. He called my attention and asked who I was, so I told him. As he was in civilian clothes I gathered he was the MI5 person and I was right. He then began a five minute lecture which involved my reports, their contents, how I was getting the information and what risks I was obviously taking. He warned me that if anything happen to me the reverberations would be felt in London, Washington and the United Nations in New York, I was to be very circumspect in my dealings with individuals (meaning Raftis and the Turks) and be doubly careful about personal protection. Then, having torn me off a strip about my previous activities like a schoolmaster to a 1st form pupil, he suddenly put his arm round my shoulders (I thought he was going to kiss me), gave a broad smile and whispered, 'But carry on, you're doing a fine job,' then he walked away.

I stood for a moment completely perplexed. One minute the governments of the world were about to descend on me if things went wrong, next minute I had to ignore them and carry on as before. It's great to pull the strings from behind a desk but I never had the opportunity. I always had to be involved otherwise I felt I was outside it all.

The days passed, highlighted as I remember by a most spectacular storm which stayed in the Polis area for approximately twelve hours. It seemed to go round in circles from the high ground surrounding the area, out to sea and back again. For an incredible twelve hours we had rain, wind, the continuous noise of thunder and outstandingly prolonged flashes of lightning. I've seen storms, typhoons and monsoons but not one like that. We took a night off and stayed in the dry. By now, some weeks later, we had been given camp beds and a WRAC Captain had finally been persuaded to hand in two sleeping bags she had acquired, so at least we were more comfortable but we had no amenities. I think I saw three films the whole time in Cyprus and we had no radio, but we were usually ready for bed and rose early so our days were full.

During a conversation one evening when the brandy was flowing, my two Turkish friends confirmed with me that I had been to a particular village and that it was surrounded by a number of rather unfriendly Greek villages. I told them that I had been there or in the area several times, when I was watching Raftis. The two Turks came straight to the point. They had to get there tomorrow and unseen, would I be prepared to take them? Doing something like this, especially if it went wrong, would really put the cat among the pigeons because civilians were not allowed in military vehicles, unless it was an emergency. Although we were often stopped at roadblocks by accident or design our vehicle was never searched and with the aid of a tarpaulin and the spare wheel we could hide them from general view (I hoped). On the bonus side I would be doing them a great favour, not that they didn't owe me already for things done, and I had plans of my own that they might be helpful with: you scratch my back and I'll scratch yours. In fairness to my driver I left him behind, and I picked them up at the school quite openly, disappeared in the wrong direction, stopped the Rover and adjusted the tarpaulin with certain ingenuity, then proceeded through the centre of Polis and then passed several 'naughty' places until eventually, without any hindrance, we arrived at the village. The reception was rapturous and with about twenty of the senior elders the meeting commenced. Occasionally I was given a resumé of a particular topic, presumably concerning British interests only, otherwise I was completely in the dark about what was discussed and they meant to keep it that way. Fair enough, I was only the driver.

On our previous visit the corporal had entered one of his usual inane language exchange conversations with the village idiot or 'brewer of vile and noxious fluids' (known as Cyprus whisky) and he had presented the corporal with a bottle complete with paper cork. It tasted awful, even the corporal refused to drink it, but occasionally out of desperation I would have a drink when I was writing my report in the evening, but not by choice.

Within five minutes of the meeting getting under way, enter the village idiot with special bottle. It was offered only to the *muhktar* and two elders, my two friends and me; they did not accept a second glass. To my dismay I found that my glass, which I placed on the floor by my chair, never seemed to decrease in its contents. It was only when I turned round that I saw Nature Boy sitting behind my chair, his face wreathed in smiles, with bottle poised, then I realized I was being 'fixed'. After some three hours or so we left amidst great excitement and countless handshakes. I was in a state of suspended euphoria, my brain was quite clear, very sharp in fact, but my limbs felt as though they would fly away. As I drove away I couldn't have cared less if I had been ambushed by the whole of the Greek National Guard. Then to another village and a much shorter meeting. I later returned them to the school. Tired, hungry and undergoing slight alcoholic remorse, I wrote out my daily report. All in all a profitable day, but my superiors were not aware of my actions. As long as they received good stuff they were happy, so I lied, or rather I didn't fully explain how it was obtained.

In April, if I remember correctly, the Truce Force became *bona fide* members of the United Nations peace keeping force in Cyprus. I thought that would let us out but we carried on and were even issued with blue beret, scarves, arm bands etc. which I didn't wear initially. I was not sure how it should be played. Then we had visitors, the advance party of the Swedish UN Troops, who were destined to take over eventually from 26 Regt. The party consisted of a Captain and two drivers, whom I never saw, a Warrant Officer, Staff Sergeant and Sergeant, who bunked down in the same house as me. The Staff Sergeant was a Regular, the Sergeant a deep sea diver, and the Warrant Officer a Professor of English and Religious Studies at Uppsala University and he was a very shrewd operator. He had quietly watched over several days my avoidance of contact with the Gunners, the daily and nocturnal wanderings, my general autonomy of authority and movements, and he was curious. One evening he sat on the steps of the bungalow with me, with a bottle between us, and told me he was not satisfied that I was solely involved in the welfare of the indigenous population. I admitted nothing, but he knew, and despite all my humorous backchat and nonchalance he was not convinced; he accepted it all with good grace and we became good friends. He invited me and the family to visit Sweden and be his guests which we almost did in 1965 prior to Borneo.

As a show of friendship the senior ranks of the Battery invited the three Swedes and myself to drinks one evening and what a shambles it turned out to be. A small block of offices now held the Stores and the Sergeants Mess and as the Swedes and I entered the Mess we were confronted by the BQMS, sprawled in a chair almost unconscious with wine trickling out of the corner of his mouth and holding the remains of a skin of local wine in his lap (you would pay about a shilling for two quarts of red vin ordinaire). The other members arrived and the drinks began to flow. Initially the conversation was healthy and full of mutual curiosity and sense. The problems began when a by now drunken Irishman fancied his chances with the Swedish deep sea diver (who had also done some boxing). This prompted his friend but ethnic enemy a Scotsman to offer himself first. In between all the talk I quickly extricated the Swedes and rather embarrassedly apologised for the antics of my countrymen, but they thought it was all hilarious and I think secretly they would have enjoyed the physical confrontation. I believe the BSM later apologised for his members' disgusting manners.

So now came the climax and it all happened over a period of four or five days. I had got to the stage when a decision had to be made for a formal introduction to the Turkish Underground Movement. I had helped, so I wanted my slice of the cake. My two friends were not fully aware (I don't think). of my far reaching plans so a letter was written and signed, and early one morning Campbell and I with the blessing of the Intelligence authorities made our way to Lefka and a particular building. Entering the rather large, wholly Turkish town of Lefka our reception was mixed; no hostility but they were not sure as to the probable actions of the British Government therefore there was suspicion. Arriving at the specific building I was greatly aware of hundreds of eyes on me. I began to feel apprehensive and rather fearful: I had really jumped into the frying pan this time. A RAEC Major who spoke Greek and Turkish and his driver had disappeared somewhere in this general area. I presume he was attempting to do the same as I. He had the languages but not enough animal cunning and intelligence to know when to back out at the right moment. Their bodies were later found at the bottom of a well; which side did the murder has never been ascertained to my knowledge. I now thought very hard about this but I couldn't back out now. I told Campbell to stay with the vehicle, and to leave his Sterling cocked but on safe, and I entered the building. Immediately two men who had obviously been watching came either side of me and prevented further movement; both were armed. I asked for someone who spoke English, I had a message and I wished to speak with Mr X. A man came down the nearby set of stairs and in English asked me what I wanted here.

I then became really worried. Suppose this bloke did not fully understand what I said, plus the fact that I had driven directly to the HQ of TNT could be thought highly suspicious and worthy of instant liquidation. Rather hurriedly I mentioned my two friends' names and that I had a letter for Mr X. A smile came to his lips and he told me to follow him upstairs. The wide and dimly lit corridor was packed with armed men in a miscellany of dress, some of it British military. Suddenly I was confronted by two rather bulky characters who were evil looking in the extreme. These were the hard men, the personal bodyguard type. One tapped me on the chest and said, 'Hey you, pistol,' meaning that I should hand it over. My confidence returning and to show face although I was scared, I told him 'to get stuffed' and tried to walk into the office my escort had entered. Hands, arms and legs were all about to go into action between us in the space of a couple of seconds and then everything died a death; a man appeared at the office door and all the Turks in some way appeared to stand to attention: obviously the managing director.

Greetings were exchanged and I clarified his name, explaining who I was, and handed the letter to him. He read it slowly, looked at me, smiled, turned round and spoke rapid orders in Turkish to whoever was in his office, put his arm round my shoulders and said, 'Come on, let's have a cup of coffee.' As we walked along the packed corridor, all was smiles, and I was even clapped on the back but what an evil bunch of characters they were. We went outside and I called to Campbell to join us and Mr X agreed. We entered a small café and our meeting began. I explained certain matters to him and it obviously cleared the air. On the basis of the letter of introduction I was accepted as a friend and could be trusted. He then explained aspects of Turkish Cypriotism and Turkey's current policy on Cyprus, and I realized that I was really in the big league, up to my neck, for as long as I could keep my head on top of it. Campbell was listening to all this with his mouth open. It was all hard to believe that two rather small cogs in a large machine had managed to pull this sort of thing off. Our newly found friend made a proposition. He was prepared or his organization was, to carry out certain actions for us, providing we (the British Government) were prepared to reciprocate in a manner he described. We went through the details more slowly, attempting to clarify certain points that I shouldn't forget. I could hardly write them down on paper and a café was not the place. It was rather mind boggling at the time and I could feel the excitement at the prospects, what a coup! Suddenly our friend grabbed my right wrist in a very strong grip, his cheerful face was now extremely serious, and his words were something like this:

'Understand this, my friend, I will not deal with diplomats or the military, you are the only person I will speak with, talk with whom you like to get the answers, then you come back here personally and give me the decision. You will be safe, but I only want to see you whom I can trust.'

With that the meeting came to an end and we said our goodbyes. We slowly made our way out of Lefka, rather stunned by it all. I had never quite expected this. I grabbed the map and told Campbell to head for Nicosia and the British High Commission. As we arrived there certain offices were being moved, so I told a particular gentleman what had transpired and he got quite excited and said I should get it down in writing soonest and that I did sitting on a stool, writing on my knee, all alone in an empty garage under one of the Commission's buildings; nothing James Bond about this rubbish.

Mission accomplished, Campbell and I drove back towards Polis. We talked incessantly about the day's ramifications and felt good. Campbell was quite mesmerised by it all which was understandable, he was only just turned nineteen years. We had passed through Xeros about five miles back and were approaching a very sharp bend to our left when a civilian car came out of the bend across our front. Campbell stopped immediately. The driver of the car, an Englishwoman, was way over the white line and scraped the side of her car on the front bumper of the Rover, which did us no damage. I left Campbell to get on with his accident report. A few minutes later he returned and said everything was in order, but it wasn't, as we later found out; he had omitted details of her car insurance and many other things. It was his first accident report and he made a right mess of it.

The following morning a helicopter was sent for me: and took me to Episkopi, a car delivered me to HQ and I hardly looked presentable. My boots were not particularly clean and were well scuffed with climbing over rocks; my one pair of combat trousers was diabolical, dirt, mud, grease, oil were in evidence, my shirt was clean but unironed, and my jersey could have smelled sweeter. In this state and without warning I was ushered into a large conference room to be faced with a gathering resembling the Army Council.

I was shown a hard backed chair which was placed in a wide open space. Facing me in an inverted U shape were twelve senior officers and the top table held Major A, someone with 'Red Tabs' as I remember, who could have been the General, the MI5/6 chap and his deputy. The conference was chaired by 'James Bond'. After the preliminaries, I was asked to explain what exactly had happened the previous day. I again did not explain how I had finally managed the letter of introduction, but faithfully reported precisely what had happened and the gist of the conversation; you could have heard a pin drop. As I finished the 'Brains Trust' really went to town; I had really captured their imagination. Order was called, and MI5/6 said: 'Don't get excited, gentlemen, most of what they are offering I could get by myself anyway and at any time.'

For a moment there was a stunned silence and like a pack of wolves the army officers went. for him. Remarks like 'Don't you know what's needed?' 'Have we been risking our lives for nothing over the past six months?' etc., etc., etc. I sat there all alone feeling as if it was the trial of the Stuarts, amused and somewhat bemused at the exhibition before me.

Sometime later MI5/6 asked me if I was prepared to go back. I said yes. But I would not be taking an answer because London would have to be consulted. In the meantime I must go back and see what else I could learn but say nothing. Someone then said, wasn't it too risky for me putting my head back in the lion's mouth, when it had not been fed. Any suspicions that they were being conned at all would result in my immediate demise. MI5/6 said all he wanted me to do was to play the 'Dumb Idiot' and say nothing definite, just maintain the contact and keep things warm until a decision was made. I was asked again if I would go and I said yes, because Mr X had given his word I would be safe as long as I could be trusted, so there was to be no con job. I was assured of this, and told to return to Lefka the following day and keep the pot boiling.

Back at the Mess I was enjoying the luxury of a pre lunch perusal of a newspaper – I hadn't seen one in weeks – when the phone rang and someone yelled my name. I picked the phone up and stated who I was. The voice at the other end did not identify itself but stated, 'Reference the place you have been told to visit tomorrow, on no account must you go there, understand?' then rang off. I was enjoying my sweet in the company of Pat when the phone rang and again my name was called. It was Jeff Hall-Roberts, one of our blokes who worked in the complex at HQ. He had been told to contact me and briefly amplify the rather terse warning call. In fact all he told me was that information had been received (from whom?) that on no account must I return to Lefka. It was vaguely hinted at that I was for the 'chop' if apprehended, but nothing was specific and I could appreciate Jeff's position: someone else had given him the dirty end of the stick. I was most perplexed. But I was adamant that I must see my friends at the School again and sound them out, and try and clear away any suspicions.

It was also going to be necessary to return to the Lefka area despite the warning, because when Campbell had had the accident and failed to complete the accident form correctly, he had been told that now we were officially members of the United Nations it was imperative that all information was obtained or else. So after a chat and for his sake, we decided to go to Lefka the following morning and early. As I remember I think the woman and her husband, a local copper mine official, lived in a village called Petra which lay to the east of Lefka. A convenient access road ran through the northern outskirts of Lefka: that would be the dodgy part. Full of apprehension, the journey was made and the bungalow located but the woman was out. To cut a long story short it was eventually all sorted out but lasted ages after my return to Germany. Now it was back to Polis soonest and fingers crossed, but it didn't happen that way. We had passed through Kato Pyrgos when we could hear the sound of shooting to the south. This Greek village appeared to be tense, you could feel it as we slowly drove through. Intermittent firing could be heard as we passed through Mansoura and Kokkina. My acquaintances were not in evidence; only old men appeared to be on the streets and in the cafés; again you could feel the tenseness in the air.

As we began the approach to Pomos Point the firing was extremely heavy and included automatic weapons. It was only when I told Campbell to stop and looked to my left, that there on the reverse slope of the high ground were dozens of Turks firing their heads off, presumably at Greeks who were advancing into Turkish owned land. This was the first day I had actually carried with me my United Nations 'Blue Bonnet' and I had it in my epaulette for effect. Obviously observed by the Turks and identified, I quickly made my way to the top of the ridge, leaving Campbell with the truck. I lay alongside a Turk and asked him what had happened and he described how the obviously planned attack had started and that the Turks were being attacked in several sections of this area that was so important to them. I then thought that if the Greeks saw the UN beret they might cease firing and negotiations could start, so I put the beret on my head and slowly looked round a convenient rock. I was exposed. The shot was three inches away from my head and my eyes and mouth were filled with dust and bits of rock. No peace pipe here, mate, this really was for real. I ducked and said a mouthful of contemporary lyrics and none of them complimentary to Greeks. I yelled to the Turks that I would go round the

Point and see what could be done with the opposing forces. Let's face it, all that could be done would be verbal. We turned the bend on the Point and there, tucked away in some dead ground alongside the road, was a British Ferret armoured car belonging to the Royal Dragoon Guards (Royals). Further west from our position some 200 yards away was a vital bridge over the Livadhi River. The sergeant in the armoured car said he had contacted his control about the shooting but had not been able to ascertain any facts from the Greeks, who obviously did not want to talk. We were 'Piggy in the Middle' again but nearer the Greek lines. The crack and thump of bullets was uncomfortably close above our heads. I said I would keep him company in case we had to abandon the Rover and use the armoured car. Near the bridge was a small collection of houses. To my interest what should arrive there but the armoured truck/bus that had been under preparation in Polis. It was possible it had brought ammunitions and some personnel.

The arrival was shortly followed by the 'Lone Ranger' or the BC who raced up to our position at a high rate of knots, I was lying behind cover trying to see where the two opposing sides were situated. When I turned round and he recognised me he damned near had apoplexy.

'Oh no, not you again, do you start these bloody battles!'

He ranted on. He ordered the sergeant to leave, who refused and the BC went purple, but calmed down when the sergeant explained that his CO had told him to remain *in situ* until told to move. He then glared at me and growled that he would see what he could do. As he crossed the bridge the Greek armoured truck lumbered its way forward to the bridge and blocked any further movement west. We were practically trapped on the fringes of a bitter battle and had neither the personnel or equipment to initiate a Cease Fire and subsequent disposal of the opposing forces. We could only play events 'off the cuff' and hope we didn't become casualties.

Suddenly round the corner of the Point came a half crouching running figure. His arms were wrapped round his midriff and his loud moans indicated he had been injured. As he staggered towards us on the road verge there was a tremendous outburst of fire which hit the verge and the road near the injured man (later known to be Greek). He fell down but I suspect mainly due to fright and shock. I yelled, 'Cover me!' and ran to the injured man. It was a stupid thing to say because Campbell could do nothing with a Sterling and the armoured car could not be placed in a firing position and so was ineffective. As I broke cover for the fifty-yard dash to the man quite a few individual shots were fired at me which hit the verge or ricocheted off the roadway but I reached him unscathed. I was then treated to a prolonged burst of automatic fire which had me making indecent postures on the earth verge and praying to God. It was obvious I had fallen just outside the firing line (again, just like Palestine). The Greek was sobbing quietly, face in the dirt. A quick look at him showed that his original injury had shattered his left forearm but it was not serious, his shirt and trousers had been holed with ricochets from the burst of fire, but he was mainly in shock. I got him to his feet and whether he understood or not told him in English we were going to make a dash for safety. The fifty-yard gap which appeared to be open to the Turkish fire seemed like a mile as we set off. Immediately, there were single shots at us, luckily no automatic fire or we wouldn't have made it, then damn me if he didn't fall down and didn't appear to have the will to get up. I was twitching with fear and some annoyance, the occasional bullet hitting the ground around us certainly not helping matters. Standing there in full view of the Turkish Forces who obviously were unaware of my status and nationality (my blue beret was back in the Rover), I thought, 'Sod him,' grabbed him by his injured arm and the back of his shirt and half lifted and dragged him towards safety.

More shots, still OK. Campbell and then the Royals Sergeant dashed towards us to bring us in. The Greek was given first aid and pointed in the direction of the bridge, I don't recall he even thanked us. In fact later another injured Greek appeared and Campbell guided him from the edge of the fifty yard gap, keeping him close to the high roadside bank.

The afternoon was passing and the battle above us continued. The Sergeant and I decided a picnic was indicated, so we brewed up and ate cheese and 'hard tack', joked and smoked cigarettes. It was an incongruous situation, but typically British Army: we just adapted ourselves and it kept our morale up.

Suddenly there was the sound of heavy vehicles, and round the corner of the Point came the 'Seventh Cavalry', a Ferret armoured car and an 'Armoured Pig' of my old friends 9 Para Squadron RE all jollied up in UNO colours and flags, and with them the Indian Deputy Commander of the UN Peace Force plus vehicles and entourage. Leaving the Sergeant and his vehicle as they were, Campbell and I returned to Kokkina to see if we could help in the talks between the Turks and UN Forces. Some Greeks had been brought in the convoy from Nicosia and it was evident that at this stage the Turks were being blamed. I briefly explained to the big blond Irish Sapper Captain what had happened to us but not where we had been, and to escape from more detailed questioning we headed back to Polis. We waved affectionately to our Royals friends as we passed and crossed the bridge; the armoured vehicle was no doubt hidden behind the houses. As we lay on our beds that night I was reading, but noticed Campbell was gazing at the ceiling, I asked him if there was anything wrong. He sat up and with a strange look on his face said:

'You know, I suddenly realized I matured today. I often wondered what it would be like to be a soldier under fire. When the Greek fell, only you reacted; we were mesmerized as we watched the bullets hitting all round you, then we both felt responsible and did something. I've seen people injured by bullets and for about five hours we were fired at or above us and to top it all when you and the Royals Sergeant started the picnic, you seemed so unperturbed, it was sort of infectious, and I lost any fear and apprehension. I knew we could cope until help arrived. Thanks for today.' He then turned over and went to sleep and I felt a glow of satisfaction. I had obviously set some sort of example to a person I thought to be an excellent young soldier and isn't that what it is all about, setting examples to others? I met Campbell very briefly in Borneo when he had taken over as FIO at Serian. I think he was only there for two or three months. We watched some casualties being flown in by 'chopper', discussed our business and I left. I hope he made himself a successful future.

The following morning I decided that with the problems at Kokkina and Paky Ammos the Greeks might be over committed and it might not be a bad idea to have a slower look around Stavros, from the south side this time. If my assessment was wrong and we got trapped up there we would have problems and probably have to shoot our way out of it, especially in the current climate. We pushed through the village of Argaca without any apparent notice. It was from this place that we were casually followed or telephone calls were made to Stavros, but this time the place appeared deserted. We wound our way without interruption to the western end of the Stavros valley. It was quiet and very still with only the occasional call of a bird. We sat there a while because I half expected to hear and see some vehicular movement. Satisfied, we pushed off up the track, took the diversionary track which would take us on the south side, and while Campbell paid his attention to driving I observed the view to the north. We stopped to look through the binoculars a couple of times but drew a blank. We stopped for the third time and could hear the unmistakable sounds of bulldozers and other heavy plant equipment above and to the south of us. Other nearby evidence showed that a new track extension was being made some distance away but we thought it unsafe to leave either one on his own while the other located the new work. Then I struck lucky and I happened to be in exactly the right place because either side was hidden by trees. I swept the valley with my glasses arc. There it was, directly across from me.

From the approximate area of the brick telephone exchange a side track

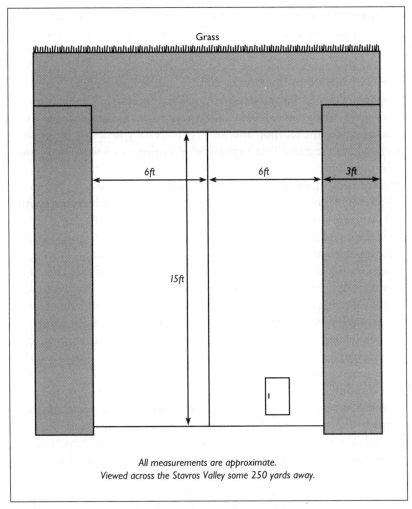

Grass

6ft   6ft   3ft

15ft

All measurements are approximate.
Viewed across the Stavros Valley some 250 yards away.

Sketch of the entrance to the underground tunnel/storehouse at Stavros as viewed from the south.

led up the steep north side of the valley to the five bungalows I had seen up there. However from my present perch I could see the track widened out a few hundred yards from the exchange and well before the bungalows, an area was available for a large truck to turn round comfortably. Set into the hillside was a large 'metal' double door, one door having a pedestrian entrance, the whole supported by two concrete columns. This entrance had been covered by soil and grassed; this was so obvious because the grass was an extremely healthy green which was unusual in that area. I had found a very large subterranean, man made tunnel/cavern/store etc., and there was now no doubt where much of that ballast had been used. The problems obviously encountered when the turnaround was constructed for vehicular access must have been considerable and so it all must have been worthwhile to the Greeks and no doubt the result of long term planning. The conclusion was that this was 'the' storage cupboard for all the illegal Greek arms or maybe only one of many. Campbell made a very good sketch of the location and we were both delighted. The intuition of the bloke 'on the ground' or 'in the field' as Intelligence terms it had proved right once again. As we said later how on earth had PI missed it on two separate runs: the grass and the turnaround were giveaways even to the naked eye; so much for science. We left soonest in case we had been spotted and our escape routes sealed off.

At the top of the valley I decided not to take a chance on our usual route back via Yialia in case we were stopped, so we went north following the River Livadhi which would bring us out near the point of the battle of the previous day, only we would be to the west of the ridge. We were happy and in no particular hurry; the sun was shining and we were about a mile away from the village of Livadhi when we took a very sharp left hand bend and nearly died on the spot. Some one hundred yards ahead the road again turned sharply to the right. In about two hundred yards of roadway and on the adjacent ground, were two hundred or more Greek irregular troops, with camouflaged vehicles, mortars and heavy machine guns. Everyone appeared to have a modern weapon. Campbell's immediate reaction was to stop so I quietly screamed at him, 'For God's sake don't stop, but drive slowly.' I followed this with invective which would have had me excommunicated. Talk about Daniel in the lion's den, what bloody awful luck or was it intuition?

These men were dressed in a miscellany of Police, British Army and shepherd's clothing and looked very aggressive. Legs were stretched out onto the track as the men rested and were very reluctantly withdrawn as we slowly approached. Campbell, white faced and no doubt terrified, paid more attention to avoiding Greek legs and therefore having to stop. I, just as apprehensive, decided on the friendly, Royal approach, having had a good background in this as a Guardsman, and so with Regal aplomb I smiled and waved with one hand giving the thumbs up sign and mouthing English obscenities to keep my spirits up. I also informed Campbell of my inner feelings and threatened him with castration if we stopped. It made him grin and he copied my actions.

The expressions on their faces were incredible. They could not believe the British Army had found them in this godforsaken place. Some lay there, others stood up, some looked aggressive and weapons were raised but not a shot was fired. As we turned sharp right, to our left from under a large camouflage net tied to a 3-ton truck, came half a dozen seniors, at least one of whom could have been wearing the regular Greek Army Officer's summer uniform. They too stood open mouthed and rigid, too amazed to issue any orders. Some fifty yards or so past the corner the troops began to thin out and still no orders were passed. Then we heard shouts and screams. Campbell by this time was increasing speed and when the shouting started, without turning I waved goodbye with a 'Harvey Smith'. We were soon out of sight and clogging it as fast as possible. The odds were too great; my fingers were white through tension, my Sterling was cocked and on automatic and I had pressed the trigger guard so tightly from tension and to avoid an accidental discharge in definitely the wrong place, but we were not out of the wood yet.

We were within a hundred yards or so of the main road when a rather familiar Land Rover came off the main road going like the clappers with four or five men on board. Seeing our dust coming down the track they pulled into the side to give me exit. About twenty yards away from them I saw who they were and nearly had kittens, and they also recognised me. It was George Raftis, obviously on his way to his men. All of them in the Land Rover, like a cluster of black dolls, rose from their sitting positions and hung there, suspended. I had the advantage as I was moving fast and downhill. I screamed at Campbell and his foot went down, the grit shot everywhere and the dust rose like a smokescreen. My last view of George 'Spirou' Raftis was of a dust-shrouded figure frantically beckoning me to return to him and with Campbell very adequately doing a Stirling Moss at 70m.p.h. we left them all to it, just happy to have got through it all with a whole skin. It was all quite a hoot and God dictated we were two lucky men not to have been caught and possibly shot.

We returned to Polis and passed on our urgent information to Episkopi and the BC. The following morning we were told not to go away from our location and a later message told us to pack up and leave for Episkopi. We had to leave our Rover with 26 Regt. at Ktima and we would be picked up by S and so it all ended very abruptly and with no warning, I suppose in retrospect it was the best way; we worked till the bitter end. Our latest news was apparently welcomed and applauded but no one said anything to us, no one was interested.

For a day and a half I did nothing, just lay in the sun; it was my first day off in five months. Just before lunch on the second day we were told to leave for Nicosia. Major A came out of his room and said we had been helpful; I believe he received an MBE for all his help. We handed our vehicle in at the UN base area at Polemidhia, said goodbye to an officer and a gentleman, Major C, the MIO. It was strange: as Major C was wishing me a personal goodbye a REME Captain passed by and spoke to Major C about a book he had borrowed. The Captain immediately recognised me, he was one of my Cadets from Mons: what a small world.

At RAF Nicosia we were documented, bedded down, did some quick shopping to keep the peace, and had a meal. S went to see a friend; Pat and I went to the Mess where I was hoping to have some pleasant relaxation with Pat, but he decided to play whist. So there was I all alone at the bar with a double brandy when through the doorway of the French windows came a mountain of a man (he was the Officers Mess Steward) followed into the Mess by two characters who could hardly stand up, they were so drunk. He sat them at the bar with tomato juice and sat next to me, introduced himself and asked who I was. This over with, he explained he was an ex Irish Guardsman, Imperial Services heavyweight champion pre-war for three years, wartime Commando, parachutist, self educated and reader of the classics; he was quiet, charming well mannered and the women adored him. He was also the hardest drinking man I have ever met. Since 11a.m. that morning he and his two disreputable companions had been on their weekly drunken spree, and they were gibbering.

In the space of an hour and a half he had bought four rounds to my one, of a double, double vodka for himself and a double double brandy for me. *There were no arguments.* I climbed down from the bar to go to the toilet and on my return saw that John McMullen, one of our chaps with the Para Brigade, plus another 'ACORN' and a RAF chap were sitting at a table behind me; we had provisionally arranged to meet.

'Why didn't you tell me you were here?' I asked.

'And get mixed up with that Irish monster, not likely, no male in this Mess will go near him, he is deadly.'

Very diplomatically I made my excuses and joined Mac and Co.

Before he left us the other 'ACORN' told us he was working in Wales and had gone home to Newcastle on leave. He was recalled, presumably because he had served in Cyprus before, sent to the Pay Depot at Worthy Down and shipped by air to Nicosia. On arrival all passengers were met and removed, but he was left on his own. Movements tried HQ 3 Division, CI Company etc, but no one knew of him so he bedded down with friends in P and SS (Provost and Security Section), RAF Nicosia. He stayed with them for a week making daily enquiries about himself but no one wanted to know, so he made himself useful with P and SS. After a week HQ 3 Division acknowledged he was theirs, but they couldn't employ him, so they suggested he stay where he was. He had been arrested three times by troops in Nicosia because he could not state an Army Unit who could vouch for him; now he was just happy someone would remember to put him on a plane back to UK!

Mac, the RAF chap, and I later had a most enjoyable meal in a tin shack on the slope of the old walled city with white wine. About 2a.m. I fell in a deep sound sleep, at 4.30a.m. we were awakened and at half past five we were ready for take off. Then the pilot came out and refused to take us all; the vehicles were loaded and had to go plus drivers, but we and some injured Paras were to be left behind to accommodate some RAF types on indulgence passes. The arguments between senior officers was tremendous and very amusing to hear. I was still suffering from the euphoria of alcoholic remorse; I was tired but not ill. The pilot eventually agreed to just one Army type who had urgent reasons to leave, John Althorp then stepped in and I was the one who *had* to go, but again I was never told why. It ended amicably and we all climbed aboard. The aircraft, a Para-carrying Argosy, was fitted with net hammocks, not seats, and at long last we left the runway. As we moved over my old stamping grounds at Polis the aircraft turned round and returned to Nicosia, then it took off again, did a circle and landed yet again. We left the aircraft and returned to it again and then we finally made it. Everyone was worried sick except me. I was not with it, all I required was sleep.

Our first calling place was El Aden in Libya; the hot sun was not good for my eyes but I enjoyed some iced orangeade. Next stop was Malta where we were to stay the night, and after a meal Pat, S and I decided to walk from the airfield to Valetta. We didn't realize it was so far but the exercise did us good. I was not impressed by Valetta and we decided to look at the renowned 'Gut', a long sloping street of bars and brothels. The absence of the Royal Navy and the American 6th Fleet failed to raise any interest in this tourist attraction. The only thing to amuse us was the unprovoked attack on Pat, who is barely 5'2", by a huge-bosomed female who descended the steps from her bar, picked Pat up under his arms to breast level then crushed him in a bear hug, expressing her love for him. When released, Pat was too stunned to get annoyed so we quickly led him away for a warm and unpalatable beer. He later saw the funny side of it.

S and I were hysterical as Pat was not that type of bloke. Our visit to Valetta lasted less than an hour; we took a taxi back and I slept like a babe.

Next morning we flew to France and it was quite a rough flight, but made up by an excellent meal at the French Air Force Station. On arrival at the UK airfield I rang a telegram to Jean to say I had arrived in UK. We all met in London and though we returned on separate flights we all arrived back in Germany on the same day, to be a family once again.

If one had to look back to Cyprus and outline comment and lessons learned it would be something like this:

a) It was outstandingly obvious that for six years the SIS and Army Intelligence had allowed a large gap to exist in our Intelligence process on the island of Cyprus and the events that occurred, though always known to be possible, were not expected, and contingency plans for UK reinforcement in this particular type of role was not catered for. In other words from the very top downwards, planning, AQ were rather shambolic with no one apparently knowing what the situation demanded. In time, and as per usual, it got into the right gear, but if blame were to be allocated, as any good Commander knows, he requires advance intelligence of the enemy's possible intentions. If people would argue that this was known and reported, it was certainly very evident that it was not correctly acted upon.

b) It was an unmitigated disaster to send a UK based Gunner unit, who for some time had been based in an experimental Gunnery School in an instructional capacity, to fulfil an infantry role under active service conditions. It was grossly unfair to all personnel; despite my comments on individuals, it is extremely difficult to change roles. Three of our small gang could not adapt. The antics of one particular Gunner Officer promoted from a 2nd Lieutenant at a Boys Unit to a Captain and a G(3)Int's job is not on. I did hear one Officer who shall be nameless put up on his wall the Fantasian (the British Army's 'mythical' enemy) Mechanized Division Order of Battle Chart to guide him, how pathetic. However, now in Ulster, Gunner units do receive training in the infantry role and this is no bad thing; they do a worthwhile job over there. I only hope the general standard of their officers and senior NCOs improves accordingly, because in my experience in various theatres the Royal Artillery is the worst officered Corps in the Army, not necessarily in their Gunner role, but as good Regimental officers and gentlemen.

c) What should I say about our little group? It is possibly indicative that in the end I was the only operational field operator working effectively on the Island; how long I would have lasted is open to debate. I still believe with the Turks it was a misunderstanding that could have been rectified; with the Greeks I was becoming too much of a problem and no doubt George would have arranged the 'concrete wellies' bit. I always felt that John Althorp did not have sufficient involvement. Pat was coping well with the Collation, Appreciative and Dissemination; maybe he should have got involved more in that and sent Pat out to a small area or vice versa, and a junior NCO was obviously needed to assist, but to have four out of seven under-employed was not good. It was also a mystery why Major C, in a senior position at the Ministry of Defence, was despatched specifically to take over from me: why not anywhere else? I don't recall any other MIO being posted to Cyprus and he also had the authority to refuse to interfere, telling me to carry on.

The whole Intelligence effort was disjointed; certain people struggled to make it work and in the end a pattern appeared to emerge: it was the odd individual along the line that was either incompetent or inefficient. The trinity of politics, diplomacy and intelligence is contentious, and the general public never understand the reasons for political and diplomatic decisions and very often neither do the Intelligence Services. Then again, what the public sees as obvious, is given a reverse decision, brought about by knowledge of specific intelligence which is undisclosed to the public. Therefore if information is directed and collected widely, intimately, sensibly and securely by reliable operators, collated efficiently, appreciated without favour or bias by senior officers or operators, and disseminated to those who need to use it, the intelligence process goes like a bomb. During our spell in Cyprus there were many question marks and the sad thing about it all was that we senior operators were never adequately de-briefed for the benefit of all concerned which badly reflects on the interest of senior Intelligence staff officers. The only person who ever asked me about my activities in Cyprus was General Frank King when I returned to 11 Brigade at Minden. He didn't get the whole story but at least he showed genuine interest in the general background and work done.

d) I was extremely apprehensive about how I could cope in the role of a Field Intelligence Operator, under active service conditions, in a hostile environment and an unfamiliar role, especially in the company of three long standing members of our Corps and with only approximately one year's service in the Intelligence field. I learned that I had nothing to fear from the SIS downwards. There is something within individuals that Universities, public schools, languages and religion cannot teach you, and that is common sense, intuition, intelligence, the ability of self preservation, sufficiency, aggressiveness and guile. If you are lucky enough to be born with a mixture of these non educational attributes and more, then you can make out extremely well in intelligence, and probably many other professions but in this, your life can be forfeit, and to be a competent survivor you need God's blessing. I look back on Cyprus and think about a job well done; as a soldier it had hiccups, humour, interest and danger. What did I sign up for? To a great extent

I was autonomous and followed my own thinking, bending the rules to suit the situation, producing the goods, and hoping no one found out how it all happened, and I followed this line of deceit to authority throughout my Intelligence work, because I would have been strangled by all the strings attached. Don't get me wrong, I was not deliberately against regulations which are essential to any organization, but I would prefer to consider them mainly as guidelines to be sensibly interpreted according to the situation, without jeopardizing any higher authority. I found it very difficult to understand the extremely insular and superior attitude adopted by a majority of my Corps officers, because many Operators were academically superior to them and had the qualifications to enter Sandhurst. In all honesty I cannot recall any Corps officer who impressed me as my superior as a soldier, or in the use of common sense and intelligence. Some impressed me academically and a few as genuinely good officers but at no time did I (and some of my contemporaries) feel inferior beings. Fortunately some of these were commissioned and retained some pride and dignity within the Corps. I was feeling all this after a year in Germany (including an upgrading course) and five months in Cyprus and after a further fourteen years or so, I didn't change my mind. Our good ones were exceptionally good, a credit to themselves and the Corps.

Extract from semi-official letter from Capt J.F.C. Althorp to Lt. Terry, Adjt. HQ Intelligence Corps (BAOR)

Now that 40 Int. Platoon has been disbanded and personnel back in BAOR the opportunity presents itself to discuss the conduct of Sgt E.I. Howard during the operations in Cyprus.

Howard was an outstanding NCO from all points of view both from the intelligence aspect and from the broader overall army aspect. He was given a difficult and acutely sensitive job of providing intelligence on Greek and Turkish Cypriot organizations and personalities, the majority violent and very anti British – in North West Cyprus, which in early 1964 was very important indeed.

On our arrival, knowledge of this part of the island was virtually non existent. In the weeks that followed Howard by hint of determination, sheer hard work and his gifted ability to seek out and assess varying types of information, had provided a comprehensive, very accurate and detailed intelligence picture of NW Cyprus.

This NCO's written reports and verbal comments were excellent and full of common sense. Because of this, both he and the Intelligence Corps were spoken very highly of at higher formation, by CB1O, and by high ranking officers.

There were several times when Howard's 'curiosity' might have endangered himself and British interests in the island but each time this NCO knew instinctively when and where to draw the line to avoid public embarrassment. On one occasion the NCO found himself in a disturbing shooting incident but good sense and judgement enabled him to quickly extricate both himself and Pte. Campbell.

At all times he maintained excellent military bearing coupled with the imagination we expect from the Corps NCOs to have, he not only earned the respect of many officers from other arms with whom he came into contact, but was a fine example to our junior NCOs.

Howard is a very quiet man but full of character.

It is for the above reasons that I would strongly recommend that Sgt Howard's outstanding service be recognised by accelerated promotion to Staff Sergeant. He is easily of Warrant Officer standard and it must be pointed out that change of arm from the Scots Guards to the Intelligence Corps caused him a drop in rank.

I am naturally reluctant to recommend accelerated promotion of any man because of the ensuing complications, but in this case I have NO hesitation whatsoever.

Capt Althorp did not submit any other personal reports on 40 Int Platoon personnel.

I wonder if he was ever comprehensively de-briefed at the Centre or did the CB10 suffice? After all he (the CB10) did get the MBE.

The Cyprus episode ends and within days of my return I return to work and normality. The only person who took any interest in my 'little jaunt' was General King, no one from the Intelligence Corps!

CHAPTER 22

Return to Duty – BAOR

An exercise which led to a document loss is now described but the year and dates escape me. The object of this Exercise was mainly movement, with Communications in a secondary role. The whole of Brigade Headquarters would move in 'Packets' via the Autobahn and other main routes to a village named Bell situated in the Mosel valley and in the French zone of responsibility. It was anticipated that this journey of several hundred miles would take between 10-12 hours and that the Russians (Soxmis), the Soviet Military Mission to BAOR, would take some interest.

It was therefore no surprise to find our Russian friends waiting for us when the first 'packet' began to leave HQ. When I approached them they drove off. They no doubt kept us under observation until the Autobahn, because when the HQ convoy as a whole was proceeding westwards near Bielefeld, the Soxmis Volkswagen with its two occupants overtook the convoy pursued by two Military Police vehicles. The driver eventually accelerated and left the Police behind. As we approached Gutersloh they re-appeared yet again. This time I gave chase and remained on his tail. The driver without indication suddenly took the turnoff to Gutersloh and I followed. We turned under the Autobahn and the Russian took the slip road to join the Autobahn east to Hannover. We were both doing about 50m.p.h. I swung off the slip road onto spare ground thinking we had finally chased him away; however the Soxmis driver had similar ideas. As a result the Russian on leaving the slip road made a tight left turn on the spare ground which brought him in a head on confrontation with my vehicle. Not expecting this sudden change of events I applied my brakes and skidded uncontrollably towards the Russian car. I recall the look of horror on the Russian driver's face and his reactions were that of a highly trained driver; having the lighter vehicle he swerved to his right, we missed by inches and the chase continued. Fortunately he did not return on the westbound Autobahn but turned right into Gutersloh and we did not see him again.

The journey to Bonn, down the Rhine and Mosel valleys, was interesting and uneventful and our arrival in the village of Bell aroused the intense curiosity of the whole village. Vehicles and personnel were quickly dispersed and a meal prepared. It never failed to amaze me how quickly the British soldier adapts himself to certain situations especially when it comes to winning the hearts of the local inhabitants. It wasn't long before individuals were invited into houses for meals, baths and rumour had it that some were actually afforded more comfortable favours? This of course could be explained when I entered the local Catholic church to observe that forty-five young men of that tiny village lost their lives in World War 2. During our time in the village only five males of eligible age were seen.

That evening the OC and I sampled the delights of the only Gasthaus in the village with only three customers, and the following morning we set off to check the surrounding area for Soxmis sightings. I was then directed by the OC to take a particular road which culminated in an extremely harrowing downhill journey of numerous steep hairpin bends before we eventually entered the Nürnburgring, the world famous racing track. The OC paid a nominal fee and he then told me to drive as fast as possible. This was fine until we reached what I would describe as the 'Wall of Death'. I hadn't been warned about this hazard and spent several terrifying seconds, trying to gain control of my vehicle because I hit this section of the track at high speed and in the wrong gear. The result could have been fatal and both of us were in a cold sweat for some time. It was quite an experience and the incident described was exciting but I wouldn't like to face it again.

The exercise was deemed a success and in the early hours of the Friday morning the OC and I brought the Brigade Major back to Minden as he had a conference to attend. We made good time and it avoided a rather tedious return by convoy. When the convoy arrived back late Friday afternoon I carried out a check of classified files used on the exercise, unloaded and placed unattended in the Superintendent Clerk's office for a very short time. When Mr Toy and I checked and re-checked, one NATO SECRET file was missing. I started an immediate investigation and certain facts were ascertained quite quickly. The file had been taken since our arrival back in the Headquarters building. For reasons which I later understood, I was ordered by the Brigade Major to hand over all my investigation notes to a colleague who would continue the investigation. I have no wish to go into all the finer details, but suffice to say that at the end of the investigation, which was inconclusive, the reports were physically removed from the Army Post Office by the General himself. My colleague, who had acted against my advice, was ordered to re-write the report omitting certain embarrassing irrelevancies which should not have been written. The end conclusion remained the same; the document had been taken by some person who had access to the Headquarters building at the relevant time when the documents were removed from the vehicle to the Superintendent Clerk's office where they were left unattended for brief moments as vehicles were unloaded. This mystery was partially explained some months later when Mr Toy found the file under a pile of paper in the Stationery Store. All papers were intact. After I had left the Headquarters for Borneo, a German female who cleaned the HQ building was apparently dismissed on suspicion of espionage some years later. She was in the building at the relevant time and apparently satisfied my colleague about her movements. Could it be that she did remove the file for obvious purposes which may also explain another matter described later, or is it feasible that for whatever obscure reason, we had an idiot on the staff who wished to cause trouble and it got out of hand?

However it would not explain the disappearance of another file from the table of the G3 (Intelligence) in the late morning, following the visit to the Headquarters building by an Italian Army Major who was visiting the Brigade on a NATO courtesy exchange, and staying in our Officers Mess. When the file was reported missing I commenced enquiries and the Major could have had access. It was obvious what should happen but how embarrassing. Several of the officers were against it but the General agreed with me: I should get into his room and make a thorough search. The General himself checked at the Mess that the officer was visiting a unit and had not taken his briefcase. The Mess Sergeant was sworn to secrecy and I entered the room. For over an hour I searched every possible hiding place and looked for any other incriminating evidence of espionage, but I found nothing. He had a magnificent trunk and it was full to the brim with extremely high quality clothing which was difficult to search without showing evidence. I had to report that I had drawn a welcome blank with our NATO colleague. Subsequent events of course revealed the obvious suspect, our elderly cleaning lady, but no one had ever reported her presence around the material time; she had free access and I suppose her continuous presence made her somewhat anonymous.

CHAPTER 23

The Girl from Hameln

One day I received a telephone call from one of the Unit Security Officers (USO) in Hameln who asked me to visit him as soon as possible as he had information of possible interest. It transpired that this particular USO had a Warrant Officer working with him and several German civilians, among whom was an extremely attractive female aged about thirty. The Warrant Officer was married and was suspected of forming a close relationship with this woman who was born in East Germany. When the USO heard of this association he confronted the WO who admitted his infatuation with the woman and when certain matters were put to him he promised to end the affair, especially as he had access to certain classified documents. The affair was concluded and taking into account the WO's excellent wartime and subsequent Army Service the USO did not report the circumstances to me, for which he apologised.

It was known however that during the previous few weeks the woman, H, had formed another relationship with a Captain from a local unit who had taken her to several military social functions. This officer had access to more important classified documents. In view of these brief facts the USO decided to ask for my help, as he had formed the impression that H was forming associations with the intention of furthering her job prospects within the British Military framework, and she had also talked of wishing to work in Bonn, the seat of the West German Bundestag (Parliament).

My first instruction was to ensure that the WO had no further access to classified documents. The USO had already taken precautions in this respect. I then asked him to contact the OC of the Captain's unit and explain briefly that the officer's girlfriend was to undergo investigation and that he should, without arousing suspicion, restrict the officer's access to classified documents.

I acquired from the USO, H's *Fragebogen* (application form to be completed by German civilians to work with the British Forces) and then conducted a long interview with this officer in order to ascertain his own personal information coupled with what H had disclosed to other members of his locally employed staff. The catalogue of reported events was quite considerable. I found it necessary to ask the officer to attempt to fill in certain gaps in the story in order to show continuity by careful extraction of information from his German staff, and within days this was obtained and a reasonable comprehensive report was compiled in order to request permission for other agencies to be involved. The following is a brief resumé of my initial report and a request for the help of other agencies outside West Germany.

In 1945, the girl H and her family resided in the area of Germany known as East Prussia, and as the Russian Army advanced, the family began to travel westwards as refugees. They were subsequently separated, and after hostilities ceased H found herself alone behind the wire of a refugee camp supervised by the Russian Army. As the family had intended to seek refuge with a close relative who resided at —, a village west of the River Elbe, H was determined to reach them. Frightened, hungry and under threat of being shot by the guards, this determined child forced herself through the wire, sustaining a long and deep laceration of the right leg just above the right knee. Some time later she eventually reached her uncle's house and there she resided for a number of years.

No trace of H's family was ever found and it was decided by her aunt and uncle that to further her educational and employment prospects she should go to other relatives in Canada. Information on these formative years in North America was sparse, and this is where the help of outside agencies was essential. My initial reaction to the unconfirmed information that I obtained was that of acute suspicion of why she should wish to return to Germany now that her relatives were dead and she had no permanent residence in Germany. From her own mouth she had stated contentment and happiness with her situation in Canada, she was satisfactorily employed and in her own accommodation, so I wished to ascertain if she had possibly been 'ordered' to return to Germany for nefarious reasons.

Permission was granted and a report was compiled and despatched to the Royal Canadian Mounted Police (who later involved the FBI), requesting their help for comprehensive background information over the relevant years. Some weeks later to my great satisfaction the report was received and both the RCMP and the FBI produced information that H, during her higher education, later employment and with relatives was involved in Communist activities. How deeply could not be completely ascertained but there was ample evidence of sympathy and contact. Both agencies offered to provide further information should their enquiries produce anything of relevance. I was now satisfied that H should be questioned at length on some pretext or other, without any mention of Communist contact. Other points such as further advancement in her employment with the British Forces should be halted and a warning to H's officer boyfriend should be held in obeyance until the interview had been completed and a report submitted to higher authority.

By now I had a new OC who was not fully aware of all the circumstances so he was carefully briefed as it would be necessary for him to be present during the interview. Alec Stevens was a former Naval Officer and senior Colonial Police Special Branch Officer. He was an experienced Police Officer but Army procedures were an unknown quantity to him, particularly those appertaining within our Corps. We had a lengthy discussion about the interview. A date was fixed and arrangements made for 'bugging' the room to enable a true transcript of the interview to be made.

At the date and time arranged, H duly made her appearance at our office in Minden. She was aged about thirty, was extremely attractive, of average height, and wearing a dark mini-skirted suit. She was of the female species who would easily turn male heads. I sat down in a chair facing Alec's desk, then brought him in. As we all sat down H appeared to make a point by crossing her legs, probably for Alec's benefit, and I could plainly see the very vivid scar above her right knee. The reason we gave for the interview was that we needed further details about her North American residence. Without prompting she explained where she was born and proceeded to give us a life history. We interposed quite frequently which we found helpful. Innocuous questions were thrown in, also more important ones to us that filled in gaps. She also contradicted evidence that we had received, and failed to disclose the contacts with persons or organizations which were of interest to us; of these she was not asked specific questions, so as not to arouse suspicion about our motives. Coffee and biscuits and a few jokes made the whole matter less official and in this I think we were successful. She only queried the reason for the interview on one occasion and appeared satisfied with our explanation.

At the end of three hours or so we had usefully exhausted our ability to continue the interview, and she left the office smiling, and in good spirits. Since the investigation commenced H had made an application for employment away from Hameln with a higher Formation, which further convinced us that H had ulterior motives; the Captain was offered as a referee. From the transcript and our information from the RCMP and FBI a long and comprehensive report was compiled by myself and in consultation with Alec certain recommendations were made and this included the involvement of the West German Security Service.

There the matter ended as far as I was concerned; certainly nothing was reported to me before I left for Borneo.

The Commanding Officer of the Royal Warwickshire Regiment was not only a fine officer and a gentleman, but took a great interest in Counter Intelligence work. We met later in Hong Kong when he had become a General. At his request two of the lads and I made a 'raid' on the barracks. While the lads covered the other areas I made a rather spectacular entry into the Headquarters building via a slightly open window quite high up; had I fallen from my makeshift 'ladder' I could have been badly injured but I suppose I proved a point. The Colonel was most grateful and no doubt he took the necessary steps to improve matters following my report. Everyone derived some benefit from these little operations.

Some of the hardest worked troops in my area were two companies of the RASC (RCT now); for most of the year personnel worked almost daily, frequently at night, covering each river crossing exercise and maintaining all their vehicles and equipment. I must admit that when I carried out the Security Survey on both units I was very impressed with the workload these units managed to carry out. It was therefore quite a shock when we received the first reports of mutiny within the units. The press had also been contacted by members of the units and it made the headlines. Some damage and an incident of violence was reported and I was asked to make some very discreet enquiries, but this was difficult. All I did was to arrive at the same conclusion as the Enquiry: that over zealous officers imposed a heavy burden of Regimental duties, 'Spit and Polish', Guard duties etc., at a time when an understanding officer would have given them time to wind down after a heavy nine months of continuous work.

The problem soon passed and a greater understanding of man management followed.

One of our infantry Battalions had joined the Brigade from another area of BAOR and requested a Security Survey. On this occasion my last job was to thoroughly check a small percentage of Confidential documents, and do a 100 per cent check of Secret and Top Secret. I had to tell the CO and the Adjutant that a NATO Secret document was missing. The investigation started immediately and later took me to Munster and latterly HQ 1 (BR) Corps at Bielefeld where I met two of the most unco-operative Staff Officers it was my misfortune ever to meet. They knew that some of the blame would fall on their plate and were deliberately obstructive. When General King asked for a quick verbal report he was fuming about the two officers and I believe took immediate action. The whole matter ended up as a Court Martial. Some time later, I am sure that I met one of those two officers in Borneo where he had an Intelligence staff job. I had the feeling he remembered me but said nothing. The unit displayed no animosity; the CO convened a special meeting of all the officers to help the investigation and complimented me on the very accurate but fair report. In this way you set the standard and trust develops to everyone's advantage.

Shortly before the previously described incident I had attended the Intelligence Centre for an Interrogation Course. The problem with a course of this nature is that you cannot teach a person to be an Interrogator, though if you have a natural ability then the Course will help to perfect technique. Great emphasis was placed on the organizing of Interrogation or Escape and Evasion Exercises and the regulations by the Ministry of Defence governing the supervision of these exercises. Since shortly after the Korea War a lot of criticism had been levelled at the MOD and the Intelligence Corps in particular, concerning the technique of Interrogation of POWs and the responsibility of MI9 in the training of specialist personnel in Escape and Evasion and Resistance to Interrogation (SAS, SBS, Aircrew etc) which of course involved the Intelligence Corps, as it provided the organization facilities and personnel, both Regular and Reserve Interrogators, which provided a method of internal Interrogation Training. The following is an extract from *Secret Armies* by James Adams:

SERE or Survival, Evasion, Resistance and Escape is specialized training to test as far as possible in a peacetime environment the ability to resist interrogation. In Britain these exercises are carried out by the Intelligence Corps and back during the Malaya campaign they reached appalling levels.

Just to try the chaps out, and it was quite amazing, off the record, how many of our big tough soldiers in fact weren't quite so tough under the skin. No physical violence whatsoever, it was purely mental. For example, you'd sit a chap down in a chair, and you'd put a latrine bucket over his head and a chap would sit there going bong, bong, bong, for half an hour with a spoon, and then he'd be taken outside and tied to a tree that had been smeared with jam, with ankle and wrist cuffs, so he had to keep away from the tree, because the ants were pouring up and down, red ants! All sorts of lovely tortures they devised, these chaps. They would take a bicycle wheel with the spindle still in the centre, and put it on the ground and make you kneel on the rim, kneel inside the rim on the spokes with your hands behind your back tied to a rope over the ceiling, and you had to keep this rim absolutely flat. You can't do it because you get cramp in the ankles and knees, and every time you moved, you got a jerk on the wrists and it was very painful. It didn't leave any mark or sign; you weren't actually beaten up and they wouldn't give you any sleep for 36 hours, or no food. You just didn't get a thing, and they'd put you in solitary confinement and you'd be in this little cell all on your own with a board on the floor to sleep on and every time you got on the board somebody would open the door and throw a bucket of water over you. Or they would put you in a pit and surround you with guard dogs and turn the hose on you from time to time to keep you cooled down. It was great fun and it gave everybody a very good insight into the sort of chaps you had. You picked out the really good and you picked out the doubtful ones.

While some of these practices have ceased or changed, the SAS still place a great deal of emphasis on SERE.

THIS DOES NOT HAPPEN NOW

Over the years, owing to Parliamentary and external pressure the holding time of 'prisoners', also the Interrogation time, had been drastically reduced to ridiculous proportions. Excesses occasionally occurred which could be blamed on seniors not affording adequate supervision; these were extremely rare but unfortunately reached the headlines. The personnel concerned generally speaking enjoyed this extremely arduous training which not only tested them initially in a physical sense but later exposed them to strong psychological pressures and this challenge they relished.

Another aspect of Interrogation which had come to light over the last two decades was the frequent necessity to use interpreters in an interrogation setting. A précis had been formulated from the experiences of Corps personnel and was mainly concerned with the selection of an interpreter and how he should behave in an actual situation. I met this problem on more than one occasion and it is extremely difficult to implement. It is not an insurmountable problem however and I managed, but at times unsatisfactorily. It was a useful course and was put to use almost as soon as I returned.

One of our major units had organized an Evasion exercise west to east across Schelswig Holstein. Unfortunately it was not emphasized that the idea was to walk and attempt to avoid the Hunter Force which was to be provided by their own unit! As an afterthought they asked Brigade for an interrogator and a Guard Force. At very short notice Cpl. S and I, with a small contingent of RMP, reported to the site, to be confronted by a subaltern whose main preoccupation appeared to be the facilities for torturing those unlucky enough to be captured: trees to tie people to or hang from, a lake where we could submerge them, etc.! I met this idiot in later years on two occasions and he hadn't changed; anyway he was quickly disillusioned. On our first tour it was all a waste of time. Personnel had 'hitched' lifts, and when walking in or even when captured were as fresh as daisies. Comments were made, and adjustments to reporting points on map references enforced which ensured that some physical stress was endured by the 'Runners'. On the second visit my Guard Force was made up of members of the Black Watch including their Provost Staff. Under the circumstances we were quite successful. With one individual we actually persuaded him that he had inadvertently crossed the East German border. We made promises and he agreed to remain in East Germany if he could bring his family over. This was no act. We had the panic, anger, frustration and genuine tears and emotion from this person; we successfully disorientated him in a relatively short time with rather frightening results.

We also carried out another Exercise with our Army Air Corps Squadron (known colloquially as Teeny Weeny Airways!). We gave them a hard time and they did extremely well. I was flown home by a Luftwaffe helicopter pilot, but my boss who stayed behind to de-brief the participants was given a most horrendous flight back by one of our 'victims': he dropped like a stone, skimmed hilltops, flew under high tension cables and used other terrifying skills. It was a very relieved and rather sick looking officer who staggered out of the helicopter to the evident satisfaction of a highly amused pilot.

During 1964 a decision was made to reorganize the military intelligence resources within the BAOR sphere of responsibility, placing more emphasis on combating the increasing threat of espionage and sabotage from the Iron Curtain countries against the British Army and their establishments. Very briefly, at grass roots level the reorganization meant the abolishment of the Intelligence Platoons at Corps, Divisions and Brigades, to be replaced by a small Section dealing only with the formations' Operational Intelligence commitments. Newly formed and located Counter Intelligence and Security Units would be tasked to carry out all Security Investigations and implement a Security Survey programme of all units, using a new and comprehensive proforma which would contain a depth of information of each unit which currently we did not hold, a point that I had advocated since my arrival in BAOR. A considerable sum of money would be made available to increase the level of protective measures, either structurally or items (safes, cupboards, locks etc.). It was to be a more realistic approach to the situation, unfortunately years too late.

I was informed that I would be transferring as Second in Command of the new unit and then the trouble started. The General and staff strongly objected to my colleague remaining at Brigade to command the section, no doubt as a result of the investigation of the missing document and the furore he had caused with his report I have described earlier. The objection was taken to the newly formed HQ Intelligence and Security Group and others; as a result I was to remain at Brigade. It did not particularly worry me; both aspects of the job were interesting and challenging, though I must admit that I had shown a natural instinct for Counter Intelligence work, being mainly responsible for doubling the case files in less than sixteen months on the ground.

As the weeks followed changes in personnel took place. General King sadly departed to reach greater heights, a fine soldier and a gentleman. He was replaced by an equally talented ex Cavalryman, General Harman, whom I met later when he was Commandant at Sandhurst during Chris's residence as a Cadet. The Brigade Major and others also left but we remained a very efficient Headquarters.

The last field exercise that I took part in necessitated the Brigade 'playing' in an area we had never ventured in before and that was towards the north-west and Bremerhaven. Brigade HQ anticipated that the Russians would afford us their close attention and it was decided that I should precede the Headquarters and 'sweep' the road route to the first location. No trace of Soxmis was observed at this stage. Our most worrying time was within a Gasthaus en route where we had stopped for lunch; local hospitality from the licensee, the local Police Chief and friends, plus some locally employed Italian ladies, could have become a drunken disaster if we had not backed out with our honour intact.

As expected, when we began to change locations the Russians were actually waiting for us to appear at the new location. Any piece of high ground was an obvious place to aim for and as soon as I or the Military Police advance party appeared, off they went. Will-o-the-Wisp characters were our 'friends' and extremely competent. As a result of their activities, and investigating sightings plus my other duties with my lads, I only averaged about two hours sleep per night and I was extremely tired. The Exercise was due to finish on the Saturday morning and early on Friday evening I gave the Intelligence briefing to the Battalion and Regimental Commanders. This was followed by an incident with a colleague, the result of which deprived me of any sleep at all. As the Headquarters prepared to move out to their final location I stripped to the waist, to wash and shave ''neath the village pump', in order to wake me up. Everyone left and I recovered one rifle and several classified documents from various positions following my sweep of the area; I then started my more direct but lonely drive to join the others.

Within a quarter of an hour I was on a traffic free main road when suddenly I was startled by flashing lights and a cacophony of noise, and there I was on the wrong side of the road with a very large 'Woofer' wagon bearing down on me, all horns blaring and about twenty flashing lights all activated. In a panic I swerved back to my right side; fortunately no other vehicles were on the road, it was only about 5a.m. I pulled into the side of the road and ran round the Land Rover briskly, jumped up and down, and, slightly revived, resumed the drive. I sang excerpts from rude, martial, and operatic ballads but within minutes I was fast asleep, across the road, and again the sound of a distant horn awoke me to spine chilling panic and a cold sweat. A repeat athletic performance and more song plus a face full of water, did the trick and I arrived safely only minutes behind the main body. Picking a large tree full of foliage I drove directly under it, ignored the camouflage net, crept into the back of the vehicle and died, having given orders not to be disturbed at any price. Two hours later the Exercise finished. I was awoken and driven back to Minden. It was a successful job done and I was extremely relieved not to have become a BAOR statistic as a casualty.

A matter partially unrelated to the Army occurred in June/July of 1965 when I received a letter from HQ BAOR via the British Embassy in Copenhagen. The letter had been written by a Hans Harald Tokswig from Jutland; he had apparently purchased an ex WD Austin Champ ¹/₄ ton vehicle for work on his farm, and required a vehicle handbook in order for a local garage to facilitate repairs. For whatever reasons the letter was passed to me. The Second in Command of the local REME Workshop was a friend and he acquired a book which I forwarded with a short letter explaining that before I left for Borneo my family and I would probably pass through Denmark en route to Sweden, where I intended contacting the Swedish University Professor I had met in Cyprus.

Some days later I received two immaculately typed pages, insisting that I should not visit that 'God forsaken place' but that I should consider visiting his home and enjoy a holiday in Jutland; he was the Government travel agent for that area. We gave the matter some thought and agreed to his suggestion, requesting ideas for accommodation and the possibility of visiting Oslo or Stockholm. By return Hans provided a route map illustrating places of interest, a Royal KRO (inn) for an overnight stay, and instructions for when we reached his home area. The journey was interesting and pleasant and the Royal KRO was a revelation. One of five Royal Inns patronised by the Danish Royal Family, this one had its own airstrip and, no doubt due to Hans' influence, we were treated like Royalty and the cost extremely reasonable. When you looked at the building it was not impressive: long and low it initially gave you the impression of a child's drawing but inside it was quite luxurious.

When we reached our meeting place destination, Hans arrived driving a huge American shooting brake. Within was Sidsel, his most charming, talented and delectable Swedish wife, plus two Alsatians. The children piled into the brake, one headache solved; the dogs were not a problem and on our arrival at the farm there were also some puppies. Hans by

profession was a very successful Commercial artist who at the height of a
very lucrative career decided to leave the 'rat race' into semi retirement, by
accepting the post of Government tourist agent for Jutland.

Hans had served in the Danish Army in an Intelligence post at NATO
HQ in Oslo during his military service. We talked long and hard into the
night during our first evening, helped by one of my bottles of whisky;
After three days of hospitality we insisted that we continue our holiday for
the children's sake. Hans obtained a magnificent bungalow on the beach
for ten days and also arranged our trip to Oslo where we stayed for five
days. We boarded the well known *Fram* in the Nautical Museum and other
items, admired the wonderful murals in the City Hall, the Olympic Ski
Run and many other places of interest. A very dour but friendly people,
the Norwegians, a well worthwhile visit, and I wish it had been longer.
What a wonderful entrance to a capital city coming down the fjord!

We spent another two pleasant days with Hans and Sidsel before we
very reluctantly commenced the long drive back to Germany. We stayed
the night in a small Danish German border town, finding a small Danish
hotel for the night. The accommodation was extremely clean and spacious.
When I was asked if we wished to eat I replied in the affirmative and the
owner said 'How about fish and chips,' and I readily agreed. We enjoyed a
small dish of soup after which in came a most enormous dish of large chips
with an even larger dish of small crumbed plaice. Jean and I ate more than
sufficient but Chris was insatiable. The owner refilled the dish and smiled
broadly while Chris demolished the lot; a simple meal but, oh boy, did we
enjoy it. You don't get a lot of fish in Germany so far from the coast.

Our journey was finally completed safely, thus ending a very memorable
holiday. Chris returned to school and Jean and I began to prepare for the
move back to UK with all its inherent problems, housing and separation,
and in between all this the lads and I had to prepare and partake in the
Northag Exercise now described.

Our efficiency was reflected following the completion of a very
important Northag Exercise (Northern Army Group) in October 1965.
HQ 11 Int. Brigade not only organized this most elaborate exercise, but
also provided the officers to fill most of the senior positions in HQ
Northag. Our Headquarters received the necessary accolades for a job well
done not only from the senior Generals but also from the foreign armies
involved. Apart from the many other aspects I was responsible for, the item
that gave me and my staff the greatest problem was the make up and
protective covering of a huge map approximately twenty feet square, which
was to be laid on a huge table overlooked by a long desk where the senior
officers supervised. All accommodation was under canvas and tight security

was the order of the day. This gave me some headaches initially, but once the routine was established as I recollect no major incident occurred, but we had the inevitable Russian interest in us.

Working in the busy yet tranquil atmosphere was noticeably less frantic and more comfortable than the spartan existence of Brigade in the field, and I think every person involved derived benefit from this experience. This in fact was my last major item of work for HQ 11 Inf. Brigade and it ended three years of my service which not only initiated me into Intelligence in the field in two overseas countries, but I also became fully qualified by examination in my profession, had experience in Interrogation, had been under small arms fire again and successfully satisfied my seniors that I was a reliable and capable 'Operator'. I look back on this posting as one of the most interesting and enjoyable periods of my service.

When the time came for leaving both Jean and I were filled with a mixture of anticipation for the future and certain sadness on leaving friends. I had to visit all my units and say goodbye to all friends and contacts. Our farewell night in the Mess was most enjoyable but also embarrassing, as leaving at the same time was a senior from the Signal Squadron, good at his job but because of his complete lack of social graces disliked by all members almost without exception. When a collection was made for our presents Mike Kelly had to ask me if he could take some of my money to pay for the minimum gift for this chap, a travelling clock, which only cost about 8DM. The embarrassment came when I was presented with silver tray, dish, and cigarette lighter. The poor chap left with his wife a few moments later; the members had made their point but it made us feel uncomfortable. I think it is sad when people are so thick skinned that despite hints they refuse to change their attitude. It was the only time I was to witness this sort of objection to a colleague.

By now the car was sold, the house cleaned and handed over and all farewells said. We spent our last night at the Kellys' house and flew back to Manchester and temporary refuge with Jean's parents in Preston.

CHAPTER 24

Borneo – the Facts

I think it was in May 1965 when I opened the unit mail and there in one
of the envelopes was the letter that I knew would horrify Jean and the
children, and it filled me personally with great apprehension.

My posting order informed me that in early November I would be posted
on secondment to the Malayan Police under the auspices of 2 Intelligence
Company which was based on Labuan. It would be of at least twelve months
duration and unaccompanied. The family's attitude was predictable. As a
wife Jean was understandably very angry and rightfully so. I remembered
that a colleague's wife had threatened divorce if they were sent to the Far
East, he would not even have been on Active Service and it was
accompanied; the posting was cancelled and he returned to BAOR.

When confrontation began in Brunei in December 1962 and the
involvement of British troops increased numerically, so the Intelligence
Corps were given an operational commitment in conjunction with the
Civil power.

In the early months of 1963 an initial visit had been made by an officer
and some senior NCOs from Singapore and Malaya to various areas in
Borneo, liaising with senior Colonial Police Officers and military
personnel, organizing the military intelligence process to the benefit of the
two Heads of Special Branch in Borneo and Sabah and the troops on the
ground, and attempting to form a basis should the problem expand, which
of course it did. The initial visit lasted a relatively short time and was very
much an *ad hoc* effort with very little pressure put on them by the
incumbent units or the military situation. From what I heard there were
plenty of trips up country to established positions and locations (no foot
slogging), parties with the locals etc. Sarawak is a hospitable place so their
few months were quite enjoyable and to some extent informative.

The following comprehensive narrative is based on my lecture notes,
borrowed and compiled from various sources, the text being available to
military personnel who had access to official figures and knowledge,
produced for general information. Some of the contents could be read in

various military publications, so to any authors or subscribers who regretfully must remain unknown, my deep and grateful thanks; many hours of research were saved.

Malaysia had its origin when, under pressure from a self-governing Singapore to join the Federation of Malaya (independent since 1957), Tunku Abdul Rahman, the Malayan Prime Minister, raised the possibility of linking Singapore, Sarawak, and Sabah (North Borneo) in wider federation. After discussion in London a White Paper in November 1961 pronounced the federation a desirable aim.

A commission presided over by Lord Dobbold was asked to ascertain the views of the inhabitants of Borneo and reported favourably in August 1962. An inter-governmental committee put forward constitutional proposals in December 1962. Malaysia came into being on 16th September 1963, after a brief postponement (see below).

Population
One of the motives for the federation had been to balance what would otherwise have been a Chinese majority if Singapore alone had been joined to Malaya. As constituted, the new federation combined:

Malaya		Sarawak	
Malays	3,910,000	Chinese	250,000
Chinese	2,880,000	Indigenous	
Indians	870,000	(Dyaks etc.)	400,000
Others	150,000	Malays	140,000
		Others	7,000
	7,810,000		797,000
Singapore		**Sabah**	
Chinese	1,400,000	Chinese	145,000
Malays	250,000	Indigenous	325,000
Indians	150,000	Malays	35,000
Others	40,000		
	1,840,000		505,000

Total: Malaysia	
Malays	4,335,000
Chinese	4,675,000
Indians	1,020,000
Borneo Indigenous	725,000
Others	197,000
	10,952,000

Brunei The British protected Sultanate of Brunei hesitated about joining the federation. The Partai Ra'ayat, successful in elections in September 1962, insisted on union with Sabah and Sarawak before any union with Malaya. In December this party led a revolt, claiming to represent all Northern Borneo, as the North Kalimantan Liberation Army. The revolt failed, gaining no backing in either Sarawak or Sabah, but was welcomed in Indonesia.

Confrontation The Birth of Malaysia had been planned for 31st August 1963. Hints of hostility from Indonesia grew from February 1963 onwards, joined by the Philippines. Talk of a summit meeting of the three leaders in April was accompanied by the first raid across the Sarawak border.

Talks took place in Tokoyo between Abdul Rahman and President Sukarno in May, Indonesia apparently withdrawing opposition but proposing a wider federation of Maphilindo (Malaysia, Philippines, Indonesia). But after final agreement on setting up of Malaysia had been reached in London in July, President Sukarno resumed his threat of confrontation, accusing the new federation of being 'neocolonist'.

Finally, a meeting of the three leaders was held in Manilla at the end of July at which a compromise was reached over Dr Sukarno's demand for a United Nations referendum in Borneo and an unofficial inquiry was instituted by U Thant. Against mounting Indonesian hostility and accusations of breaking the Manilla agreement, this mission reported in favour of Malaysia and the postponed date of 16th September for Malaysia was adhered to. Attacks on the British Embassy in Jakarta gave an ugly character on Indonesia's attitude.

Defence Treaty This was first signed in September 1957, between Malaya and Britain. Australia and New Zealand became 'associated' by an exchange of letters and confirmed in July 1963, to apply to the whole federation then about to be formed. It provided for full military co-operation by Britain to meet any threat to Malaysia, at Malaysia's request.

Bases Singapore now HQ, Far East Command. The number of British soldiers committed was now rising to 10,000. Warships included two aircraft carriers, one commando ship, one guided missile destroyer, three escort squadrons of frigates, one submarine squadron and mine-sweeping and support ships. The RAF had Javelin Squadrons, Hunter Squadrons and a V-Force capability. There was also a Commonwealth Brigade stationed at Malacca, but a British battalion was initially withdrawn to deal with infiltration. Australia and New Zealand each had a battalion at

Malacca, and in addition Australia had six warships in the area full-time, with an aircraft carrier paying periodic visits. New Zealand had a frigate.

Developments 1963-4 Indonesia cut off trade with Singapore, restricted or expropriated British business in Indonesia, and broke off all diplomatic relations. Indonesian raiding across Sarawak and Sabah borders increased. In January 1964 Mr Robert Kennedy, United States Attorney General, was sent on a mediation mission by President Johnson, and a cease-fire was proclaimed. Foreign Ministers met in Bangkok in February but talks broke down in March.

Elections in April in Malaya nevertheless showed strong backing for the Tunku's Alliance Party. In May Dr Sukarno said Malaysia would be crushed by January 1965. Another summit meeting in Tokoyo in June broke down because Indonesia refused to withdraw guerillas as a preliminary to political talks. Raids now increased and took a new turn in autumn with landings and air drops in Malaya itself. None of these had any military effect. There were minor naval engagements in the Strait of Malacca until a much larger build up of forces was detected and confirmed.

In September Malaysia took the issue to the United Nations Security Council, when the vote was nine to two on a Norwegian resolution deploring Indonesian landings and calling for respect for territorial integrity. This UNO support for Malaysia and rebuke for Indonesia only inspired Sukarno to fully commit his regular forces in the battle to conquer East Malaysia and extend the situation to a full scale battle for the jungle.

CHAPTER 25

Borneo – the Job

Limited war had been going on continuously in South East Asia, in varying degrees of intensity, for the past twenty-one years. There had been eight important conflicts: eight years of war in Indo-China; Indonesia's fight for freedom against the Dutch; the twelve year Malayan emergency; the Korean war; the conflict in Laos; the three and a half year Indonesian confrontation against Malaysia; the 1967 security operations in Hong Kong; and the large scale fighting in Vietnam. This is a brief introduction to the Indonesian confrontation against Malaysia, which was concentrated mainly on the island of Borneo and lasted more than three years.

Until September 1963, Borneo had consisted of three separate and independent states, Sarawak, North Borneo and Brunei. Then Sarawak and North Borneo (later called Sabah) joined the Federation of Malaysia with Brunei electing to remain outside as an independent state under British protection.

Lieutenant General Sir Walter Walker, KCB, CBE, DSO was appointed Commander British Forces, Borneo, on 19th December 1962, and later became Director of Operations. In April 1963, the Indonesians crossed the border and annihilated the police station at Tebedu, uncomfortably close to Kuching. The British Army were given the task of identifying and defeating Indonesian aggression, or 'confrontation' as it came to be called, over a land frontier of 1,000 miles, a coast line considerably longer, and the air space above. The aim was to prevent the conflict from escalating into open war, similar to that in South Vietnam. To do this, it was necessary to win the opening rounds of the jungle battle and also, at the same time, the psychological battle in the kampongs and villages of the up country tribal peoples. In addition, there was an internal threat of clandestine communist subversion and of armed rebellion in the mainly Chinese urban areas. These dangers had to be tackled with the same energy and expense as the external challenge, for the Chinese-run Clandestine Communist Organization had a membership of 24,000.

In December 1962, the forces available consisted of one brigade of three battalions, six naval coastal minesweepers and some fifteen naval and air force helicopters. In March 1965 there was a combined multi-national force consisting of:

a) Coastal minesweepers and naval and maritime police fast armed patrol boats, for both inshore and up-river patrolling.
b) 70, later 80, helicopters (which was about 40 short of what was required, and some 2,700 fewer than the troop-carrying helicopters available in South Vietnam).
c) About 40 fixed wing aircraft.
d) Four regular infantry brigades – totalling 13 infantry battalions: British Gurkha, Malay, Australian and New Zealand.
e) The equivalent of one battalion of SAS (Special Air Service Regiment) – the squadrons being British, Gurkha, Australian and New Zealand.
f) The equivalent of about two battalions worth of police field force, or police jungle companies.
g) About 1,500 border scouts, recruited from the indigenous tribes.
h) Two regiments of armoured cars – British and Malay.
i) The equivalent of two regiments of Artillery – British, Malay and Australian.
j) Two regiments of Engineers – Gurkha, Malay and Australian.
k) An excellent joint communications system, which gave rapid inter-communication with the troops in the jungle, the aircraft in the air and on the airfields, the ships at sea, the four joint Army, Navy, Air and Police, Headquarters of the National Operations Committee in Kuala Lumpur, as well as the Commander-in-Chief Headquarters in Singapore.

There were few motorable roads in Borneo outside the urban areas, and no railways. In addition, there was only one deep sea port – Labuan. From there everything had to be in small coastal cargo boats and lighters across the twenty miles of sea, and up river to Brunei. Initially there were no Service stocks in the country, such as rations, medical stores, ammunition, clothing, tentage or transport. All these had to be brought in some 900 miles by air and sea. There were no camps for the troops, no generators, no pumping engines, no workshops and no local military forces from whom one could get assistance. Every battalion, camp, company base and platoon post had to be built from scratch.

Ninety per cent of the logistic supply within Borneo was by air, both air-landed and air-dropped. This was dictated by the lack of roads and also by our operational concept, which was one of complete mobility and flexibility. In guerilla and insurgency operations in really dense jungle country, roads are not only deathtraps, but they give advance notice to the enemy of your presence and intentions. To give an example of our air supply efforts: during the year from November 1964 to October 1965, in each month we lifted an average of 19,000 troops, we airlanded an average of 1,900,000 lbs of supplies, and we air-dropped an average of 2,000,000 lbs of supplies. Few people in England at that time, or indeed since, can have realised the magnitude of our airlift.

General Walker drafted a Directive. It was based on his experience of the twelve-year Malayan emergency (1948-60) and a study of insurgency in Indo-China (Laos and South Vietnam) from 1946-62. It goes without saying that the Malayan emergency influenced him tremendously, because it was there that Field Marshal Templer forged that unique and successful system of unity – between the armed forces themselves, between the armed forces and the police and between the security forces as a whole and the civil administration. It was this unity, joint planning and joint operations at all times and at all levels, that defeated the communist guerillas in Malaya.

This directive said that the ingredients of success would be five-fold. Unified operations; timely and accurate information, which means a first class intelligence machine; speed, mobility and flexibility; security of our bases, wherever they were and whatever they might be (airfield, patrol base, etc.); and domination of the jungle. After about one month a sixth principle was added: winning the hearts and minds of the people, and especially indigenous people. This was absolutely vital to the success of operations because, by winning over the people to your side, you can succeed in isolating your enemy from supplies, shelter and intelligence.

The sixth principle entailed winning the local people's trust, confidence and respect. We set out to speak their language and respect their customs and religion. Small highly trained patrols were sent to live and work among them, to protect them and share their danger, to get to know them and gain their confidence. These troops were as friendly, understanding and patient to the villagers as they were tough and ruthless in the jungle. It was sought to give the villagers a feeling of security by day and night, through the presence of phantom patrols and through constant visits by the civil administration, the police and the army. We helped their agriculture, improved their communications and trading facilities, improved their water supply, provided medical clinics and a flying doctor service, established schools, provided transistor wireless sets and attractive programmes, and so on.

The army went to any lengths to keep its hands clean. For example the security precautions for offensive air support, for artillery and mortar fire were as foolproof as it was humanly possible to make them. It was indelibly inscribed on our minds that one civilian killed by us would do more harm than ten killed by the enemy. Every time we defeated the enemy we took every possible precaution to ensure that he could not exact retribution on the nearest village. The Army gave that village protection either visible or invisible. If the latter, only the headman was told that troops were in ambush nearby. In addition, each village had its own alarm system and local defence plan. At all costs the enemy had to be prevented from capturing a village and digging in, because this would have meant a battle to recapture it and, in the process, its probable destruction. If the price a village had to pay for its liberation from the enemy was to be its own destruction, then the campaign for hearts and minds would never have been won.

Winning the hearts and minds of the indigenous inhabitants is not just a question of direct aid. People must be given the will to help themselves and the necessary expertise to do so. This is something which the British Army is good at because they have so much experience and know-how. But this can so easily be lost. The British Army had to start from scratch because the lessons of the Malayan Emergency had been forgotten in a space of three years. Good though our record had been in several insurgency campaigns, on each occasion we have had to play ourselves in, all over again.

Giving Effort to Unified Command

There remained the all important question of unified operations, about which both the Services and the civil administration still had so much to learn. In Borneo, the Army and RAF were in separate and widely separated headquarters, and there was no permanent Royal Navy representation ashore. In order to bring everyone together, the first action was to take over a suitable building and establish a Joint Headquarters. This set the pattern for similar headquarters at all levels throughout the country.

To give practical effect to unified command, a Director of Operations Joint Headquarters had to be set up at the earliest possible moment. This had to consist of five elements – the civil administration, civil police (including Special Branch), the Navy, Army and Air Force. Then there had to be joint operational executive committees set up at every level throughout the country state, with the chief minister in the chair, division, district and local.

There were various pitfalls to guard against. It was all too easy to forget that the armed forces were in support of the civil administration and the police, and would continue to be so. There had never to be in committee a 'heavy front row of military brass'. On the contrary, the civil administration had to be seen to be conducting affairs and should not be kept, or allow themselves to be kept, in the background. If the country was newly independent and short of experienced administrators (as was the case in Borneo), the civil officials had to be particularly encouraged to take the lead. Some army officers could be far too dictatorial and unbending in their manner. They had to overcome this failing and go out of their way to be diplomatic, patient and courteous, and they had to have a complete grasp of the functions, capabilities and limitations of the civil police and civil administration. Only in this way could they win the respect and confidence of their civil colleagues.

It is too easily forgotten that civil officials see battalions come and go at short intervals, whereas they themselves spend the whole of their working lives in the country. They speak the language and know the people, Internal friction is bound to be generated if military commanders ride rough-shod over political implications. Especially is this so if the operations are being conducted in an independent sovereign country, such as East Malaysia.

Holding a 970 Mile Frontier

The speed, mobility and flexibility of the British forces was all important in the operations as they developed. This immediately became obvious when one realised that a frontier of 970 miles (equal to the distance between Liverpool and Warsaw) was held by only 13 battalions against an enemy two or three times their strength who had no constraints about violating the frontier. To dominate and own the jungle over 1,000 miles to a depth of 100 miles, against this enemy, and smash him every time he attempted an incursion was no mean achievement on the part of the thirteen battalions concerned. There were those who argued at the time that more battalions should have been kept back concentrated – 900 miles away in Singapore and on the mainland – ready to be flown in when an incursion took place. Such a policy, General Walker considered, would have resulted in the arrival of too little too late. One just could not dominate the Borneo jungles from Singapore, let alone win the hearts and minds of the local people from that distance.

The frontages of the four brigades were 181, 442, 267 and 81 miles. Before a fourth brigade headquarters arrived in January 1965, the front of the most westerly brigade was 681 miles. (In comparison, a brigade's area of responsibility in Europe is about 9-12 miles square.) With this tremendous frontage and depths, and almost complete lack of roads, railways and navigable rivers, how were the infantry, in this really thick, mountainous jungle country, to maintain the momentum of operations? Their job was to anticipate the enemy's intentions, cut him off and destroy him before he could retreat to the sanctuary of his side of the frontier. The solution lay in a combination of good intelligence and all types of air support.

It was mainly helicopters that provided the Army with the necessary degree of speed, mobility and flexibility. They proved themselves over and over again to be real battle-winners. They flew tirelessly over the mountains and along the valleys, placing men exactly where they would do most good. For example, reconnaissance patrols were positioned along the frontier to find and report the enemy, and sections were set down neatly in depth to cut off unsuspecting raiders. A clever company commander with a few 'choppers' could so block guerillas at every turn that they would think an entire army was on their heels. We hit the enemy so often the moment he put his nose across the frontier that we were credited with having some special form of radar. To take the strain off the helicopters and off air-dropping, we were always building short jungle airstrips, or improving existing ones, for our light fixed wing aircraft. The Beaver is a wonderful aircraft and was certainly one of the best buys the Army ever made.

Another means of transport which really proved itself in Borneo was Hovercraft. Trials were completed with the SRN 5 which could take about twenty troops or two tons of freight, and has a cruising speed of 50 knots. We found it suitable for patrolling rivers and coasts, for routine surface transport, and for quick movement of small parties of troops, particularly at night, when the helicopter was not at its best.

Anyone who has operated in the jungle will know that there is no front in the accepted military sense, and this is even more the case when there are dissident elements within, lying low, prepared for armed rebellion, as was the case in Borneo. Unless commanders take a firm stand, they can very soon have all their forces tied down defending their bases. We dealt with this problem by making everyone responsible for his own protection, wherever he might be, in front or rear areas. Every man in uniform had to be a potential front line infantry soldier. Officers and men of armoured car, artillery, engineer and signal units, were all trained and ready to fight as infantry. The same applied to the services in depth – RCT, RAOC, REME and Medical. I use the term 'in depth' deliberately, and not 'in rear' for there is no 'rear' in counter-insurgency operations. Great use was made of deception and guile, never doing the same thing twice; all forms of lethal and warning devices were used: armoured cars, mortars, dogs, booby traps, claymore mines, trip flares, seismic intruder devices, and so on. Time and time again the enemy tried to infiltrate into villages and towns and to get within mortar range of our airfields. But our intelligence was such that nine times out of ten we knew his every move and we brought him to battle long before he had reached a point from which he could mortar a village let alone a town.

In the forward areas we adopted a mobile defence, keeping our forward posts to the minimum. Such forward posts as there were had to be properly dug in with overhead cover and capable of being held overnight by not more than one third of the post's garrison against any opposition – artillery, mortars, rockets, Bangalore torpedoes or direct infantry assault. The other two thirds of the garrison was always out in an offensive role, dominating the jungle and ambushing tracks by day and night, so that the enemy never knew where we were, and was always liable to be contacted and savaged.

General Walker insisted, and how right he was, that results could not be achieved merely by attacking and shooting the enemy and then returning to base. He had to be played at his own game, by living out in the jungle for weeks on end, by winning the hearts and minds of the people and by placing our own agents in villages known to be unfriendly. In these conditions, your base must be carried on your back, and that base consists of a featherweight plastic sheet, a sockful of rice and a pocketful of ammunition. The jungle has got to belong to you, you must own it, you must control and dominate it.

Special Fighting Skills

What, then, is the technique of domination of the jungle? In really dense jungle, it is the individual fighting skill of the soldier which has to make up for the difficulty of providing him with conventional forms of fire support from both ground and air. In Borneo, the army made sure a soldier was properly acclimatized and given jungle training at our jungle warfare school in West Malaysia. With the odd exception of myself, all FIOs were from Corps personnel with the Commando Brigade, or already in the Far East. Troops could not be precipitated from Salisbury Plain straight into jungle operations against regular soldiers (who had been trained as guerillas since 1945) in a tropical climate unless a very great deal of realistic and really tough preliminary training, particularly night training, had taken place. *(Unfortunately I was).*

These Indonesian regular soldiers were the people we were eventually up against, not the ill-trained volunteers whom we met in the first year. While he was no 'jungle superman', he had earned his freedom against the Dutch the hard way in 1946, fighting in much the same fashion as he fought in Borneo, but now he was a great deal better trained and equipped than he was in 1946. He possessed a variety of modern weapons, and those of Iron Curtain and US manufacture were of high quality. He used such weapons as artillery, medium mortars, anti-personnel mines and rocket launchers with considerable skill. All in all, he was a thoroughly competent adversary. Against him, the Army established complete mastery by fierce aggressive patrolling and ambushing – always searching for and hunting the enemy, and soldiers living as guerillas, when on patrol.

The objective was to dominate and own the jungle and the frontier, week in, week out, day and night. There was no galloping over the jungle canopy in helicopters. Pilots used all their cunning and guile (for example, contour flying) to get within striking distance of the enemy by helicopter, but without being seen or heard. Then the Army tracked him down, stalking and closing in on their feet for the kill. The sure way to beat a guerilla is to operate more quietly, smoke less, talk less to possible enemy agents before an operation. In Borneo, it was nearly always the Indonesians who fell into booby traps and triggered off the claymore mines and trip flares set by patrols. OCs did not allow any forward troops into any shops, cafés or bars. When they rested they did so in their jungle base, miles from any bright lights.

We avoided tying up troops in static posts. Decentralization was the order of the day. For example, the gunners deployed thirty guns in single gun positions over nearly 1,000 miles. The 105mm Pack Howitzer could be picked up lock, stock and barrel, with ammunition and detachment, by a Belvedere helicopter; the assembled gun was slung underneath and was switched twenty miles to a platoon post in well under an hour. Our artillery was as mobile and flexible as our infantry. The same applied to the sappers. Heavy bulldozers were airdropped by Belvederes or flown in by Twin Pioneers and assembled on the ground. Gradually we acquired light air-portable earth moving equipment. We were completely air minded and allowed no obstacle to stand in our way.

Lightweight Weapons for the Infantry

The final element in establishing jungle mastery was by lightening the soldier's load. After two years the Army began to discard some of the heavier type weapons and equipment. The infantry's main weapon became the American armalite rifle – the AR15 – a really lightweight automatic weapon with a first round hit capacity which pole-axed the enemy at 50 yards in the jungle.

In 1965, the changes in our weapons and equipment were sudden and extensive. The infantry, in addition to being armed with the AR15 rifle, were issued with the 88mm mortar instead of the 3 inch; the Carl Gustav in place of the 3.5 inch rocket launcher; and the General Purpose Machine Gun (GPMG) replacing the medium machine gun. They also had claymore mines, M79 grenade launchers, M26 grenades, seismic intruder detectors, Australian light weight jungle-kit, and new British and Gurkha light weight rations.

The irony of the situation was that it was the British Army who had trained these Indonesian officers at our jungle warfare school in Malaysia and at our School of Intelligence in England.

They had artillery to support them, and all infantry NCOs had to be experienced in directing artillery and mortar fire, calling for air support, talking-in air support aircraft, constructing helicopters pads, and so on.

Many of us in the West have in the past been guilty of underestimating an Asian guerilla-type enemy, often with disastrous results. This is really unforgivable for we have only to remember the toughness of the Japanese in 1942 and of the Communist terrorists in the first three years of the Malayan emergency, to realise what a mistake this is. Those with little experience of Asians should speedily remove from their minds any notion of the inherent superiority of the white man as a soldier, as Field Marshal Slim has pointed out.

The Asian fighting man is at least equally brave, usually more careless of death, less encumbered by mental doubts and not so moved by slaughter and mutilation about him. He is better fitted to endure hardship uncomplainingly, to demand less in the way of subsistence or comfort, and to look after himself when thrown on his own resources. He has a keen practised eye for country and the ability to move across it on his own feet. He has no inherent disinclination to move through swamp and jungle nor to climb hills. Jungle fighting is similar to night fighting in that, although men may be close together, they see little, and they suffer the fears and anxieties of isolation. The more civilized we become, the more shall we draw our soldiers from well-lighted towns and the more frightened shall we be in the dark and in the jungle. The greater, therefore, will be the odds in favour of a more primitive foe. The European can, at present, more readily design and produce new weapons and equipment and find the skilled men to maintain them. Being superior in education he is also able to find a higher proportion of potential officers. But the Asian learns as readily as we do how to handle complicated new weapons. Our soldiers must be carefully indoctrinated and highly trained for guerilla and counter-insurgency type operations in battlefield conditions which are almost unimaginable in their demands on human endurance. In Europe, our climate is too temperate and our life is too urban, and our peacetime training areas are only of limited space.

Exercises on Salisbury Plain were in no way a suitable rehearsal for jungle operations. Nevertheless, there was a great deal that could be done in Britain. For example, because jungle conditions are similar to night conditions, our preparedness for jungle fighting would obviously be improved if half of the tactical training of troops to serve in the Far East could take place by night. There were always good reasons why night training could not be carried out, but there were many better reasons why it should. The Russians did a tremendous amount.

Secretly in Small Groups

In the West, the army is trained in nuclear and conventional tactics, and it depends for transportation primarily on roads, railways, water and, to a more limited extent, air. In guerilla warfare, roads, railways and rivers are the ambusher's paradise, even when convoys observe all the safety rules. On the other hand, an army that travels secretly, mostly in small groups, making rendezvous only at the precise moment of battle, cannot be ambushed. That is the way the Viet Cong usually travelled. It is the way our soldiers learned to move and they did it better than the enemy. They out-guerillaed the guerilla in every department of the game through sheer good training, based on operational experience.

The ambush is at one and the same time the guerilla's most potent enemy and his most potent weapon. Whether on a small or large scale, it can be the key element even when guerilla warfare shifts gear to full-scale mobile warfare. After all, an ambush is merely another word for 'fighting from ground of your own choosing' but with the difference that it depends entirely on complete surprise. The enemy must be unaware that he is walking into a trap. An ambush requires all the tricks of the infantryman's trade, an eye for country, track discipline, concealment, camouflage, silence, alertness, fire discipline, marksmanship, guile, cunning and, above all, self discipline. It requires constant training and rehearsal. For example, you will never pull off an ambush if you smoke, chew gum, wash your hands, clean your teeth, Brylcreme your hair, whisper or cough. In ambush, a man is lying in wait for a dangerous hunted animal whose sense of smell and keen eyesight are phenomenal.

Let us now look back on the course of Indonesian confrontation and trace the changing demands it made on an infantry battalion. In 1963, the threat was from small, ill-trained and poorly armed gangs of so-called 'Indonesian border terrorists'. To meet this threat, our tactics were similar to those of the Malayan emergency, platoons operating independently from country bases. In 1964, the Indonesian government stiffened the border terrorists with regulars and we had to contend with much stronger professional opposition, calling for closer control at battalion level and a start to company operations. Helicopters, until then small and in short supply, became larger and more numerous.

The War of 1965-6

In late 1964, Indonesia stepped up her campaign and trebled the strength of her regular garrisons in the border area, particularly in West Sarawak. In 1965 and 1966, we were therefore dealing with the regular Indonesian army in a real war, akin to fighting the Japanese in Burma. It was long range patrolling often in company strength, ambushing and attacking relatively large bodies of enemy, often dug in. It had become a company commander's war. The enemy fought with tenacity and skill. He had mortars and guns and used them efficiently. Gone were the days when the immediate reaction to a contact was to charge the enemy. During 1965 and 1966, only the highest standards of patrolling, battle craft, fire and movement, and the fullest use of our artillery and mortar support could win the day.

In mid 1966, the 'war' ended and the wheel turned full cycle back to 1963. Once more battalions were chasing only terrorists, mostly Chinese from Sarawak, trained in Indonesia. Terrorists infiltrating in twos and threes, demanded the redevelopment of platoon and section patrols and ambushes. And then, suddenly, in August 1966, there came the attempted Indonesian incursion of fifty insurgents at a time. It took one battalion a full month to smash one such incursion in the most appalling jungle and weather. A whole battalion was stretched overall about 200 miles, deployed as follow-up platoons in cut-off and deep ambushes, with the helicopter as usual doing a superb job. By that time, however, the British Army in Borneo were such masters of the situation that such an incursion was annihilated to a man.

All this goes to show how versatile the infantry soldier had to be. One day he was fighting terrorists, the next he was attacking sophisticated, well-equipped, highly trained regular soldiers, dug in and supported by artillery and mortars. The superb performance of our security forces deserved much more publicity than it received.

The effective use of such fighting forces depended on timely and accurate information – in other words, intelligence. Before the formation of Malaysia and before confrontation, both Sarawak and Sabah had been peaceful countries with practically no crime. Indeed, the size of the combined police forces of Sarawak and Sabah was smaller than the strength of the local police force of the smallest state on the mainland of West Malaysia. There was no locally-raised army or navy, just a small maritime police force. Most serious of all was the grave shortage of Special Branch police officer and inspectors.

Immediate measures were taken by the Government to overcome this shortage. Then, against some opposition, a force of 1,500 border scouts was raised from the upriver tribes, who became our 'eyes and ears'. They provided company and platoon commanders with early warning of the movement of enemy on both sides of the border. New battalions sometimes took a very long time to learn the technique of how to use their border scouts properly, but in the end everyone came to realize their worth. This is yet another example of failing to profit from the lessons of the past. These same tribes were the very people whom our special forces organized against the Japanese in the Second World War. It was because we won the hearts and minds of these people that they supplied us with reliable information. Their tribal areas, land, relatives and friends extended on both sides of the frontier, regardless of the international boundary.

In counter-insurgency operations, certainly in a sovereign independent country possessing a sophisticated Special Branch, military intelligence should be the servant and not the master of the Special Branch. This is because Special Branch officers and their staff and agents live in the country, speak the language, know the people, and are of the people, whereas army intelligence staffs are here today and gone tomorrow. Good intelligence depends on continuity at every level.

Political-Military Co-operation

In the current climate of world opinion, any military action had far reaching consequences. The political factor had, therefore, to be paramount and the Services had to accept this. Unilateral military action would eventually lead to disaster. Joint operations entailed control by a triumvirate – civilian, policeman, soldier – all under the single direction of a 'military' Director of Operations. It was the job of the Director of Operations to make sure that the system operated as two blades of a pair of scissors, neither subordinate to the other, but each making it possible for the other to succeed.

The directive given to General Walker by the National Operations Committee in Kuala Lumpur charged him with 'stimulating and encouraging the civil administration'. Although this did not entitle him to give orders direct to the civil administration, it did enable him to cause orders to be given to the civil administration through the National Operations Committee. Once the National Operations Committee were satisfied, they invariably gave their support. It was then his business to ensure that these orders were carried out to the letter with the minimum of delay. It was very seldom necessary to crack the whip. Once one began to win battles and in addition, produce civic results, one had won the confidence of the country as a whole, and from then on all should have been comparatively plain sailing.

I will quote again from Field Marshall Slim's book *Defeat into Victory*. In it he says: 'I believe that jungle fighting is today, strange as it may seem, the best training for nuclear war.' He goes on to explain this by saying that formations will be compelled to disperse and that dispersed fighting will require skilled and determined junior leaders, and self-reliant, physically hard, well-disciplined troops. He ends with these words:

> In nuclear war, after the first shock of mutual devastation has been survived, victory will go, as it does in jungle fighting, to the tougher, more resourceful infantry soldier. The easier and more gadget filled our daily life becomes, the harder will it be to produce him.
>
> In Borneo, the British, Gurkha, Australian and New Zealanders did produce him, and victory was ours, with a loss of life which was less, over three years, than the slaughter on the roads in Britain on a single Bank Holiday.

On 27th November 1967, Mr Denis Healey, the Secretary of State for Defence, paid this tribute to our Forces:

> When the House thinks of the tragedy that could have fallen on a whole corner of a Continent if we had not been able to hold the situation and bring in to a successful termination, it will appreciate that in the history books it will be recorded as one of the most efficient uses of military force in the history of the world.

CHAPTER 26

Intelligence Corps Commitment

During the latter months of 1963, as confrontation spread to the areas of 4th and 5th Divisions of Sarawak and into the North Borneo state of Sabah, the need arose for more Intelligence Corps assistance to Special Branch and in April 1964 No 2 Intelligence Company was formed.

The establishment was designed to provide Field Intelligence Officers (FIOs) as a supplement to Special Branch, Malaysian Police. These personnel would be seconded to the Malaysian authorities and under their direct control (a matter that was to be so controversial at the end of 1965). There were two military interrogation teams (one each for Sarawak and Sabah), and an operational intelligence element for staff work at HQ Director of Borneo Operations (DOBOPS). Some UK Brigades brought out their own Intelligence Platoons; other Brigades had Int. Corps personnel for operational intelligence.

FIO posts were allocated and established on the direction of DOBOPS and Heads of Special Branch, in areas affected by the threat of armed incursion, sabotage and subversion from Indonesian territory. FIOs were deployed along nearly 1,000 miles of jungle border. I don't think at any time more than ten posts were operative, and as the threat concentrated, the posts were decreased in number. A few posts were made to assist Special Branch on the internal threat, and certain MIOs had assistants. The photographic intelligence interpretation requirement was met by a detachment of two officers and a technician from JARIC (FE). JARIC is a joint service organization who produce intelligence following the interpretation of information gained from air photographs, a fascinating job.

So the scene was set, but staffing was the problem. Two other FIO posts were solved by long standing bachelors in the Corps, one where I eventually ended up and the other in 5th Division. The third bachelor held an operational intelligence job in SIBU, 3rd Division. The remaining FIO posts were by necessity having to be given to personnel of any rank who happened to be available, irrespective of background or experience, and this inevitably caused problems. Although they were all acclimatized, few if any had been to Jungle Warfare School although all had some slight experience of the jungle, mainly coming from Malaya postings.

The Intelligence Corps has always maintained that their personnel did a first class job under arduous circumstances (made more difficult because choice was limited) and who am I to argue with this? However, could the job have been done better all round? From my own experience, talks to Corps personnel and comments by certain Army and Police personnel the answer is definitely in the affirmative.

How could you hope for continuity and a successful Intelligence set-up when unqualified NCOs were moved in and out of areas every few months? They did not have time to know geographically and understand the ground they were responsible for, nor did they always make themselves known to the indigenous population in the area (in the nearest village maybe) and they certainly did not have the time to recruit and establish a team of cross border agents.

In certain areas FIOs made home in a military base or an adjacent bungalow and wandered down the road to the border village whenever traders crossed the border in order to question them; such was the limit of their efforts. It may have been geographically difficult in the odd area but I feel sure that many FIOs lacked the confidence and incentive to get on their flat jungle feet and cover their area. If this was not deemed feasible then I would suggest the FIO was wasting his time and was badly placed. I was told of one FIO who did a weekly walk to his border village for a chat to 'crossers', a distance of about a mile, and left Borneo with a Commendation and the reputation of having the most well stocked fridge of tinned beer in that area. What a way to win a war. Lucky chap – he even put on weight.

I recall meeting a Colonel (GSO 1) who came out to Borneo on a directive from the Director of Military Intelligence (DMI). He was a Corps man so he should have appreciated the problems. I often wonder if anything ever resulted from his findings and subsequent report. This officer was involved in Planning and this aspect requires vast amounts of information, both positive and negative, which you may cast aside after perusal. However information must come from all sources to be successfully collated with particular emphasis at grass roots level, and in this I think he failed, otherwise his brief summary was excellent.

As the person in charge of a particular Wing this officer had checked all previous Emergencies and it was obvious that from the point of view of Intelligence handling no two operations were alike. The operations in

Borneo were unique, they were not internal security duties nor counter insurgency operations either, and this required emphasis.

The main object of this visit was to assess and possibly update the process of handling information and intelligence through the various Formations and Establishments by the introduction of ADP (Automatic Data Processing) and the replacement of extremely outdated office equipment. Some ten years later I had not seen or heard of any significant changes. I expect financial constraints might have been a contributory factor; it may be different now.

During the three or four weeks the team spent in Singapore and Borneo the main effort seemed to be concentrated on the observation of the intelligence process from Intelligence Staff Officers at Brigade level upwards, which from the ADP and office equipment point of view made sense. I would submit that more attention should have been paid to the Intelligence gatherers (the FIOs) and all other sources of information, because it happened to me in Cyprus and in Borneo that correct and balanced assessment fell down at G3 (Int) level.

When an officer attains the (doubtful) distinction of Staff Officer Grade 3 he quite rightly believes that this is the first step on the rung to his Field Marshal's baton as he was told at Sandhurst, and by God he is going to prove himself worthy. His Commander is 'Hitler' to be followed implicitly and his doctrine rigidly adhered to, but the man to be feared is the Brigade Major who is 'Himmler', right hand man and 'hit man', who runs the Headquarters like a well oiled machine.

So this young officer, wanting desperately to impress, is made well aware of the Commander's requirements and peccadilloes, and so to voice an opinion, no matter how well balanced that may be, contrary to the Commander's view would be ill advised. Remember the Para Major (G2 Int) of the 1st Airborne Division prior to Arnhem; he correctly collated all the information and similarly assessed it and in his view there was a distinct possibility (at the time *not* definitely confirmed) that German armoured units were re-grouping or stationed in the Arnhem area and that the operation should be delayed. General Montgomery was in favour of this use of the available Airborne Divisions (US and British). All Airborne Commanders from Battalion upwards were demanding action to prove their worth, and no way did they want interference in the glory that was to come. They must all share the blame for the débâcle in Holland; they behaved like demented bulls trying to get to the herd. Who the hell was going to listen to the lone voice who with great sincerity and efficiency proposed a temporary postponement? The concept was brilliant, the organization excellent, the result diabolical; no one wanted to listen to adverse intelligence and weather prospects therefore so many died to satisfy the ambitions and self glorification of those who should have known better. The tragic sequel to all this was that the G2 (Int) subsequently committed suicide because he felt he had not done enough.

In Cyprus, Borneo and China I was often faced with assessments of dispositions, units, weapons and personalities totally alien to what had been reported and moreover frequently assessed in a categorical manner when confirmation had not been obtained. It all looked good, sounded good at briefings and usually justified action to be undertaken by the formation's units, and this is where the intelligence process usually fails (if it does) by the failure of an individual to fairly and without bias, collect, collate and assess information correctly before he passes it on down the line to higher authority. A computer is only as good as the information it is given, despite the microchip, ADP or advanced office equipment. Intuition, common sense and the human element are still the most important elements of intelligence work.

The Colonel admitted that those in command on the ground knew what they were about and were grateful for the excellent work being done by FIOs. I quote: 'Concerning these, I could not shake off a feeling that we were not preparing them for their tasks with anything like the thoroughness necessary, and that they were surviving more because of the artificially/ politically controlled tempo of operations than by use of the junglecraft they knew, because few if any had been trained in it. This might not be the truth of the matter, nor do justice to the men concerned, *but bears thought.*'

His final comment in general states that it would be better to debrief *key* intelligence personnel more fully when they come out of the area of operations, and require a report on the period to be sent to the Intelligence Centre.

When we wined and dined in the Borneo Hotel maybe some of my comments were remembered by the Colonel, although in my experience few Corps officers ever seriously considered the comments of their senior ranks. As they normally do not undertake field work this is possibly understandable. I was never de-briefed or submitted a report following any of my operational tours or incidents.

I say this because to place a relatively young, inexperienced NCO on a civilian secondment, working autonomously in an environment completely strange to him and for which he has had no training, is asking a lot, plus the fact that instructions issued at that time said that they were *not* under command of the local military commander but the Divisional Special Branch Officer.

What joy to the immature NCO to be able to tell some captain above to get knotted (with impunity) because he was not under military command. That comment may sound tart but in effect it did happen and no doubt in some instances more than once. In one particular area the FIO (not Intelligence Corps, I believe) did not enjoy a good rapport with the G3 (Int) he should have liaised with. It was a Colonial unit, and as a result of this friction the FIO refused to impart information even verbally to the G3, which considering we were on active service was quite ridiculous and John Althorp had to fly out from Labuan to sort the matter out.

Another item which was of paramount importance was that quite a number of FIOs were incapable of maintaining their own healthy environment and self sufficiency in a physical way. Some FIOs fell victim to diseases not necessarily because they exposed themselves to the regions of jungle living but because they ignored common sense, military health guidelines and they didn't eat correctly or clean themselves properly, and as a result FIOs had to have mandatory two-monthly check ups with the nearest military Medical Officer.

Faced with these operational and yet administrative problems something had to be done on a more permanent basis and I think I was the first person to be posted direct to an FIO post for a tour of at least twelve months from a UK or BAOR post. The posting of personnel is never an easy task especially when you should be more selective for active service intelligence jobs. Bearing in mind that Cyprus had intervened in 1964, it was taking time to regularize the posting plot and give the FIOs a chance to organize their areas of responsibility and learn more quickly from the horrors that their predecessors may have made.

The one thing that the Intelligence Corps could not concede was to give Operators the time for acclimatization and some knowledge of jungle warfare which I think would have been of great help to the Intelligence effort and made far more effective Operators for the future.

There is a grave misconception in the Intelligence Corps, and quite a large percentage of Officers and Operators share this view, that because they form part of a Corps with a distinctive title they are the God-given holders of a superior intellect and as such are a class apart. They frequently consider Infantry, Ordnance etc. slightly inferior beings, which is a sad mistake to make. In my humble view the really effective Field Operator (remembering that officers very rarely indulged in this 'rough work') should be almost as highly trained as a SAS Trooper, capable of looking after himself, and confident of his ability to do so. (This is an old hobby horse of mine.)

So the Corps now appeared to be choosing Operators with some proven background. They were not to know that we would all be out of Borneo by

November 1966. John Althorp was already Commanding 2 Company from Labuan. Staff Patrick should have been in Malaya by 1965 but would no doubt have followed later on to Borneo; I was about to go; young Campbell eventually had a few months in Serian; and another one of the Cyprus crowd was due to follow after a language course. In my estimation that was the reason I was selected for Borneo as the beginning of a more stable effort by the Corps in this particular theatre. None of this would have made sense to my wife; the exigencies of the Service meant nothing to her, only separation and the added responsibilities of an absent father.

The most instant of problems, as October approached, was to find accommodation in the Preston/Blackpool area. Married quarters were available but only desired if absolutely necessary. Hirings were seen and refused. When we started making the rounds on our arrival back in UK, initially we stayed with Jean's parents in Preston. Then the good Lord smiled on us and we found the ideal flat in Bazley Road, Ansdell. The owner lived below us and she was an angel and so good to Jean in the long months ahead. It was a great relief and comfort to me to know that despite the separation Jean and the family were housed adequately, happier despite the circumstances, and near enough for relatives and friends to call; and of course Chris was close at hand from his boarding school in Blackpool.

To add to my limited knowledge of what lay ahead I was rather reluctantly granted an 'audience' at the Counter Intelligence Unit at HQ Western Command, Chester, to see a particular officer, who formerly commanded 2 Intelligence Company at Labuan. When I had written to him from Minden to ask for any helpful information, in a flippant and terse manner he said everything would be provided and you didn't need much in a grass hut. That is what was known in the Intelligence Corps as leadership from the front. I doubt if he ever saw a native hut except from the air; still, administrative types remain the same the world over.

The briefing was varied and informative. He spoke of the locations and backgrounds of indigenous tribes, what 2 Company had achieved during his tour as OC, but very little about the way of life and practicalities of working as a FIO, because he didn't know, and wasn't particularly worried so long as nobody got on his back. After about half an hour I was ushered out of his office as he was about to meet the G1 and argue as to whether he should be entitled to a Staff car which would be larger than his unit one so that his legs would be more comfortable! I left him with mixed feelings, but I must add these further comments.

We met again in Singapore and we had a clash, which almost led to violence. I stayed with his unit for a few days after treatment for my bad eye, and not by choice was brought into a unit briefing on their role in an

Internal Security exercise. I was asked to comment on what had been outlined, so I did so bluntly and honestly, adding the consequences if they didn't re-think. With one exception (a Warrant Officer) all the officers and senior ranks howled me down. Events that followed proved me right in every way and the unit was not only censured from higher authority but hated in most service establishments; they behaved quite stupidly.

When I left Borneo and stayed with them in Singapore for a few days I developed a slight fever. Walking from my room to the toilet some five yards away I was observed wearing only a jungle green towel round my waist. The erstwhile Captain accused me of being a savage, lacking manners, a possible insult to women who worked in the unit. Two nights later I was sitting alone at the unit Bar waiting for Mick Courage and his girlfriend to have a final drink when in came the Captain. He had had previous drinks but began a conversation with the barman (a lance-corporal) and a corporal, addressing them by their Christian names and discussing matters of a personal and military nature which he should not have disclosed.

Suddenly he stopped talking and looked across at me, then, turning to the NCOs at the bar he pointed to me and said, 'He is probably the most dangerous bastard in the Corps; he says nothing but hears everything and makes a mental note of it. On top of that he is probably the best soldier in this Corps and I don't f—g like him, give him a f—g drink.' Inwardly I was very angry but did not feel fit enough for a physical confrontation so the matter ended. I saw him once again in Edinburgh when I arranged some accommodation for him. He apparently behaved in his usual obnoxious manner and the hotel said they would not entertain him again. He later resigned his commission, acting most beneficially to the Corps – a pity several more didn't do the same.

I tried to explain to my brother John, without disclosing anything, that my work in Borneo would be odd and that he should try and explain matters to Jean if anything happened to me. I don't think I was very successful as he never asked me about it at all, even when I came back. Whether he was being discreet or just had no interest I shall never know.

CHAPTER 27

Initial Reactions

The last few days at Bazley Road were very traumatic. It was hard to guess how the children felt, but Jean and I were dreading the separation. She was obviously thinking of my safety and that she would have to cope yet again with all the problems of a divided family. I was full of apprehension and some anticipation of the job ahead, the challenge of the work to do, the perils of a jungle (which I suppose I was in fear of), and the possibility of contact with the enemy without the usual support.

I'd already said my farewells to Chris, told him to work hard and not to worry, and that I would no doubt see him somewhere in the Far East a year the following Christmas. It was therefore a very choked and close to tears soldier that carried his suitcase to Ansdell station, leaving behind a brave but tearful wife and daughter. I had known about my posting and duties for too long and this is what made it harder. I was glad to reach London with all the time consuming problems of catching an aircraft at Heathrow.

Most of the personnel travelling on the plane were in small unit groups or married families, I was alone and felt isolated; this was probably a good start as it set the pattern for the next year. Following nine-hour hops to Kuwait, Columbo and Kuala Lumpur we finally arrived at Singapore. It was around midnight and reasonably cool. By 2a.m. I had acquired a bed in the Transit Camp at Nee Soon and slept till 9a.m. I contacted Jack Pitt at HQ SIB who picked me up and took me to his flat, and I met Pat and the kids once again. Their welcome and familiar faces did a power of good to my morale.

At 7a.m. the following day I was flying over the South China Sea to the island of Labuan, Headquarters Land Forces, Borneo. The heat and humidity were overwhelming but my room at the hotel was air-conditioned which helped. I also took the opportunity to have a quick dip in the sea on the east side of the harbour; it was most pleasant. Luckily I didn't swim far from the shore; I was told later that the harbour area was a favourite haunt of the highly poisonous sea snake. *Lesson one*, you are not at Blackpool,

266

acquire local knowledge. I later had a haircut and shampoo, ably carried out by two rather attractive Chinese girls, *Lesson two*, Great, Eh!

I drew certain items of jungle kit from the Quartermaster, had an administrative and operational briefing from the OC 2 Company, Captain John Althorp, from Cyprus days, and was taken over to HQ to see the G1 (Int) who then informed me I was not going to Pensiangan as originally thought. It was now a possibility that I would be despatched to a nomadic border tribe of Muruts, who meandered around the triangle formed by Sabah, 5th Division and Indonesia. My mind boggled at the thought of this lunacy, anticipating all the various problems especially the matter of communications. I kept my mouth shut, understanding the need for information in the area, but this was surely not the answer: there were too many complications. Back in my room I formed the opinion that this was no doubt the brainchild of some desk bound warrior who had had no experience of intelligence in the field and where the operator would have to rely solely on the whims and fancies of primitive tribesmen, who would obviously put tribal matters before my operational commitments. I began to have some nagging doubts about the Staff Intelligence set-up down the line; I hoped that this particular scheme was not indicative of the problems I would undoubtedly face in the coming months.

Within 24 hours I was informed that I was going to Bau in 1st Division as the FIO. It was the busiest and most interesting post in the theatre; my morale soared. I met a Signals Warrant Officer at the Catholic Mission Church whom I had served with in 11Bde and he asked me to the Mess that evening, I was leaving the following morning for Kuching so I could afford a celebration. It was a mixed service Mess and we had a great evening.

I don't wish to be critical, and as I well know, there have to be Headquarters personnel to keep the pipeline flowing, but it seemed so unreal in the Mess that night; dozens of 'single' men having one hell of a bachelor type night out, which they probably did several times a week. They swam, sunbathed, water skied, sailed and so on, and did their office work of course, but at the end of the six or nine months unaccompanied, they still received the same piece of purple and green ribbon to show they had served in Borneo. What a contrast to the lot of the lads at the blunt end: infantry, gunners, engineers, cooks, etc. I always maintain that combat medals where applicable should accompany a theatre 'gong'. All have their jobs to do but it is the conditions under which the duty is performed that should be taken in consideration and in this theatre, what a contrast.

A pleasant surprise at the airport the following morning: who should walk in the lounge coming from Tawau en route to Terendak Camp, Malaya, but Bert Rainford and Johnny Johnson of ISG. We had a pleasant ten-minute chat before I boarded the Fokker Friendship for Kuching. From the aircraft, the view of Sarawak was awe inspiring and formidable, a large mass of trees and vegetation. I began to feel apprehensive; was I too old at forty for a lark like this?

I was met by Jones (MIO 1st Division) and the chap I was relieving. On arrival at Police HQ I was taken to see Jones 2 (MIO Sarawak), a career officer, well spoken, every inch a gentleman, a smoothie who put the knife in within a minute. Neither he, Jones 1, nor the CO of 2/10 Gurkhas wanted me there, and they had fought all along the line to obtain their wishes but had been over-ruled, I had an idea that John Althorp had used his persuasion. Jones 2 made his briefing short, wished me luck and dismissed me. Leaving his office I then knew where I had seen him before: Germany 1964. I had been investigating the loss of a NATO secret document by one of our units. The particular document had in fact been lost, stolen or destroyed for more than nine months, and the unit admitted negligence by several officers, but the depths I had to go to in order to complete a comprehensive investigation had led me to a senior formation HQ where Jones 2 was employed with another officer.

These two reverted to type, indirectly reminding me that *they were officers* and to watch my questions. They were unco-operative and evasive. I gave up after a quarter of an hour with the words 'we are only a post office' ringing in my ears. My subsequent report on this part of the enquiry held nothing back. I believe General Frank King had something to say to the higher formation when he read my report. I wonder if Jones 2 recognised me?

I then met Head of Special Branch (HSB) who would be my boss, a career Colonial Police Officer of sound reputation. He was a very nice bloke and we chatted about former Ex PP chaps we both knew. He made me feel welcome, a fact so appreciated.

Leaving HSB we went to Jones 1's office near Central Police Station and had a more detailed briefing about my area of responsibility. Jones 1 was RCT (SAS), a tall, laconic individual who didn't like driving a desk and who was apt to take off on occasions and indulge in a 'walkabout'. I don't think these excursions were for the purpose of intelligence gathering, but they kept him in touch with the countryside and maintained his physical fitness. Things were revealed later that suggested he would have been better concentrating on his desk work. He was a good, capable soldier and as he did not have a Military Assistant at that time he would have been more gainfully employed in his office. It was some time later when I was checking some details with Ssgt. F, the newly appointed MA, that I pointed out all the discrepancies in his briefings. He was still talking about enemy units and locations that had been long gone, or been evacuated further to the rear, confirmed by 1/10 Gurkhas and myself.

The character I was due to relieve, we'll call him S, was an extremely odd character, an extrovert, I had met him briefly at the Centre where he had worked in 1962-3. He was about thirty years of age, a bachelor and a very unsociable type. Inclusive of leaves and Courses he had been at BAU for about two years and to some people he had created the myth that he was indispensable: James Bond, Kissinger and Sanders of the River all rolled into one. Hence the antagonism on my arrival. He expected Special Branch to fight his corner but they knew better. He adored the Dyaks and thought they could do no wrong; this was mutually returned on the surface but he would have been hurt had he heard their comments about him when he had left.

However one concession the Pro S lobby had obtained was that he could remain *in situ* and await the arrival of an agent of his with 'special' information. Within three weeks of my arrival I had ascertained that the agent was already serving three years imprisonment in Indonesia for theft; the bubble had burst. He left the house almost immediately, took local leave, then UK and Berlin. I was glad to see him go but in the initial week the following occurred.

A guide/bodyguard/interpreter named Patrick had been found and accepted by SB. In order to introduce me to military and civil contacts we first flew by 'chopper' to Serikin, the busiest trading village in my area, meeting the Company Commander of the 2/10 Gurkhas, the Headman and Border Scouts. The following day I was introduced to the Commanding Officer of 2/10 Gurkhas and others, then went across the road to meet the Battery Commander of 129 (Dragon) Bty, of 40 Light Regiment RA, two of his officers and several senior NCOs. Then we flew to Stass, a large village close to the border which had been attacked on occasions. Again I met the military and was shown the defence locations, then we walked to the village and I had my first introduction to the precarious, tedious and at times painful chore of crossing swampy ground by means of logs laid end to end. I was never a circus act, being too tall; carrying a heavy pack I frequently lost balance and my ankles and lower legs became black from continuous bruising over the next twelve months.

We stayed overnight with the Headman. Our meal was rice and some green stuff, backed up with the native drink tuak, not a drink I ever enjoyed, it also gave you quite a headache. Next day we flew to 'Buckit Knuckle' an ingeniously designed military position on a ridge of high ground. All the trees had been laid on the surrounding low ground to form an effective barrier, suitably mined. The location was re-supplied by parachute and by air-lifting. An old Land Rover with winch, secured on top of 'knuckle' made a very effective winch system and was erected from the Dropping Zone (DZ) enabling all stores including artillery ammunition to be handled comfortably the hundred feet or so to the top of 'knuckle'. Four or five huge trees laid end to end made an aerial footpath from the top to join the track to a village called Gumbang which lay some two miles away and high on the watershed, some two hundred yards from the official border. We did not visit the village on this occasion, but Patrick and I came the following week.

Introductions were made to the Gurkhas, then we went off to visit Tringus and Tringus Matang. I think S was attempting to drive me into the ground five days out from England and he bloody near succeeded. To my surprise we had a fifteen-year-old Chinese boy with us who was a *friend* of S, who apparently paid his school fees, I did not query his presence as I was the new boy, I just watched points. As it was the rainy season we scrounged groundsheets and other items from the Gurkhas then set off along a track deep in mud but climbing all the time. The rain fell and so did the leeches. The heat and high humidity made me feel stifled and I sweated terribly, asking for frequent stops. The leeches, despite precautions, entered jungle boots and liberally helped themselves to the chest, back and mainly the neck; did I suffer. Patrick removed them with a lighted cigarette, at least the ones I couldn't see. I reciprocated but rarely ever found them on him. European blood must be more palatable. It was a chore that neither of us enjoyed but it was done so many times in the months to follow (we once removed what was known as a bull leech from the back of a Gurkha and it was about the size of an Havana cigar, quite fantastic).

To approach Tringus from the mountain necessitated a sheer descent of 600 feet. It was dangerous and even worse to climb. On our arrival we met the Headman, had a bathe in the mountain stream and ate our rice. Anticipating an early night to rest my weary bones, would you believe, they laid on a 'Dance' for my benefit. The ladies gathered in a corner of the Headman's house and played the drums, they don't dance; the men, mainly young ones, displayed their sensuous gyrations then I was dragged up to participate. I'd never danced with a 'fella' before! I was not drunk, as most of the tuak I had managed to pour through the cracks in the floor. After some ten minutes I pleaded insanity or something and managed to remain seated on the floor without offending anyone. Sleep was short but blissful.

The morning brought further pain. We began to climb the mountain and into Indonesia. As we climbed we were confronted by a series of sheer cliff faces up to eighty feet or so in height which could only be ascended by means of large trees, branches trimmed, and steps cut into the trunk. To aid travellers, makeshift handrails of bamboo were somehow attached to the trunk. It was hazardous enough to climb up but the descent was really quite frightening; to fall on one side would have been bad enough but the other side would have ensured certain death, a drop of hundreds of feet to where the mountain stream was the source of the Sungai Pedi. Reaching the summit completely exhausted I asked for a short rest before we continued over the border to locate the hut of an Indonesian witch doctor who apparently had two wives who adorned themselves in a unique way with bangles on legs and arms which effectively crippled them. This family had one son who attended the School on our side at Pengalan Tebang, and this is where S had made contact with the father, who travelled widely in the Border area and was maybe a useful source.

We reached a cleared area of ground where the lone hut of the witch doctor lay close to the trees. The two ladies waved a welcome and I gratefully collapsed. After a welcome bathe in a nearby stream the husband returned and we were introduced. Owing to the attitude of S I was unaware of what he had said in order of tasking so I told Patrick to tell him quite forcefully that I was now his best friend, precisely what information I would like and that I would pay him well if it was useful. He was a thin, emaciated looking individual who did not strike you as a particularly intelligent character and it was known that he disappeared for six to eight weeks at a time so he could really not be considered as a reliable source.

After a meagre meal of rice and some kind of vegetable we talked until the light failed then the seven of us prepared to sleep on the floor of the hut. Then suddenly the thirteen-year-old son made an appearance; he had been told(?) that we had intended to visit his father so he had made the journey from PT, which had taken me two days. He had managed it in failing light in under two hours. Our age gap was obvious and of course he wasn't bothered about meeting enemy soldiers. More talk, then sleep, which was interrupted by the abrupt drop in temperature and I shivered uncontrollably, not a good night.

We made an early start and then had the frightening climb down the mountain with a grateful rest once again in Tringus. You do not need telephones in this environment. As we munched bananas we were joined by Ang Hoi Poh (AP) a person who was employed by another Chinese gentleman Ang Soon Cheng (AC) who was a storekeeper in PT, the village to which we were heading. AP volunteered to guide us there. Unaware of my physical condition we crossed the Sungai Pedi no fewer than thirteen times. It was at its seasonal height with huge hidden boulders and a fast tortuous current which caused loss of balance and frequent duckings, and when we reached the last flat stretch I sat on the bank completely exhausted, a bowed, wet, bedraggled figure unable to move. A curious AP looked at me and conversed with Patrick who then dashed into nearby trees and entered a small hut, returning shortly with a fist size lump of rock salt, I ate this like an apple at the request of AP, both he and Patrick watching with tolerance and smiles. I told them to go on and I would follow but they refused. S and the boy sat there talking making no comment. Within half an hour I felt much better. We finished the journey and entered the tiny village of Pengkalan Tebang.

Ang Soon Cheng was the most charming of Chinese gentlemen. He owned a local store and had been involved in cross border trading for many years. AP worked for him on a regular basis and he also employed the local villagers when necessary. I was a welcomed guest if I was passing through, and I also spent a couple of visits at his home in Kuching; we became good friends. He made the point that I should never have been taken on such an arduous trip nine days out of England, and he insisted that we travel to Krokong, a village near Bau, by his boat the following day. I made my weary way back to the nearby river, stripped off and enjoyed the lazy luxury of a relaxing bathe, heeding the warning that small crocodiles sometimes swam to these upper reaches. I have always had a fear of snakes and other such creatures, unlike my father, uncle and brother who all found them fascinating, and who frequently regaled a company with stories of incidents and hunts for snakes. I found it interesting but I could never find any enthusiasm deliberately to go out and search for them. If I had to take risks let it be by accident or enemy action.

I must confess that that first week cancelled out any basic fears of the jungle. I imagined the worst: nothing happened, I was so tired during those early days of 'jungle bashing' and keeping up with the others that I did not think about any natural dangers around me and so it was a good start to my jungle survival. As we walked Patrick and I, between gasps, talked, and over the early weeks I learned quickly on the spot provided I asked all the questions. Patrick's annoying habit was to wait until something happened, then he would explain. The two incidents now described are indicative of his lovable but most perplexing personality.

On two particular occasions because Patrick did not offer helpful information I nearly fell to my death.

The route to the area of Tringus Matang in Indonesia was a perilous one. I had an agent there, previously described. He had been recruited by S but was really too independent and isolated to be of any great use. He could not faithfully be tasked but he did bring back information of an area facing Bau and Padawan Districts which was helpful and was worth the occasional visit.

From the kampong and helipad at Tringus the little used track was rough, overgrown and very steep. At four or five points where the traveller was confronted with a sheer cliff face and a four to five hundred foot drop down to the river, huge tree trunks probably eighty feet or more were placed against the cliff face. Steps were hewn out of the trunk and a bamboo handrail somehow attached to either side. The most difficult part was negotiating these tree trunks on the way down. As Patrick usually avoided carrying any weight in his pack I carried blankets, First Aid kit and food, plus two weapons, grenades, and ammunition. It was top heavy; add to this muddy and wet jungle boots and as you can imagine the descent was dodgy to say the least. The handrails were essential to give confidence and help your balance, but they were made of bamboo and therefore always suspect. Bamboo can crumble at a touch after so long from cutting, and this is what happened to me on my second trip down this route. As I placed my hand lightly on the right hand rail it disintegrated at a touch and two six-foot lengths disappeared hundreds of feet below. Panic, and did I pray; my left hand hung on to the other rail and it held, no problem. How I kept my balance is a mystery; add to that I was frightened to death of falling. The remainder of the descent was quite an experience, and Patrick just smiled, saying, 'Well, it does happen like that sometimes.' The annoying thing was that he didn't appear to be worried about the consequences, to me or any other traveller. It still hadn't been repaired on our next trip.

The other incident occurred when we were crossing the Sungai Pedi, heading for Pengkalan Tebang. We had been along the foothills of the Bungo Range that formed the eastern extremity of my allotted area. This range only extended for approximately twelve miles into Sarawak and was so rugged it took a platoon of Gurkhas seven days or so to patrol the ridge and they had to be completely re-kitted on their return. Flesh was torn and clothing ripped to shreds: quite an horrific journey considering it was so short. It proved one thing, that Indonesian regulars or guerillas were unlikely to use the high route, so I took the low one, visiting kampongs and isolated huts en route.

As we reached the bridge (of native construction) I wondered why it had been built so high above the rocky river bed. Patrick explained that when the river was in high flood it was necessary to have a bridge that reached the high ground on either side. As I boldly started to climb the bridge Patrick conveniently started to relieve himself. I was two thirds over the bridge almost above the opposite bank when the handrails and the footrail started to crumble and the whole bridge collapsed. Yelling in terror I managed a foothold on something and launched myself towards the steep opposite bank. I hit the sodden bank like a ruptured crab, losing my Sterling SMC on impact; it slid into the depth of the river and so did I. Not without a struggle I may add; I think I grabbed at every leaf, blade of undergrowth or crevice on that twenty-foot descent, hands, feet, chin, nose whatever, but to no avail; I slid decorously into the murky depths. Luckily my Sterling had stuck just below the surface and I recovered it, but to rub it in, when I looked across the river, Patrick was doubled up with laughter.

I contravened the Race Discrimination Act and called him some well established Anglo Saxon names which only seemed to make it worse. Eventually he was persuaded to cross the river which he did in a series of leaps from one rock to another and short swims when necessary. He finally pulled me up the bank with the aid of rattan or something, and then we both had a laugh. I asked him why he hadn't crossed first and he said, 'The locals wouldn't use the bridge because it's unsafe.' I said, 'Why didn't you tell me?' and he said, 'You didn't ask me!' There's no answer to that, but that was dear old Patrick.

A few weeks before I left I decided to buy him a good watch as a farewell gift and something he would remember me by. Within a week he had given it to his younger brother. When I asked him about this as I felt slighted, he said, 'We always give to people we love, the thing we love best.' I could find no answer to that either.

To conclude my description of Patrick, we shared that year day in day out and I led him into all sorts of dangerous situations, but I only scratched the surface of his Dyak character. In the brief periods we were home, within minutes he would disappear behind the small bunk I had arranged for him in the bungalow, then, washed and changed, he was off to his home which lay in the jungle some distance from Krokong. I knew he had land and rubber trees and was using this job to save his salary and secure his future. Although a schoolteacher by profession, he was not over intelligent, and he never developed a sense of involvement in our operations; he just allowed himself to be led. Naturally lazy like the majority of Dyaks (understandably so) he had to be closely watched especially when it came to interpretation. He spoke Malay and had a knowledge of four or five other tribal dialects. I found that after a prolonged conversation I had to question him about the text of the exchange. He was not forthcoming and this presented problems when the object of the exercise was to gather information, although continually reminded. He was hard work at times; I knew what I wanted and so did he, so it was hard work when he continually digressed. Apart from this fault he was my right arm, leg too. He just lacked the necessary motivation. We were an extremely effective team, but with more interest on his part I think we could have been better.

The journey down-river was quite fascinating and I enjoyed being the lazy traveller as I lay on top of AC's goods. They filled his boat which was more awkward to handle with additional passengers. The high jungle trees formed a canopy over the river blocking out the sun and keeping it somewhat cooler. It was like travelling through a long tunnel. The boatman had frequently to leap out of the rear of the craft to guide us round or off the unseen boulders on which we frequently balanced rather precariously. Our load of Indonesian rubber demanded utmost care in navigation, but I couldn't care less. I wasn't walking and I felt great. We scrounged a lift by road from Krokong to Bau and that ended my first hard trek. We eventually arrived back at *my* bungalow which it now was, still tired but pleased that I had managed to stay on my feet. I was going to insist that Patrick and I would work on our own forthwith, and my fitness would have priority. S never came out again. It would be feet before 'choppers' and at my pace. Within a month I was as fit as a butcher's dog, but I was rapidly losing weight. The intense heat and humidity, plus hard exercise and a rice diet reduced me to skeletal proportions.

I stayed out for longer periods than S who apparently used the 'choppers' like a taxi service and didn't spend long periods out, preferring to wait for his friends to make their regular visits to the bungalow when he paid for their lies and 'duff' information. It was a matter of assessment. S was not a soldier or a policeman; the job was secondary to him. However for a couple of days after our return he melted somewhat. In between one 'chopper' trip I made, I attempted to pick his brains and then he closed up. We shared the same bedroom (when I was in residence) for another month and he rarely spoke or entered conversation. He wasn't aggressive or obnoxious in any way; he behaved quite childishly, knowing the writing was on the wall. SB didn't want to know him and he didn't wish to know me. It was at this stage that I met three persons who made the Borneo period something to remember.

From a Depot at Bau, the Public Works Department commenced a road project through primary jungle linking Bau to Lundu, the most westerly town in 1st Division. It was a necessary, ambitious operation that would enhance the lives of the indigenous tribes in that remote area affording access to medical facilities, the law, trade and other aspects of civilization. A road engineer supervised the practical construction, but the maintenance of all plant and stores was the responsibility of a gentleman from Salford called Peter Slowe. He was ex RAF, in his mid thirties and a very competent and experienced engineer. As the project was through thick jungle you can imagine that the plant equipment, operated mainly by locally recruited labour took a hammering, and Pete was kept busy on the ground and at Bau under very harsh conditions.

Pete was fortunate; he was allocated a charming bungalow next to the District Officer, situated on high ground to the south of Bau, adjacent to the airstrip. He had been most fortunate to acquire an excellent Amah (servant) named Chin, whose uncle worked for Pete and had suggested that she would be a suitable employee. Chin was Chinese, very attractive, and pregnant; apparently she was being forced into prostitution by parents until the uncle intervened. Pete and I met within days of my arrival and formed a friendship immediately which, with interruptions, has lasted to this day. On an intellectual plane he enjoyed the company of S but not in a social context, whereas with me when I was 'at home' over a period of seven months we enjoyed a unique rapport. We shared many interests, but were diametrically opposite in others. The most amusing were the alcoholic escapades which helped to relieve my loneliness; it was a straw he grasped and I was grateful, but these are stories for the pub. His house was near and within minutes of arrival at my bungalow (a hovel in comparison) by chopper, road or on foot, Pete would arrive in a cloud of dust, cheerful and full of suggestions on how we should spend the next few hours together. He was envious of my undoubted culinary accomplishments with frozen steaks and we were usually 'three sheets in the wind' before we ate. A wonderful, generous character.

Paddy Kelleher was Battery Quartermaster Sergeant (BQMS) of 129 'Dragon' Battery, 40 Light Regiment Royal Artillery. Four of the Battery's six 105mm Howitzers were *in situ* on the forward positions the other two remaining at Bau to reinforce if necessary, Paddy operated from Battery HQ working a unique wartime/peacetime accounting system which he thoroughly enjoyed! He was a 'bogman' pure and simple, humorous, warm and generous to a fault; he was a scruffy edition of Barry Fitzgerald. He had offered S friendship, kit and food and had been totally rejected. S preferred Dyak company which to Paddy was the unforgivable sin. He was a lapsed Catholic, although he did come with me to Mass on one Sunday and repeated the whole Mass in Latin! Married to a Spanish girl they had two lovely children. The OC and two officers remained at Bau in Bty HQ, with four senior ranks and fifteen to twenty junior ranks. For one dollar Malay per month I was mysteriously on attached strength. A bed was available, I could eat if necessary, and pay for as much beer as I desired. They all knew I was engaged in 'strange duties' and operated differently to S, but not one person ever asked an embarrassing question. A visitor one evening began to get curious and he was taken to one side and told to mind his own business. Paddy's hilarious escapades in the 'Ice Van', on the Lake, and with Capt. Correa are pub stories in themselves; what a person, a soldier and a mate.

Peter Lim was the Chinese Police Inspector, Special Branch, who shared my bungalow, a very charming, talented University graduate, who was serving on a short term contract, later to become a Regular. Born in Sibu, 3rd Division, his parents owned a large store there, Peter was earmarked for Special Branch duties before completion of his studies. He married after I left and had a family. He was a person I would love to see again and I managed this in 1994. In this sphere of police work he was more than competent, highly intelligent, dedicated and enthusiastic; one could not wish for a better partner. My area of responsibility was five miles our side of the border and beyond into Indonesia, and Peter was responsible for the remaining internal area of Bau District, which also contained the largest Communist dominated village in the country, Tundong, which controlled small cells throughout the District. He had a room next to mine and we worked closely together throughout my tour so successfully that in the last few months with my 80 per cent and his 20 per cent we practically wrote the SB Intelligence Summary (Int Sum) for the whole of 1st Division. He was a person I was proud to have known.

To summarize: at this stage I had arrived in station, met all essential military and police personnel, with one exception visited all border villages, got S out of my hair, extracting as much information as he was willing to impart, and had survived my first taste of 'Ulu bashing', so why was I here? Field Intelligence Officers were seconded to the Sarawak Constabulary, now the Royal Malaysian Police Special Branch, and it was the duty of FIOs to obtain information on all Indonesian military activity, Sarawak born Indonesian based terrorists (IBT) and any other relevant information of use to the Malay Government.

CHAPTER 28

Duties of FIO

Briefly (although I have official copies) the Sarawak Constabulary Special Branch of the Royal Malaysia Police Standing Order outlines the duties of an FIO as follows:

Special Branch Field Posts will be established as directed by Head Special Branch in areas affected by the threat of armed incursion, sabotage and subversion from Indonesian territory.

Personnel to man the posts will be Intelligence trained Army NCOs, designated Field Intelligence Officers (FIOs) assisted by English speaking auxiliary police officers.

The object is to collect, collate and assess information concerning the threat of armed incursion, sabotage or subversion and to disseminate such intelligence to the local Security Force Commander and to the Divisional SBO (Special Branch Officer).

The FIO will collect information from all available sources in his area. Included are:

Agents/Informers Recruited by the FIO or a previous 'Handler'.

Border Crossers Persons who cross the Indonesian border (who originate from within either Sarawak or Indonesia) for *bona fide* reasons e.g. trading, visiting relatives etc. and refugees from Indonesia. Talent spotting should always be carried out to recruit regular informers.

Government Officials Police and District Officers, Penghulus, Tuai Rumah etc.

Military Posts in Area Ascertain info gained by military in their contact with local population.

Prisoners FIOs will interrogate prisoners for immediate operational intelligence.

Collation Kept very simple:
a) an operational map – enemy locations and movements.

b) Records – carbon copy of Intelligence Report Form.

FIOs should be very selective in recruiting agents. Treat agents as casuals until information is of sufficient quality to upgrade them to regular informers.

Ensure reverse of Report Form is compiled accurately.

Identifying marks of agents, and observers forwarded to DSBO.

Maintain a card index.

All information held under secure conditions.

Assessment By virtue of FIO background knowledge of enemy, and his training to reason logically, he should be able to assess the value and validity of information and comment accordingly on the reverse of the Report Form.

The FIO should make assessments of enemy dispositions, strengths, activities and further intentions.

Dissemination

a) Original report form to DSBO.

b) Copy retained.

c) Local Security Forces operational Commander (VERBALLY) a copy of the report may be passed to the Commander *if the FIO considers it necessary*, but the particulars on the reverse side of the report form will not be completed.

Tasking FIOs will be tasked, and briefed for intelligence tasks by their local Military Commanders. Tasks and briefs may be also given by Divisional SBOs and MIOs.

Administration

Command and Liaison FIOs are part of the Special Branch machine and *under operational command of DSBO*, but liaise with SF Commander from whom they take tasks and briefs.

DSBOs MIOs and ASP E2. Will visit FIOs to update their intelligence and guide their work.

FIO's will normally wear civilian clothes *and will be armed at all times*. Housing will be provided by the police or in a Security Force post.

Victualling FIOs can be provided by food from nearest military unit or draw ration allowance and provide own messing.

Arms Constant range practice, and when moving in an area where contact with the enemy is possible, they are to be escorted by police or military. (This never happened at any time.)

Transport Use police transport when available, the military may assist.

Helicopter transportation should be requested through the local SF Commander.

Finance FIOs will maintain a No 1 Account for payments.

General The role of the FIO is to collect, collate, assess and disseminate intelligence concerning the threat from Indonesia. The internal threat to Sarawak posed by Communism is not to be regarded as a Task to be tackled by the FIO, but any information concerning Communism or any other threat to security which is obtained by the FIO will be reported to the DSBO who is the authority for assessment and dissemination.

Special Branch Field Posts are established to serve local Security Force Commanders and Divisional SBOs. FIOs will perform this task and will remember that they are *not* under command of the local military commanders and are answerable to the Divisional Special Branch Officer.

September 1964

CHAPTER 29

The Serious Work Begins

I was given the names of approximately ten agents who were officially on the books; within a relatively short time I kept one and got rid of the rest whom I had found to be completely unreliable and the information offered was not true. In fact I ascertained that on the dates they stated they had obtained this particular information these agents had not left their villages, so they were dismissed and I recruited afresh. S had been squandering 'the Fund' for a long time on worthless information, acting as a benefactor to certain native individuals for his own personal reasons. When I explained my actions shortly after Christmas to the Chinese Chief Inspector, my Divisional Special Branch Officer, he looked at me in an old fashioned way, smiled and said, 'It's only what I expected.' Although my agents were fewer they were well briefed, reliable, and I met them regularly; more important *they did not come to the house*, an S habit I had found quite incredible.

At the time of my arrival the resident military unit at Bau was the 2nd Battalion 10th Gurkha Rifles (2/10) GR, with three Companies in forward positions at Stass, Serikin and the newly prepared Bukit Knuckle. A reserve Company and Battalion HQ at Bau completed the unit's positions. 2/10 was commanded by Lt. Col. Myers, a tall, thickset, bespectacled individual who on initial introduction resembled a headmaster. He was definitely his own man and used to obtaining his own way, and although polite he had strongly resisted my arrival in the middle of a tour and told me so. Our rapport was never strong, in contrast to the three succeeding Commanding Officers I had to deal with.

Facing this excellent Battalion across the border was a unit of the Indonesian Army known as 438 Bn (Diponegoro) who had shown that they were prepared to conduct an active role in the border area. The District was distinctly contained within two high ridges, to the north the Bungo range, and on the south the Raya ridge. Two other ridges of high ground ran in between these two, the Brunei and the Jagoi. All these high features ran into Indonesia and were obvious incursion routes, although most tracks for border trading or in between kampongs were through primary jungle on the more level ground. Sited at strategic points were helipads with metalled bases; they gave the Commanding Officers an opportunity to move troops into an area quickly to search or act as a 'step' in the event of an incursion.

129 Battery (Dragon) of 40 Light Regiment, Royal Artillery with their six 105mm howitzers had a support task to 2/10GR as previously described, and also carried out a Direct Fire (DF) plan each day on selected tracks or track junctions to keep the enemy on their toes. At a fixed location on the west bank of the Sungai Tepong close to the junction of the Serikin/Stass track was a permanent gun post position of a 5.5 inch howitzer known as Pejiru. A military road was under construction by the Malay Engineers from this point to Stass. Over the river at this point was a relic of World War 2: a Japanese type of Bailey Bridge, rather narrow. Anything larger than a Land Rover had to cross via a ford and hereby hangs a tale. A *kedai* (café) was situated adjacent to the bridge.

Some weeks before my arrival the young officer in charge of the small armoured car unit based at Bau had actually driven down the river on both sides of this bridge. He described the journey, as the river was low, like driving down half a drainpipe, on semi circular bed rock, most extraordinary. During the heavy rains and flooding, two young soldiers drove their heavy Leyland Recovery vehicle into the flooded river at Pejiru and in the middle of the ford, it stalled. Scrambling out of the cab they leapt onto the opposite bank and ran for help to the men on the 5.5 position. Some minutes later the rescue party returned to find the vehicle had disappeared. They enquired at the nearby *kedai* and searched the area downstream from the ford, but no truck was found. It was some months later that a helicopter pilot crossing the Sungai Tepong many miles from the ford observed this upright vehicle standing majestically in the centre of the river, lonely and surrounded by thick primary jungle. It would have been physically impossible to lift it out by helicopter and a waste of manpower to extricate it along its previous path so it was written off. This mysterious disappearance was the subject of much discussion in the subsequent weeks; it did have humorous connotations, and embarrassment to the crew.

The frontier of Bau District to Indonesia was only fifty or sixty miles in length but it was the shortest distance from any part of the border to the capital of Sarawak, Kuching. This part of the border contained more regular trading routes from Indonesia than any other part of the country, a fact which in itself presented advantages and disadvantages in the intelligence and security context. The advantages were obvious. The main disadvantage

Helicopter has just left us on the 'pad' prior to crossing the border.
No Gurkhas present; we had to jump from the aircraft.

was that there were a large number of trading people from Indonesia who knew the known and lesser known tracks and that many indigenous tribes were often split geographically between the two countries. Local guides were numerous but oddly enough very few volunteered to guide the Indonesian regular forces or the guerillas into Sarawak territory. In general the border population in Indonesia were not well informed of the situation.

They distrusted Indonesian officials and military personnel and appeared to have more faith in the British, no doubt due to their influence in pre and post World War 2 times when the border status was extremely fluid.

My 'unofficial' powers were enormous. As the 'No 1 white man' in the border area I could use the advantages in many ways. The indigenous population, in spite of the possibility of getting involved on either side of the border in firefights, ambushes, checks and detention, were still very dependant on mutual trading established over the years; it was a necessity of life and it was encouraged under the control of myself and the military in a far greater way than before. With the connivance of my newly cultivated agents on both sides, frequent parties of twenty-five persons were allowed to cross the border at specific times and to certain villages, in almost all cases supervised by me. My contacts also benefited financially, in business or in kind. In this way a tremendous volume of information was obtained, even from places as far away as Pontianac, the main port on the west coast of Indonesian Borneo and the main centre of military movements. It also helped me to recruit new help, by favours, threats, or even blackmail. It was a dirty game to play but it paid off. It was amazing what followed after you had flown a sick child with parent for hospital treatment in Kuching; that gave immense satisfaction. In other ways one had to be a devious bastard. In matters of personal safety, no weapons, knives or *parangs* were allowed to be carried by the parties; these people still took heads on odd occasions and could decapitate or seriously injure a person in a second if provoked.

To help in the general control of the border area a quasi military group was formed known as the Border Scouts. Recruited mainly from border villages the Scouts attended a small training school at Bau commanded by a British Army Captain, a pleasant 'cowboy'. Here they received some elementary military skills, jungle tracking, gathering and reporting information and some police procedures, thus becoming a sort of Special Constable. They patrolled areas near their village in civilian clothes and carried shotguns, all the time looking for signs of possible enemy movement. Eventually they became more effective when wireless sets were issued and although communications were dodgy, a regular reporting schedule to their HQ at Bau or the nearest military base made them more effective. Inevitably this also posed problems. In my time some of the Scouts began to feel envious of the growing affluence of some of their village neighbours who were engaged in trading. Some, with friends, attempted to start in opposition and their duties suffered; at one particular village two Scouts began to waylay trading parties and order them to visit friends rather than the village Chinese trader who was married to the

Headman's daughter. Although using intimidation it didn't work and I was informed; the Indonesians couldn't obtain the goods they required to justify their journey. I had to step in officially so the problem didn't last long although it interfered with the flow of information for a couple of weeks.

My instructions to anyone trading or their employees, some of whom worked for me, were that only certain goods could be offered in exchange; money was rarely used. The more attractive items such as transistor radios, batteries, cameras, films etc. could only be obtained with my permission. In this way my agent and I held an enviable position of power and could dictate terms. The persons who generally required these goods were the senior Indonesian officers or senior ranks; this meant that my man was cultivated for a favour. He could enter military premises, talk socially to personnel and, being well briefed and concerned for personal safety, he kept his eyes open, listened to conversations and asked careful and judicious questions. Thus with great care information flowed in. Some of it had to be cross checked, but frequently it was unnecessary, such was the degree of reliability the agent achieved.

In fact I kept the Colonel commanding the Battalion of Brimob (a crack military/police unit) waiting for a camera for four months; he only got a film for it a week before I left. My man was a welcome visitor to the 'Officers Mess' on many occasions, bringing stuff for the 'boys'.

Let me then describe the main indigenous group of people in my area. The Land Dyaks enjoyed an increasing population of over 60,000 persons and they inhabited the interior and high ground in Sarawak's 1st Division. As the mountain ridges and high ground extend on either side of the watershed, which is commonly accepted as the border between Sarawak/Indonesia, so these people also live in the adjacent regions of Indonesian Borneo. The reason for the increase in population was because since the advent of the Rajahs and the suppression of the brutal Brunei Malays and the aggressiveness of the Ibans, the Land Dyaks have been free to multiply and prosper. In about 1850 they were almost in danger of extinction.

Taken as a group they are quite distinct from any other people in Sarawak. They have a language which is associated with Iban but is quite distinctive; they enjoy a quaint system of customary law, and live in a special style of house. As a group they are yet again divided into smaller groups which are characterized by differences of dialect and why I never attempted to learn the language. There were four or five different dialects in my area alone.

Generally speaking the Land Dyak is inoffensive and has a gentle nature but as an individual he does not lack courage. In fact officialdom claimed head hunting was finished but I had proof that Land Dyaks in the Bau area took Indonesian Army heads after a raid on a Kampong. Unlike the Iban who had infiltrated to most parts of the country, the Land Dyak was not a gypsy and yet there was a land shortage because of their long held habit of shifting cultivation of their rice crop which is wasteful and the land becomes infertile. They closed accessible areas, hacked down the trees and undergrowth, allowed it to dry, fired it, dug it, planted padi and waited for the harvest. If they had over planted the excess was not harvested. Unlike all the other tribes in Sarawak, when padi was harvested they plucked off the head with their fingers; all the others used knives.

Emphasising their uniqueness, remains of Hindu culture have been found in parts of Sarawak inhabited by Land Dyaks. I was told that some of their spirit beliefs are similar to the Hindu pantheon and another strange custom is that they cremate their dead which is unknown to other tribes in Sarawak.

The Land Dyak is typically short in stature, slim and round faced. His villages vary in style, some with individual huts, others with longhouses without the open verandah like the Iban. They usually construct a detached high roofed building which is know as a Rest House; usually the bachelors congregate here and socialize, village ceremonies are held within, and visitors are usually accommodated in its spaciousness. I avoided them to sleep, because snakes had a habit of living in unfrequented huts. The Headman or Chief was called an Orang Kaya which I believe means a Rich Man. As they have been close to Europeans for some time a fair percentage have become Christians, mainly Roman Catholics, but they have not embraced this faith as ardently as the Ibans.

Many years ago it was a characteristic among the females to wear brass rings round their legs; again it was a custom unique within Sarawak to the Land Dyak. I never saw any of the tribes in my area who practised this and did not hear of any examples in other areas of 1st Division. However in Indonesia in a remote area opposite my patch of ground was a useful contact, a witch doctor (previously described), who had two wives and who was friendly towards the white man; his son attended school at Penkalan Tebang. S had met him initially and I visited him quite frequently in the late stages. Both his wives had rings which covered the legs from mid calf to above the knee and also on the arms; these rings were quite heavy and very uncomfortable to wear. It deformed the calf muscle, was not particularly a graceful adornment and was I should imagine painful. When I took Pete Slowe to see these people is another story.

So although the jungle had been deprived of a lot of the old timber by

Dyak cultivation methods, nature reclaimed its own and it could be damned hard going even with a track.

In the areas away from the border lived the Chinese and Malays (and in my area even some Indonesians) who mainly cultivated rubber and grew pepper. The Land Dyak sometimes planted banana trees near his house and very occasionally pineapple, but the more popular fruit tree in season was the rambutan, a small sweet whiteish fruit, and another similar sized fruit, sweet, segmented and deep orange in colour which made very potent wine (and well I know it). The Dyak was by no means the best of agriculturists and it would take years of re-education to encourage him to change the habits of a lifetime and join the twentieth century.

The other favourite fruit is durian which the Chinese and the Dyaks also used as an aphrodisiac. Plucked, it has the most distinctive and disgusting smell to Europeans. Roughly oval in shape with a thick skin the fruit is divided within to four to six segments which resemble a pliable plastic bag covered in French chalk. The fruit is sickly and over sweet but trees are highly prized possessions, and the fruit is easily sold or exported. When I refused this fruit I'm sure the locals thought I was 'gay', or not wishing for sexual incentive/stimulation?!

Having discussed the indigenous people, how do we describe the environment in which they live, an area that I had to learn to exist in, a situation totally alien to the average white man's way of life? In my humble view the jungle was almost indescribable by words, it had to be seen and lived in to be believed; there was so much to warrant description that mere words don't mean a thing.

As a child I was brought up on Tarzan, King Kong, the *Adventure* and *Hotspur* (comics). It all seemed terrifying with only the nasty horrors described, snakes, insects, reptiles, man eating trees and so on! But it was not like that. There was great beauty and interest in the foliage. Sadly I never had the time or interest to enjoy the fascination of a botanist's joy.

In my particular area of Borneo conditions varied but were not too extreme: mountains, high ridges, many rivers, extremely dense primary and thinner secondary jungle which usually contained the tribal kampongs, although there was one kampong which literally sat on the top of a sharp ridge, a higglety, pigglety wooden form of street divided huts of various shapes precariously supported over a steep drop by stout wooden pillars. This was one place I had no wish to spend the night. Although the Headman's daughter, married to a Police Officer, was most insistent that I should stay, we decided to move on.

The Bornean jungle is full of a bewildering assortment of plants, trees, insects and wild life. Even now though much is known it could take thousands of botanists many years adequately to catalogue the species that are there. The upper storey of the forest mass when observed from *terra firma* appears to be composed of high crowns like mushrooms which belong to single tall trees which monopolise a high percentage of life giving sunlight. Probably the two most distinguishable trees are the red belian, which is a favourite wood for Dyaks to build their houses with if available, and is the mengaris, very distinctive because its top looks like a crown of feathers. It can grow well over 150 feet; in fact I read 250 feet is possible.

In the middle of all this, shaded and deprived, are trees that adapt themselves to existing in the shade, also saplings, all waiting for a large branch to break or a huge tree to fall down so that the sun can penetrate this almost immovable canopy. If a break happens the young trees grow at an alarming rate trying to reach the top, spreading out laterals, and so the weaker ones are relegated yet again.

On the floor of the jungle, the light is dim, almost like dusk; you don't develop a tan in this place: with the heat in the upper 90s and the humidity not far behind, the jungle floor is a sweat box. There is no grass, but usually dense undergrowth which is difficult to travel through, and only occasional plants living among the litter of fallen leaves and decaying organic matter. The leaves of trees fall all the year round, for there are no fixed seasons.

Some plants and even flowers grow from trees with no connection to the ground; some even grow like a parasite, inside another. I can only recall seeing one of these and that was not close to, because I was initially attracted to a peculiar smell like rotting meat and I thought we had a body on our hands. I have since learnt that it is called rafflesia, after the founder of Singapore. This huge plant which has a flower over two feet across, is red, white and brown in colour and weighs about 15-20 lbs.

The Borneo jungle usually receives two monsoons a year, one from the north-west and one from the south, giving a minimum of 120 inches of rain, an average of 180 inches and in some places even 220 inches, so the air in the jungle with the intense heat above is always saturated with moisture. No one would ever starve to death if they knew what to eat.

What strikes you initially is the noise, louder by day but never ending even at night. You become used to the buzzing of cicadas and crickets, burps from frogs and lizards and a constant chorus from birds and other creatures of the forest. I must admit I missed the noisy primitive peace (an Irishism) when I left.

The bites of flies, mosquitoes, ticks, leeches, heat and humidity all added to the hardship of life, but as time went on I gradually became accustomed to the various discomforts and became extremely physically fit for moving around the jungle. However a healthy physical specimen I was not; within a couple of months my weight had dropped from just over 13 stone to under 10 stone. I was beginning to look like a Belsen inmate. My eating habits generally were as a native, hopefully one meal of rice per day with possibly some vegetation! I was bordering on starvation in European terms, but that was my choice in how the job should be done. I did occasionally supplement the diet by a meal with Pete Slowe or 129 Battery, but my stomach had shrunk enormously and a small normal meal took me an hour to eat. On rare occasions a scrawny chicken would be produced between eight to ten persons; wild pig when hunted was really delicious. I remember once being extremely greedy and devouring during an evening a bowlful of diced pig containing two to three pounds of meat. Various snakes were also enjoyable, and delectable as chicken but only in small quantities, possibly because the flesh was shared between families.

By prior arrangement Patrick and I arrived late at night in a particular kampong to stay with a family who were greatly honoured that I had graced their particular house; they had even provided me with mosquito net! After a warm drink and some talk I was assured that breakfast was to be a special feast for me, so, tired and hungry, I lay on the floor and slept well. I washed and shaved in the nearby stream and through the walls of the hut could be observed curious villagers. Whatever was coming, it had to be a 'hearts and minds' job, said Patrick. Through the doorway two of the women brought in a huge metal dish, three foot in diameter, containing a hot mountain of large bones. Hanging threads of meat lay limply in this steaming heap, the smell was atrocious and a yellowy mass of liquid scum moved sluggishly in the bottom of the dish.

Cries of anticipation came from the family and we all sat crosslegged around the dish. Rice was piled into small dishes and handed round, then I got the first real inhalation of the stench from the dish and I was almost physically sick. It was so obnoxious. By motions I was offered first choice and very reluctantly grabbed the nearest which was probably a rear femur bone, amid cries of approval from the family, who then with Patrick fell on the dish and in the 'free for all' chose an item of carcass and amid squeals of delight began to suck and gnaw at the bones, and I had to imitate. In a low whisper *with venom* I said to Patrick, 'What the bloody hell is this, it tastes rotten?' With a delightful twinkle in his eyes and an impish grin (I'm sure he enjoyed telling me this) he explained that nearly a month earlier a hunting party had wounded a huge wild boar but it had disappeared in the jungle. Three days ago my host and others had found the remains of the boar, and when he had met me, he offered the invitation to join them at this rare feast. The bones and the remainder of the decomposed flesh was brought back to the village to await my arrival. God knows what that carcase looked like having been lying on the jungle floor for approximately three weeks, in that atmosphere, with the possibility that every animal and insect had had a go at the remains. Here I was having to enjoy eating it to win the hearts and minds of the local populace. Ugh!

Back to the feast!

To say it was painful was an understatement, to keep my stomach steady was a miracle in itself, but I moved the bone up and down towards my mouth which was kept filled with a mixture of rice and the 'Sauce Disgust'. I could not describe the actions and sounds emanating from the other eaters, grunts and snarls as their mouths and noses worked round these huge, hot animal bones and the licking of mouths and hands as the sauce dripped down, not helped by the insertion of bare hands into the dish to remove the liquid. I had the only spoon.

Eventually and thankfully the meal ended and our host volunteered to guide us to the next kampong I wanted to visit. He would leave us before our destination as the two kampongs were not particularly friendly to each other. Our host, though a cripple, moved through the jungle like a gazelle. After about two hours slog along tracks through thick jungle, he said his farewells and left two gasping travellers gulping the air. I was also sodden with sweat.

In the kampong we were offered cold drinks, and I watched as this liquid, which resembled in every way pure orange juice, was poured from a pipe of bamboo, into a pan, then to a teapot and into a glass. I accepted a full glass. It was, amazingly, almost ice cold and tasted exquisite. Patrick had barely an inch in his glass, he said it was enough, but again no explanation. I finished the glass and more was offered. Patrick refused, making hidden faces but not speaking. I accepted another half glass. Finally we left the kampong to climb a section of Gunong Jagoi which was about 1200-feet high. I asked Patrick what the drink was and he told me the name of the fruit from which it was derived but I can't remember it. In a quarter of an hour as we started the long undulating climb I was as drunk as a monkey's uncle, taking three steps up and losing two as I slipped back. Patrick got uncontrollable giggles and I giggled with him. I was alert enough, I had to be, but my body and legs felt like jelly. My jolly little friend explained that it was one of the most pleasant of the jungle 'hooches' that the Dyaks made from fruit, but it was also one of the most potent.

'Why didn't you tell me?' says I to Patrick.

'Because I wanted to see what it would do to you,' says he.

'I needed a drink to get rid of that horrible taste, after that bloody awful breakfast you knew about, you little —'

'Ah,' says he, smiling and most knowledgeable 'That drink will have killed anything that is bad in your stomach.'

What was the use? I know I had a terrible head for the remainder of the day and night but I don't think I suffered too much from the experience. When you think about our behaviour, we were going back over two thousand years when our ancestors had existed in like manner, feasting off the carcases of wild animals, fresh or otherwise. Here was I, a product of modern civilization, reverting to type of an age gone by. I know there are several places on earth today where the inhabitants still emulate ancient man in many aspects, but never in my wildest thoughts did I ever think I would be 'privileged!' to partake in it.

On the day of my arrival in Singapore when I had seen the specialist about my eye problem, I was being led away by two nurses back to the ward when I was seen by a former colleague of mine from the Scots Guards. He couldn't believe his eyes. Checking that the person he had seen was me, he returned to the Battalion at Terendak Camp telling everyone he was convinced I was dying, I looked so thin and emaciated. The members of 22 SAS who served in Borneo all suffered from this terrible loss of weight.

So much for the culinary jungle laughs, now back to the more distasteful, I mean leeches. What was known as a bull leech was mainly found in the deep swampy areas and if undetected for any length of time could swell to the size of a cigar. There were two common species, one a dirty brown colour that remained on the ground and attacked the feet and legs. God knows how, but they climbed through tight fitting jungle boots rolled over socks and fed with impunity. Sometimes the first indication you had that they were present were when your boots turned red with your own blood when you had unknowingly killed them slipping off a rock or logs. For a year my ankles and lower legs were black with bruises caused by slipping off the logs that were laid end to end to facilitate a track across swampy ground.

The other type of leech was, I believe, slightly larger and a bit more colourful. It used to attach itself to a leaf and adhere itself to anything or anybody that passed. This one could also leap, and it moved in a series of loops across the ground. They used to drop on my jungle hat (rarely Patrick's) on to my shoulders then to my neck and back, and this was when we had to help each other to remove these loathsome things, usually with the gentle application of a lighted cigarette end and a size 10 boot. Leeches are equipped with three circular teeth inside the front sucker, and when they finally adhere themselves to flesh, they cut a fine 'Y' shaped hole, pump a anti-coagulant into the wound and start to feed. As a lubricated bit of surgery it was excellent, you didn't feel a thing; you might if it touched a nerve though.

A patrolling Gurkha had the misfortune of having a leech in his penis with disastrous consequences. Durex were always available if patrols were going into swampy areas or water for long periods. I carried them but never used them, although on one occasion I found a leech had passed my belt and was on my stomach. It hadn't been there long; it was quite small.

During all my period in the jungle I never saw any wild animals although they were no doubt about and much to my great relief I was not really bothered with snakes. Many were seen but at a distance. Pythons over twenty feet in length will attack deer or pigs but rarely go for a full grown man. Those who know state that in Borneo there are upwards of two hundred different species of snake, the most vicious being the various cobras, kraits and pit vipers. Thankfully snakes will usually avoid confrontation, though I was never convinced. Before I left the country I always wanted to visit the snake museum in Kuching but never managed it. I was also told that considering there are so many different species of snake in the country the incidence of snake bite is lower than any other tropical region; maybe the natives cure themselves.

Patrick knew I disliked snakes and he liked to tease and bait me when we slept in the open air in a hut, about snake noises. He always tried to convince me that they were all around. I was very gullible and I never knew if he was telling the truth. Snakes aplenty were seen but at a distance, usually getting out of our way. When sleeping in the jungle they probably came close to share the bodily heat but never harmed Patrick or myself and probably slid away when we started to wake up. (Patrick had a brother who stepped on a sleeping snake and was bitten in the foot, through his shoe, but survived OK. Try as I might I could never find out if he cured himself or came to the Dispensary at Bau. Dispensing information was not Patrick's forte, he rarely volunteered what he knew or had heard; invariably it had to be coaxed out of him.)

The most interesting snake story I heard concerned an acquaintance in 129 Battery RA. a Capt. Correa. This officer was born and bred in Kenya and was of Asian origin. A very forthright and down to earth chap, he could not be described as a 'typical Gunner'. He was a soldiers' man and behaved like one; the other ranks adored him, he was a good field soldier and was obviously no stranger to wild life, which in this instance was most helpful.

In Borneo, Gunner officers in forward Batteries usually performed two functions: 1. FOO (Field Observation Officer) who accompanied infantry companies on their long patrols along or in the border area. The FOO and his Wireless Operator kept in touch with Battery HQ on the Gunners' net ensuring that the Battery's guns situated at the infantry bases or moved to Helipads knew minute by minute of the patrol location and that support fire could be given almost immediately if they were attacked. 2. GPO (Gun Post Officer) was the officer or senior NCO in charge of a gun team, which in Borneo was more important than normal, as you operated almost independently and your margins were very narrow. Errors could not be accepted; the killing of your own troops or civilians would not be accepted either, so you had to be professional.

On this particular occasion Correa was a GPO and to support a particular patrol, a single 105mm pack howitzer had been moved forward by helicopter to a site on the helipad. (These were usually prominent geographical locations, cleared of jungle vegetation, flattened, and given a steel carpet which would support a 'chopper'. They were given a colour prefix, in our area Red, followed by a number.) The border area had numerous helipads and several were constructed inland; these were also helpful during a incursion when the troops could be landed to seal off an area.

Having set up shop ready for action and posted sentries etc, Correa eventually crept into his sleeping bag which was placed in a position slightly isolated from his men. He slept well and woke up to the usual cacophony of sound which only the primitive jungle can make. Instinct made him be still and listen before leaping out of his bag to start what could be a very interesting day with the possibility of action. He suddenly became aware of an unusual weight on his stomach. Carefully raising his head and nothing else he glanced down towards his nether regions.

Lying quietly in a somnolent posture, no doubt enjoying soft and heated comfort on its coiled body, was a snake. Correa's first reaction was panic as in effect he was trapped. Experience, discipline and training then took over. As he carefully looked around not one friendly sleeping bag could he see; calling out in a soft voice didn't raise anyone either. Another careful look at the reptile made an identification. It was a species also common in East Africa with somewhat of a reputation but not necessarily against humans: it was a spitting cobra.

This reptile is unusual because it has the ability to blind its adversary at a distance of six to eight feet by ejecting from its mouth a jet of poisonous substance which blinds a victim most effectively. The cobra is then at liberty to kill in its normal fashion of oral injection without any damage to itself. This blinding substance is held in a special sac in the jaw area and the snake is uncannily accurate in its aim and invariably strikes in between the eyes of the victim. As the jet of poison reaches its limit it turns into a spray which is even more effective.

Correa made up his mind to throw the snake off his body and hope for the best. The first job he had to do was to slowly bring both his hands, which were folded near his upper chest, to a position within the sleeping bag underneath the snake without disturbing it. The imagination boggles at what must have been going through this chap's mind as slowly and painfully his hands moved into the throwing position. He had a last look round for possible help, saw none, took a deep breath and heaved, turning his head away to avoid the snake's possible reaction. It was too late: he was blind. His shouts brought immediate help. I presume the snake disappeared in the jungle. Apart from bathing the eyes very little could be done for him. A call over the radio eventually brought a chopper in and Correa was taken to hospital in Kuching, where after several days treatment he was back to normal.

I once saw a film documentary, part of which, some five minutes or so, depicted a man and wife team who wanted to record on film precisely what happens when the spitting cobra attacks. Filmed in East Africa this intrepid couple located the 'star', set up the camera, and the *woman*, protected by a plastic face shield, approached the snake from a 90° angle to the camera and deliberately taunted the reptile. The reaction was too quick even for the camera, so it was done a second time, advancing more slowly but with plenty of taunting movements. The filmed reaction was quite amazing. The roused cobra with hood extended is a fearsome sight, but the courage of this woman to provoke it for a second time is deserving of great praise and it proved to me the facts which had only been described to me verbally. I wonder if the snake hit him while it was in mid air? Certainly it makes an interesting tale.

I acquired a beautiful python skin from a trader on one occasion. It was about 13-14 foot long and 16"-18" wide. The chap wanted two dollars for it so I gave him five and told him I wanted another one soon. I presented the Sergeants Mess of 129 Battery with the skin in appreciation of their generosity to me, especially 'the Bogman', also to mark our close co-operation workwise. I always tried to find them an alternative target if my information was accurate. Some time later I picked up the same trader. He was rather stupidly on his own. He offered me what appeared to be a roll of parchment, but it was another skin 23 feet long and 21" wide; he wanted the equivalent of £1 for it. My intention was to use a skin as a household decoration, not cover a wall with one, so I refused this lovely monster. Later in Hong Kong we saw an anaconda skin 12 foot long for 1200 dollars HK (£75). I was a fool, I should have kept it, if only to tell tales, lies as well!

One day as Patrick and I laboured slowly up the mountainous track into

Indonesia between Matang and Brunei mountains, head down, watching the track and breathing heavily, I stopped suddenly when I saw this creature scuttling across my path. It was a centipede and must have measured ten or twelve inches in length, with a body and legs some two inches in wide. It was enormous and I was fascinated with the sheer size of it. Patrick said they had a vicious bite. I had never heard of a biting centipede, and I assumed this was another of Patrick's 'tales', but I have since read that he was quite correct: they have pincer like jaws and poison glands.

Rats were also a jungle pest and as I well know they are disease carriers. It was when I was cleaning my teeth in a small stream that two dead rodents passed my face. There was no doubt they that were responsible for my dose of cholera that started my eye problem.

One evening we arrived at a village and refused the use of the Rest House, preferring to stay in the house of the Headman who had a wife and six small children. We ate and talked to many people and anything worthwhile was noted. When it came time for sleep we were offered the use of the top of a huge 'coffin' which lay in the corner of this large hut. It measured some 12' x 2' x 3'6" deep. Everyone else including the babies slept on the floor. I was told the wooden structure held the family's rice. With my large pack as a pillow, fully dressed and covered by a light weight blanket, Patrick and I lay head to head on the coffin. I immediately fell asleep, but some time later I was awakened by loud noises inside the 'coffin'. I could tell my companion was also awake.

'Patrick, what the hell is that?'

'Rats,' says he.

'Noisy sods,' say I.

A few moments later a little squeal and a movement from Patrick.

'What's wrong?'

'One on my legs,' says he, and within minutes I had one on my chest which I heaved to the floor, then one on my legs, and that's how we spent the night, writhing, kicking, cursing until dawn broke. There was no room on the floor and in any case I think the odds were better on the 'coffin'. What sort of an environment to bring up small children!

In the forward bases rats became as big a problem as the Indonesians or boredom. These locations varied from above ground Wild West type forts in cleared jungle areas, to World War 1 type dugouts, or deep underground or cleared ridges where the felled trees served as a perimeter fence or at least a barrier that could be booby-trapped. I only slept in a couple of these bases on the odd occasion and the dugouts were made quite comfortable and as airy as possible; some in fact had unserviceable parachutes festooned from the ceilings and walls plus the unmentionable 'pin ups'. Snakes were about but they kept the rats down. Strangely enough when the Aussies re-designed one particular base, filling in the dugouts for section perimeter posts completely eliminated the problem of the rats.

These forward bases all varied slightly by design but generally had their own attached 105mm howitzer, volley ball court, some even a football pitch, and usually a covered area to show films. Ingenious hot showers were installed which helped to keep down tinea and other skin diseases helped of course by plenty of powder. Even I didn't have hot water in my bungalow. I was lucky I never developed any skin problems because some I saw among the natives were quite hideous.

One of my agents had a friend who used to porter for him to various areas in Indonesia. He physically resembled an Ancient Briton or even a gorilla; his body was thickset and immensely powerful, his arms and legs short and well muscled, but with the exception of his face which was not pretty, the whole of his body was covered in fishlike scales and hideous to look at. He was such a nice person to talk to but apparently a terrible man in anger. I attempted to lift his load one day and could not do it singlehanded; I would estimate it weighed between 150-200 lbs, such was his strength. He travelled over extremely rough ground, rocks, tree roots etc. in his *bare feet*; now that was a hard man.

The oddest jungle phenomenon I experienced was on a trip near the Stass area where the Security Forces base held by 1/10 Gurkhas was situated approximately one mile from the border. They had a large 'Claret' patrol unit in ambush position and I was checking on their position with the Company Commander before I also crossed the border. Suddenly there was a yell and radios of the Gunners and Gurkhas began to spout words. Within seconds the 105mm howitzer had whipped off half a dozen shells followed by more; the Gun Post Officer (GPO) was a Sergeant, and in his enthusiasm snapped the lanyard which fires the gun. He then attempted to keep the gun firing with the aid of a stick which meant he couldn't turn his head away and he suffered accordingly. The gun fired altogether 76 rounds in the short engagement and the Sergeant fired most of them. He staggered into my arms with blood pouring from both ears and in a bad state of shell shock. It was his duty and he was very brave but in retrospect stupid. In a few seconds a new lanyard could have been fitted and he would not have been injured. He never came back to his beloved gun or the Gurkhas he supported; he was no doubt medically discharged.

Patrick and I went like the clappers over the border to meet the patrol which were about to leave and make a hurried withdrawal. Two civilians had wandered into the area and later we located them and took them prisoners with the Gurkhas. From what they said, and movement that the patrol could observe down the track, there was possibly a large force of Indonesians in the area hence the request for artillery fire to discourage any attempt to follow up.

The two bodies had been draped with jungle ponchos so Patrick and I grabbed a hand apiece and covered by two Gurkhas we hurried them through the jungle at a swift pace until we reached comparative safety. One of the Gurkhas with a puzzled look on his face drew my attention to one of the captives' feet which were badly deformed. I sat them both down while we waited for the helicopter and could see that both feet had extremely high insteps, the foot was divided like a wedge, and on each side of the wedge were *three toes*. We asked him about this and he agreed he had been afflicted since birth, then he brought his hands out from his dirty shirt and it was almost a repeat performance without the wedge. Each finger was only $1/4$ inch in diameter and no more than one inch long; the thumb which was miniaturized had an additional finger attached to it making six digits in all. Throughout all the questioning no way could I get a logical answer to his tragic affliction. No other member of his family or his kampong were crippled in this manner so it didn't appear to be hereditary.

It was necessary to get them both into my bungalow for interrogation and without the world knowing about it, because technically they had been kidnapped although they could have been acting as scouts for the enemy;

We brought this disabled 'scout' back to the bungalow with his comrade for long interrogation before returning them to Indonesia.

this we had to ascertain. So we rolled up to my bungalow through the police compound in a Gurkha Land Rover. With the escort we hurried them inside, then the Gurkhas left. It was over in seconds but we were not quick enough. Within minutes Peter Lim came to the door – the prisoners were stuck in my bedroom out of sight. I could trust Peter but I couldn't tell him the truth. He understood this but said that Superintendent Bill Olley had told him to come and find out who I had got in there. Unfortunately I had to be blunt and told Peter to tell him that the matter was my business and that he should speak to HSB (Lt. Colonel McAlister had told him what I was doing). This interfering policeman would not contact HSB but became very abusive on the internal phone, though it didn't make any difference. He continually interfered in matters that didn't concern him. Eventually both the Australian Battalion Commander Lt. Col. Thompson and DSBO had to get a higher authority to speak to him. He jeopardized two little jobs of mine, and started detailing the junior ranks of Peter Lim's team to unofficially visit in the border area. This was a stupid and dangerous action and my life was at stake so he was reprimanded.

The more immediate information was passed on to 1/10 and DSBO, the general background came later, and as it was so late I decided to keep them overnight, feed them, and 1/10 could pick them up about 0800 hours and deliver them back to Stass. I also emphasised that these two had to get back to their kampongs, I didn't want any 'accidents'!! to occur in transit, they might be useful to me in the future. People have been known to fall out of helicopters! The two were very nervous and frightened but eventually were co-operative. They admitted that the Indonesian soldiers had 'forced' them to act as scouts but didn't know how many there were in the party. We got quite a lot out of them, fed them, then I handcuffed them round the rear door banister and went to bed. Peter Lim was highly amused by it all, even helped us to bring in some food for them, and he was very intrigued by the crippled limbs. And so they were returned 'safely'. I later found out that they did a 'Grand Tour' round the villages, describing 'flying in a big bird over the jungle' (actually they cried when I took off their blindfolds and let them see where they were); they were petrified – cruel but they were co-operative later. They had never seen a white man before, so Patrick was held with some respect, but I was described in great awe, the all powerful white chief who had a 'noisy bird' and knew many things, lived in a big house with water, with a Chinese servant and bodyguard (this amused Peter Lim) and so the incident ended but there was a sequel to be told later.

Patrick and I had returned by helicopter very early one Saturday morning. I immediately wrote out my reports and Patrick disappeared back to his village for the day. Shaved, washed and changed I had something to eat at Boon's *kedai*. Boon was a Chinese gentleman, a cook, who enjoyed a drink. Bent of back, shaven haired and dour featured, he spent at least sixteen hours every day of the week behind his stove by the doorway of his establishment dressed only in shorts and flip flops cooking quite passable native food. He had three very attractive daughters and two sons. His son in law was a Detective Constable in Special Branch with Peter Lim. I was told they were all out working (meaning the SB lads). So I returned to my bungalow and sat relaxing on my verandah watching some of the Malay Police Field Force playing volleyball.

Suddenly I heard the sound of a vehicle braking hard and a few seconds later a very warlike looking Peter Lim, obviously very excited, ran across the compound shouting instructions to the Field Force before entering the bungalow. He quickly explained that during the morning they had picked up a suspect Chinese terrorist whose presence in a village had been reported. The prisoner had eventually agreed to lead a patrol to where his pistol and hand grenades had been hidden. Peter Lim was not happy with the size of his own party so leaving the prisoner with his two men he had returned for more men. He said it would be helpful if I would come along even though I had only just got back, so I got changed and 'tooled up' and off we went, reinforced by two sections of those renowned jungle fighters the Malay Police Field Force commanded by an Inspector.

We reached the spot on the new Lundu Road (that Peter Slowe was helping to build) where the prisoner was being held and after a brief conference we set off into the interior, heading in the general direction of the Chinese village of Tundong, who almost to a man were all rabid Communists and suspected terrorists. It didn't take long before I was completely disillusioned about the reputation of the accompanying members of the Field Force. During the Malayan crisis in the late 1940s and early 1950s this force of Malays, Chinese and Indians was raised and by reports achieved some success; this particular Company stationed at Bau had been drafted in from mainland Malaya to supplement the normal police force and concentrate on anti terrorist patrols in rear areas away from the border and out of military jurisdiction.

They were noisy in the jungle, and shouted ribald and insulting remarks to each other without censure, some even smoked and few of them appeared to be observant. Weapons were carried in a nonchalant manner and I in the middle of all this was not impressed. Our prisoner was a wily bird and after 45 minutes of jungle bashing to locate the position of the hidden weapons he said he was lost. After a short talk we set off again coming eventually to a river, the Sungai Sarawak Kanam, some thirty yards wide and quite deep. Apparently volunteers were asked for to take a rope across, but no one stepped forward. What the hell, I was feeling annoyed and went forward, but by this time Peter Lim, also unimpressed, had grabbed the rope, left his kit on the bank and swum over. I even had to tell the patrol to watch the opposite bank, and be alert. The rope was secured and not waiting to be detailed I grabbed Peter's weapon and kit, slid into the water and hand over hand reached the opposite bank. Three or four men who by now had 'learnt to swim', including a Bren gunner, scrambled over and yet had to be told to take up defensive positions while the patrol was so vulnerable.

Eventually, as the rope grew slack through use, I had to wade up to my neck in the river, hold the rope up as high as possible and literally drag all the non swimmers across. It was hard work and the swift flowing river didn't help. Then came a mini disaster: the rear half of the patrol with the Field Force Inspector and myself lost contact with the other half with Peter and the prisoner. God, what a mix up! The idea was to head for Tundong anyway, to pick up transport there so all we could do was to head in that direction.

We carefully approached a large house through some pepper gardens. Four men of the patrol were ahead of me spread out, and I was alone following up. From the rear of the house I saw two figures running to my right into the rubber. The four men in front all appeared to be going to the right but no alarm was given. I pointed to the right, yelled something and dashed round the left side of the house, where nothing was moving. The Inspector wanted an explanation for my actions. I explained, but the four men said they had seen nothing. A policeman at the rear said after I had yelled he vaguely saw two running figures disappearing in the shelter of the rubber. The house was deserted so we moved out. After several minutes the silence was shattered by gunfire but not near us. Now really on our toes the patrol became professional. We searched some isolated huts and their occupants; all were closely questioned and the Inspector was not happy.

Eventually we reached Tundong; our arrival was greeted with open hostility and even a reluctance to sell us soft drinks! Peter arrived some time later and explained that two, possibly three, men had tried to escape from a hut they were approaching and had fired at them. The patrol had chased, Peter had fired first at one man, missed with two shots, the man got caught in the undergrowth and as Peter lined him up to squeeze the trigger, a Field Force chap stood up directly in front of him, blazed away at the man, missed hopelessly, and the man disappeared. Peter was livid, not that he had not personally shot the man but that another body or prisoner might have broken up this gang that Peter had been interested in for some time. He was not pleased about the actions taken by over half of the patrol and was very critical about their reputations. So it was a very angry and frustrated patrol that returned to Bau empty handed and tired. I was angry because I don't like inefficiency or apathy, call it what you like. It was supposed to be my rest day, I'd volunteered to patrol and we should have had two kills.

There was a happier sequel. In the following three days with the Field Force, Peter's group arrested all the people we had questioned and some more; they were interrogated and eventually a number of men were arrested and charged with terrorist offences.

Some weeks later Peter also located a most ingenious terrorist HQ which consisted of a series of tunnels into a small hill which culminated in a large underground room with adjacent storage spaces. Needless to say it was not far from Tundong and was destined to be the HQ of the local CCO and it would have been extremely difficult to locate under normal circumstances. However Peter had the bit between his teeth and with the help of good police work, energetic patrolling by the PFF and good information from informants he had some success in subsequent months. When the chips were down the Malay, policeman or soldier, could do an excellent job, but to a European they had a lovely natural charm which denoted lethargy and lack of interest; a boot up the backside was frequently necessary. Their outlook on life was totally different.

On my arrival at Bau two operational incidents occurred within a week. 'C' Company, 2/10 GR had set off along the Jagoi's ridge from their company base at Serikin to carry out a 'Claret' patrol led by their Company Commander, Capt. Maunsell. Leading the patrol along a steep sided ridge was Lance Corporal Rambahadur Limbu who located an Indonesian position. He crept towards it with his support group. A sentry gave the alarm and was promptly shot by Limbu. He moved his group to a better firing position, but unfortunately both men received serious wounds. At great risk and under enemy fire Limbu, with fire support from his comrades, made two journeys under fire and retrieved both his wounded companions. He then joined in the final assault when four of the enemy were killed. Limbu was awarded 10th Gurkhas' first Victoria Cross; the OC received a Military Cross.

I consider it was a great honour to have served alongside both Battalions of 10th Gurkhas in Borneo, also 1/10 and 1/7 GR on the Chinese border in Hong Kong. In their chosen role they can be equalled but never surpassed. Their bravery, dedication, and professionalism is well registered; they are a credit to their Regiments and Nepal, and since their inception they have been a most honourable force within the British Army. It will be a sad moment for me should we lose them.

A more humorous aspect of Gurkha life occurred some weeks after the battle on the Jagoi ridge when a large parcel was sent by 'C' Company to the forward enemy troops facing them. It was carried by a trader who knew their location. In the parcel the Gurkhas had placed a volleyball, cigarettes, toffees, chocolate and toothpaste plus some copies of *Playboy*, on the centre page of one a most attractive naked girl posed in a kneeling position resting on her heels. It was the Gurkhas' appreciation of a brave enemy and no hard feelings.

In the enemy base at Koruh the Indonesians were commanded by Company Sergeant Major Untong of 438 (Diponegaro) Battalion and to show their appreciation a very talented wood carver had made three copies of the girl depicted on the photograph. One for the trader, one for Capt. Maunsell and one for myself. In a brief note given to me, Untong said he didn't know why the magazines had been sent as none of his men understood English! but they were grateful for everything else. I have some photographs of these soldiers who appeared to be a happy bunch. A strange, honourable and ethical war, but not when the chips were down.

Further humour involving the officers of 10th GR occurred when they perused the various 'peculiar' magazines that ended up in the forward positions. Camouflaging by abbreviation and numbers, an individual would select a fellow officer as the victim and apply by letter for various sex aids, intimate items of clothing, cuddly companions to be met, aids for bed wetting problems, corsets and lingerie for use in the tropics; the list was endless and it was good for morale. Some expense would be involved, but to see a rather large, handsome Captain wearing nothing but jungle green underpants festooned with a Size 40 A Cup bra and matching panties in shocking pink for use in tropical climes had me doubled up laughing. Army humour at its best.

The other incident involved a RAF chopper pilot who was relatively new to the area of Bau District. I don't think he had been out from England all that long. He was detailed to fly to the SF position at Stass, a place he had never been to before. He was no doubt given a compass heading to fly on and told to look for a prominent identifiable feature of twin high ridges behind which lay the SF position. Flying with him to Stass was a Lance Bombardier of 129 Battery, 40 (Light) Regt RA whose gun was based there. The pilot was flying a Whirlwind; he had no co-pilot or crew and he obviously had to back his own judgement in a strange area. It will never be known what height he was at but it could so easily be done, knowing how the jungle can hide features from the air if the height and distance are not

Bottom right is Bau 'town'; to the left Police compound including accommodation, clinic and my bungalow top right. It's still there!

exact. Unfortunately for the pilot several miles south of Stass near Kindau in Indonesia were two even more prominent geographical high features and the pilot headed for them. Indonesian Army Troops with 12.7mm anti aircraft guns were stationed near Kindau and the chopper was shot down, and both men posted missing presumed dead.

The end of March saw the return of one of my chaps from the Indonesian Army main supply port of Pontianak in Sambas province. We shared his rather crude shelter as we de-briefed him on military movements etc. As night wore on he asked us to recall the incident when the British helicopter was shot down at Kindau. He said he had been told that when the soldiers opened fire the gunner was hit and fatally wounded; the aircraft was badly damaged but somehow landed. Troops rushed towards it but the pilot took out his pistol and shot a sergeant and a private; both died. The pilot was killed instantly by other troops, and as a trophy the pilot's flying overalls were shown round various villages and were last on exhibition in Boembong in December 1965. The bodies of the pilot (and possibly the gunner) were buried by Dutch Catholic Friars in the cemetery of the Mission at Singkawang near the Sungie Kawa and a cross was erected.

I told him that when he went again to Pontianak he should try and visit Singkawang and find out what happened to the pilot and his passenger, and if both of them were buried there, and if possible obtain photographs which I would pay for. He had said that there was a military cemetery at

Singkawang and that he had counted over sixty graves all with helmets. To get accurate information was always a problem, but I informed the two senior RAF Officers at HQ West Brigade and OC 129 Battery. Over the years I have always been curious to know what efforts were made by the MOD and British Embassy in Jakarta to ascertain the whereabouts of their final resting places.

Subsequent enquiries by me began in November 1993 and is the subject of another story. Hopefully in the fullness of time both the families of the missing men and the authorities will be told by the Indonesians the full story of the incident in every detail.

Whilst discussing the Borneo workhorse, the helicopter, a tragic incident occurred during the changeover of units based in the neighbouring Lundu district, between a Gurkha Battalion and the incoming Royal Marine Commando. The Bau helipad was being used in this operation and as a Naval helicopter approached Bau town and the pad from the east, it suddenly lost blade power, engine clattering ceased, and the aircraft turned over and crashed in a padi field fifty yards from the main street. The three occupants, all naval pilots, were killed instantly. What a sad waste. The townspeople were shocked. I believe disciplinary action was taken aboard the Commando carrier following a subsequent enquiry.

Towards the end of February I began to hear information about a possible change of enemy battalions facing Bau District. It was imperative that I was well informed and I briefed my agents accordingly. In the meantime Lt. Colonel McAlister of 1/10 GR had ideas to discourage any enemy aggressiveness in the border area by using practically every soldier in his unit for a 'Claret' operation on 1st March. The two most westerly villages facing us and almost totally occupied by the TNI were called Kindau and Belida. They were the nearest jumping off point for the enemy to use the Gunong Raya ridge into Sarawak. So nearly a thousand Gurkhas of 1/10 plus artillery support from 129 Battery and the 5.5 gun at Pejiru would take out and test 438 Bn Diponegoru's defences around Kindau-Belida because within the villages were many civilians.

I found out later that the infliction of casualties was slight and 1/10 suffered none, but as a well executed operation it was first class. It was almost cancelled at the last minute especially along the Jagoi ridge facing Babang as the evening before I had learned of a party of TNI who had been observed carrying antipersonnel mines and wiring to protect certain tracks along the Jagoi. I even knew the approximate position for which they were intended. I arrived back at HQ 1/10 in a sweat and told the Colonel, who said not to worry, his men were already past that point and in any case maybe they hadn't been sighted yet. He went off in his chopper to direct the operations and I scurried back to the border area to see what I could pick up after the operation ended.

The operation lacked a head count, but 1/10's efficiency was 100 per cent and morale was high; they dominated the area. 438 Battalion were demoralised especially by the artillery support. The villagers were frightened of dying but not frightened of the Gurkhas; they were aware that the TNI were the enemy, so they tried to keep out of the way of trouble. Poor old 438, they ran into A Comp 1/10 on 17th April when they were being transferred by boat along the Sungei Koemba. In separate ambushes several boatloads were annihilated; the OC A Comp got a well deserved DSO for the job. First, I heard of relief of 438 on 8th-10th March but nothing was confirmed, then came news of a Brimob unit passing through a rear area called Sangau. (Brimob is short for Brigade Mobile, a very highly trained infantry/police unit of excellent reputation; as an offshoot they also had several special SAS type units, and they were the finest in the Indonesian Army, known as Resemen Pelopor.)

By 20th March I knew that Brimob had definitely taken over and even dispositions were suggested. Some days later I had a positive identification, Kobrimobda II Bandung 203 (Bogor) Battalion and the name of the local Commander around Babang, an officer called Rasidi. More disturbing were the various reports of more than a hundred members of a special force who were distinguished by their different dress and deportment and were destined for operations/patrols only. They wore a distinctive type of camouflage uniform, different jungle boots, wore neither Red or Green sweat rags, carried Armalites and generally impressed the civilians; even we thought we had seen them from a distance. I therefore reported the possible arrival of Resemen Pelopor facing Bau area; these were as previously described, the best. McAlister was interested because if this was so, the border area would really be contested and he and 1/10 were going to win the fight, so patrols were strengthened and despatched. My reports were ridiculed at West Brigade, laughed at in HQ 17 Gurkha Division in Malaya, and a priority signal from the Ministry of Defence in London, as advised by the Military Attaché in Djakarta, stated that as they were aware of all troop movements, all Resemen Pelopor were accounted for and none were in Indonesian Borneo.

I read the signal plus a photograph of some other Indonesian soldiers they had suggested might be facing us, when I walked in off patrol. Then my phone rang and it was McAlister; he sounded excited and said he'd send a Land Rover for me. In my scruffy condition I entered his office and he immediately shouted a Gurkha Sergeant's name and the man entered. In Gurkhali the Sergeant's story was repeated for my benefit as follows.

While on patrol, the area was immaterial, voices were heard and the patrol went to ground as the enemy were not far away. The Sergeant did not particularly want a confrontation unless he could pick his ground and it was too late for that, so he wanted information. Leaving his weapon behind and armed with wire cutters he literally, slowly and painstakingly, cut a tunnel through the thick jungle undergrowth until he was in a position to partially observe the enemy group. There appeared to be about a dozen of them and the position could be a regular patrol base, but more important was their dress and equipment. The Sergeant described in detail what he had seen, and apart from his failure to see correctly and identify the upper arm badge, he had bravely identified my 'Pelopor' enemy. This NCO then slowly returned to his patrol. His couple of dozen yards of tunnelling cost him nearly three hours and much sweat and not only from the heat and exertion.

McAlister and the Sergeant were then shown the photo from MOD and the affiliated unit signs and the Sergeant said no, they were not similar. The CO informed West Brigade etc, and apparently got the same solution as I; he was livid, and for better or for worse some days later he suffered again.

On the 28th or 25th March in the area of Belida a Gurkha patrol decided to sit in ambush at a particular point with its GPMG (General Purpose Machine Gun) in an excellent position to fire down the leafy jungle track. Their vigil was eventually rewarded; an enemy patrol of twelve to thirteen men was approaching dressed as I had described. The silence was shattered as the belt fed machine gun opened up, killing instantly the two leading Indonesians, then everyone started firing. The Indonesian third in line dived to his left and in a most professional manner killed the two Gurkhas manning the GPMG. In the few short moments the engagement lasted two more Gurkhas were hit and badly wounded; hits from a Kalashnikov or Armalite at short range do terrible damage. Some five or six of the enemy appeared to be casualties but it was all very confusing. One thing was certain: the Gurkhas were full of admiration for an enemy that could extract themselves from an extremely difficult situation, and they would have loved to have captured the one who killed the two on the MG, not to take his head or injure him but to congratulate him on his bravery and soldierly ability; they thought he was great. They all agreed that these were good and to them were 'Resemen Pelopor'. I later learned that the villagers nearby disappeared when the shooting started and that the following day were asked to bury three dead, and nearby found a helipad made of logs and said they had heard a chopper around 7p.m. when dusk had fallen. What they didn't know was that the RAF refused to evacuate the badly wounded Gurkhas at that time and in that position. Eventually Teeny Weeny Airways (Army Air Corps) ignored regulations and did the job; the Gurkhas built their own helipad.

McAlister had mixed feelings. The total Indonesian casualties were not known and he had two dead and two badly wounded and the ground had been in their favour. He could only assume honours were even; he knew he really had a scrap on his hands and reported all the facts accordingly. Even after all this the desk-bound warriors or bagpipe players refused to acknowledge the presence of these excellent troops facing Bau area: they had never been committed before, why now? We knew but they wouldn't accept it.

So it was now back to me again. It was getting to be a challenge and I had to obtain irrefutable proof of the presence of Resemen Pelopor. I was never asked and I never disclosed how it was all done but I used in all four cameras and a lot of help from the people of Serikin who were unaware what it was all about. A celebration was to be held in Babang and some villagers from Serikin, including some girls, volunteered to go across if their safety was assured. The Gurkhas were told to keep away from certain tracks and early in the morning the journey began. Everyone was rather tense. The villagers from Serikin had never been over since Confrontation began, and gossip was that special Indonesian troops were in Babang, presumably to counteract the activities of the Gurkhas. Serikin was very pro-Gurkha and enjoyed the close presence of a forward Company base near the village, so everyone was apprehensive. But most of all I knew all the facts and wondered what we were going into.

Many hours later, having left Patrick at Bau, I took the films into Special Branch and placed an order for at least five sets of all the photographs taken as early as possible. A few hours later the first proofs were ready and Eureka! – out of the eighty or so photographs taken two of them, one in particular, showed without doubt a tall, slim, heavily moustachioed Indonesian Army Major wearing the tell-tale epaulette insignia of Resemen Pelopor; some other lesser mortals had Pelopor arm insignia, and dress was previously described. Colonel McAlister was delighted when I rang and told him.

The following day I was visited by a Special Branch Superintendent, a Malay whom I had never met. He brought me my five sets of copies and I told him I might need some more to offset any suspicion that I or the villagers had been involved in anything underhand. The Superintendent (who had a very beautiful daughter, Miss Sarawak 1964) looked at me rather shamefacedly and informed me that the negatives were already in London, so no further copies could be made. This could have put me and my agents in a very awkward position. It gave me personally and no doubt Col. McAlister great pleasure to know that after all this time the egg was going all over the faces it should do, but I have no doubt they worried very little about it: only we at the sharp end derived the satisfaction of knowing we were right from the beginning. It was a pity lives had to be lost, and our lives put at risk to prove a point. Some juggling of the photographs and some wonderful excuses to the Indonesians gave me my complete set. I presented 1/10 Gurkhas with a special set of copies to commemorate the action, and the remainder were to be spread out between the Indonesians and the Serikin villagers.

How often are these circumstances repeated in civilian or military surroundings, when seniors refuse to accept the facts or submissions of juniors because it would upset the preconceived opinions held, and to change would be against the grain. To me I lived through it too many times; the ideal modern example is the Yorkshire Ripper.

Probably the most amusing tale to tell concerns the American Peace Corps contingent who were stationed at Bau. The American Peace Corps was the inspired brainchild of President John Kennedy, formed to assist the development of Third World Nations in such matters as Education, Agriculture, Medicine, Building and so on. Selected young graduates volunteered to spend three years in a country of their choice, where they would be housed, fed and receive spending money; in return they should assist in the successful pursuance of various projects to help the nation's economy and its continued progress. If originally this was solely the President's object, then the scheme was laudable. It is generally accepted by some of us that the organization was formed or was later integrated (not necessarily wholly) into the CIA (Central Intelligence Agency).

Two males and one female, all in their twenties, shared a small isolated bungalow just off the Lundu Road. All were involved in agriculture, trying to encourage the locals in the rear area kampongs to be more self sufficient in poultry and eggs and other matters. They were strictly forbidden to enter the five-mile border area and generally I think they adhered to these restrictions, but they certainly cultivated the well placed English speaking locals and were always evident at social functions and parties. Occasionally they would be invited to British Sergeants Messes, but not Gurkha; mainly they socialized with groups of soldiers in a particular *kedai* in Bau's main street opposite Boon's. Generally I managed to keep out of their way, but I was frequently waylaid en route from Boons' to my house and so was not always successful. The woman was the problem; she was attractive but rather too heavily built to attract the average man, but out there to speak to a white woman was a bonus, and it was difficult to insult her.

On this particular day, a Saturday, Patrick and I had not returned until late afternoon, so after report writing and a general clean up it was 8p.m. when I ate at Boon's. At 9p.m. I was crossing the road on my way home when I was hailed by the 'Three Stooges'. The REME Sergeant from 129 Battery was also with them, and I think he wanted moral support. The conversation was kept on a general level with the girl commenting that I must be busy as I was never seen at various social functions. Her bait was ignored and the beer flowed and I began to enjoy their company; being with a female made it more acceptable. I noticed she bought the rounds but only drank pop, though at parties I had seen her scoffing hard liquor with no apparent effect. One of the male Americans made a rather flippant but academic comment about food and the world population and the subject of birth control was introduced amid various stories from the Americans.

By this time I must have felt the need for comic relief as the subject was becoming very technical. With a serious face I began to explain how I thought English Morris dancing could help reduce the world's population if it was introduced into countries of high birth rate such as India, Turkey or South America. The Sergeant's mouth began to twitch and his eyes were laughing but he kept his face straight. I said that Morris dancing was a medieval form of birth control commonly used in England until the Industrial Revolution. All the young men danced, and were generally garbed in a white ensemble, with coloured sashes, bells attached to their legs and hand sticks with bells or streamers. There were of course certain dress variations depending on the area of the country you came from, but the dancing, to quick and lively music, was most energetic and at times bordering on the frantic. Couple this with a few pints of potent mead or such like alcoholic beverage and you had it made. Three hours of this madness before bedtime would make any man impotent and incapable of performing his natural marital functions. The woman naturally encouraged their menfolk to dance with skill and vigour and praised them well, plus their drinking process. The men reacted to this flattery with renewed enthusiasm to impress, and left their wives alone in the sexual sense. I praised the guile and commonsense of the English women of those days who sensibly were trying to escape from the problems of child bearing and rearing, illness, poverty and feeding. Wasn't I a lying sod! A magnificent embellisher.

I continued to elaborate and lie through my teeth to a very attentive audience of three. The Sergeant swallowing hard had excused himself and returned to camp before he laughed hysterically and spoiled it. The beer still flowed. I was questioned quite sensibly but I was beginning to run out of anecdotes of medieval Britain which I could barely remember. I did explain that the dancing was still performed but only by societies for posterity, and that I myself as a small child had been a member of a Morris dance troop. There was doubt in their eyes but to them it possibly made sense; only a bloody silly Englishman would give up sex for a dance and physical accolades. The Sergeant had confirmed that Morris dancers did exist today, but he was not fully aware of their origins, and so the matter rested. I went home happy with booze, content that I had enjoyed company, and satisfied that I had helped to further cement Anglo/American relations!!

To my shame and horror it was only years later that I read that in certain parts of England, morris dancing is considered to be a *fertility* rite. It is of course possible that I had read of this beforehand and just twisted it round as my warped sense of humour dictated on the night. Who cares, I thought it was funny.

The following Thursday the Sergeant, who came from Wiltshire, received from his wife the local paper, and there in the centre pages were several photographs of performing Morris dancers at various country functions. They were dressed as I had described them almost to perfection, and the photographs showed them adopting movements that could be described as energetic. The scene was set. My friend the Sergeant had told the half dozen members about my tale which curled them up, so when he produced the paper and photographs Paddy and one other came into Bau to show them the proof that Howard was not lying. They were totally convinced and the whole matter made sense. A report was submitted, so I was reliably informed, to their reporting centre and forwarded to Washington for processing and evaluation. My apologies to the Cultural Attaché serving in the British Embassy at the time, if he was bombarded by requests for details of the Durex book of Medieval Contraceptives, or 'Dance with Morris and keep Britain tiny'. No wonder the CIA get some stick; still it all helped to improve morale. Was it indicative that shortly after all three left Bau and we got a schoolteacher instead?

I suppose I should carry this on. The replacement was a typical all-American boy, not large in stature, but handsome and clean cut. He had US of A printed right through him. His first social function was at the presentation of a Malay Government propaganda film held in 1/10 Gurkhas Mess. He had one glassful of Henry's special punch and he died for two hours, which did not help his introduction. Later I lent him some books and he confided he was an avid reader of World War II history, so I asked him if he had read *The Struggle for Europe* by Chester Wilmott, now deceased, which I considered one of the finest books written about a period of the war. He made a note and left.

Some ten days later I returned to my house and went for a meal. The American was waiting and ambushed me in the street. He had purchased the book in Kuching and had never read such an anti American publication; it was provocative, insulting, full of lies etc. and how dare I have recommended it? I explained that the book was factual and that no general of any Allied nationality had made any adverse comment about it, and if the truth hurt, well, hard luck. He looked hard at me, stamped his foot, did a ballet turn and left me. It's hard to believe but he returned my books when I was absent and never spoke to me again. The last I heard he was engaged to a local Dyak teacher.

The 1/10 Gurkhas were to be relieved in May 1966 by the 4th Battalion Royal Australian Regiment and I was sorry to see them leave. Pete Slowe threw a party for the senior ranks and the RQMS Henry produced his delicious but highly potent hot punch. We met up later in Hong Kong and they all came to bid farewell to Jean and me when we left Kai Tak Airport. They were a great bunch of blokes.

However it was a more amusing party when the Advance Party of 4 RAR entertained the 1/10 Rear Party, Pete Slowe and me, and Paddy plus three from 129 Battery. The Gurkhas fell out almost following supper. By 10p.m. we thought the party was swinging. The jokes and the songs started, the beer was flowing and at about 1.30a.m. we were rudely interrupted by the very angry and irate voice of 1/C Advance Party, the Battalion Second in Command who summoned the RSM to the door. We looked around to find that our fifteen Aussie hosts were fast asleep or drunk and had been so for some time. The RSM (formerly of the Welch Regiment) gave us the 21/C's compliments but would we f— off, he couldn't sleep and we didn't sound like the Luton Girls Choir. These hard drinking Aussies don't like prolonged drinking sessions, only 'Happy Hours'. Luckily the Commanding Officer of 4 RAR, Lt. Col. Thompson did not hold it against me and we worked together very successfully. He was a good soldier and was prepared to listen; he did not suffer fools gladly, and was only too pleased to help sort out my 'friend': the interfering Police Superintendent Bill Olley.

4 RAR immediately set out to conquer hearts and minds and promised new furniture for the school at Serikin. On the day it was to be handed over officially, we had had a tremendous downpour (Far East style) of rain in the morning as Patrick and I walked into Bau having been out for several days. About lunchtime I had a visitor who told me a trading party had arrived at Serikin from Babang and the Headman was not happy; would I come to the village as soon as possible and check the party. There was no transport available at the Police Station, but 4 RAR said they would send

a driver escort, as their official party had already left for the village. Two rather large, energetic young Australian privates arrived at the bungalow and off we went. I was astonished to see water lying in the more sparse areas of primary jungle adjacent to the rough vehicle track and the small streams were very high; usually even in heavy rain the streams appeared to cope.

We parked quietly near the new school and the two Aussies said they would join the official party and enjoy the subsequent food and drink. We entered the Headman's house from the rear, and spoke to the Border Scout who brought to us one of the Indonesians who began to tremble. I had to resort to subtle or not so subtle threats and he admitted that one of the party was an Indonesian soldier but would I please not disclose who had informed. Reassured, and having disclosed a description and location in the village, he crept away, his identity secure. To impress the Indonesian civilians the 'lift' had to be done melodramatically. Patrick entered the hut to cover me as I moved in behind the suspect and cocked my pistol by his ear. He fell over sideways on to his back and the look of horror on his face was enough, he was petrified. His mouth was open and his eyes bulged like organ stops. He was beckoned to his feet and unobserved taken to an upstairs room in the Headman's house. Neither Patrick or I had said a word, the wonders of psychology. The Border Scout was told to watch the party, slowly get them all together and wait for my instructions.

Our 'victim' was sitting cross-legged and shaking involuntarily but he looked defiantly at me, not knowing what to expect. As arranged, I sat in front of this individual and cocked my pistol again at the same time that Patrick said, 'You are an Indonesian soldier dressed in civilian clothes and captured on British territory, you are a spy and can be shot without trial.'

I almost shot him there and then; he made a swift move inside his jacket to his shirt and that could have been fatal. He had quickly been frisked so had no weapons but he shouldn't have moved so quickly. What he threw at me was a set of rosary beads and he shouted in English, 'Please, I am Catholic.' I was stumped for words, and across Patrick's face crept the inevitable grin. Seeing he had scored a point he quickly explained he could speak and write a little English but preferred to speak Malay/Dyak. I gave him pen and paper and he wrote – 'Faustimus, Larentimus, Dorani' plus the name of his unit (I still have the original).

He was twenty-five years of age, a Staff Sergeant in the Indonesian Army Intelligence and had volunteered to be a member of the trading party with a view to regular visits and then hopefully to be allowed to visit Bau and possibly Kuching. Credit it to him, he had guts and should be a Colonel by now. We talked for about two hours, and the longer we spoke the more confident of his life he grew and when he started to be evasive and even smiling, the decision had to be made.

The Malaysian and Indonesian governments were currently holding very sensitive talks in Bangkok about the possible cessation of hostilities. The Malays have never been particularly warlike, so ethnically and economically a solution was imperative. When the Indonesians had removed Doctor Sukarno from office and many Left Wing elements were eliminated, the new leader Suharto wanted an early end to confrontation without losing too much face. It was desired that the regular Indonesian forces stop the war as soon as possible and then they would attempt to disarm, disband or eliminate the TNKU (Tentara Nasional Kalimantam Utara) and other organizations formed against Malaysia.

It all sounded good, but I had been in written contact with the Commanding Officer and Intelligence Officer of 203 Brimob Battalion since June. In July an incursion party had passed through the Aussie positions to set up the beginnings of offensive operations (more about that later). The officers wanted to talk peace; at the same time specialized highly trained RPKAD troops entered Sarawak; it didn't make sense. If I took Dorani to Kuching for detailed interrogation and further processing then it was almost a hundred per cent certainty that the peace talks in Bangkok would have been called off. To keep it at Special Branch level and release the prisoner might be the more judicious action to take. The incursion in July had caused quite a hiccup but since then the dialogue had improved and everyone was hopeful.

It was not an easy decision, I was not a politician or a diplomat, neither was I a Commanding General. I decided to let him go and take my chances with authority. Dorani would eventually have talked more, but what would he have told us that we didn't really know already, following Manjar 1 and 2 (the incursion into Bau District). Dorani was rather forcefully reminded that should a similar attempt be made to cross the border without my permission by any member of the Indonesian Army in Bau District the consequences would be severe. If captured they would just disappear without a trace – a case of summary jurisdiction. He had to tell his Commanding Officer that I was willing to talk to them at any time providing it was with the permission of higher authority and that no further operations like Dorani's or Manjar 1 and 2 were contemplated.

The Headman called to Patrick. After a short discussion Patrick said that Sgt. S, a Special Branch man from Bau, had unofficially (ordered by the Superintendent to snoop) accompanied the official presentation party but spent most of his time talking to the villagers and some of the traders consequently had heard about Dorani's 'removal', and now wanted to make an arrest. Quickly Dorani was smuggled out of the back door, across the river, reminded what he had to say and in the company of the Border Scouts was escorted to the border in some haste.

Eventually Sgt. S and I met and he demanded this and that (he had a reputation for viciousness and had a vile temper) and became most angry when told Dorani had left. I also had to tell him about his area of responsibility and that I would not have any more interference either by uniformed or Special Branch Officers in the forward areas, otherwise I would go direct to HSB and make it official. The poor chap was only carrying out orders from a senior, he had little choice, and he knew that Peter Lim did not agree. However on my return I spoke to Colonel Thompson and he agreed: now was not the time to pick up POWs even though technically Dorani was a spy. This incident was a good bargaining factor at Bangkok (if it was ever used) and when Colonel Thompson spoke to HSB on the matter he had a long think about it, rang us back and agreed the decision had been right and that he would deal with Bau District's Police Superintendent in his own way. The man still tried to interfere and it was only when all British and Commonwealth forces were withdrawn in August and operations in connection with 'Claret' had ceased that he began to be told a little more of what was happening in the border area. He was a menace to my operations, my agents, and my life, and I strongly resented it. I can't blame him for feeling parochial and I knew he resented the fact that he was not 'in the know', and that a junior person i.e. the FIO, had the ear of very senior police, military and Government officers and he was not included. As a former senior RAF Officer he was very conscious of seniority; frankly I thought he was a snob and a great believer in self preservation. How well I remember the death in custody of the man (a Chinese I remember) who had butchered his wife with a *parang*, and had decapitated and hacked to pieces the policeman who came to investigate. There must have been some slick talking done and the ultimate responsibilities was his.

But to continue. We left the village in the early evening with the two Aussies in a state of euphoria or should I say drunkenness. The officer representing the unit had left much earlier, so 'Bill and Ben' without supervision had over-indulged. The first part of the return journey was erratic to say the least, accompanied by lewd Aussie songs. Suddenly we ran out of road. The whole area appeared to be one vast lake. The driver decided to push on; the water was higher than the floor of the Land Rover but remained steady. With a whoop but without his weapon the escort took a header into the water and proceeded to swim to the front of the vehicle. He stated it was his duty to see that I got safely back and that he would walk/swim in front and guide us along the submerged track. Between songs, comments and frequent disappearances under water it was quite hilarious; I didn't know whether to laugh or cry. When the driver, not to be outdone, decided to join his mate for a swim I gave up. The waters could have been filled with all sorts of dangers, snakes, rats, etc., but they couldn't care less. Patrick with a straight and noncommittal face turned to me and said, 'I think they are both very happy,' that sounded more like the address to the bride and groom. Eventually the driver returned and we continued. I have had much safer rides but none quite so amusing and difficult to describe. As I went in to see Colonel Thompson we bade farewell to 'Bill and Ben' who were wet, bedraggled, full of alcoholic remorse and, knowing the local hooch, would have the beginnings of sore heads and stomachs. They probably thought I was a real 'Pommie bastard' with no sense of fun, but I had other things on my mind that they knew nothing about.

At the time of handover between 1/10 and 4 RAR, 'D' Sqn 22 SAS had handed over to a squadron of Australian SAS and they were about to commence operations. I arrived at Bukit Knuckle mid morning by helicopter in order to carry out a particular job in the Gumbang area and to wait for someone. The 'Knuckle' was a feature of high ground, felled of trees and undergrowth and fortified with *sangars* and dugouts, protected on the lower fringes by Claymore mines and the felled trees. An Aussie SAS patrol of six (I think) was about to leave on patrol, and the changeover was due to take place over the next twenty-four between 1/10 and 4 RAR. Some forty hours later at about 0530 hrs, Patrick and I with our prisoner reached the edge of the 'Knuckle' perimeter and I was apprehensive. I had told the 1/10 and 4 RAR officers that I should return in two or three days but to approach a fortified position at that time of the morning was risky especially as the resident troops were new and were not familiar with the 'Terrible Twins'; we were such a contrast in size. From the side I was approaching from, access to the position was an upward climb along the carefully placed trunks of several very large trees laid end to end.

Approximately a quarter of a mile from the position I very carefully blindfolded the prisoner and he was not happy, and pedestrian wise very reluctant. On reaching the trees I told Patrick to tell the prisoner why the blindfold was used and where he was about to walk, and that he must trust us, but he was not convinced! Because of my height and dress and the identifying 1/10 sign on my jungle hat I hoped I would be recognized. I placed the prisoner in front of me while Patrick guided and cajoled him. After the second tree I felt happier; the early morning mist was moving a bit and I wasn't sure if I'd been seen and recognized. Thankfully we got to

'Fred' and me about to board the 'chopper' prior to interrogation.

the top to the great curiosity of the Aussies. We were not Gurkhas, no unit
signs, badges of rank etc.; it certainly helped the reputation. I handcuffed
our friend near the Camp HQ dugout; Patrick went to eat with the few
Gurkhas remaining and brought the prisoner some food back. Meanwhile
I spoke with the Gurkha Captain who asked if I had heard any explosions
or gunfire during my wanderings on the previous day. I replied in the
negative, explaining that I had not returned to the Gumbang area until the
early evening with the prisoner and had heard nothing.

Patrick and I with two 1/10 Gurkhas bring back the two 'scouts' of the Indonesian incursion party.

When the Gunners fired their regular DF tasks each evening you could hear the explosions for miles and small arms fire could be heard over a fair distance too, especially if you were moving quietly and slowly or on high ground. The Captain explained that as I left the position to reach the high ground in the Gumbang area, the Aussie SAS group left in another direction. Some two hours later the Gurkha Company Commander and his Aussie equivalent were flying above the jungle tree line in a Sioux helicopter doing an 'air recce' of the forward border area, more on the Indonesian side than our own. Down in the jungle to their amazement they saw two figures in a small clearing waving to them; a closer examination revealed two members of the SAS patrol. Without hesitation the pilot picked a spot, landed, picked up the two soldiers and returned to 'Knuckle'.

The subsequent story told was too incredible to believe and all in two hours or so of leaving the base. Briefly they said that they had had close contact with a forty strong (approximately) Indonesian patrol. They had been spotted and short fire fight followed, with no SAS casualties. They decided to run for it. An RV (rendezvous) was arranged. The rescued two set up a grenade booby trap, it was sprung, they opened fire and ran. They did not RV with the others but had heard further prolonged gunfire being exchanged and were worried about the fate of their comrades. When they heard the sound of the Sioux they took a chance of early rescue as the patrol was finished anyway. The Gurkhas led a composite patrol along the track allegedly taken, finding nothing to substantiate the story. Both I and the Gurkhas knew that until December 1965 Indonesian troops had occupied Kampong Siding some seven miles from the border, but owing to aggressive Gurkha patrolling they had withdrawn even further to a kampong some fifteen miles or so from the border.

It was known by me that no Indonesian military patrols had been in that part of the border area since December (and in fact my prisoner could verify this), but where were the other four members of the patrol? Later as dusk was approaching the Sioux was having a last 'swan' over the area and saw four gesticulating bodies in a clearing. They were picked up and eventually the patrol were returned to Kuching. The Aussies' Company Commander was, in loyalty, rather noncommittal, but it left much to the imagination. I often wondered what the eventual outcome was. Knowing the Aussie character they probably decided among themselves that they couldn't be bothered with all the hardship and aggravation of a patrol and concocted these unbelievable series of events; pity they didn't do their homework with me.

To return to my particular problem. The sun eventually penetrated the mist and low cloud, the weather improved but the chopper was delayed because it was imperative we land at Kuching and were met with secure transport, not to the SB Interrogation Centre but to Central Police Station, so we sat on the 'pad' and sweated. I could have released my prisoner at Gumbang after I had questioned him, but he was aggressive, cocky and rather unco-operative. If he was frightened he might talk more and he might even work for me, but he would have required payment, so first we had to teach him a lesson and see what his reactions were, then get him back across the border and await results. Placed next to Patrick in the Sioux and against the window he had to be manhandled because he was so frightened. The engine noise was enough, especially blindfolded. We left the pad vertically and circled, and I told Patrick to take off the blindfold. When he saw where he was and recognised the tiny figures on the 'pad' he was absolutely terrified. When we flew higher and he could see the jungle panorama he was hysterical; he grabbed my shoulder from behind and grabbed Patrick's right wrist and never let go. Patrick's wrist was very bruised for several days.

I must confess that to land at Kuching Airport was for me a giggle. It was largely occupied by the RAF with minimal aggressive aircraft, and some RAF Regiment defence units. The main aircraft were RAF Argosys for re-supply by parachute to forward position, Belvederes and Whirlwind helicopters and 'Teeny Weeny Airways' or the Army Air Corps' Sioux 'choppers' and Beaver 'Spotters'. So as we landed and walked to the transport, the RAF RCT (Royal Corps of Transport) loaders all stopped work to look at these two disreputable figures in some form of jungle uniform dragging a rather reluctant scruffy figure with a blindfold on: all very mysterious especially to people who slept safely in their beds every night. We did this several times. I think it reminded them that forty or fifty miles away people were fighting a real war.

In the quietest of cells the interrogation began again. Reluctantly he talked but had little information of value, even with my pistol in his mouth and Patrick putting on the verbal pressure. His wet shorts and bulging eyes told us he had nothing further to offer; we had no time for the finer points of interrogation with this particular one. Eventually he agreed to visit certain areas for me and come in to Gumbang to report, but we did not believe him and he never did. He was a gutsy little character, and enjoyed the trip back to 'Knuckle' with Patrick and was deposited over the border by Patrick and the Border Scouts. Like the two from Kindau he did a grand tour of the area (well away from the border) telling all the tribes of his extraordinary adventures in the metal bird with the big white man. He did have difficulty in describing his journey by motor vehicle, which is understandable. Oh, that life is so simple and we take so much for granted.

CHAPTER 30

The Saga of Manjar 2
4th-24th June 1966

A story with some aid from a military document

It was early morning and the mist started to rise above the jungle as soon as the sun's rays started the day's cycle. Individually the seven men awoke and took several moments to remember where they were and the situation they were in. Each one in his own way felt the momentary grip of panic and apprehension which receded as the sleeping brain activated itself, and reality, training and common sense brought on a calming effect. At intervals the men left the hide to wash in a small stream that flowed some fifty yards away, and after their ablutions were completed they sat on the jungle floor singly or in groups, quietly talking or cleaning their equipment and weapons. A noise and low voices brought instant reaction; it was now about 0800 hours and food was expected but elementary precautions had to be taken.

Two young and attractive Chinese girls, both dressed in light cotton blouses and trousers, came nervously towards the hide, stopped at a pre-arranged spot and laid the food on the ground. It would be hot as the hide was only some two hundred yards from the Chinese kampong. The one Chinese in the group slowly emerged from the jungle and rubber trees and held a conversation with the girls who spoke vociferously then lowered their eyes and adopted a shy but coy poise. When they left, both had long and curious glances towards the jungle surrounding the hide. The Chinese have a natural curiosity and this worried Private Benny; he was not anti Chinese and when he was stationed in Djakarta he and his comrades had had fairly good relations with them, but in Indonesia many Chinese are Communists and as a Christian he personally did not have strong feelings for them. He was not even angry with the Sarawak Chinese guides who had been stupid enough to lose the way and the circumstances which split the patrol which at the moment was only 50 per cent effective.

Now fed and feeling more content, Benny attended to his pressing toilet needs, washed his hands, and lay on his own quietly smoking a cigarette. Seeing the two young girls stirred his reminiscence of home and his family and he felt unhappy but began to recall his early childhood days.

Benny was born in Djakarta in December 1941 and his family, father, mother and brother Johanes, lived on and farmed a small plot of ground in the District of Djalan Djatonegara. He attended Primary School in the District for six years, but at the age of thirteen years he left because his parents could not afford to send him to Secondary School so he helped his father on the land. There was not a great deal to look forward to in his life so on or about his eighteenth birthday he applied to join the Army at his local Police Station. Within a fortnight he and other volunteers from the area were taken by army lorry to a camp at Bogor.

He recalled his initial apprehension but he quickly settled in to the routine of physical training and how to use weapons like the FN 7.62 rifle, grenades, Bren guns etc. They enjoyed the obstacle course, did Section attacks, and had opportunity for sport. The latter he did when ordered but he was not enthusiastic despite all the facilities. If he was honest with himself, he was a bit of a loner; after seven years in the Army he had never written home nor had they written to him. He had no particular friends in the unit. Now the girls had made him think of home. His initial training lasted three months and about six hundred recruits were trained at the same time. When training was completed Benny was told he was now in 1 Battalion RPKAD (Resimen Para Kommando Angkaton Darat) or Army Para Commando Regiment, one of the elite of the Indonesian Army. They were initially formed by the amalgamation of four para battalions and in 1965 were issued with a distinctive type of camouflage uniform plus a bush hat, though normally they wore red berets.

1 RPKAD embarked on a ship in Djakarta which took the unit to North Sulewasi and for six months they carried out operations against the Permesta rebels of Colonels Semual and Kawilarang. He knew the rebels were against the Government but never knew of their reasons and aims. Over the next few months after they returned from Sulewasi the unit practised sea-borne assaults and he successfully completed parachute training, a fact of which he was intensely proud, and as he lay there he could not conceal a confident smile and feel satisfaction within himself.

He was now a fully fledged member of RPKAD but for the next five boring years he remained in barracks close to Djakarta. In September 1965 he was sent for three months to Magelang in Central Java to undertake Passandha training. (Pasvkam Sandyi Yudha – Secret War Team.)

He certainly hadn't volunteered for this, and had no idea why he was selected.

A voice called to him, it was his time for duty sentry.

Since the loss of the other guide and ten of their team including the leader WO Moentahar, the senior soldier was Djamaluddim and he took charge of Benny, Wimoto, Tjini, Santanto and Suwarno; the last three were not RPKAD. The guide was confident enough after a couple of days to go and do some shopping and try to establish contact with the North Borneo Fighters who were to give them local help. The guide was given money to buy cigarettes and clothing. Benny bought socks, trousers, cigarettes and even a fountain pen; the guide probably got them from Tundong. The seven had been in hiding for about a week when they were visited at the hide by a young Chinese man who was dressed in blue shirt and trousers, a blue hat and brown rubber soled shoes. Benny was becoming very observant in this situation. The newcomer was introduced as a representative from the Commandant of the North Borneo Fighters or TNKU (Tentera Nasional Kalimantam Utara), the North Kalimantam National Army, and he wanted to know what unit the team were from. Djamaluddim was suspicious of this and did not admit to being RPKAD. Nothing firm appeared to have resulted from the visit.

Djamaluddim then announced that if the Fighters or the other members of the team did not contact them within a fortnight they would return to Indonesia. Benny came to the conclusion that it had all been a waste of time despite all the preparation and training. It was the 24th June, because they had checked and was a fortnight since they had arrived at the hide and they were all wishing the time would pass quickly so they could return to Indonesia. The early morning routine had passed; it was becoming a boring exercise. This comparative security and inactivity could make them careless and vulnerable. The team had done so well initially, crossing the enemy's well patrolled border through the Australian positions on the Raya Ridge and finally to this place some fifteen miles behind the lines.

It was probably about 1000 hours when the Chinese guide looked into the small clearing near the hide. His eyes were wide with excitement but mainly intense fear was making his body tremble. In a strangled whisper he said, 'Quick, get out, troops are coming here.' He gesticulated behind him then disappeared into the all enveloping jungle undergrowth; he was never found. Benny grabbed at his stacked weapon and kit and blindly followed Santanto and Tjini into the protection of the undergrowth and trees. In blind panic the group fled in different directions. The first group had scarcely left the hide when the first shots were fired followed by a more intense and concentrated fusillade; within seconds one lay dead, his head and body ripped apart by Armalite bullets, another was losing great quantities of blood through a gaping wound, while the other, unscathed, lay still on the ground and prayed for his life. Through almost closed eyes he saw his weapon kicked away by a green jungle boot, something hard was forced against his shoulder and he was turned over very slowly on his back and through hazy eyes saw two grim brown faces under jungle hats. 'Gurkhas!!' He babbled greetings, salutations and his eyes became full of tears, he even passed water without embarrassment; he was beyond care but he wanted to live. He was quickly searched and saw the tattered remains of his comrades as they lay on the ground. His hands were tied behind him and his eyes were bound; he began to realize he was lucky to be alive.

The initial outbreak of fire gave Benny and his two companions a slight advantage. Over the sound of firing, Gurkhali voices could be heard calling to each other. In between hurried gasps of breath the three exchanged words that they might have escaped through the net. Thorns, brambles and low branches of rubber trees tore at their clothing, they threshed about at obstructive items in frantic desperation as their progress was impeded. Carrying equipment instead of wearing it made speed an impossibility.

Suddenly a loud cacophony of sound burst all around Benny. For a moment he witnessed a huge red hole appear as if by magic in the middle of the man's back in front of him. At the same time the heads of his two friends twitched violently from side to side and he was horrified to see portions of their skulls disappear in a bloody mess. Leaves, splinters of wood, branches of trees appeared to fall all around him like bread from heaven, his companions' legs collapsing, bodies sinking, arms waving wildly at nothing, releasing weapons and kit; they fell heavily to the ground. At the same time Benny felt a searing pain and a blow to his head, a frantic, fearful cry came to his lips and he reached for his right eye to hold it. Unconscious, he fell to the ground.

He regained consciousness within seconds of his falling. He was lying face down and was aware, through his good left eye, of a pool of blood, his own, that was becoming increasingly larger. He had no other pain. The jungle floor was warm and damp and as the sun's heat began to extract the evening's wetness from the ground, the smell entered his nostrils, sweet and fetid. Suddenly he was assailed by severe pain in his eye and an involuntary groan came from him as he tried to turn on his back. Through his blurred and painful vision he saw two shafts of sunlight, like heavenly corridors penetrating the jungle canopy. Figures broke the symmetry of the corridors and he was quietly surrounded by small dark-skinned men who moved and acted with practised ease; he assumed they were the fearful Gurkhas. Hands felt at his body, pockets were checked, his wound was attended to by sympathetic hands, he badly wanted the toilet. The bandage covered both his eyes and he was carried through the jungle for some distance. A familiar sound told him a helicopter was near and he was borne away from danger and to the comforting hands of white and dark skinned nurses. The welcomed prick of a needle and he fell into oblivion.

Benny awoke, aware that he was lying between cool clean sheets in the security of a hospital ward. The dimmed light made him feel at peace but he was fully aware of a very sore eye and head with no doubt more pain to come.

'Oh God, why did all this happen to me?' he pleaded, hoping for an audience. 'Couldn't I have been left alone in Djakarta, to quietly soldier on?' He heaped bad wishes on Passandha and in particular General Sarwoeddy and as his mind cleared slightly he began to remember:

The Passandha training had been completed by December 1965 and with his twenty-three companions he had returned to Djakarta. Their leader WoI Mindaja briefed them on an operation they were due to carry out on the Indonesian/Sarawak border. They were told that the operation initially would not be aggressive and that battles with the enemy were to be avoided; only group leaders were told of the operational details. So on 29th December 1965 the twenty-four flew in an Auri (Indonesian Air Force) Hercules plane from Djakarta to the staging post at Pontianak. From here, by helicopter and on foot, they reached Sentas where they were met by Lai Pak Kah, a Chinese who commanded twenty-five members of KOPS (Kommando Perd Juangan Serawak) Sarawak Struggle Command. In mid February some Passandha and KOPS personnel left to carry out an operation in Sarawak; they did not return until the end of the month. They stayed a month in each of two further camps in the area until at the end of April they were sent to Sangau Ledo by army lorry to train some members of 514 Brawijawa Battalion for an operation with the Passandha team.

Out of sixty-four members of 514 only twenty-five were selected for the operation and on 29th May 1966 the 4 RPKAD (Passandha) and 514 members walked to Seluas opposite Bau District where they were later joined by the remainder of the Passandha team. The whole party rested for two days and on 1st June 1966 Benny took part in a small parade to welcome the Brigadier General Sarwo Eddy who had marched up from Sangau Ledo, about twenty miles. After the parade a briefing was held by the General who personally visited the Passandha team with WoI Mindaja, a Colonel, a Major and a man in uniform but no rank was evident. The following morning Benny and the others cleaned their equipment, and at 1100 hours a selected group were called together by a WoI Moentahar who was to command them. They would be known as 'Manjar 2'. Each man received three hundred dollars Malay to buy food in Sarawak and it was explained that their task was to train people in Sarawak who were friendly towards them. At 1700 hrs that day the sixteen members of Manjar 2 plus two Chinese guides left Seluas. Sarwo Eddy waved them off and wished them a safe operation.

When they stayed at a small kampong called Kindau, WoI Moentanar gave them each a further sixty dollars Malay which he described as tactical money and not for food. Then for the following five days they made their way through the slopes and foothills of the Raya Range. During this journey Benny recalled their bodies had been soaked with rain and the crossing of many rivers, and negotiating for all those days that almost indescribable ground, and knowing that the enemy (the Australians) were thick around them, it was all quite fearful. It was dark and almost 2000 hours when they came to a kampong occupied by Dyaks (Kampong Senian). As the guides were leading the group round the edge of the kampong, a number of villagers carrying lights came out of a house, alerted by a barking dog. Both guides were at the head of the Manjar file and they hurried quietly on for approximately half a mile. To their horror and panic the team had been split; there were only three RPKAD Passandha and three of 514 plus the two remaining guides.

The leader, Moentanar, and all senior group leaders had vanished and no one could understand why they had not continued as a complete team despite the obvious curiosity of the villagers who had not approached them.

They waited a very long hour for the remainder to join them but no one appeared. Djamaluddim, the senior soldier, assumed command of what remained of Manjar 2, and said they would continue to their destination. At 0200 hours on 10th June they suddenly came across a wide road. At this point the guides said they were confused and had forgotten the way. It was decided to turn right which they did and after an hour's careful walking the guides admitted they were totally lost. Djamaluddim ordered them into the jungle beside the road before it became light. At about 0500 hours one guide said he would go and find out where they were and was told to hurry back as quickly as possible. They spent an uncomfortable day on the roadside and it was somewhat nervewracking listening and watching the pedestrian and vehicular movement on what was the Bau-Lundu Road (by courtesy of Peter Slowe). They never saw the guide again. It was decided to press on without him.

The group continued to walk down the road, but after half a mile the remaining guide decided they were going in the wrong direction so they turned about and walked back the way they had come the previous night. Eventually they came to a track leading off to the right (east), which the guide said went in the right direction and after a short rest at the road/track junction they started to walk along the dark narrow track which led through jungle and rubber plantations. They crossed a shallow river and suddenly reached a kampong; they had not travelled much over two miles from the road. The guide motioned them to hide off the track and said he would contact his friends. Half an hour later he returned and led them to the safety of the hide and relative safety and comfort.

Benny looked up to the ceiling or God; he uttered a prayer to give him strength and was given added confidence when a dark skinned nurse accompanied by a grim faced Gurkha questioned him in Malay on how he felt and if he was in pain. He was made comfortable and left alone. A rising fear suddenly gripped him, his stomach muscles knotted and his bowels protested violently. Soon he would have to face the 'Interrogators'.

As the dogs barked and the villagers appeared from their hut lights flashed all around but no one approached. WoI Moentahar motioned those behind him down to the ground and they made a slow crawl back the way they had come. They waited patiently while the jungle maintained its normal noisy nocturnal habits and carefully continued along the track to regain contact with the forward part of the team. To Moentahar's disappointment and frustration he could find no trace of them, so he decided to continue east. They finally reached a good and wide road (the Bau/Lundu Road) and hid in the jungle till daylight. For the remainder of the 10th the group just watched the road and waited. On the 11th Moentahar sent out teams of two men in civilian clothes north and south of their position to find their comrades. Gratefully they all returned. Feeling more confident the two-men teams crossed over the road to the east side. The following day again they returned, one team reporting they had been helped to cross a river by a Chinese youth who thought they were Dyaks. Another group had asked questions about buses from people at a bus stop; one man appeared to be suspicious but nothing happened. Moentahar now had to make a decision. A third of his military strength had disappeared, he was without guides for safe movement and probably more significantly, their contact with the local Chinese and their assistance to the team which was so important. He decided that the ten men remaining should split into two separate teams, A and B, and at first light on the 13th move on to the Raya Ridge and return to Indonesia.

Team B, again despite wet conditions, traversed the ridge on alternate sides through jungle and along tracks and on the morning of the 15th heard the sounds of a violent fire fight and later artillery being carried out in the misty foreground below them. At that time they were heading north. Tired and hungry they carried on, hoping their comrades were safe. They were feeling very confident now as they approached the border. They could hear the noise of enemy helicopters and occasionally one would fly very close to the ridge but they were not worried. The party had reached a point south of the junction of the track to Stass and the high ridge track when it happened. A high velocity bullet hit one of the 514 men and lifted him off the ground; he was dead when he hit the jungle floor. This sudden shock galvanized them into action. The enemy appeared to be all around and the group tried to move further south down the ridge to give them space, exchanging fire all the time, to manoeuvre. The contact with the Australians was fierce and bitter. It lasted for half an hour. Only one of the group, nursing a nasty wound in the right hip, managed to crawl away into the safety of the jungle and head for the border that was only about a mile away. His four companions, their bodies shattered, lay at peace in the jungle, one Australian died and another was losing his life's blood rather rapidly despite the efforts of his comrades; a helicopter was the answer. More Aussies arrived to seal off the west edge of the Raya.

Team A followed roughly the high line of the Raya. Little did they know that Team B had been so close when they had rested on the 14th. At about 0800 on the 15th, following the undulating foothills of the Raya, they heard noises and went up to higher ground. They were fortunate to stumble across a deserted area, no doubt formerly used by troops. Suddenly fire was opened up on them. It was not accurate but it did wound an RPKAD man in the hand. Using the high ground to advantage, good fire and movement and heavy accurate fire pinned down any outflanking movements attempted by the Australians. Team A used the old SF positions in the rocky outcrop to good advantage, but were sent into a panic when they were shelled, though for some reason it was totally ineffective, possibly caused by the terrain. By 1130 hrs when the Aussies had re-grouped and advanced on the outcrop Team A had gone. The troops spread out to search and tracks were seen heading north, so troops and tracker teams headed north then west and met Team B and success. Elated by action and their skill in extracting themselves out of serious trouble, Team A, covering their tracks, decided to hide for twenty-four hours and keep out of sight.

Knowing sanctuary was not far away they did not wish to take unnecessary risks at this stage. In the late afternoon as they lay quietly close to a stream in thick jungle they heard the sound of gunfire, lasting about half an hour. They were not aware but yet another third of Manjar 2 was being accounted for, permanently.

While daylight lasted enemy helicopters buzzed around like furious bees. The Aussies were in full cry and caution was the watchword. On the 16th less than a mile was made through thick jungle but they were safe, and on the 17th they recrossed the border and headed for Kindau. A cry from the side of the track revealed a mud and blood splattered comrade from Team B who could hardly walk. They carried him into Kindau, then later met Manjar 1 and returned to Seluas.

Such was the fate of the Manjar operation.

Let us now look at other events that linked up, and subsequently contributed to the virtual destruction of an adventurous and daring Indonesian operation. Had confrontation continued this would have been a very serious threat to the internal security of Sarawak. Dedicated, highly trained and well armed soldiers, succoured and assisted by the indigenous population, would have been difficult to trace and could have inflicted terrible casualties on the Security Forces. It was the intention to establish Manjar teams in Bau and Matang with an approximate reserve of twelve initially to concentrate on subversion and later on offensive operations. From an unofficial source it was stated that the FIO Bau was top of the hit list closely followed by Peter Lim. Reinforcements and equipment were subsequently to be infiltrated into the pockets. There was indication of a form of receipt and transmission of messages. It was later in July that I first began to hear about the groundwork necessary for the establishment of a Manjar team in the Matang area but nothing was ever discovered; the Dyaks had no time for the TNKU and the Indonesian Army.

These now are the events:

At about 1900 hours on 10th June 1966 a Chinese was walking north along the Bau/Lundu road when a man stepped out in front of him and in Malay told him he was a Border Scout and that he was arresting him. The Scout was armed with a shotgun. The Chinese was taken to Bau Police Station and interrogated by SB Inspector Peter Lim. Initially the Chinese lied to Lim but subsequent interrogation revealed that he had been briefed at Seluas with about fifty other people, TNI (Army), TNKU, and Chinese. He had crossed the border with Manjar 2 on 4th June 1966 (16 TNI and 2 Chinese guides). For some reason the team was split on 9th June 1966, the guides and 6 TNI trying to get to Tundong. Before his arrest he was trying to rejoin his seven comrades who were waiting for him on the roadside.

At approximately 2300 hours on 11th June 1966 a local from Kampong Plaman Semaya reported to the police at Bau that a party of ten uniformed men had come to his house at 2200 hours that night. They asked if SF visited that area at night and if he was armed. The local replied no to each question. Then they asked for food as they had not eaten for two days. Before the man's wife had cooked rice the armed men ate durians and salt and drank boiled water. They asked the local to guide them to Tundong.

He refused but showed them a track which led in the right direction then without waiting to eat the cooked food they left at 2230 hours. The local carefully counted ten men.

These men were described as non-Chinese who spoke Malay with a peculiar accent. They wore jungle hats similar to SF and green or khaki uniforms which were wet and mud spattered. They wore a thin waist belt which held a four-compartment magazine pouch; also on the belt were carried two grenades. Their weapons were all Soviet Kalashnikov 7.62mm assault rifles.

Shortly after midnight on 12th June 1966 these two items of information were given to 4 RAR who immediately sent a Company out to check the Sungei Selalang if it could be crossed. They established it could, then moved into Tundong, and by first light Tundong was sealed off. As the Company moved into Tundong a young Chinese was questioned and he admitted that two strangers whom he addressed in Dyak but who spoke Malay had asked him to guide them across the Selalang which he did. They were not armed. Some time later a policeman said he became curious about two strangers at a bus stop at Grogo. They were asking for a bus to Tundong and when told the bus only went to Bau they left. The policeman thought they were Indonesians, but didn't arrest them because the bulges in their pockets looked like grenades. These were from the party of 10 TNI who were searching for the guides and 6 TNI.

At 1600 hours on 13th June 1966 a Border Scout reported he had seen tracks of five men at Gunong API on the Raya. They were heading west and had been made that morning. He also said that the same track had been used a few days earlier by a larger number of men but heading east. (This was obviously the same track used by Manjar 2 as it headed for Kampong Senian and the eventual split.) A tracker team and Border Scouts were lifted on to API at 0730 hours on 15th June 1966 and tracks followed until they were washed out by rain. The subsequent contacts have already been described.

To summarize, it had been a very courageous enterprise by well trained troops, who unfortunately were confronted by equally well trained and experienced troops, police and Border Scouts. Many brave men died and at that stage should it ever have been attempted? Who am I to comment!

CHAPTER 31

The Sheriff of Bau

My *nom de plume*, the Sheriff of Bau, was given to me following an incident which was amusing but which could have led to serious problems had I not nipped it in the bud.

I had called in at Serikin to quickly run over a visiting trading party when I was told by the Headman that one member of the party held a 'Leave Pass' issued by the Indonesian Army which 'entitled' him to travel to Serikin, Bau, Kuching and return via Kampong Opar. In other words he was having a run round for Brimob's Intelligence boys. It also asked for the Pass to be countersigned by Authority on our side. The man was told he did not have my permission, and if he disobeyed he could be jailed or even shot.

I then left to visit another kampong and some twenty-four hours later Patrick and I called in at the little *kedai* near the Japanese bridge at Pejiru only to be told that my friend from Serikin who had the Land Rover had called in on the way to Bau and he had with him an Indonesian who had been given permission to visit Sarawak by a uniformed Police Inspector and Special Branch Sergeant, who had yet again visited the forward areas without military agreement and had interfered in my work. A 3-tonner from the Gunners' 5.5 Camp was passing so we scrounged a lift. Now Bau was like a Wild West town, one street only, so Patrick and I took a side apiece to locate our 'visitor'. He and my friend were just about to leave a store when I confronted them. Their faces were a picture, a crowd gathered, and Patrick joined me. I demanded the 'Pass' and it was hurriedly produced. With great ceremony I tore the document into pieces. There was a murmur of approval from the crowd. Telling Patrick what to say: 'You've got half a minute to leave town!' I pulled out my pistol, cocked it, and the pair of them were off. My friends' decrepit Land Rover made very funny noises and vicious bangs and as it started off amid dust, bangs and mechanical mysteries the vehicle swayed from side to side and from the back resembled one of those old 'prairie schooners' as it negotiated the badly rutted main street of Bau. It struck me as humorous and my report

Indonesian SAS equivalent: 'Resemen Pelopor' with some Serikin villagers I'd persuaded to visit Babang. Confirmation!

on the matter was both pointed and funny and apparently quoted all down the line. The Indonesians didn't try that again and the police yet again had to be reprimanded.

About this time John Althorp had left and Major Jago had taken over 2 Company at Labuan. I had already received confirmation that at the end of my tour, whenever that was, I would go to Hong Kong Counter Intelligence Platoon. I then received a signal from Major Jago via the Australian Battalion to state my preference in postings on leaving Borneo; an immediate reply was required. Some hours later I had hurriedly to leave by helicopter for the border, so I asked the Aussie Intelligence Officer kindly to reply and I quoted the letter I had already received. When I returned some days later a letter was waiting for me from Major Jago who tore me off the most vicious 'strip' for the tone of my signal, and that he could not wait to confront me when he would visit in a fortnight's time. I was absolutely grief stricken being 'sorted out' by a person I had not even met. I was even more horrified when I saw the Aussie IO and saw the contents of the signal. He had more or less, in very abrupt terms, stated that idiotic officers should not send idiotic signals to hard working soldier boys at the sharp end who had more to do than send back information that was already known if they would care to look for it and it was not even signed.

I then wrote a long letter of apology and explanation but received no reply. On the day of the expected visit I had been out and was rather dirty. Major Jago and a Lt. Colonel from Singapore were meeting Brigade personnel, Head of Special Branch and his seniors and as I was trudging down to my bungalow the white Land Rover pulled up alongside and two very jovial characters leapt out, shaking my hand, asking, 'And how is the Sheriff of Bau feeling today?' I was rather overwhelmed; my first reaction was to start apologizing. Major Jago with a huge grin held up his hand.

'No need, old chap, your letter explained it all, I know what Aussies are like, forget it.'

We had a long chat, a few beers in the *kedai*, lots of thanks for doing a good job and being an excellent example for the Corps, then they left. The next time I saw Major Jago he was on his back in Woolwich Hospital and I have never seen him since. He was one of the few really good officers in our Corps, a fact verified by many senior ranks.

I lay in bed shortly after 10p.m. one Sunday night. I was thinking about my week ahead, trying to keep two jumps ahead of all eventualities, a habit I have never been able to break. I've always found it pays especially when dealing with senior officers. The two policemen who manned the compound gate could be heard chatting quietly to themselves above the normal jungle noises of cicadas and frogs. I should explain that the Bau-Tundong road ran passed my bungalow and police families accommodation; we were all within the police compound, the road gate near my bungalow was closed during the hours of darkness and all vehicles and pedestrians closely scrutinized. On the opposite side of the road a further fence had been erected making a effective inner compound which housed the police station and accommodation for the Police Field Force, single men, and near to me families accommodation. A small pedestrian gate gave access to the inner compound and this is where the two policemen stood.

The relative quiet was suddenly shattered by crashing glass, the banging of doors, screams and frantic cries in Dyak and Chinese. I put shoes on my feet, my sarong round my waist, grabbed my pistol from under the pillow and ran out on to the road. Patrick had not returned from his village, Peter Lim was out and neither of the two Dyak policemen spoke English. All I could get was 'prisoner', so I gathered that one had escaped. I am not sure that at this stage a shot was not fired which increased general nervousness. The night was black, with no moon; observation was almost non existent, I told the policemen to lock the small gate and leave me outside on the road. As the minutes ticked by, vague shapes could be seen in the inner compound. Torches flashed intermittently and the voices of the searching policemen became more frantic and higher pitched. Quarter of an hour passed with no obvious results. I was about to call it off and go back to bed when low peculiar Dyak whistles were heard and whispered shouts; the two policemen disappeared. Not knowing what to expect, I had seen the policemen cock their rifles, so I cocked my automatic (my own P38) and waited. Round the end of the families accommodation came a dodgy, crouching figure. I yelled out to stop in English and Malay, and in English that I would shoot. The figure dodged under the huts while my finger was on the trigger. There was no movement for several seconds and then this huge apparition left the shadows of the hut and leapt towards me carrying what appeared to be a *parang* (jungle knife or sword) in his right hand, I crouched protectively, raised and steadied my gun with both hands, took deliberate aim to kill this running figure, when I saw it was a white man. Instinctively I came out of the aim. I suppose I was expecting to see a Chinese or other local. There was a maniacal yell from this white creature, and he leapt up on the chain link fence holding on with all limbs. First the *parang* fell and he lost his right hand grip, then both feet slipped. As he was hanging by one hand the two little policemen came from out of nowhere and courageously dragged him from the wire and piled into him, later joined by four more. Our white friend was shrugging them off like children but they kept coming back for more and I could do nothing behind the fence. Finally a familiar, gasping, dishevelled (as usual) figure arrived, pistol in hand. It was Paddy Kelleher, and in no uncertain terms he stopped the man from resisting, and, surrounded by police, he walked quietly back to his cell. I explained to Paddy what had happened and how close the bloke had been to death, because I was not sure if the man was a terrorist or a prisoner.

Paddy explained that the Gunner concerned was over six foot tall and weighed 14 stone. He had been brought back to Bau to see the BC about a personal domestic crisis. He had had a drink in camp, walked into Bau and had more, picked a fight with two Sappers, wrecked the bar and it had taken eight policemen (they were rarely over 5'2") and the two Sappers to bring him to the Station. As Paddy walked in the door to take him back under close arrest he grabbed the *parang* (evidence in another case) and smashed his way out. A very contrite Gunner offered apologies to the Police Station and particularly myself because of his narrow escape. It could have been fatal.

I remember Patrick and I once had to fly into Kuching either with a prisoner or some urgent information. We had been out for some time and we were not clean; in fact with sweat and dirt our jungle clothing was 'high' and I don't think I had shaved for a few days and looked rough.

We had to wait for some reason and as it was lunchtime the MIO's assistant, I shall call him F, took Patrick and me to the Sergeants Mess. He took Patrick round the back and told the English and Gurkha cooks to feed him, then he and I walked into the Mess. Both in the bar and the dining room the silent reception was mixed. Some members, no doubt in admiration and envy, thought 'Ah, a soldier,' others, in the majority no doubt, thought, 'Dirty, scruffy sod, shouldn't be allowed in a respectable Mess.' So at the rather long Mess table and armed with a pint of beer I slowly ate a civilized lunch with F. Not one Mess member came and sat near us. I felt like a social pariah, I was in the British Army, wasn't I?

I had to wait while F obtained an interim report and further instructions, so I entered the lounge, sat in a chair, and with my pack at my side and pistol and *kukri* on my belt across my knees I immediately fell asleep. My nap was interrupted by a blow to my muddy jungle boots. Through narrow sleepy eyes I glimpsed the epitome of the RSM at peace. There he was, immaculate in pressed jungle greens, Sam Brown gleaming, hosetops, puttees and shiny boots with his badge of rank very evident.

'And who are you?' demanded the voice of authority. (I wore no insignias or badges of rank.)

The resting members of the Mess sat up in gleeful anticipation, of a topic of conversation that would delight the Mess for many nights. As I stood up I towered above him. I mustered the correctly military bearing, and quietly told him who I was and who I was waiting for. I was explaining what had brought me here when the MIO and F arrived in the white Rover and shouted for me, I bade the RSM goodbye and walked out. He was looking for trouble and to impress. I have no doubt I might have satisfied him about dress and appearance but he would certainly have dug in about loaded weapons etc. in the Mess. Its not easy being a base wallah and they frequently do not know or understand what is happening outside their little circle and especially at the sharp end. They never saw infantrymen, sappers or Gunners, so I must have looked like something from Outer Space. To some extent it was similar to the situation in Cyprus: if I ever had lunch in the Episkopi Mess. I did not look tidy and I often saw people looking across and talking about me, because I was the odd one in the Mess and I was obviously doing something different and dangerous.

One of my agents, HP, was a casual trader and was a close associate of my friend SC at Pengkalan Terbang. He was introduced as a possible agent on a regular basis. He had previously helped S but the matter had never placed on solid ground; now it became a business proposition. He would be tasked, briefed and debriefed in the correct manner, payment by results and strict obedience. A Chinese like his friend, he welcomed the security, an odd expression to use with a spy. The strange thing was that he was willing to work for no cash incentive, he was just being patriotic. I told him I admired his patriotism but if I was to task him and he had to obey, then he should accept payment for the obvious dangers involved. As a patriot he had an option, with me he did as he was paid. A mutual compromise was reached and he was always reluctant to accept cash but we became good friends in the end, and in the spy business this is not necessarily a good thing.

First I did him certain favours in my official capacity and this cemented our relationship. His information initially was sketchy and contained no depth; with better handling his information improved and gave me a better overall picture. HP was involved in two particular incidents which were important.

The first was a chance remark he had overheard in mid August, and he mentioned it in a nonchalant way to me. It concerned sickness in various villages. These people were all the same, you had to drag information out of them. Apparently several deaths had been reported from at least two Indonesian villages close to the border. Did he know what the symptoms were? Had the Army said anything about the cause of death and so on? His first priority on his next visit was to verify certain matters and make an early return; this was important. In between his journeys, my wanderings and meetings with two other sources confirmed reports of many dead, cause of sickness unknown but possibly smallpox. HP returned and reported smallpox, and that the population of one village all died, forty in all. He confirmed the disease at Lawang, Sebujit, Kapoet Tokot and others. HP was advised to be inoculated and I would pay, I had been in the company of three possible carriers but I was up to date with my inoculations, but the Chinese doctor with the Malay Regiment gave me another, just to be safe.

I had reported my original information but added I wanted confirmation. Now this was available, something had to be done and fast. Medical teams descended on Pengkalan Terbang and Gumbang initially, all were inoculated and two carriers were discovered and evacuated to hospital. We were just in time and an epidemic was prevented which could have claimed many lives. I received no acknowledgment from either the Government or Police on the matter; it was as though no one shared any interest in our actions.

One of two Sarawak-born leaders of the TNKU based in Indonesia is our next subject. The two were very violent and dangerous men, politically motivated towards Communism. They were very powerful and held a widespread reputation. One was named Dadang and the other Penglima Guntor. One was born in Bau District around the Buso area, of mixed Malay/Dyak parentage. He still had close family relatives in the area not far away from Bau.

On a trip, HP was detained and to his horror was taken to this person and as he confessed to me HP did not think he would ever return alive to Sarawak. This person was extremely clever. He closely questioned HP about his movements over the past couple of years, whom he worked with, where he got his supplies from, and so on.

Having ascertained this he then intimidated and threatened HP with all sorts of dire tortures and punishments if he did not help. He was sent away and told to report back the following day. He did as he was ordered and this person was extremely cordial and friendly. After a long conversation he handed HP a packet to deliver to his brother near Bau and a further warning was given. HP reported direct to me, I talked to Peter Lim and the two of us went to HSB. The letter was opened and its contents noted, but not in my presence; this was mainly internal stuff. Re-sealed it had to be delivered and HP had the twitches. He was not happy and I couldn't blame him, walking into the lion's den. It took a lot of threats, cajoling and persuasion to make him go to this village but eventually he agreed. I told him to say as little as possible, keep his eyes and mainly his ears open, insist on a reply and wait for it.

When this was achieved he should return to me unobserved with the package which would be opened, the contents noted and the package re-sealed. HP could then resume his normal activities. Peter Lim and I spent several anxious hours during which time a very frightened HP did as he was told, was again threatened by the brother if news of this got about, but left his assignation in one piece, a very relieved man. We did what we had to do and HP was sent on his way. Special Branch seniors were very happy with this breakthrough, although I never asked for details as it was mainly a matter for locally based Special Branch Officers. I was just responsible for the whole operation working smoothly; the end product was none of my business. It only happened twice before I finally left which was a pity; from a military point of view it could have been invaluable had it happened many months earlier. When HP, SC and I spent a couple of days together prior to my departure I had the feeling that HP was not happy about being handed over to another Master or 'Control' and I wonder if he continued to serve. He was an ideal agent, as previously described. I had great admiration for his dedication to his country. Was it wrong that he felt safer because I was also his friend? – no doubt not a situation advocated by the various Intelligence services but for us it worked successfully. For a Chinese it is unusual to show emotion to 'white skinned pigs', but HP had tears in his eyes when I left which proves that human nature foxes us all.

The following story is really in two parts and one is the sequel to something previously described.

Thirsty work crossing rivers. You save on the laundry bill!

Two of the leading IBTs (Indonesian Based Terrorists) in the area of 1st Division were Ah Joo and Ah Jas, both Sarawak-born Chinese from the Bau area. They had defected in 1962/3 and were known ardent Communists. Early in July one of my agents spent quite some time with Ah Joo who had stated his gradual disenchantment with the ideals of communism, the support offered by the Indonesian Regular Army, life in Indonesia and so on, and that he would like to return to Sarawak but without harassment. Some of his companions were also feeling disillusioned; their conversation frequently suggested this.

I spent a long time with my man briefing him carefully on the terms of surrender, supplying him with leaflets to distribute surreptitiously, but also explaining that following interrogation and debriefing we would expect Ah Joo to return to Indonesia and that he would be expected to try and persuade the estimated two hundred plus IBTs who were reported to be strung out in small bands along the 1st Division border area to defect. This would be the first breakthrough achieved by the Government and British Forces, and could be the first sign of a weakness in the makeup of these dedicated Communist Terrorists. I had talked it over with Peter Lim, HSB and the MIO; all I could do now was to be patient and when the time was ripe go over (unofficially) and bring him back in great secrecy, transfer him to Kuching, let him go through the process and if he was still willing, return him secretly to Indonesia then wait for results.

My diary on 18th July 1966, reads, 'Source briefed to bring Ah Joo over to RV' but I recall there was a hiccup. I was in charge of the operation and was instructed by HSB/MIO to write the Op Order. Briefly, at a time laid down Patrick and I would cross the border near the Serikin/Babang track RV at a specific place with my agent and Ah Joo. The terrorist would be disarmed and I would move him like the clappers over the border to Red 441, a helipad close by. Patrick and the agent would cover my withdrawal and join a protective covering party on the border made up solely of SB men in case an ambush had been laid on for my benefit. The helipad and the track also were secured by SB, the chopper would be radioed in and Peter Lim and I would remove him to Kuching. So far so good.

The MIO's assistant was the Sergeant who had stood in for me when I was in Singapore with my eye problem, we'll call him F. He was a hell of a nice bloke but never a soldier, a linguist, yes. On the day arranged. F said he wanted to come, but at the time arranged to leave my bungalow he had not appeared. The MIO said he was on his way. An hour later he appeared, to spend possibly three days in the jungle, dressed in white shirt, light coloured trousers, black shoes and forty fags only. Peter Lim and another SB Sergeant gazed in amazement. He was quite prepared to soldier on as he was, however, what a character.

I reclothed him and gave him a weapon, jungle boots were scrounged for him, plus pack, water bottle etc. and then we set off. From the transport we carefully circumvented Serikin kampong and headed for the border. Patrick was ahead, and waved us down, then beckoned to me, I moved forward to find Patrick chatting to my agent. Ah Joo had had an arrow from a pig trap enter his leg and could not walk for at least two weeks, so after all that, back we went. The next entry in my diary which could make sense is somewhere about the 23rd August 1966. Ah Joo was fit to travel, the RV was at an isolated hut. I had to take a chance because the stakes were so high. Patrick and I would not have stood a chance if it was a set-up: we would be on our own and sitting ducks; death or capture faced us both.

At 0500 hrs we were making our way carefully by the border to the RV.

We expected them about 0700 hrs but I wanted to look around first. All appeared in order as much as one could tell in the dense jungle and the early morning sun heralded another beautiful day if we lived to enjoy it. We both lay on the floor of the hut, Patrick nervously puffing at a cigarette while I was just nervous. A noise, safety catches off, dampness in the armpits and crotch and a tenseness at the back of the head. People began to climb the ladder into the hut.

It was all such an anti-climax: my agent's beaming smile followed by this thin emaciated, scruffy Chinese man. He looked as if he didn't know whether to laugh or cry. I suppose he was just as frightened as we were; he was given a fag and sat down. We three quickly discussed the arrangement for the return of Ah Joo, then the agent disappeared. We were not far behind him and I suddenly felt safer in the depths of the jungle. On approaching Serikin we carefully negotiated our way round the west side near the old military base. In the jungle on the edge of the old DZ and near to the track we sat and waited, Patrick taking the opportunity to photograph Ah Joo, which came out badly. I was apprehensive because F was going to make the pick-up in the MIO's white Land Rover and I was not happy. However, we passed the time questioning 'our friend' but nothing serious, he would have enough of that where he was going and we wanted his help and co-operation. The noise of a vehicle was heard and the engine switched off. We crept off and frightened F to death when we appeared out of nowhere. In seconds Ah Joo was under a canvas sheet in the back out of sight, F was puffing contentedly on a fag, and Patrick and I were relaxed to some extent over the body of our conquest. We had been out for several days and were tired and unshaven. At the Interrogation Centre Ah Joo was taken away for 'chats', Patrick was taken back to Bau by F while I was instructed to stay in F's room at the Palm Hotel until the preliminary interrogation had been completed.

F's room was air conditioned and had hot water and a shower. I hadn't enjoyed this luxury since November. I took my boots off, lay on the bed fully clothed and slept. I awoke about midday, and had a shave and a hot shower by courtesy of F. A knock on the door brought me back to reality. My visitor was the OC 99 Brigade Int. Platoon. He said the interrogation was progressing OK, he had checked with the MIO, but the real reason for the visit was two-fold. First, was there any reason of a domestic nature why I had not written to my wife for some six or eight weeks? I informed him that I wrote to my wife at least once a week, sometimes twice; they always found their way to Bau Post Office even from the jungle. Apparently he had had instructions from the Intelligence Centre to check my whereabouts. Jean had apparently not heard from me for the past six weeks or so which was unusual and it was making her ill, so she asked the Adjutant for information. He reassured her that as far as he knew I had not been reported 'Missing' although it was not unusual for me to be absent for long spells. The officers having finally convinced the MIO that he had to see me was now satisfied and would signal accordingly.

He also said that I had been selected, and the MIO had agreed that I should take part in a film being made by the BBC. Several servicemen had been picked to film and describe their duties in the Borneo theatre. I burst out laughing and refused point blank. The officer smiled and said that I had to report to Major Gahan's (the new MIO's) bungalow at 7p.m. the following night to discuss the matter. How on earth could I openly describe my duties which were classified SECRET and frequently TOP SECRET on film to the viewing millions? I returned to Bau a very puzzled man. Patrick said he would shave and should he have a haircut! Bloody comedian!

The following night I returned to Kuching and began my moan to the MIO and A.N. Other; I was in a very aggressive mood. The MIO provided two very stiff whiskies and a more mellowed Howard listened to the con job that was to follow; they also conned me. Apparently the BBC types, four in all, would arrive in Bau and I would take them through to Stass. They had been told my duties were somewhat secret, but not that agents were involved and where I wandered to, just that I visited friendly kampongs, talked to the natives and was sometimes given information, end of story. On the basis of this they roughly knew what film they wanted to shoot. It was no use objecting: the order for me to perform had come right from the very top, all I had to do was lie through my teeth and disclose nothing of what really happened and certainly nothing of 'Claret'.

Initially the team took film of us both walking through the jungle, then negotiating tree trunks over swampy ground. They began to look a little uncomfortable when on entering the kampong I told them just how close to the border they were and that this particular one had been attacked several times. It was also where the last 'heads' had been taken when the inhabitants went out to inflict retribution. So for some time the camera man busied himself taking situation background material. The headman was absent, so we made up the usual greetings afforded us when we visited, using a passing male villager.

As young girls and the old people were 'chatted up' by Patrick for the cameraman and the producer, I started munching sandwiches provided for them, and lounged about on the long verandah. One of my favourite little boys, only about twelve months old, came up to me naked as the day he was born, and just looked at me. The producer got excited and brought the cameraman over but I don't know if he took it all. I knew what my small friend wanted but I tempted him first with bites from my sandwich which we shared. His facial expressions and his bodily movements were full of humour and expression and no doubt made good camera. The climax of course was when I took out of my top breast pocket the dirty, damp and sticky object, an Army barley sugar fruit sweet. I teased him as normal but this time he was close to tears. Throwing caution to the wind he grabbed the sweet and disappeared into the dark depths of the long house. The producer was delighted, it was completely off the cuff, but time was running out so down to the river we all trudged. The river in which all the villagers bathed and drew water was about six feet deep at the widest part we chose, and that wasn't excessive. Patrick and I crept out of the jungle 'all warlike' much to the amusement of numerous married and unmarried women and children who were congregated at their usual bathing point some thirty yards downstream. I entered the water, weapon above my head, and slowly walked along the river bottom to the other side, emerging like a drowned rat but very soldier-like. I covered Patrick as he commenced to emulate my face-on confrontation with the camera; this was his big moment. To his native consternation he suddenly realized that he was a foot short for walking on the bottom; he went down like a stone leaving his hat floating on the surface. When he re-surfaced, preceded by his No 5 rifle, the sodden jungle hat covered his face. Frantically he pushed it to the back of his head with one hand while his little fat legs were going like pistons in the upright position trying to reach the opposite bank.

Patrick was desperate for fame and fortune. He needed to be seen and this was really his opportunity, but the more frantic he became the more frequently he disappeared beneath the surface. I was in hysterics on the ground while the others yelled encouragement to Patrick. It was a very apprehensive, sodden but spluttering body that left the water and was reassured he hadn't to do it again. He then realized why I was so amused, then we all had a laugh. It was really the only time I ever got the laugh on him. Two more sequels were shot, one talking to a rubber tapper (another bloke 'kidnapped' from the village) and our pedestrian efforts struggling through a foot of mud.

We crossed the river again and the cameraman asked if it was OK to film the bathing women. Acknowledgments to the affirmative greeted Patrick's query, so the cameraman got to work. My gaze was suddenly drawn to a passing woman and her child. Both her feet were split like the man from Kindau and likewise she had six toes in miniature but her hands were normal. Her child was perfect and she was in the early stages of pregnancy so she informed us. Between us, Patrick and I remembered names but the woman had no relatives of that name in Indonesia although the tribes were vaguely associated; she said her parents were physically normal, also her relatives; she could not explain the deformities and didn't seem to care. The BBC team were intrigued and the cameraman used more film when the other story was told. It really held their interest but they could not offer a solution either. I have wondered over the years, and I must say the woman was not very helpful over this: did her mother ever take or eat anything that was unusual during her pregnancy, for an illness or discomfort that was attributed to carrying or even concerning a child? The woman could not remember or help in any way; even local wives' tales proved negative.

When you consider what the contents of thalidomide tablets did to those unfortunate children some years ago, the results were not unlike the ones I witnessed, only much more drastic. I still feel it is possible that when the women went to gather leaves from the trees, roots or plants to eat as a vegetable they picked a 'wrong one' which inflicted these terrible injuries to the unborn child. The male and female concerned were in the same age group; could it be that the jungle had thrown up a rogue plant similar to a known one which unfortunately for the parents had such disastrous yet somehow uniform results on the physical appearance of their children? Dyaks never seem to be able to state an accurate date of birth so I would put DOB for both persons between 1935-40 and at that time the border, recognised generally and officially as the watershed between the two countries, was very fluid and geared to the convenience of the indigenous population for legal, administrative and medical problems. Could it not be that a travelling doctor, nurse, botanist, explorer or writer had dug into an elaborate medical pack and dished out some tablets for an acute stomach problem possibly unaware that the problem was pregnancy. Let's face it, I saw this sort of thing happen, in good faith I may add, many times when I was there and I also contributed.

I had a fairly elaborate jungle pack made up for my medical needs, labelled in Gurkhali and English, and it catered for the head, throat, skin, stomach and so on. I had also morphine and needles and scalpels for real emergencies. My initial reaction had been, 'Bloody hell, this is a right DIY kit, where would I start?' I wasn't clueless first aid-wise, but you need some training before using scalpels and needles and I had not had any. The only time I used morphine was to enable Ah Joo to overcome his injury after the pig trap incident, and it prevented infection.

But I have been as bad as others following bad language interpretation, and given individuals tablets not knowing their full medical history but attempting to be Christian and relieve pain. It was all an interesting talking point and I was glad I had experienced it, but it's always nice to get an answer, to remove the dark areas.

We left the kampong of Stass as the light was beginning to fade. The team were not happy in the fading light as night closed in. I could not offer them food but said we could eat food if they preferred it. This certainly did not appeal to our BBC city dwellers, who said beer would be fine. So Patrick disappeared to Boon's for a dozen bottles and the producer asked if we could sit quietly together in the garden which we did. Having lit cigarettes and quaffed a little beer my friend then produced a leather jacketed tape recorder and stated that we'd better get the interview taped as quickly as possible. I exclaimed my ignorance of this but he said he had official permission and proceeded to ask questions to which, had I had time to think about, I could have prepared an answer without giving anything away or blowing my own trumpet. As it was I paid too much attention to the possible disclosure of information on my real role and also the producer's manipulation of the button on the recorder, as I was wary about what could be pieced together. I did realize later after they had left that I had made a *faux pas*. The producer had spent some time trying to get me to agree that wandering around the border area on my own with just a diminutive Dyak guide was highly dangerous. He seemed to be well informed and stated that SAS Patrols were usually six to eight strong and that infantry patrols were up to a hundred strong, sometimes more, so being on my own was dangerous and I agreed. I then realized that as the tape would be played in conjunction with the film Jean would probably see and hear it, which was what I was trying to avoid as she hadn't a clue what I was doing out here. Luckily, in some respects, she didn't see it and neither did Chris. Some people I know said they recognised me and really enjoyed it, but I would have felt better under the circumstances to have had knowledge of the questions and then my manner would not have been hesitant and my answers more explicit and unclouded. The public were conned but so was I, and I never forgave Major Gahan and others for that.

To return to Ah Joo, he was processed and carefully briefed by SB, and when I saw him some days later he looked a different man. He felt he had made his peace with the authorities but was apprehensive about returning to Indonesia, not only for hardship and inconvenience he would have to endure, but if he was 'discovered' by the Indonesian authorities acting as a spy or aroused the suspicions of his more dedicated former IBT friends he would definitely get 'the chop'. However as he travelled around he had a good idea who possible candidates were and he had been briefed carefully by SB and lastly myself on how to keep the suspicions away from himself.

In the last few months of my tour I was very much on my own. Pete

Slowe had left for Miri, the British and Malay Engineer detachment disappeared almost overnight, then the Aussies followed by the Gunners were evacuated to be replaced by the 3rd Battalion Malay Regiment. I felt a little naked and not happy about my back-up. It wouldn't be long before the Indonesians and IBTs knew the Aussies had left and might try to infiltrate more Manjar parties into Sarawak despite the rather tenuous Cease Fire and subsequent Armistice that was signed, which did not include the IBTs, although their existence in Indonesia was admitted. Then began a period of harassment and shooting of IBTs by the Indonesian Army in isolated incidents so there was a need for me to encourage Ah Joo to greater efforts and soon, before the IBTs started to return to Sarawak in gangs, armed and without discipline which could have been disastrous to the Government. It was also damned dangerous for me. I was always very aware that Patrick and I had no chance if we bumped into Indonesians or IBTs; we couldn't match them for firepower, but with the knowledge that aggressive patrolling was always performed by British or Commonwealth forces, it meant that we were less likely to meet trouble. All I could do was fling my unofficial grenades followed by a smoke one, run like hell and hope for the best. There is a time and place for Gung Ho heroes, I've experienced it; it's very much off the cuff and on the spur of the moment. I would do no one any good trying to fight it out; discretion to an Intelligence man is certainly the better part of valour. So as I knew the Malays were not going to patrol vigorously, I was very wary.

The weeks dragged on. News from Ah Joo was intermittent and less than encouraging and as it was approaching November my time was running out. A Detective Inspector Nathan Ha was earmarked for my job; we had met several times, but the handover was not to be smooth as he had Court appearances in his former post and he had to find a suitable house. Then suddenly I had a date and possibly an estimate of numbers who would surrender. To my surprise it was ten, a good start, and livened everything up. As I was jokingly called the Sheriff of Bau, when I was asked to write the Operation Order I called it 'Operation Nottingham'. I handed my notes to the MIO who was in fact *ex*, as his job had finished in the September but he was waiting about for domestic reasons. He, as is usual for high ranking officers, decided to add words for impact and summarise paragraphs for brevity, which only confused the Malays, Chinese and Dyaks, then we were ready for off. Then there was another cancellation, but finally the day before I left in early November when all my official kit had been handed over and I had been paid a nominal fee by the Pay Office which would last me till I arrived in Hong Kong, I received word from my agent that they hoped to make the RV if they were not

Our last 'Op'. Patrick, SB Insp. Nathan and I about to return to Bau, following our last abortive trip into Indonesia. An hour later Patrick and I said goodbye.

interrupted by the Indonesian Army. So Patrick and I, Peter Lim and his lads shared the jungle floor on my next to last night in Sarawak surrounded by a full company of the Malay Regiment. By 0500 hours Patrick and I were across the border, the SB back-up party were on the border ready to move and the Malays were deployed in case it was all fixed to get me.

As I lay there on the jungle floor with Patrick several yards behind me on the opposite side of the track I was very apprehensive, tense and excited. If it all came off, what a fitting climax to a year of damned hard work, but probably the most satisfying work I would ever do in the Intelligence field. We lay there until 0900 hours. They were two hours late and I was not waiting; we carefully walked back to the border and with Peter's approval I cancelled the 'Op'. In a letter from Peter some months later he told me that eventually the party did come across (about twenty strong) successfully, and more followed so it all ended well.

CHAPTER 32

The Last Hours

I entered my bungalow for the last time, dirty, tired and unshaven, I put my jungle boots and soiled OGs in a plastic bag inside my case, bathed and shaved, and changed into civvies with my P38 automatic still around my waist; it was habit. Patrick came up, also changed, and with a strange expression on his face said, 'I have to go to my farm urgently, have a good journey.' He shook hands and walked away to the door. I went to the door and looked down to the road. He stood there as if he were waiting for me to appear, looking at me through the wire with that strange look in his eyes. He raised his arm and said, 'Goodbye,' and walked off. I felt I wanted to cry. This was not the sort of farewell two people should make who had lived, worked and shared so many dangers and problems together for twelve months, it seemed so shallow. I felt empty and so very sad as I gazed on his little figure walking down the dusty track into town. I was standing there a little choked when Peter came up to me from his room and I tried to describe my feelings towards Patrick and that I was shaken by his abrupt departure, especially as a bare three hours earlier we were both in danger, yet again, of losing our lives, not in heroic circumstances but just doing our job. Peter said I probably didn't understand how Patrick felt; he loved me like a brother and did not want to see me go. He would not show emotion at any price (he never did) so he left to avoid it.

Peter said he had spoken to Patrick a couple of weeks before, asking him if he would stay on with Nathan Ha. Patrick had said maybe for a week or two but now that Mr Howard was going he did not know what to do. He then opened his heart which was unusual; he was quite upset. Even after a year I couldn't weigh up the Dyak mind. It was the same with all my agents. Considering the risks they had taken our farewells were almost business-like (no doubt the best way); there again I suffered from European sentimentality. Two of my Chinese agents were different. I stayed two days with them in a house in Kuching and they really looked after me. I briefed them for the future and Nathan Ha, and de-briefed them from their last job. I enjoyed that two days with a family again, ate well and relaxed. Our parting was more emotional, they were friends as well as agents, not advocated but it worked. I was sad to leave them. Peter was the last to say farewell. He had arranged transport to the hotel in Kuching and as we shook hands he had a laugh and a smile, said all the right things and left.

The Land Rover arrived and I had a final look around this building that had been loosely called home for a year. I felt numb and empty. Here I was losing everything in the space of a few hours; my job, comrades, house, colleague, and many many friends. I had to leave or I might have cried. We stopped outside Boon's *kedai* and I yelled cheerio to his almost naked figure. Within seconds he and his son-in-law were outside shaking hands only to be joined within a minute by seventy or eighty people from the shophouses including my laundrywoman. Some I vaguely knew from kampongs; everyone was smiling and cheerful. I felt better as I left town. 'The Sheriff is dead, long live the Sheriff.'

As I passed the Catholic Mission I made a sign of the cross and said a quiet prayer. I was thankful I was safe and would soon meet my family. It had been quite a year. I was forty-one years of age, too old for hard jungle bashing, but I'd made it with a few scars, loss of hair and almost four stone in weight and the satisfaction of knowing I had done my job well and above the call of duty.

I was in my small hotel by midday, had a light lunch and decided to fulfil my ambition and see the Sarawak Museum and all Tom Harrison's hard work. So by 1.30p.m. I was entering the Museum to relax for a few hours. I had entered the first room on the right when I heard the noise of a vehicle being braked hard on the gravel outside. In seconds who should burst into the room but Cpl. Roberts, one of our chaps from Pedawan, the neighbouring FIO. He had with him a local Police Superintendent who was ex Palestine Police. He said he had seen me entering HSB's office some months earlier and had asked who I was. He said he knew me from way back but I couldn't recall him. My objections were overruled and I think we travelled the whole of Kuching having drinks in cafés. It was a good thrash and a fitting end, I suppose. I have not seen either of them since but Roberts was still serving, I think, when I left the service. At least I wasn't left on my last night to brood and become morose. When the RAF chap the following day checked my documents he said I couldn't leave because I had not had the necessary injections. I was in the horrors but not to worry, he would fix it. God knows who he was but I'd had the needle, the document was backdated and a signature forged, one of the few times the RAF ignored regulations and used common sense. What a bloke to have on Movements, Medical and Provost. And so I left this country that I had grown to love, despite all the problems.

I had lived at times like an animal, experienced a way of life in these modern times which the large percentage of our civilized society will never be privileged to witness and learn by. For indeed there were a lot of lessons to be learned about human nature and the quality of life. The Dyak was backward, almost primeval, and mostly steeped in tribal history and habits, but out of this came the occasional entrepreneur, uneducated but with an eye for business, full of animal cunning yet very gullible in the ways of modern society. Basically they were lazy, living life to a set natural pattern and it had a quality. Not for them cancer of the brain, the lungs or the stomach, very few heart attacks here, and certainly ulcers were not common through worry. Admittedly they had certain medical problems but mainly it was lack of sensible diet and hygiene. But of course you cannot eradicate generations of an accepted way of life in one fell swoop and it should not be attempted. Although many nations in the Third World have tried to achieve it, invariably it fails because of lack of patience and adequate teachers.

I was once in the house of our District Officer who was a Sarawak Malay, a capable and charming person; there was a party and the house was crowded. 'Hadji' came to me and said he had a friend visiting who was from mainland Malaya and about to take up the post of Chief Agricultural Officer for 1st Division. We were introduced and he immediately started to tell me what his plans were for reorganizing the agricultural development of the border tribes. Now only a couple of months ago I had seen a Malay Governmental Information film which outlined the difficulties facing the Government when they tried to persuade the more well informed and educated mainland Malays to change their traditional methods of agriculture to one which would both benefit them financially and promote better health for the population. It also included more hard work and it wasn't totally accepted.

My newly found friend was expounding his theories for a quarter of an hour or so when I finally stopped him and asked, 'Have you visited any of the Land Dyak kampongs in the area?'

Shamefacedly he answered, 'No, but I intend to.'

I told him of the great power and influence that I had officially, *but* that even after twelve months of this if I wanted any particular kind of help or action it generally had to be introduced by subterfuge, getting them to trust you initially, then introducing them to actions that would be acceptable as habit. I told him he should start walking as from tomorrow and that five-year plan would possibly not be off the ground in that time, never mind as a viable experiment. He was a terribly disillusioned man after our talk. Most graduates are full of the same misguided ardour and it is such a pity; ardour should not be stifled and neither should potential, but Universities should also teach and advocate more use of fundamentals and common sense. A problem need not necessarily require a PhD solution. I wonder how my Malay friend eventually coped; maybe he returned to Kuala Lumpur a frustrated and disillusioned man which would be a pity. Remember the old Chinese saying, 'Sofly sofly catchee monkee.'

So in twelve months I lived among and observed man in a now almost forgotten but natural primitive role. It also showed me that the veneer of civilization was extremely thin. Without any preparation or training I had accepted this existence which would quite frankly have revolted me weeks earlier. I learnt a great deal about me and how I was made up. During that year I suffered and enjoyed physical and mental stresses, eventually finding that all my faculties and senses of intelligence, animal cunning, deceit, courage, fitness and decisiveness had all been put to the test and I felt a better person for it. Borneo was an unforgettable experience I'm glad I did not miss. Hopefully generations to come will never have to undergo the hardships suffered by Gurkha, British and Commonwealth troops under active service conditions in this beautiful but harsh country.

CHAPTER 33

Hong Kong

As I sat in the aircraft bound for Singapore I took my last glimpse of Sarawak with mixed feelings as I had done when I left Cyprus. Had it all been worth it? Had I made a worthwhile military contribution? My job had been unusual and I knew successful, but how was it viewed from 'above'? As usual there had been no comment, no de-briefing or submission of a report; the job was over. I was the last one out and no one cared a toss. Obviously there must have been lessons to be learned, had they a crystal ball and knew all the answers? I doubted it.

I was deposited at C1 Company, Singapore and allocated a room, feeling extremely tired and with a touch of fever that lasted a couple of days. It was all helped by the resumption of the friendship with Mick Courage and his girlfriend whom he later married. Much younger than I, and very much in love, they helped in my rehabilitation as I patiently waited the few days for my flight to Hong Kong and to be reunited with Jean and the family again. I was taken to various places on this island and it is quite a fascinating place. It's hard to believe that it was only some 150 years earlier that Stamford Raffles arrived at this tiny fishing village in the middle of mud and marshes to find that it could boast of an extremely deep harbour. The population at that time consisted of 120 Malays and 30 Chinese; within 3 months 5,000 Chinese had arrived but no more Malays; now there are over 2 million people in Singapore, 75 per cent of whom are overseas Chinese.

The island became a colony and in the early 1960s joined the Federation of Malaysia. Unfortunately Prince or (Tunku) Abdul Rahman, Malaysia's political leader, had no trust in the Chinese from whatever background, and he disagreed politically with the rather radical Socialist views expounded by Singapore's elected leader, Prime Minister Lee Kuan-Yew. This Cambridge-educated politician was considered pro-communist by many people but he had foresight, imagination, ruthlessness and above all else political acumen, a talent not usually associated with Asians. He spoke Chinese, Malay and English fluently and was somewhat of a spell-binding orator. When the alliance began to experience difficulties Singapore left the Federation.

Lee Kuan-Yew gave the British military a time limit to remove their bases and influence. With dictatorial efficiency he offended many Western sympathies by imprisoning his Communist opponents, inflicting a one party system, curbing Trade Unions and the birth rate, initiating radical social laws and reforms; he also would 'trade with the devil' (as he was once described); he confused and bemused the world's statesmen but he made a success of it all. When I was there the PM's ideas were in their infancy; social conditions were not good but the people were industrious. I was impressed but it was not a geographical location in which I would have enjoyed living. I was used to the jungle type of high heat and humidity and it didn't affect me, but I found in Singapore that the atmosphere was too humid. It lacked a freshness even after rain. I always felt sticky and uncomfortable. I have no doubt I could have got used to it but I was glad I was not remaining there to finish off my Far East Tour.

On my arrival at Kai Tak Airport I was pleased to see a friendly face. Bill Ward was a former colleague from Minden, a tall, bespectacled bloke from the North-East who was extremely reliable and had a sense of humour. My first impression of Hong Kong was not earth shattering as many writers or visitors describe it. Having experienced Sarawak and Singapore the general atmosphere is very close. Hong Kong appeared to be busier. John Sheldon drove us safely through the milling traffic to the HQ of the Intelligence Company that was situated in Whitfield Barrack off Nathan Road, Kowloon. The bed was made down in the single men's quarters and after a wash and a quiet drink in the Club with the lads, I began to feel the cooler temperature. Even though it was 65°F. that was some 30° less than I had been used to and I shivered. We went out for a light snack and then a very welcome night's rest.

The following morning I met the OC, Capt. Waters; the 2/IC, a recently commissioned 2nd Lieutenant; the Warrant Officer, Harry Dunne who sadly died some months after leaving the Colony; and my other three senior colleagues: Winterton whom I had known in Borneo; 'Dusty' Miller whom I knew from Maresfield; and Alec Davis, a great character who had done extremely well in the Corps, he was a Cantonese speaker and he originated from the Manchester area. Sadly he died in 1987, when he had achieved the rank of Lieutenant Colonel.

Winterton had the New Territories; Miller Kowloon; Davis drove a desk in the Main Office and attended to matters civil; I was to be responsible for Hong Kong Island where military HQ was situated. The OC said that John Sheldon would stay with me for a few weeks. He was to give me a guided tour of Kowloon and the New Territories for interest's sake, but obviously I should concentrate on the Island, the location of military and civil establishments and the people of interest within them. Within a week I was happily settled in, driving the Section vehicle, coping with the traffic and feeling more relaxed. I had been allocated a lovely flat at 13 Edinburgh Mansions on the fourth floor of an eight-floor block in an area known as Kowloon Tsai which was situated on the slope of the range of hills which separate Kowloon from the New Territories. We lived directly under 'Lion Rock', the highest point at 900 feet. This small military complex of officers and other ranks were housed in seven blocks of flats complete with NAAFI, children's playground and communal building for meetings, entertainment and so on. Two Brigadiers lived in houses on the road approaching the complex. There was a more than adequate bus service and taxis were readily available, it was ideal. All I wanted was Jean, who was due to arrive a week after me so I had arranged for us to spend a couple of nights in an hotel until I could take over the flat on the departure of the occupant to UK.

Reunions after enforced separation were really quite wonderful affairs, full of emotion, looking at each other and just wanting to touch or be in touch with each other. A year is a long time. There was a strange atmosphere of accepted intimacy and yet we were temporary strangers. Only people who love each other and have experienced this length of separation or more can understand what I'm trying to say. A poet would enthuse in words; I just felt happy holding my girl in my arms again. Ignore the sexual connotations, it was heaven just to enjoy her nearness and listen to her talk (non stop!).

The hotel we obtained a room in was the only convenient one that I could afford. It was also staffed and owned by the Communists but I didn't tell Jean this. It was comfortable and clean and as we were only there for two or three days it didn't really matter. We seem to spend most of our time gazing at the wonderful shops that surrounded us in the vicinity of Nathan Road. After the life I had been leading this was almost therapeutic and to be able to thoroughly relax with Jean and away from work was good for me. I took over the flat and it was reasonably clean. The occupant and his wife were still 'under the influence', and he was unshaven and scruffy so I presumed the cleaning was probably done by the amah (the Chinese female who usually lives with you and who cleans and cooks).

Having an amah was not obligatory, but an allowance was paid to each occupant of a quarter for the amah's services. For the wives' sake it was sensible to have one, especially in the hot weather. Families who did not have one invariably spent the money on booze, cigarettes, clothes, or other forms of entertainment and as a result their accommodation was usually dirty and the wives became sluts because everything was too much trouble in the heat, including their children. The odd exception did manage of course but they were in the minority. Many wives just did not adjust to a different environment and the heat, which at times could be quite oppressive; it shortened tempers and patience, and as a result quite a high percentage of wives and mothers became the victims of depression. Husbands must share most of the responsibility for this situation, often spending too much of the spare time in messes and bars, etc. when they should have been sharing this almost idyllic lifestyle with their families. I do not wish to dwell on this matter but soldiers have a difficult profession and it is necessary to spend time away from home and family. They need to know and be reassured that fidelity and stability is secure at home. They themselves must also reciprocate by devoting as much time as is available to their wives and families. It is well known that military wives resent the fact that the women who have first call on their husbands are Madam Britannia and the Queen; total allegiance is sworn when you sign on and that is how is should be. But that does not excuse the military husband from encompassing his wife and family with all the love, care and devotion they should expect from a husband and father. If not, why the hell did you get married? Prospective military wives should be well informed of what the life entails, but even then the problem will never be completely resolved.

In Hong Kong social functions were many. Some were 'stag' and Jean accepted these (as most wives did) with reluctance, providing they were not too frequent; on the other hand she (and many other wives) had the very frequent opportunity to dress in their 'glad rags', and wine, dine and dance at some of the smartest hotels and clubs in the world. It's a question of being fair, and everyone was entitled to do his or her thing if they could save and afford it. Hong Kong offered the opportunity of a lifetime; Jean and I took it and thoroughly enjoyed it. Whilst on this subject one aspect was tolerated but never really accepted, and this was the views and fears of the wives involved. The fact is that soldiers or any other Servicemen are vulnerable to approaches by agents of foreign powers for various reasons, but usually it is for reasons of espionage and/or subversion. These approaches are usually made in the leisure haunts of Servicemen and women and it is the duty of the Counter Intelligence personnel of the Intelligence Corps to supervise these places and the personnel who frequent them to ensure that appropriate action can be taken if undesirable contact is made. I personally made no difference in the rank structure either; this supervision included officers, as in Germany, UK or elsewhere, and there were several who have cause to be grateful for a timely and sometimes unofficial word in their ears.

Hong Kong Island boasted the largest bar and brothel area in the world; the area was known as Wanchai, well publicized following Richard Mason's book *The World of Suzie Wong*. In a relatively small acreage there were probably more than 150 bars and God knows how many brothels. The streets are illuminated with garish neon signs which by old colonial law are not supposed to move or flicker. The unsuspecting visitor, or should I say hopeful, is tempted by the lights and previously consumed liquor to take the nervous, faltering steps into these dens of iniquity, which lack the sophistication of similar areas in other lands, but which stay open till 2a.m. and are only concerned with the dexterity of how you open your wallet and not your sexual prowess. To me Wanchai was a harder business centre than Wall Street. As one of the world's largest ports, a military garrison town, a renowned tourist centre, and at that time a 'Rest and Recuperation' centre for servicemen from the Vietnam war, Hong Kong had to provide for all the carnal aspirations of these sex deprived stallions of no fixed age group, many of whom were drug addicted. Wanchai coped adequately with its responsibilities. It appeared to bend and sink appreciably each evening as its pavements were hammered by the feet of thousands of visitors. Its fascination was contagious. I don't think the authorities ever had any accurate idea how many whores, call girls, dance hostesses or bar girls were involved in Wanchai or Kowloon but they always appeared to be gainfully employed especially with the Americans.

A senior American service officer was the official 'pimp' in one aspect of 'R and R leave', which lasted for five days. Each serviceman was allowed to bring in a nominal amount of American dollars into the Colony. On payment of a set amount of cash, this officer and his staff arranged a hotel room and a presentable and 'clean' girl, who had a medical and Health Department 'Blue Card' (it was white) and who attended a weekly clinic to have the card 'chopped' (official stamp). The serviceman was responsible for feeding himself and his 'friend' and he had ample spare money for his sightseeing, entertainment and presents for 'back home' which he procured from the American PX which was situated at the British Serviceman's Club on the fringes of Wanchai. Some people comment that this particular action was morally reprehensible, but it must be admitted, the participants on both sides remained 'clean' which medically was admirable, and the serviceman enjoyed a leave in a sober and agreeable manner. I just could not envisage the MOD using military personnel in this manner to control this 'racket'. How do you recruit, or under what guise, do you obtain personnel to 'pimp'?

Considering the reputation of the area visitors behaved themselves, as all their wants, be they social, thirsty or sexual, were readily available. Occasionally the waiter, girl or pimp became greedy by stealth or theft but the police were very efficient and parties were reconciled. This then was the area of controversy with my wife or wives of colleagues. At least one evening a week the area had to be covered, as many places as possible visited while one drank as little as possible; funds were limited. It was essential to be known to bar owners and managers, especially the ones used by our servicemen. I achieved this with the help of the British and Chinese CID staff from the local 'nick' on the seafront and the officer in charge of the Naval Provost Unit who was in plain clothes. I was introduced as a military person, not RMP, Navy or Air Force, and not police or CID. The air of mystery always intrigued the Chinese; they probably guessed who I was and as they were safe from prosecution they usually co-operated because I had 'friends'. Originally this was done in the afternoon when the area was quiet and people were available. To be seen as a person (a white skinned pig!) who desired talk and information in preference to drink or the other 'hospitality' helped enormously, especially as I towered above the diminutive Chinese. With my build and stature no way could I 'fade into the background' so I played a different role and it paid off. Almost without fail these denizens of the Chinese underworld were helpful whenever it was necessary, or if it suited them.

One other main factor that helped me to settle into my job quickly was the Hong Kong Guards Association. This was brought about by the arrival in the Colony of an Irish Guards RSM to take over the Kowloon Garrison RSM's position. His arrival was publicised and he received an invitation to the Association's monthly meeting. By this time he knew that I was an ex Jock so the invitation was extended to both of us. We could not have been made more welcome. All were ex Guards officers and need I say gentlemen. They were involved in every aspect of business throughout the Colony but mainly on the Island. The President was the Head of the Hong Kong Tourist Board, an ex Colonel of the Grenadiers, the Secretary was an ex Major of the Coldstreams, a leading Solicitor and President of the Hong Kong Law Society, and later we were joined by Henry Keswick (now Sir) an acquaintance from 1 SG who ran Hong Kong's largest trading conglomerate, Jardine Matheson. From this pot of gold I was introduced to so many people who could and did help if I required information or an introduction to open so many doors. It was nice to know that this assistance was available. When I did ask, and that was not often, the support was always forthcoming and what's more, they never asked questions. It was also via the Association that I met an ex Palestine policeman whom I shall not name nor his status or job, who was a great asset. He offered me his deputy's job in preference to the two Brigadier Generals in the Colony who were shortly due to retire and had stated their interest. I was flattered and tempted. He was frank and stated his standards and responsibilities. I could have coped admirably with the post but the financial and other aspects deterred me so I refused, I shall never know if I made the right decision. I suspect it was MI6.

So I was once more suitably housed and with my family, I had acquired a Ford Consul Coupé from a ship's Captain, the job was falling nicely into shape, with a good bunch of colleagues; Christmas was coming and so was Chris. I was putting weight on and felt good. We had already made friends with two REME Warrant Officers and their wives and we were both looking forward to an enjoyable tour in what is arguably the most fascinating area in the world. I shall briefly describe the Colony of Hong Kong and what my work entailed.

Hong Kong island is approximately 11 miles long and 7 miles wide, about 30 square miles in total; it is mountainous with twisting heartstopping roads on which you can never relax when driving, but they are maintained in first class condition. In the uninhabited areas it is tropical

The border at Sha Tau Kok: no barrier or wire, just a white line in the middle of the road. Was this sentry one of the group who killed the seven policemen?

and beautiful. Most of the detached houses belonging to *Taipans*, Government officials, businessmen, or Communist millionaires are out of this world and their gardens could only be described as exquisite. These terraced, hanging gardens supervised by enthusiastic Chinese labour are overlooked in almost majesterial splendour by superb houses and villas, reminiscent of Hollywood at its best. This is 'The Peak' area which overlooks not only the island on which it stands but to the north Kowloon and the New Territories, a superlative view on a clear day.

Not a million miles away, however, towards the Lymune area the hillsides are littered with human debris, mainly refugees from the mainland. With the ingenuity that only the Chinese appear to have, dwellings are constructed out of oil drums or any other metal container, wood, plastic and tyres: quite remarkable, I've seen TV and fridges in these ramshackle abodes. It's a disgrace, and the blame is not wholly on the head of the British administration; most of it is self imposed as indeed are most of the world's problems and there is no quick and easy answer. Eventually by rota these people are re-housed, but not even Chairman Mao could wave a magic wand. During the typhoon season these 'squatters', the 100,000 or so who live on sampans and the tens of thousands of individuals who illegally subsist on the rooftops of tenements and sleep in stairwells, really suffer. These blocks are so overcrowded that during the seasonal weather it has been known for blocks to collapse resulting in injury and loss of life. Fire and old age also contribute to the hazard either on the squatter site or in the blocks. It is a tragic and very precarious way of life but some prefer it to Communism, so what price freedom.

A tunnel has now been constructed linking the Island with Kowloon and facilitates a quicker turnaround of vehicles; however, for the vast thousands of commuters, crossing from the island to the mainland or Kowloon side is normally performed by ferry which takes about five minutes. The ferries operate from approximately 6a.m.-2a.m. continuously; it's a wonderful service.

Kowloon was taken from the Chinese to protect Hong Kong island and the harbour area, and is about $3^1/2$ square miles in area ending at Boundary Street which is the official line where the Colony ends. Leaving the Star Ferry the first building to catch the eye is the Peninsula Hotel, a magnificent reminder of the Colonial splendour of a bygone age and having sampled its opulence I would say it's one of the finest hotels in the world. Though flanked on one side by a large Communist emporium and the YMCA building it still stands supreme.

Flanking the Peninsula Hotel and splitting Kowloon in two is the regal and rather stately Nathan Road, a thoroughfare interspersed with banyan trees that divides this complex, overcrowded piece of land full of skyscrapers, tenements festooned with household laundry, shops and factories. The garish shop signs in Chinese and English overwhelm you and the further you walk the less English you see. From Boundary Street travelling north you become more aware of the huge blocks of resettlement housing and the density of the population; you could almost say that you had stepped into mainland China. If you walk alone in this environment as a 'white skinned pig' you have a feeling of vibrancy and great excitement, and at the same time you feel you are about to be overwhelmed by the people about you and are always apprehensive. Even the airport of Kai-Tak is different; there is insufficient land so they built it into the sea. It is quite unusual to land with water on either side of the plane.

During my time in the Colony two tragic incidents happened at the airport, the second of which I witnessed from my flat, within a couple of weeks of each other. In the first incident a plane about to land suddenly dived into the water some 150 yards from the end of the runway. Five people were killed as I remember and several injured. Some suggested the plane had hit the rock which protrudes from the bay and lies directly in the flight path; I never heard the eventual outcome of the enquiry. The second incident happened on a Sunday morning when I was in our bedroom looking directly onto the runway some two to three miles away. I saw the aircraft start its run towards the sea at the normal fast rate, then it appeared to slow and lose power. I momentarily looked away as I thought it was a practice run; pilots had to do seven or eight practice take offs and landings as it was such a difficult airport. When I glanced again the aircraft was just leaving the side of the runway and falling into the sea. This time no one was killed, but I never heard the result of this enquiry either. The quickest joke to emerge by some comedian said, 'Travel Cathay Pacific, the only airline in the world that guarantees you a bath before you land.' The Chinese were amused but it was rather sick.

As you leave the overcrowded housing blocks you reach a line of hills which stretch across the Kowloon peninsula, the highest feature of which is Lion Rock at 900 feet. These hills effectively separate Kowloon from the New Territories. A first class road runs along the southern slopes and a tunnel makes easy access to the New Territories. From these hills begins the rolling Chinese countryside with mountains and fertile plains containing small farms. From Kowloon to the border is approximately twenty miles in depth and in places thirty miles wide, altogether about 340 square miles. The border with China is formed in part with the Shum Chun river and hilly border country. To prevent mass exodus into Hong Kong this fifteen miles or so of border is heavily barbed wired and patrolled.

A rail link is maintained between Kowloon and Lo Wu, the official border crossing point into China. Nearby is the huge water pipeline which Hong Kong relies on for a substantial amount of her water supply from her neighbour during the dry season. Although the New Territories grow a large amount of vegetables they could not cater for the Colony's needs, so most fresh fruit and vegetables come from mainland China via Lo Wu.

Surrounding Hong Kong are hundreds of small islands; over two hundred belong to the colony but are rocky, barren and uninhabited, but one large island called Lan Tao is much larger than Hong Kong. It has a monastery and is only sparsely settled because of the nature of the land. I suppose if the future of the colony was settled some enterprising conglomerate may seriously consider a future for Lan Tao. All this then was the British held colony of Hong Kong virtually surrounded by occupied Chinese Communist islands whose garrisons observe all movements in and out of the colony.

The British garrison maintained in Hong Kong consisted of HQ Land Forces on Hong Kong island, 48 Gurkha Infantry Brigade in the New Territories, and HQ Hong Kong and Kowloon Garrison which commanded units in Hong Kong and Kowloon and an infantry Battalion in each place. HQ was in Whitfield Barracks, Kowloon, where Counter Intelligence Company (HK) was situated.

To operate effectively, military Counter Intelligence must assess the current threat not only to the area but also to the military, in order that effective action can be taken. The main threat to Hong Kong was the creation of internal unrest deliberately fostered by the Chinese People's Government with the aim of embarrassing and discrediting the authorities. Disorders might be also incited to provide a pretext for intervention by the People's Government and alternatively, although it may not have been an original intention, if internal disorders occurred arising from some other cause were in any way prolonged, the People's Government might decide to take advantage of a deteriorating set of circumstances and intervene at short notice.

So it was explained to me that my role and that of CI Company (HK) was to carry out Counter Intelligence operations with the object of detecting and forestalling hostile intelligence operations, subversive activities, sabotage and malicious damage directed against military installations and personnel by agents or groups operating on behalf of foreign powers or hostile sections of the indigenous community. Quite a mouthful, but really no different to the role of CI personnel in UK, BAOR or any other part of the world. Our task was to gather security intelligence from various sources, ensure that military units were Security Surveyed and personnel supervised, and that all civilians employed by the Army, Navy or Air Force inclusive of the Ministry of Public Buildings and Works, were vetted and issued with passes or permits. I could enlarge on all of this but what I have said is common knowledge. To effectively implement the task fell squarely on the shoulders of the individual Section Commanders. Obviously there was much more to it and that is not for disclosure; so much of intelligence work depends on the individual and his dedication to the job in hand. During all the years in the work it never failed to fascinate and challenge me. It was time consuming but I was never a clock watcher, much to Jean's chagrin. Too many persons in the Intelligence Corps only pay lip service to the job; they do what they're told and well, but like a first class detective you have to give more and that's when the job grabs you. The area is so vast you can spread your wings and unlike the detective you are not hidebound by tedious reports, Judge's rules and so on. I suppose I was the object of criticism from my colleagues because I put more time in than they did, but it was my choice and the OC was unaware of it. In the basic job our reports were comparable; the difference came in the other items of interest. Owing to this extra time spent on the job, information was always forthcoming and that's what I was paid to do. At no time did I work with any ulterior motive, to crawl, impress, or 'brown hat'; I did the job the way I thought it should be done and I know I was right, results proved it.

Details of a possible threat are now outlined.

The Triads and the British Army

In my brief period in Hong Kong the obvious menace of Triad involvement in matters military only surfaced on one occasion and it concerned an approach to a loyal member of the Hong Kong Regiment. It was reported to me with a subsequent short report. No further action was taken owing to a reluctance on behalf of the person concerned. His attitude, as the Police told me, was understandable. Patience was a virtue, his Commanding Officer should be made aware, he should be watched and if possible kept away from arms, stores or clerical duties. As I recall that was the only brief involvement I had. As the following entries will show the organization was mainly criminal therefore in the capable hands of the RHKP (Royal Hong Kong Police).

Triad Societies began to assume their present form in the seventeenth century. The Chinese of old considered the three elements of Heaven, Earth and Man as containing magical properties, so the word 'Triad' is related to the figure 3. Four hundred years ago the Ching dynasty ruled

China, and the Ming Dynasty had been overthrown. Partisans of the Ming Dynasty still assembled in enthusiastic groups agitating for the Mings to return to power.

'Shades of Kung Fu': among these various partisan groups assembled a party of Chinese monks, just over a hundred in number, and they had a power base at the SIU Lam Monastery, which was a hot bed of Ming sentiment. Although dedicated to meditation they also, as a farm of militarism, were extremely well trained in the noble art of self defence!

When the reigning Ching Emperor heard news of this enclave of dissidents he sent troops to destroy the building and its occupants. Apparently this group had a Judas, and owing to his information the troops captured the monastery and all but eighteen were slaughtered. These were hunted down until only five were left. This small group founded the Hung Mun, a society whose name incorporates the name of the first Ming Emperor (Hung).

The Hung Mun attracted many supporters. To ensure strict allegiance a series of rites was devised for the initiation of new members. In the following years these groups attempted to overthrow the ruling Manchus and restore the Mings, but the former were extremely ruthless in their repression and gradually the political motivation of these societies fell drastically and they degenerated into criminal gangs. Even after the Manchus were deposed in 1911 and the Republic of China was proclaimed, these societies did not disband but continued to be involved in well organized crime. Hong Kong, before the British arrived in 1842, formed part of Kwangtung Province, and this was the area the Triad Societies retreated to and formed their power base. The British came with their Laws, culture, customs and language and the local Chinese, or at least a percentage, opposed the infliction of rules from the 'white skinned pigs'! Thus Hong Kong became an excellent breeding ground for the societies, especially after Chiang Kai Shek was deposed when thousands of these villains arrived in the Colony.

Triad societies have one abject in mind – to make money. Today as in the past the Hong Kong Police are faced with innumerable gangs closely involved in drug trafficking, prostitution, illegal gambling, protection rackets etc. The societies are not particular how they make their money although the members take great care not to become implicated for instance in drug trafficking. One of the main tactics used by Triad Societies to make money is terrorism and not only against rival gangs competing in the operating of opposition cinemas, gambling and drinking joints. When there is rival tension it is the innocent patrons or bystanders who are killed and injured. The general public hold the Triads in healthy fear, hence the reluctance to impart information. Strict Mafia type territories are well defined and woe betide the transgressor.

In former times the societies were divided into 'lodges' and 'chapters' (that has a familiar ring!) and numbers were used to designate rank in the hierarchy. The numbering was a code and the two highest ranks were 489 and 438. The former was held by the Sham Chu or First Route Marshal, the other by the Heung Chu or Incense Master, the person who was in charge of the initiation ceremonies. Each number had a hidden significance. Every number began with the digit 4, which was symbolic of the four seas the Chinese of old believed surrounded the world, with the implication that the Triad Societies' influence would encompass and bathe the universe.

The numbering system is now 'old hat'. The modern gang elect or have a self chosen leader for a defined term of office, who is known as the Cho Kun (the person seated within the lodge). He is the top man and has a number of deputies who are known as Tai Ko Tou. The thirty-six oaths of loyalty to the Society are concluded by: 'May five bolts of lightning strike me dead if I ever break this oath.' Each oath not only concerns the taker but his family as well, it is total commitment. Treason, or the slightest indiscretion connected to the secrecy of the system, is punishable by death: 'five bolts of lightning' or a myriad of swords.

In the middle of the nineteenth century the authorities tried to remedy the Triad problem through legislation, and made it a punishable offence if membership was proved but the laws were ineffective. Even today the Societies Ordinance forbids membership of Secret Societies, in particular the Triad.

There are in fact laws preventing Triad societies meeting, recruiting members or exacting membership dues. A first offence carries a maximum of three years imprisonment, subsequent convictions could carry seven years. The RHKP considered that the Triad Society problem so acute and complex that it constituted a very serious threat. Consequently, in 1957, the Triad Society Bureau was initiated to collect, collate and assess the data, then take executive action as required. This unit contained several hundred personnel. The spectre of corruption lurks in the background of this enclave of free Chinese. The enemy may be contained but I doubt if it will ever be beaten. There are many areas in the world where societies are active including UK, Holland, USA and Canada, in particular 14K (Sap Sie Kee) and (Wo Lee Kwan).

My first priority was to check the unit files and create some resemblance of order and make a plan of priorities for security surveys. It was soon evident that comprehensive surveys had never been done and that annual inspections were extremely cursory and lacked information; they had probably been done over the telephone! It was blatantly obvious that the current procedures in BAOR and UK had not penetrated the thick blind of holiday atmosphere that existed south and east of Hannover, Detmold and Bielefeld. The Near and Far East were a world apart. With an armful of files I went to see the OC, expressing my dismay and astonishment that the accepted procedures for surveys had not been implemented in the Far East. His excuses laid the blame squarely with the various Headquarters in the Far East who were dragging their feet and there was also the fiscal problem to be considered, but he agreed that if I could produce from my BAOR notes an aide memoire to fit local procedures I could do it, but he would not produce anything official until Singapore said so.

There lives within HQ Land Forces Hong Kong a military intelligence organization with far-ranging tentacles and a wide brief. I suggested that a warning of impending doom should be given them, and within a month I would descend on them to tear the place apart. The OCs face was a picture and he stuttered, 'You can't do that,' 'I don't know if you'll be allowed in to do it,' 'It's too sensitive.'

'But they are a military unit,' I replied, 'And unless they have a dispensation from MOD I don't see why they shouldn't endure a visit, it's the most important area in the Colony.'

'I'll see what I can do,' replied the OC.

I said that I would work nights and keep out of people's way but it made no difference. OCs came and went; some two years or so after I left the Colony a team of eight I believe came from Singapore, and the disclosures sent shivers down the spine. Call it apathy, carelessness, laziness, incompetence but my original impression formed when I first arrived was correct: the incumbents were a law unto themselves, their actions were those of a Civil Servant not a soldier who is governed by stated procedures. I should have been allowed to make a start four years earlier. The disclosures were horrific. I don't think there were any allegations of document loss or espionage, it was just that established procedures in registration and accountability accepted throughout the Army were flouted and deliberately ignored. What is even more vexing, especially to people like myself, is that no heads appear to roll. So many seniors had been involved over a prolonged period that a fair 'head hunt' would have had to be far reaching and way back and the old boy net hates to accept blame in retrospect.

However, a start was made with the Signals unit and the more sensitive Branches of the Headquarters and after several weeks I was joined by a Sergeant from the Australian Intelligence Corps who was to be attached to me for an eighteen-month tour of exchange duty, to undergo training in

aspects of intelligence work he could not obtain in his own military sphere.
John Castle was a former British Army soldier from a Highland Regiment.
Following service in Korea he decided to join an East African Police Force
with which he served for some time (it was my belief that for some reason
he left before his time expired) and emigrated to Aussie-land where he
became more Aussie than the Aboriginals; he was completely captivated.
He had only just finished an unaccompanied tour in New Guinea and got
another to Hong Kong, and apparently following Hong Kong he had a
tour in Vietnam. He was a bit of an introvert. Workwise I could find no
fault in John. Although he lacked imagination and flair and his social
graces did not help him, he insisted that he should be responsible for the
military survey programme of unit/barracks as he would never again have
this opportunity. I agreed but insisted that if I was not otherwise engaged
we should work as a team. When John Sheldon left to work with Alec
Davis we were later joined by Martin Brown, a humorous and talented lad
from Fleetwood. John Castle was thoroughly efficient, honest and
painstaking. Like me he did not concern himself with hours, and enjoyed
the job. I would say that he was probably one of the most proficient
operators I have worked with on survey work, but he would never make a
counter intelligence man; he was not the right type of character. I enjoyed
him (in small doses)!

As work began to settle into a routine so our social life increased. We
had regular functions within the unit and were fortunate to have a small
club and bar. As a unit we were also responsible for the training of the
Intelligence Troop of the Hong Kong (Volunteers), a local TA unit. Most
of the members of the troop were Government employees and the others
were self employed in high places, so all were reliable, keen and above
average intelligence; as a result the social aspect was of a high calibre,
enjoyable and helpful. Jean and I also made good friends of two REME
Warrant Officers. Bill Pearce was the senior Armaments Inspector in the
Colony, a large, taciturn man who loved his football and social activity. His
wife Joan was a darling; she came from North Lancashire and was the
librarian in Whitfield Barracks. Ken Hamblen was a senior technician with
the Army Air Corps at RAF Kai Tak; he was a small humorous man and
we shared many interests. His wife Betty was a lovely girl whom Jean got
on famously with. They had three small children, so most weekends we
spent at one of the many beaches in the New Territories and so we shared
the many social ventures available from the REME and RAF. As we all had
amahs, baby sitters were no problems of an evening and it was not
uncommon for us to wander out after 11p.m., maybe have a meal or a
snack followed by a drink and bring home fresh bread from Kowloon at

2a.m. It was a good life. As a family we explored, especially when Chris was over on holiday from UK, every corner of the Colony; we saw everything of interest that was possible and enjoyed every minute of it.

At this point I must explain how we changed amahs and why, also the subsequent heartbreak. On our arrival at Edinburgh Mansions we left the problem of selecting an amah for a few days until we knew the form. Eventually by recommendation from other occupants and our Chinese grocery 'boy' we agreed to have Ah Lee, a widow with three children; she did the job well enough but was rather miserable, she did not like to babysit on a Saturday and she tended to gossip during the day. One Sunday we went up to Fan Ling to visit a Catholic priest whom we had got to know in a rather roundabout way. On this visit he had two male visitors and a nun who was a very talented orthopaedic surgeon and as we sat drinking his beer in his tiny lounge Father Polletti and the nun were discussing the problems of the local Chinese women who would not visit the newly built medical clinic provided and staffed by the Catholic Church, because a baby boy had not been born there. When this did occur the women came in droves and it was now a thriving unit.

Father Polletti then turned to us and said, 'But I have my own family, you know, with the help of the nuns, I look after an orphanage. Would you like to see it? Good, I'll ring the Mother Superior and tell her you will visit.'

The dear Father was like that. Some twenty minutes later we found and entered the orphanage and were welcomed by the Mother Superior who explained to us that they based the organization of the orphanage on Doctor Barnardo's and had a series of houses of ten to twelve children under the supervision of a resident House Mother. Unfortunately Father Polletti was the only male person the children came into contact with so my reception would be unknown. The Reverend Mother also explained that they found homes for many of the children, some even to the UK; she told us that one child was to be adopted by an English couple and was due to leave for UK in a few weeks. We were shown round the home and ended up at the house containing the child due for adoption who without shyness introduced herself and proceeded to speak the few words of English she had been taught. Little Helen was gorgeous with beautiful eyes. As we walked away from the house I suggested that it would be very difficult for the child suddenly to be moved from one environment to another and in between a nine thousand mile journey by air on her own. The nun agreed but nothing could be done about the journey. Could we help, I suggested, and take her to our home on visits to get her used to European manners, food and habits. I don't know if there was some misunderstanding but within ten minutes the child was ours. Names, addresses, telephone numbers were exchanged, and Helen, her hand tightly clutched by Carolyn, was in the car complete with half a dozen items of clothing in a plastic carrier bag and she never returned to the orphanage.

Jean and I looked at each other in amazement. I have never seen an offer of help so readily accepted. The UK Social Services would have been appalled. Our recommendation from Father Polletti must have been extraordinary. On the Monday when Ah Lee was due at the flat for work Jean cheerfully produced Helen and briefly stated what happened. Ah Lee was not amused and later that day Jean took Helen down town and bought her dresses, shoes and underwear to fill the gap until her journey to UK. When they returned Ah Lee became even more vocal, stating if we wanted to spend money on a Chinese child why not her three children not 'THAT' (indicating Helen as a very inferior being). Jean was furious and over the next few days saw Ah Lee behave in a very cruel manner both vocally and physically towards Helen. I dispensed with her services almost immediately and until we acquired Ah Jan, Jean managed all the household chores; in the cooler weather this was not so arduous.

Considering Helen had never been close to a man before, she never left my side when I was in the house, and she copied Carolyn in every way. Within days she was eating European food with knife, fork and spoon. She was clean in her habits, kept herself tidy and was the most lovable of creatures. We were all captivated by her and I could see that Jean was close to ringing the Convent and asking for Helen to remain with us for adoption, and ask that the people in UK wait for another. Helen was quite content. We presumed later that she probably thought that we were in fact the people she was to live with; she had been told that she was going on a journey and would live with white people who had white children.

We received some very curious glances as we walked around the streets. Being so tall every Chinese looked at you and carrying a Chinese child which invariably I did, it naturally aroused a lot of curiosity. Helen brought us a great deal of happiness in our brief association; I wish we could see her again. I forget precisely how many weeks we had her but inevitably I received a telephone call and the following day two nuns arrived and I drove everyone to the airport. Poor Helen was confused but reassured by the nuns. It was a tearful farewell when Helen was handed over to a stewardess to be transported into the great unknown. Her UK address was given to us and I have since tried to contact this address via the Post Office but unsuccessfully.

Oh, Helen Lee Hoi Lun, where are you now?

Johnny was the 'store boy', a chap in his thirties who called almost daily to ascertain if you needed specific items of food. If it was urgent he would be back within half an hour, otherwise later in the day. He was the most reliable tradesman I have ever met, helpful in every way. He warned us about undesirable 'Look See' callers who sold inferior goods, those he recommended he knew, and they could be found again and their goods were always worthwhile. Johnny arrived at our door early one morning with an elderly amah. He knew all about Helen and why we had booted out Ah Lee; he applauded this because he didn't like her. Johnny explained that the amah had a daughter whom she had trained in the work of an amah and she wanted her to work for us, mainly because she also worked in our block and she could keep an eye on her and supervise her work. She would live in and babysit. Sunday she would have off to visit her home in Yuen Long. This sounded fine but the mother explained that Ah Jan was only fifteen years of age and should not really be employed as an amah. I said we'd like to see her, and as she disappeared upstairs Johnny explained that he had known the mother for many years; she was extremely honest and reliable and the daughter would be the same.

Ah Jan was tall for a Chinese and though she was only fifteen she could be taken as much older. She had an attractive face and figure with a lovely smile. She spoke some English and her outlook was very cheerful. She said she knew her duties and understood them. The wages were satisfactory and I said she would be paid more (normal amah pay) when she became sixteen and proved satisfactory. Ah Jan was perfect in every way, the flat was spotless. Jean would have to lie in bed to keep out of her way as first thing in a morning, she was like a whirlwind. If an item of clothing was taken off, on return home it had disappeared and within minutes was up on the roof drying: shirts, dresses, underwear. She prepared vegetables, watched Jean when she baked and when given permission to have a little baking session to prove that she had learned, she produced not a cake but scores of the little tiny mouthful cakes that the Chinese adore. Ah Jan, much to her mother's chagrin, became a member of the family especially when Chris was home; we took her with us on trips and she saw places she would never see left to her own devices. The mother thought it would affect her work and discipline but it never did, and she stayed with us until we left. Ah Jan was honest, hardworking and humorous. I'm glad we didn't treat her as a servant for she was a friend, and for a Chinese showed unusual emotion when we left. I hope she has had a happy life.

It would be almost impossible to attempt to describe the more enjoyable social aspects of life in the Colony in detail but briefly, work was mainly routine within fixed hours, with the occasional evenings involved in duty visits to Wanchai or observations and investigation in a more involved case but this was rare. So the weekday evenings were spent at home or attending other military social functions, farewells etc.; we had so many invitations I had to politely refuse many. Two nights a month we lectured to the Intelligence Troop of the Hong Kong Volunteers, which could almost be described as a social function. At the weekend it was different: we worked Saturday mornings, our wives and children usually came down to do some shopping and we all met in the Club for sandwiches and drinks. After this Jean and I usually did more shopping in 'Stinky Market' near the airport, an area renowned for its street market, with meat and vegetable stalls. Jean was fascinated by it all. We bought delicious frozen meat from New Zealand and the ham and bacon were a delight, then to a wonderful rice shop where you were spoiled for choice. A quick visit to collect fruit and vegetables probably fresh that morning from the Republic of China and as tasty as at home and loaded down I would return to the car and deposit them in the boot, then to return to Jean and Carolyn for the routine hour or more round the street market. Strangely enough, few Europeans visited this area and so the stall holders came to know us, and the visit was usually very convivial, interspersed by the occasional excitement when a police patrol attempted to round up the scores of unlicensed traders. They were rarely caught, people stared for a moment, grinned at nearby on-lookers, and carried on; they had probably made a purchase from him minutes earlier. The goods were cheap, usually well made (probably from China) the stall holders basically honest, and it all made up to an enjoyable and colourful couple of hours. In the evening with our REME friends we could visit any one of several military or RAF Messes if something special was on, otherwise we would just have a meal with a difference or visit a nightclub for a dance. Saturday night was very free and time did not matter.

    Sunday morning gave us a choice of churches for Mass: the military, Portuguese, or the 'Factory' as it was commonly called, St Teresa's Church in the heart of the Chinese housing estate, which was huge and was filled to capacity at every Mass. Communion was likened to a line in a factory, hence the name. On our return home, after a hurried change of clothes the midday meal would have been prepared, and off we would go with our friends to 18-mile Beach in the New Territories or to cross over to Artillery Bay to swim, sunbathe, relax and listen to 'The Archers' on the radio. I really enjoyed this. After Borneo, to be able to enjoy the simple things of life that other people did was absolutely great. Of course this was not possible from my arrival because it was quite cool from November to February or March; mind you, Chris when on Christmas leave thought it was wonderful and swam quite contentedly; to him 60-70°F was heaven. I was used to the 90°s and the water correspondingly so. Sunday evening was usually cards and games with the children followed by a walk and a casual drink. We attended films, searched out Festivals or other items of cultural interest and visited remote villages to see how the other half lived; this was fun and broadened your knowledge of the Chinese with a look into their way of life. In this way we enjoyed every minute of our free time and were thoroughly enthralled by it all, 'You pass this way but once.' So we took advantage of it and apart from petrol and time we did not waste our money.

I suppose at this time I should mention 1/10 Gurkhas who were stationed at Sek Kong in the Territories. I had of course an open invitation to visit them at any time and I did so on my arrival, meeting again Lt. Col. McAlister. When Chris arrived at Christmas I took him, Jean and Carolyn to meet my friends and they made such a fuss of them all, I was so pleased. Lt. Junbahadir Limbu, known as JB, Wo II Krishnabahadir Thapa, known as KB, the Chief Clerk and Edward the RQMS were special friends whom I shall never forget.

My next big social visit to 1/10 was when Pete Slowe called in Hong Kong on his way home for leave. In the late afternoon we sat in regal splendour in the Mess recounting the days in Bau. They were always over generous when dispensing alcoholic liquor and I had had sufficient, to drive sensibly. When it was time to depart, however, I had to accept a final glass. Pete was surrounded by Gurkhas but saw my glass being filled by half a pint of brandy topped up by lemonade. He made efforts to attract my attention, but I was closely attended by men who had met me in the forward positions and intended that I should finish the drink which I did. It is very difficult to detect a 'spiked' drink after a couple of strong ones in a pint (a Gurkha quirk) and so we left the Mess to a noisy farewell with me at the wheel. Pete started to tell me of the trick but it was too late; there was no point in stopping. We came into contact with an overladen, swaying goods vehicle which brought me back to earth. The Chinese in the Territories are notoriously bad drivers but I was under the influence and I would say it was probably my fault and completely out of character. I was usually most capable of having a drink and driving with caution; it becomes an occupational habit in my work and I always behaved with circumspection. Further danger and embarrassment was avoided within minutes. The car just stopped; we had run out of petrol! (or had the Gurkhas emptied it as a joke!) but we had gone too far. Pete was white faced and so relieved. We hopped aboard a bus which dropped us in Kowloon, where I was promptly sick which helped. When we arrived home Jean was not pleased. Even Pete's pleas of understanding were not accepted, I should have known better; going to visit those 'lovely little devils' for a reunion would inevitably turn to disaster. The car was recovered without incident the following day and eventually I was forgiven. JB did ring the following day to ask if everything was OK; I suspect it was all a put up job.

Our next visit to 1/10 followed a rare invitation to Jean and me to attend Dashira, the Gurkhali feast which takes place over a week or more, the climax of the ceremonial being the beheading of a goat by the youngest member of the unit with a huge ceremonial *kukri* and it has to be clean cut otherwise it augers bad luck to the Battalion. Presence here is a privilege. Jean entered the Mess with some trepidation. She was overwhelmed; a pint glass was placed in her hand, the brandy bottle was produced and she had to fight to keep her drink minute and filled it with lemonade. We spent an hour chatting among the other guests, Jean fighting all the while to keep away from the brandy. She looked across at me at one time in supreme enjoyment and resignation, indicating her large glass; I think she understood the reason for my *faux pas* months before. KB's wife was a nurse and looked after the families' clinic; she spoke very good English and became our official interpreter with other Gurkha wives and their husbands and children. We eventually left the Mess to attend the open air theatre complete with stage. To Jean's amazement the monsoon ditches contained the unconscious bodies of drunken Gurkhas, and they were ignored. Our hosts were highly amused; it was accepted within the confines of the barracks at Feast time. They did no harm, it was a form of 'drunken decorum'.

When the officers and their wives arrived I recognised Sue Dady who used to be the Brigadier's PA in 11 Bde in BAOR; she was now married to a Rhodesian chap who was a Captain and 'chopper' pilot attached to the Gurkhas. Susan was a lovely girl who used to 'bend my ear' frequently when we were at Minden. From the time she left home to work in UK and during my time in Borneo she wrote newsy letters and informed me of her forthcoming marriage. In Minden Susan was affectionately known to us 'Intelligence chaps' as 'Albert' which amused her no end. I asked JB to approach her and say, 'Does the name Albert mean anything to you? an old friend says hello!'

Her face was a picture; she leapt up, spotted Jean and me and in a very unofficer's wife manner dashed over and hugged and kissed us both. We had a long chat and she later visited us in Kowloon, a very pleasant reunion.

The entertainment was quite enjoyable but performed only by men; explanations were given by JB and KB and it came as a welcome break when with due deference I was escorted to the building where the beheading ceremony was to take place. Without going into detail the ceremony was successful. People may find the action as cruel, obnoxious or barbaric, but until you travel around and mix with different nationalities you cannot understand their way of life, customs and religions. So I did not find the ceremony distasteful; it was carried out with dignity and to their beliefs, which should be respected. It did not make me jump for joy (I have seen death too often) but I deemed it a privilege as I was somewhat of a special guest and I would never refuse if invited again. I think JB and KB were pleased that I showed no adverse emotion, realizing that it would be abhorrent to most Europeans.

The entertainment was still going strong when we left about 3a.m. We had had a wonderful time and royally entertained. It was so nice to meet old friends and show Jean off; she thought it was wonderful and was so impressed by the Gurkhas' friendliness and hospitality that I was at least partly forgiven. When we left Hong Kong a party from 1/10 came to the airport to see us off; they had gifts for us and I felt a little choked knowing it was unlikely that I would ever see them again. It was just nice to know that in addition to the chaps and their wives from the unit other friends had made the effort to say goodbye. I had a Christmas card from JB and KB in Penang, Malaysia and replied but nothing since; someday I shall contact them again.

The next important event in this tour was the beginning of the Cultural Red Revolution in Communist China. For some time in mainland China reports had been received about the cultural takeover by the youthful Red Guards in accordance with the procrastinations contained in Mao Tse Tung's *Little Red Book*. The Red Guards carried out a purge throughout China on a scale that Europeans would equate with the Nazi persecution of the Jews. Thousands died and were imprisoned; people from the professions were forcibly cleansed by enforced periods working as peasants. No one escaped.

Further south, confrontation with the 'white skinned pigs' began in Macao in 1966 where the Portuguese authorities eventually lost executive control and were forced into humiliating capitulation. So successful were the Chinese in annexing the Portuguese enclave, that the temptation to attempt a repeat performance in Hong Kong must have been quite irresistible.

Eventually, in May 1967, the Chinese Communists planned and organized two particular strikes at a plastic flower factory and the Green Island cement establishment. These were followed by political intimidation of students in leftist schools and apprentices in leftist factories. Children were actually paid to throw stones and professional 'hit men' murdered individuals, and made and planted bombs causing casualties which included children. For several days marches were made on Government

In 1967 the Hong Kong Police were probably the finest riot control group in the world. Just imagine the living conditions in this typical block of workers' flats.

House where the gates and walls were liberally plastered with Maoist slogans. On one particular day in a ludicrous demonstration of support thirteen local Chinese millionaires drove past Government House and the chanting throng in their Rolls-Royces! to show their distaste of British fascism, imperialism and tyranny within the Colony. How two faced can you be.

All this agitation failed to rouse the majority of the population in support. A general strike was advocated which included public transport, ferries and seamen; this was a flop. When riots were organized the Police dealt with them superbly; they were probably the finest, best disciplined riot police in the world. Police raids, both Special Branch and my friends' team, were carried out on Union premises and suspect houses with creditable success which gave the population confidence in their Police Force which was well merited. Some subversion was initiated from Radio Villa Verdee in Macao and Chinese mainland Communist press in Hong Kong, and as a result some Communist newspapers were closed. The Pakistanis in the Police were vilified, the Gurkhas were defiled as mercenaries, and efforts by the Unions to undermine the loyalties of members of the Police, Armed Forces and civilians attached, also hospital workers, failed miserably.

Some arms running, explosives and saboteurs came from mainland

China but there did not appear to be any central planning. Control of terrorist activity was localised and therefore not successful owing to efficient Police activity and information from the public.

Then it happened, out of the blue, surprising all the authorities. A mini riot at Sha-Tau-Kok was followed by an attack on the Police Post and seven policemen were killed. Sha Tau Kok lies on the eastern side of the border with mainland China and a road from Hong Kong skirts the fringes of the village which is mainly in mainland China. At one point, where the road turns west, half the road is in Hong Kong, the other half in China, then it all goes into China.

Two days after the attack I was summoned to the OC's office told to pack a few military items plus washing and shaving kit from home and that I was off to Sha Tau Kok with a company of the 7th Gurkhas. It was not possible to state how long I would be away but I would be performing similar duties to those I had done in Borneo. I would be briefed at Brigade HQ in the New Territories and the less said to my wife the better, was advocated. I did what was necessary at home and just over an hour later I was at Brigade HQ receiving a briefing which was quite frankly grossly inadequate. The administrative aspects were extremely vague; I would just have to make out with the help of the Gurkhas. Operationally, an assessment had been made by an Intelligence Corps Sergeant from Brigade HQ that approximately eight hundred Chinese troops had been despatched to Sha Tau Kok and that the lines of Chinese trenches in the Black Hills which overlook the border and the New Territories were being cleared and re-activated. Brigade, and I suppose the world in general, wished to know if it was all a prelude to an invasion of Hong Kong. That was the immediate problem. If it had been possible at the time to think of what the international ramifications could have been had this happened I doubt if we would have slept easy.

On the British side of Sha Tau Kok the tallest building was a small factory of three storeys, adjacent to the attacked Police Station and the Customs Post. The Gurkha company had made its Headquarters there, and the remainder of the Battalion was strung out in Company locations along several thousand yards of the twelve-mile border. Batteries of the Gunner Regiment were deployed in support. If I remember correctly the Armoured Unit consisted of a Tank Squadron and we also had the assistance of the British Army's 'Mule Company' to transport supplies to Gurkhas who were busy digging in and selecting good fire positions. Not a realistic opposition to the millions of Chinese on the other side, plus me of course.

On arrival I introduced myself to Major —, the Gurkha OC who gave me a quick operational brief and took me on a quick tour of his positions. The more questions I asked the more I became aware of the complete lack of firm intelligence to suggest that the Chinese had reinforced the border to such an extent. When I ascertained how this intelligence was obtained and the lack of corroboration, I was convinced the threat was over exaggerated. With a warning I then walked on my own down the road to China. As the road turned left to the west I was faced by a shop house. Two armed men in civilian clothes watched me from the shelter of the shaded shop front. Hanging by its neck was a crude replica of the Governor of Hong Kong, a written symbol around its neck confirmed this; it swung lazily in the warm breeze. No one else appeared to be in the area, no sandbags or fortified positions. It would have been extremely foolish to have chanced my arm by walking any further on my own. Having had a glimpse at first hand I turned round and walked back the 150 yards to relative safety, but with a funny feeling in my back. Speaking to the OC, we both decided that it would be more helpful if we had something more powerful than binoculars. The powers that be even jumped one step ahead, they sent up the latest model Pentax with an enormous lens, which when properly set up could double as a powerful telescope. So began my seven or eight days of China watching and photography, averaging eighteen or twenty hours a day: very tedious, tiring, but interesting. When my OC came up to visit me I told him I was wasting my time; the troops on the ground were quite capable of reporting anything of interest. The person sent up to relieve me only stayed two days before he was withdrawn.

When it was decided to erect a fence along the border months later things really got out of hand in a military sense. My Corps sent out from UK young NCOs to observe the border. These characters wandered about festooned with small arms, grenades hanging from belts etc., but no enemy! Even incidents of children throwing half bricks across the wire were afforded a report classified SECRET! It grew completely out of hand and quite ludicrous; there was more action on the streets of Hong Kong Island. From an intelligence point of view the border area should have died a death within the first fortnight and carried on as normal. Someone, somewhere wanted to keep the pot boiling; I wonder why? The trenches were being tidied up by small parties of militia men, small cadres under arms training were observed on several occasions in the early evening. The house in which the handful of regular soldiers lived was identified, and the occupants spent most of their time with their feet up, eating, drinking, laughing and joking: not the obvious signs of a potential invading army.

I suppose the more humorous side of life occurred in our effort to

Sha Tau Kok. My wasted eight days of 'China watching': an enemy that wasn't there.

survive. A small group of us consisting a Signals NCO for Rear Link Communication, and a sergeant, driver, and Wireless Operator from the Gunners, were allocated a small hut to live in. This 'shanty' was about seventy yards from the Gurkha Company HQ and my observation position. The five of us gazed at our accommodation with mixed feelings; it measured about 12' x 8', four walls and two apertures, no doors! Dusk was closing in. We were discussing the food situation and what to do about future feeding arrangements when the driver yelled, 'Look at this bloody lot,' and we were confronted by an army of rats, good sized ones too. Our hut was at the end of a small muddy creek, and on a promontory facing us and overlooking the creek was a line of ramshackled Chinese huts, about twelve in all, now deserted. The fear of invasion had encouraged flight, anywhere away from the border and possible death.

The average Chinese peasant is not well educated in general hygiene. Food, particularly rice, was unceremoniously heaved through the open windows on to the turgid sea and when the water receded the food remained on the mud and down came the rats to eat, twice a day.

We hurriedly pooled our resources, made a meal, placed our camp beds and bedding in the hut and I climbed up to my eagle's nest to see if China night life was interesting, but it wasn't. We had one evening show when a political pantomime, including dancers, entertained the small border town inhabitants. We could only observe the fringes of this show but at least it relieved the boredom. We were also very alert. The Gurkhas were extremely aware of the monumental odds facing them if an invasion took place and they would ensure the enemy would pay a bitter price.

That first night in the hut was a hoot. We kept the Tilley lamp lit, because the Gunners had to have one man awake to keep the radio link open, and throughout the night we fought the rats. They even leapt up the walls to try and grab the bread we hung there. Success was supreme when one of the Gunners transfixed one of the miscreants with his bayonet and left it there as a warning and it worked; but it started to smell the following day so it was removed. They still wandered in but infrequently. We ensured that our food was high and safe. I also met a former Officer Cadet of mine who was a Gurkha Company Commander, Captain Eyres. His men held the high ground to our left. He had become a very competent officer; it's nice to meet your products as you grow older, fruits of hard work.

By the end of the second day I was satisfied in my own mind that the eight hundred Chinese troops were a myth. It was true that on the day after the killings of the policemen some thirty-plus Chinese trucks had driven into Sha Tau Kok; all the vehicles were covered and the only thing that any observers could state was that two, possibly three, Chinese soldiers were in the back of each vehicle. It was impossible for anyone on the British side to see inside any of the vehicles. So a very foolish assessment was made: 30 plus x 25 = approximately 800 personnel and everyone gets their knickers in a twist. When I stated my point of view the Gurkha Officers guardedly agreed; inwardly, they knew, Brigade did not want to know. After all it was one of our people who had initiated the presence of the 'enemy'.

As the hot, humid days progressed, I and the Gurkha sentries baked on the hot roof, and I photographed and observed every moving thing I could see of interest in this shabby border town. On the outskirts in the cool of the evening weapon training Cadres were held for the local militia and miles away in the Black Hills, small fatigue parties of militia could be observed clearing the long lines of trenches on the forward slopes facing the Colony, and everything was done in a very leisurely way, there was no urgency.

I shed no tears when after eight days Norman Miller came as my relief. He stayed for two days then our involvement ceased; the responsibility went back to Brigade. If they wanted to play 'silly buggers' they were welcome.

One matter I must mention. On or about the third day, two Padres arrived. One was Roman Catholic; I immediately recognised him as the priest from the Military Hospital in Singapore who never visited me in the ward and didn't even condescend to speak to me when I attended Mass

with my eye covered, obviously an in-patient. This was the first time I had
ever met a forces Padre that I disliked and I met all denominations. 'Hello
and who are you?' one of them cried. I told them and we chatted for a
moment or two. Then the Company Commander walked in and spoke to
the Church of England Padre; after a couple of minutes he walked over to
the Roman Catholic Padre, introduced himself and said he had been
brought up a Catholic but didn't go to Mass now. With no excuse or
apology the Padre took the Company Commander by the arm and walked
away without a word to me. I considered this the height of bad manners
and only confirmed my original assessment of the man; his Ministry was
purely social. I turned to walk out in disgust when the Company
Commander asked me to stay and have a drink with him. I made an excuse
and left; not my idea of a Forces Padre and a very ignorant person to boot.

Back again in harness at the unit, work was a-plenty. I think by this time
John Castle had arrived and had been keeping himself busy in my absence.
I had rewritten a Security pro forma based on the BAOR format for annual
surveys on units; this helped our reports to be far more comprehensive but
would also necessitate more finance to bring specific buildings and other
items up to higher standards. Although not officially adopted in the Far
East, the OC decided we could make a start and see what local reaction
developed in comparison to BAOR. The Far East was a Teddy Bear's Picnic,
way behind in awareness to 'The Threat' and yet it was there all right and
many people from the top downwards placed their heads in the sand and
didn't wish to know. Security always appeared to affect social life at all
levels. I considered if my lads and I had to be involved, so should everyone
else; our social life was affected also, and we had a job to do.

I also heard of Jean's onslaught on the OC while I was away. Her
indignant outburst was untypical of her. On the Saturday morning she had
walked into the boss's office to ask where I was, what I was doing and how
long I would be away. The answers did not satisfy her.

'Do you mean to tell me that you have two seniors at Brigade, three
more here doing Counter Intelligence work plus Harry the Warrant Officer
and several competent junior operators and yet my husband who works on
the Island and has just finished a twelve-month unaccompanied tour has
to go and do this job while they are in that other office drinking coffee?'

The OC, somewhat flustered at being abused by a female, replied, 'Ah,
what you don't understand, Mrs Howard, is that the General asked for him
personally as he is the only one who has worked with Gurkhas under active
service conditions and has the experience on operations.'

'Then I suggest you get some of this lot outside to go and gain some
experience,' says Jean, and left the office at a high rate of knots to seek

solace with our next door neighbour who ran the nearby library. Joan Pierce dried her tears and took her shopping; later Jean said it made her feel better and she apologised to the OC who with a wry smile said it wasn't necessary, he fully understood. As I've said, he was a gentlemen.

It wasn't so long after this that the OC and Harry the Warrant Officer were posted. Both were nature's gentlemen, competent but in my opinion they needed to assert more discipline without being obsessive about it. Normally it is not necessary but with this unit people took advantage, particularly of Harry. Poor chap, within twelve months of leaving Hong Kong he was dead; it was a terrible shock to us all. You could not have met a nicer person, also his lovely wife.

We now continue with Hong Kong's mini revolution. As a unit we were not particularly involved unless the security of military units could be a possible target and I could only think of one occasion when most of our unit turned out to reinforce the Ordnance Depot which was surrounded by blocks of flats, which as photographs show were bursting at the seams with bodies. A full alert was on throughout the Colony. When we entered the Depot the majority of the staff appeared to be in a drunken state. God knows what would have happened if the crowds had suddenly decided to rush the wire, but I cannot recall any particular incident which involved a military establishment. It was put forward that the last time rioting took place and the Gurkhas took to the streets, the Chinese had a very healthy respect for the Army and its capability. Thank God they didn't test the RAOC at that Depot. I believe the situation changed dramatically following our arrival, and certain disciplinary actions were taken. In the weeks and months that followed it was all Police action and I would consider their Riot Drill was the finest in the world: highly trained and disciplined, it did not take long to disperse a riotous crowd.

I recall an incident on one of the main thoroughfares on Hong Kong Island when a Superintendent with a relatively small squad of police confronted a huge demonstrating crowd who were damaging vehicles and shops. The officer, using a loud hailer, called on the crowd to halt which they did. He nominated the ringleader by description, who was waving his 'Little Red Book' and urging the crowd on. He told the crowd he would give three warnings to disperse, and if not, he would shoot the ringleader. The three warnings were ignored and the vast crowd began to move again; the officer took a rifle from a nearby policeman and shot dead the ringleader. To ensure the body was recovered the police Land Rover ran over the body to prevent the crowd from retrieving it but they had disappeared like magic. I cannot recall any further riotous crowd problems after that incident until the end of our little revolution.

Of course we had bomb problems and many hoax calls, but the population behaved very stoically about it all. The Communist taxi drivers bombarded you with Mao music and open hostility but didn't refuse your custom although they were ill-mannered; suddenly it was almost back to normal. We had bombs on Lion Rock and on many main roads, and Gurkhas patrolled the Married Quarters area, but then incidents began to be spasmodic and to all intents and purposes the Colony slowly returned to normal. A fitting climax was the helicopter assault by the Welch Regiment (whose CO was an Ex Grenadier) and the Police on a Communist commercial building on the island. This building was well reinforced on the ground floor and the Police were sure it was being used for illegal purposes. When the troops slowly made their way downwards entry was eventually gained on the ground floor and concluded a very successful operation.

Surprisingly, Jean did not let the situation worry her. With her friends, shopping continued with the occasional scare, and even in the large Communist stores they were served in almost empty premises with sullen good manners.

Also during this time we had the water problem. Hong Kong has limited facilities for water storage and had a annual agreement with mainland China for the supply of fresh water via a huge pipe into Kowloon. As the summer progressed the water in the existing reservoirs became almost non-existent and then China decided to turn off the water and only turned it back on after urgent negotiation. After this it became a rather macabre yet childish political game; they turned the water off and on as they saw fit. The fire hazard in the Colony, especially in the squatter areas, was acute, and people did die because of lack of available water. At the height of the problem we were rationed to *four hours water every six days* and at a specific time. You do not realize how much you miss the habit of turning on a tap. I did, of course, because I'd lived in the jungle for a year but everybody coped amazingly well.

As soon as the water came on, baths were taken and huge amounts of washing done, then the baths were thoroughly cleaned and fresh water stored mainly for washing and the toilet. In the kitchen initially plastic bags were used, rather precariously, then enterprising characters produced larger plastic open drums which generally solved everyone's problem in normal accommodation. No sooner had households solved their problem than China decided it had proved a point: Hong Kong needed China's water and we shouldn't forget it and they resumed normal supply.

During the problem prayers were offered for rain: please send us a typhoon to fill our reservoirs. Now the last thing we wanted was a storm but we got one. In the season, typhoons are formed in the Pacific and nature propels them usually in a north-westerly direction, sometimes hitting the Philippines and dashing across the South China Sea to hit the south coast of China. Some typhoons are isolated but occasionally several can gather in quick succession and play havoc with the weather forecasters' predictions. It's not the eye of the storm you should worry about hitting you but about 50-100 miles from the eye can be a disaster. Damage deteriorates the further you are away from the fifty-mile limit but it can still be extremely severe.

The media advised close contact with radio and TV and warnings were given on a scale from 1-10. It progressed through sufficient food, schools close, shops close, everyone goes home, seal the house, ferries stop, don't drive etc. Then you hope to God it is not too severe. The winds are vicious, the sea rises, and the rain enters your house in places you would not think possible; it is quite an experience. We also found out what those huge circular holes were for on our balconies: they were to allow the wind access through the structure of the building and therefore relieve the stress. Needless to say our reservoirs were filled, and there was general talk about a desalination plant to be built using one or more of the coastal creeks, as much water was wasted during the rainy season and a scheme like this could possibly help to alleviate a growing problem with an increasing population.

Chris, being at boarding school, looked forward enormously to his visit. The first one at Christmas 1966 was excellent for us all. I took him all over the Colony to anything of interest. At 70°F I found it cold and would not contemplate swimming in the sea, but just after Christmas Day at Artillery Bay he stripped off and enjoyed a swim, ugh! The summer holiday was long and enjoyable but I had anticipated a holiday away from the Colony for us all. I had made serious enquiries about a visit to Japan, and via one of my contacts with a shipping line where I had been making enquiries on another matter, I was offered a 23-day cruise to Borneo for the equivalent of £44.00 each. Only ten passengers could be carried on board this trading freighter; accommodation was adequate but not luxurious and food all in. The ship called at Jesselton (in Sabah), the island of Labuan, and all the ports to Kuching, staying there three to five days (sufficient to visit old haunts). Then it was to return in reverse order. What an offer, everyone was quite happy with it, but of course when the trouble started in May I was not allowed to leave the Colony on any pretext so we never had an Asian holiday, a fact I bitterly regret because I think they would have enjoyed a visit to a country very few Europeans would visit as tourists.

I am now struggling to recall any matters of importance that I can relate and create interest. As a group we shot to keep up our proficiency in small arms, we kept fit with a mixture of Orienteering (not me), Football, Volleyball (Minor Units Champions) and concluded Physical Efficiency Tests, very taxing in 80°F and of course I swam every Saturday and Sunday. I was as happy as a sandboy: work hard and relax well.

Recently I read Jones Clavell's *Noble House*, and it brought back names, streets and buildings long forgotten. Rather over-exaggerated, the story was interesting, I met the new Taipan in 1968 and renewed old acquaintance. The devious Chief Superintendent Crosse was in fact a Chief Inspector of Celtic origin and he and his small staff had nowhere near the resources in the book. In fact we both became very friendly; we exchanged information and helped each other. There was in existence a file which he held in strict security. Any disclosure from this would have caused a diplomatic uproar in London, Washington and Hong Kong. I ascertained from a reliable source that the investigation carried out by certain police officers outlined the existence of a homosexual 'fairy' ring, that if exposed would have been political dynamite and from a high level it was deemed necessary to suppress its damning contents. Knowing that my Celtic friend could give me a brief decision because he trusted me, as I uncovered names of personalities in a particular investigation he would say, 'You're right, he's in the file.' He knew that I knew to what he was referring because I had told him I knew of the file's existence. He was more interested in keeping 'his file' up to date with the current information I was imparting, and by my actions he trusted my integrity without question.

The following incident is recorded because the connotations recall sadness and bitterness over a relatively short period and it indicates how rapport between working colleagues can deteriorate over a short spell and seriously influence a person's sound judgement concerning work, social activity and personal relationships. In this case it led to unnecessary bias and downright lies and as the recipient of these actions it took me almost twelve months to exonerate myself. This also necessitated the promulgation of a letter sent worldwide to all senior Corps Officers that they must adhere to the laid down procedures for the completion of an individual's Confidential Report. In conclusion, the individual concerned achieved his objective: owing to age limitation he had successfully blocked my possible Commission.

Some weeks before the departure of the OC and Harry Dunne we had no seniors in the unit; the OC and 2 IC were on temporary attachment to Force HQ, and Brigade HQ, New Territories, respectively and Harry was on Corps leave. At this time I had a very complicated enquiry concerning a highly vetted Royal Signals NCO who had previously served in a sensitive unit in BAOR. It was necessary as a matter of some urgency that CI personnel visit in this unit and obtain specific and comprehensive answers to thirteen questions I had painstakingly formulated. I signed and despatched my report as Commanding the CI Section Hong Kong Island, addressing it to the Officer Commanding the CI unit in BAOR (a Major); in this I contravened all the laid down rules of office procedure, within and between units. I did wrong, but, in mitigation, with all the right motives. My report could have sat on the OC's desk for days, even two or three weeks, for the monumental pile of files and reports requiring personal signature by our absent OC. Action and a quick reply was required, so I took the short cut, and in retrospect I think I would do it again and damn the consequences.

When the relevant report arrived from BAOR, the enquiries had obviously been completed by a junior or very inefficient senior NCO because the answers still required amplification. The Major spent more time in the report commenting on my horrendous breach of etiquette than on the important facts before him, which didn't say much for his efficiency. It was a prevalent sore within the Corps that in Counter Intelligence matters 'brevity is best' and officers pedantic in its application. Despite the length of a report, a summary had to be compiled in case a busy Staff Officer did not have the time to digest the full text! As a former police officer this irritated me. Any report submitted by CI personnel should be as brief and comprehensive as possible, *dot the i's* and *cross the t's* and this should eliminate the necessity of further amplification by the recipient and how often did this happen; it was unnecessary and time wasting.

Now in the chair, the new OC, Capt X, received the report from BAOR and hit the roof. He ranted and roasted me for ten minutes and rightly so, I needed reprimanding but not sufficient to bring on a heart attack; he was purple with unsuppressed anger. What made it worse was that his tirade was having little effect. He was more concerned about rank status. Given the opportunity I explained my reasons and actions, he then added that he had now read my initial report which was excellent, comprehensive and very interesting, he could not fault my thirteen queries, but he would never forgive me for my terrible breach of etiquette – and he never did. From the moment I left his office we ceased to be 'best mates'. There was no outward sign of animosity, he was more subtle; the more profound manner he found to embarrass me was his attitude toward my draft CI reports. Although never thought necessary by Capt. W, my reports were slashed, the text completely altered, and names of officers, members of the Corps, although not directly involved but essential for continuity, were deliberately omitted, giving the contents an air of confusion.

I could never obtain from him a satisfactory explanation for his alterations especially as they also had to go to Singapore for information. He was more concerned with how I had obtained my information and from whom. My reluctance to impart the names of my contacts, some of whom had high positions and wished to be anonymous, made him angry and, I suspect, jealous. Just before I left I submitted my 19th Security of Personnel (SOP) report (British Vetted Personnel) which was always a very delicate subject. This particular initial report was very comprehensive owing to reliable information from my contact, which is unusual in the interim stages. It forced Capt X to look at the relevant file only to find that since my arrival fifteen months earlier, twenty reports of this nature had been submitted and I was the author of nineteen of them. They covered Officers down to Privates including WRAC (possible prostitution), and some GC HQ personnel and dependents. He had never known such a situation, particularly from one Operator, how did I justify this? I was forced to tell him that I did not work like other personnel; I was fortunate that I had good contacts that I maintained, and unless it was absolutely necessary I never stayed in the office: there was always something to do or someone to see. My reports had covered possible allegations of homosexuality, prostitution in Wanchai, excessive drinking, undesirable associations and unbecoming conduct.

Capt X gave me the distinct impression that it was *I* that was being disloyal; we had reached an impasse. I was not guilty of dereliction of duty, and probably should have been complimented. SOP reports are difficult under any circumstances because in the initial stage it is usually hearsay; when the information concerns vetted personnel it justifies thorough and balanced investigation, because a person's future may depend on its authenticity. Subsequently vetting status could be removed with obvious ramifications. It is the duty of CI personnel to report any suspicious iniquities of vetted personnel. If one studies closely any of the many post World War 2 spy sagas, many lives were lost and highly classified information given to the Eastern Bloc by spies whose conduct was suspicious and was never reported, or if reported no one in authority took executive action. I was always fully justified; the ultimate decision in any SOP case is taken by a higher authority. Only in certain circumstances would the investigator be justified in making any form of recommendation for future action. We had reached a stalemate. I couldn't win.

Two other incidents occurred that widened the wound between Capt X and myself. A vacancy had opened at the Kindergarten where Jean worked and she was asked if she knew a possible candidate. We did, the wife of a Captain QM of the Lancashire Fusiliers who had taught Chris in Germany was a close acquaintance; she was University qualified and a very nice person. Jean offered her name. The wife of Capt X queried Jean about the vacancy some days later and she was told to apply. The school made the decision and the teacher was appointed. We were told later that OC and wife were livid that the appointment had not been filled from within the unit; Jean and another lady already worked there. We had been disloyal!

The second incident really began soon after the arrival of the new OC. We were told that he had, for whatever reason, seriously upset the Brigade Major and other Staff Officers in Kowloon Garrison. The comments of various officers were no doubt transmitted to our new Brigade Commander, an old friend of mine from Minden days when he commanded the Royal Warwickshire Fusiliers. I had worked closely with him and he knew me well. On his initial visit to the unit (we were now at Argyll Road), as the OC was about to announce my name when opening the office door, the General brushed past, saying, 'That's all right, we're old acquaintances aren't we?' Shaking hands with me and Bill Ward (ex Minden) he sat himself on the corner of my desk, ignored the OC completely, and talked about old acquaintances, my time in Borneo, his family and mine, times of Mass and various Churches etc. The OC was visibly annoyed at his exclusion. Including Bill in the conversation he stayed for ten minutes or so and I think that was the straw that broke the camel's back.

It is laid down in Army procedures that before *any* personnel leaves a unit on posting, the contents of his Confidential Report are shown to him. This is compiled by his immediate officer, Warrant Officer or Senior NCO, and is then counter-signed by a Senior Officer. In this case it was the OC and a Lt. Col. G at the HQ in Singapore. This Colonel interviewed me two months before I left Hong Kong, and congratulated me on my forthcoming promotion when I was due to take command of the CI Section in Scotland. He also mentioned Borneo and my work in Hong Kong. (I came face to face with the Colonel in Millbank Hospital, London, in 1971; I addressed him, he appeared surprised and very embarrassed, mumbled a greeting, turned his head and walked away. I found that sad.) I must confess I did not consider anything untoward in the fact that I was never shown my Report before Departure, I just forgot. I had never had anything less than excellent during my service; it was the last thing to worry about, in between packing, despatch of possessions, flight arrangements, handing over the flat and farewell visits. Handing over the Section, posting and promotion were settled: why worry. In order to apply for a Commission which I fully intended to do, it had to be before my forty-second birthday and with a recommendation for promotion. The retribution of Capt X manifested itself *four months* after my arrival in Scotland when my Report finally arrived. I was praised for my honesty, integrity, smartness and devotion to duty and then the roof fell in. He criticized my command of the Section, said that I had an aversion to the world of Security Surveys (we all worked to my pro forma!) that I delegated this 'chore' to junior ranks while I concentrated on the more glamorous aspects of Counter Intelligence! My reports were badly written, said Capt X; the Colonel said he had read them and endorsed those comments. The laugh was *that Capt X re-wrote all my reports*, and until the day before I left I still retained all the altered draft copies before I destroyed them.

Had I been shown my report prior to posting and disagreed with it I would have had recourse to higher authority, in this case the General at Kowloon Garrison, and Capt X would have had to prove his comments and I know who would have won. At that stage I would have had the altered reports, the Australian Sergeant who had stated his desire to do all the surveys though I refused him. The Surveys of the Commander British Forces (CBF), the three inter-service aides to the CBF, 'G' and 'A' Branches, Signal Squadron in Cypher Room, 1st Bn the Welch Regiment, The Hong Kong Regiment, and the newly installed Chinese Language School were all done by me and Cpl. Brown; John Castle assisted us on a couple of days but he did all the other branches of the Headquarters. The adverse comments of Capt X were all false and could have been adequately disproved, so without the documentary evidence and not in location I had a battle ahead.

I first appealed to the G2 (Int) at HQ Scotland who offered no help at all; he would not accept that an officer would lie. Subsequently I was granted an interview with the Adjutant at the Centre. He listened sympathetically, put the problem down to a clash of personalities, and stated that the two officers concerned refused to change their comments(!) and would not accept that procedures had been contravened. I was disappointed at the total lack of support to right a blatant wrong; no one was prepared to hold their hand up. I returned to Scotland, my morale at a low ebb. I had not related all the facts to Major R who had been appointed to command the Section instead of me mainly because I thought it unfair to involve him in a matter that had occurred outside his jurisdiction; now I told him all and he was quite upset. Some days afterwards and I suspect after some phone calls he told me that our Corps Brigadier's Personal Assistant, a Major with a sound Regimental background, was due to pay a visit to Scottish Command and he had arranged an interview.

This gentleman listened carefully to my grievance. I spoke non stop for some twenty minutes. He made notes and made no attempt to hide his

disgust and was appalled at the circumstances I outlined. As we were both
Infanteers this was a situation that would never occur in a Regiment,
especially with a Senior. Some weeks later I received a posting order to HQ
6 Inf. Bde. and promotion to Warrant Officer. So ended the sad and
disgraceful saga of Capt X, one of only two persons during the whole of
my military career that I actually had a major difference with, and lost all
respect for as an officer and a person. Throughout life you frequently meet
people of either sex with whom you may experience a difference of opinion,
and you can take them or leave them. He was the only one who cowardly
put the knife in my back and turned it even when I wasn't there. Later I
was shown a letter sent worldwide to all Supervising Officers of Corps
personnel reminding them of their responsibilities to ensure this did not
happen again, but it was too late for my Commission application; he won
after all but I was exonerated.

To return to Hong Kong and the final weeks: another old friend had
arrived and joined SMIS as G2 (Int), Major Hugh Laing from 1SG. He
sent for me and we had a long chat. I told him my fears about his new unit.
I wonder if he was caught up in the big Survey. The job was so tremendous
that had I done it on my own I doubt if I'd have surfaced in time to depart
the Colony. I cannot recall any particular case that merited a prolonged
and challenging enquiry. Small investigations were undertaken for the
Royal Navy, especially when certain ships were in; HMS *Tamar*, an Aussie
lesbian prostitute involved with RAF and GCHQ personnel who later
attempted suicide; a former disreputable ex member of the RMP; and a
highly placed member of an important utility, mentioned in the 'Fairy'
ring, who was formerly Intelligence Corps. There were so many persons
and incidents I received information about. I reported those of military
interest and gave the others to my contacts in Departments or Stations in
the Police. I was a very small cog in a large wheel.

Regretfully the Hong Kong posting came to its conclusion. It had been
a wonderful experience in every respect for us all as a family. For me the
change of environment from Borneo to Hong Kong was an unimaginable
contrast, but quite enjoyable. As always the departure came upon us quite
rapidly. We bought and packed, said farewells to friends and colleagues. At
my farewell one person was conspicuous by his absence, pleading a previous
engagement, the least said the better. Bill Cheong, our photographer, did
me proud with the buffet. We talked and drank a lot, played 'clag', our
favourite card game, and concluded with a 'fives' of 21 aces. The players
throw the Chinese dice in rotation, and whoever throws the 7th ace
nominates five drinks of his choice in a pint glass. The thrower of the 14th
ace pays for the drink and the lucky boy who throws the 21st drinks it in

one! Some of the concoctions can be most vile. I nominated one, paid for one, and drank two, drove the lads home, woke up at seven o'clock fit as a butcher's dog. I must have had the stomach of a rhino; after Borneo that was understandable.

As usual all the lads turned up at the airport, with wives and girlfriends, with one exception! There were also farewell gifts from a group from 1/10 GR, I was choked. Prior to takeoff we had to endure an extremely heavy and violent storm and of course, remembering the two aircraft accidents at Kai Tak we witnessed from our flat, Jean was most apprehensive. However seconds after takeoff we cleared the low cloud and had a tiring but uneventful flight by RAF VC10 to Brize Norton.

Owing to flight postponements Jean's passport was out of date which caused some humour with Immigration but was successfully concluded. I handed in my personal automatic weapon to Customs so we were not unduly delayed. The train journey was tedious but eventually we were bedded down with Jean's parents at 56 Winckley Road ready to start a new job in a fresh house.

CHAPTER 34

CI Section, HQ Scotland

During my leave period I made arrangements to visit Edinburgh to sort out the allocated quarters and visit the unit. This was done without problems, mainly due to the Warrant Officer I was replacing; he was extremely kind and most helpful. With his help I also purchased a Saab car therefore the move from Preston to Edinburgh was relatively painless and we soon settled in.

Soon after my arrival Major R assumed command. I had met him briefly at the Intelligence Centre at Maresfield. He was a pleasant, inoffensive person who didn't wish to rock anyone's boat, particularly his own. I had found time to check the unit files and was very disappointed. The standard of Security Survey reports was poor, and without information, units were termed 'Satisfactory' in a security context. Yet again, like Hong Kong, the more comprehensive BAOR procedure had not been adopted for whatever reason, and the filing system contained a fair amount of useless paper, so I suggested to Major R that a clearout and re-assessment should be initiated forthwith; this was agreed and completed. Units throughout Scotland were informed that surveys would be more comprehensive and that TAVR and Cadet Associations should be prepared to allocate more finance to bring units up to the standard required. In some respects we proved to be closing the stable doors. In the case of Scotland all involved must share the blame for the inherent lethargy in their attitude involving security, principally the Corps, HQ Scotland, Commanders of Highland and Lowland Divisions and individual units.

My first major investigation into a Loss of Guns occurred near Inverness. Twelve .303 rifles had been stolen from a Cadet Unit. I was accompanied by the head of the area's CID, a Detective Chief Inspector. I could not argue with his local knowledge or his theory, but at the back of my mind I felt that vindictiveness was at the back of this, and that the use of a frogman in a nearby small stretch of water might reveal the weapons. The matter was totally in his hands in the follow up investigation. In my report I outlined both theories in the matter. To my knowledge the weapons were never recovered during my tenure but I was mainly interested in what procedures had not been adhered to and whether improvements could be recommended for the future.

The next loss of arms was infinitely more serious, and some days later the investigation was concluded satisfactorily, much to the relief of all concerned. The new housing conurbation of Easterhouse lies to the north-east of Glasgow and in 1968/69 it was subjected to a serious outbreak of gang warfare. It became total media headlines. The Lord Provost of Glasgow, MPs and many other civic dignitaries expressed serious concern, hoping that a death would not occur. The popular singer Frankie Vaughan, who was a champion of boys organizations, paid a visit to the area in order to negotiate between the warring factions, but whatever success he may have achieved was suddenly shattered.

My telephone rang. It was a senior Staff Officer from HQ Lowland Division. The Cadet armoury at Easterhouse had been forcibly entered and five .303 rifles and one .22 rifle plus a quantity of ammunition had been stolen. The General wanted results and a report on his desk by the next day; an SIB officer would join me later.

Entry into the Cadet compound had been easily effected. A small window had been smashed and after entry with the aid of a shovel a large hole had been made in the door of the arms chest, which was made of solid wood and several inches thick. The weapons had been easily removed as they were not chained, and the ammunition lay next to the weapons when it should have been in a separate store; there were other procedural misdemeanours. Eventually I contacted the Captain who commanded the unit. He initially refused to attend, and when he did arrive he began to verbally abuse the SIB officer and myself for our insistence. I had the greatest pleasure in reducing this loud mouthed, bombastic individual to a whining mouse. When all his administrative errors were told to him, he later resigned. I also met the very hard working, harassed head of the Divisional CID and I was very pleased for him and his colleagues that all the stolen items were subsequently recovered owing to an anonymous phone call. They deserved a break after all the hard work they had undergone plus the media and Council pressure.

Both of these serious incidents only reinforced my argument and insistence that a more comprehensive survey procedure was quickly adopted for the UK, despite the fact that the risk element concerning arms, ammunition, and classified documents was assessed as considerably lower than in other parts of the world; but it should generally be standardized. In respect of Cadet armouries throughout the UK, many are in isolated localities and it was my contention then and later that the only weapons to be held by Cadets should be Drill Purpose Weapons. Weapons required for the range should be held in a higher grade environment i.e. a TAVR Armoury, and years later the authorities in UK were attempting, without interruption of training, to bring this more acceptable procedure within the whole of the UK.

Another matter at this period of time was that of the recruitment of mercenaries and it was necessary to make enquiries in the Edinburgh area to ascertain details of named former ex Servicemen with as much background as possible. I was helped in this matter, particularly on one occasion, with the Brigade TIE. As soon as the media ran out of mileage on this matter it gradually died a death, and agencies, mainly in the South of England, either closed or reduced their activities. I think the lack of support from the agencies, and in some instances the non-payment of promised high salaries, made a lot of would-be mercenaries think again. If the truth were known a large percentage of persons showing interest in overseas employment of a military nature were military cast-offs, and would be of very doubtful reliability and competence to any worthwhile agency.

Following the last item and reading a small article in the local paper I spoke to Captain —, our resident ATO (Ammunition Technical Officer), who had been involved in making safe and removing a quantity of explosive discovered on railway property in a certain part of Scotland. The officer gave details of the incident but out of interest showed me a file that he had compiled, outlining several reports concerning him and his predecessors. All these reports involved the reporting, at times under the most bizarre circumstances, of explosives, arms and ammunition from secret dumps along the east coast and border area of Scotland. He also referred me to a book called *The Last Ditch* by David Lampe. The text of the book refers to events following the fall of France in 1940, when the British Government, fearing invasion from the Continent, authorized the formation of the Local Defence Volunteers. As an offshoot of this organization, personnel were recruited to form a nucleus of a guerilla army should the United Kingdom be occupied by German forces. Initially these potential guerillas were organized on a rather *ad hoc* basis, but they were sworn to the strictest secrecy under the Official Secrets Act; even wives and close relatives were not to be informed on any activity undertaken. Men died in later years and never disclosed any details of their proposed duties. It was only after their demise that wives then began to ask the authorities, police and ATO, to remove highly dangerous explosives, arms and ammunition, radios and so on from wartime dumps in houses, outbuildings and specially constructed hideaways in woods and fields.

The organization of this mini army was initially concentrated on the high risk areas of possible invasion, i.e. south-east England, the Kent and Sussex coasts, East Anglia, the Wash and the east of Scotland from Inverness south to the coastal areas of Northumberland. One must presume that the organizing of these activities would have been enlarged should invasion have taken place, to cover the whole of the country. However as the risk of German occupation diminished, interest was maintained by the authorities but rather superficially. They had of course been incorporated into the Home Guard, but as stated their training was mainly related to their peculiar role should the Germans invade.

At the end of the hostilities an effort was made to safely collect all the arms, ammunition, explosives and radio sets that had been issued for concealment in dumps known only to the minimum of personnel. It should be appreciated that many of these key personnel were old or unfit for military service, therefore after five years or more some of these persons were deceased or there was no record to whom the equipment etc. was originally entrusted to.

Interest in these hidden caches of arms began when in various parts of the country, mainly on farms, items were discovered in old barns or ploughed up fields. Road schemes unearthed barrels of lethal high explosives on important road junctions. As a result of these isolated discoveries the War Office made enquiries and in addition the author of the previously described book began an investigation with access to certain information held by the War Office. The most astonishing aspect of all these enquiries was the complete reluctance by the Home Guard personnel to disclose any information as to their proposed wartime role, the names of personnel, location of dumps etc. Whatever information was extracted from individuals was only obtained by persistent persuasion and explanation that the Official Secret Act was no longer relevant under these circumstances. The book was interesting and informative but, as the author relates, the facts could have been more comprehensive if all the participants interviewed had been co-operative. All credit to them, however: 'Mum's the word.'

Two fairly recent incidents had been recorded by ATO, and both concerned people who had been recently widowed. One lady wheeled a pram through the streets of a small town to the local police station; the pram was full of small arms, ammunition, and hand grenades with detonators. She told the police there was more in an attic room and that it was something to do with what her husband did in the war! The second lady called the police to her late husband's business premises, a bakery in a small Lowland town, ATO was called and to his horror in a room above the ovens was a huge haul of ammunition and explosives, with a few weapons. Some of the explosive had in fact melted and was running down the oven chimney! ATO could not believe how a disaster had been avoided.

What interested me were certain names that the book casually mentioned. These subsequently tallied with names we had on file as members of organizations of possible security interest; the implications are obvious.

Routine work continued and the standard of our basic procedures improved, consequently our installations and units appreciated that security standards were improving. They co-operated and did not hesitate to ask for our help which was readily forthcoming. By now we had a new G2 (Int), a Sapper Major who initiated a new and necessary interest from all Unit Security Officers.

In between all this activity a rather interesting case was initiated which lasted until I left to join HQ 6 Infantry Brigade who were stationed at Barnard Castle and due to leave for Germany for approximately four months training. This saga actually continued during the time I was in BAOR.

One afternoon I received a telephone call from an area south of Glasgow. Mrs S needed help and advice and could I come and see her? I agreed to do this the following day which would give me the opportunity to make some brief enquiries on background which should be available from records.

The following morning I arrived at a very pleasantly situated council house and was welcomed by Mrs S and her married daughter. She explained that the events she was about to describe were fully known to her husband and he had stated that he wished to dissociate himself completely from the situation. He was described as a person of strong principles. The three of us settled down to tea and biscuits and the background was unfolded.

In 1961 1 KOSB (Kings Own Scottish Borderers) were a regular service Battalion serving in Berlin. Private S, Mrs S's son was a member of this unit and was currently listed as a deserter and was resident in East Germany, now married with two children. A recent letter from her son gave an indication that the East German authorities were prepared to allow Pte. S to visit the UK as an individual. He wished to verify the situation concerning his desertion, possible Court Martial and imprisonment, and if the British authorities would permit his return to his wife and family. Our talk was based on these queries.

Pte. S had settled into military life quite satisfactorily, a tall, well built young man. At the time of enlistment he was inclined to shyness, did not drink and had no current girlfriend. The Army and Berlin changed all that. As he matured his confidence grew; he was an adequate soldier and on his first UK leave in early summer of 1961 he told his mother he had a girlfriend. What he omitted to tell her was that his girlfriend was a bar girl in East Berlin and this is where he had formed the relationship. It was apparent that he was infatuated with this girl, who was his first sexual experience. He produced photographs taken in the bar, one of which he left with his Mother; it was endorsed with the girls' name and, as I recall, her address. According to Pte. S's sister he had thoroughly enjoyed his first UK leave but was anxious to return to military life and his girlfriend.

When he returned to Berlin in the August of 1961, international relationships were strained between the super-powers, and East and West Germany. Soldiers were warned that the freedom they enjoyed to travel into East Germany for social purposes should be curtailed, and units therefore issued orders forbidding entry into East Berlin until the situation was rectified. Pte. S chose to ignore the order and continued to meet his girlfriend. Without warning the East German authorities sealed off the border and the isolation of communities began. The Berlin Wall was about to be erected; Pte. S was stranded. Briefly, he was arrested, and was later charged and given a twelve-month sentence of imprisonment and despite the efforts of the military, the West Berlin authorities, the Foreign Office and BRIXMIS (The British Military Mission in East Germany) the imprisonment continued. At the end of his sentence the East German authorities appeared to delay the process of his return and Pte. S rather stupidly attempted to cross the border without the necessary papers. In the argument that followed he assaulted a Police Inspector and subsequently received a further term of imprisonment of twelve months. It could be that it was during this term of imprisonment that he decided to remain in East Germany voluntarily or perhaps some persuasion was introduced. No reference was ever made concerning the bar girl.

Pte. S subsequently met and married a young lady and commenced employment, if I recall correctly, as a motor mechanic. He was placed in a comfortable flat on the outskirts of East Berlin and two children were born, a boy and a girl.

I was shown letters from Pte. S to his mother which began to arrive erratically in 1962. Not being a person of high intellect these letters were ill composed and not particularly informative, and as he began to learn the German language during his incarceration so his letters in English confusingly were written as a German would speak, as he was by now quite fluent in the language. He stated by letter that he could not leave the GDR (German Democratic Republic) but invited his mother and sister to visit him, and also extended the invitation to his brother who was a Serving

Police Officer. The mother admitted that Pte. S was aware that his father had completely disowned him. As a former military man he could not accept his son's desertion from the Army and his residence with the 'enemy'; he classed it all as disloyalty to his country.

In 1967, mother and daughter visited Pte. S, followed some time later by his brother. All described him as a happy husband and father. He had spoken of being approached by a English speaking person near his flat, who had been going through the notions of making a temporary repair to his car. He gave a name and an address in the Midlands, said he was a visitor and attempted to draw Pte. S into a general conversation. After several minutes Pte. S began to worry if this was a Security Police trick or if he was contacted by British Intelligence. He panicked and hurried home.

Within the year of 1968 Pte. S's letters to his mother became more frequent. His affection for his mother was pronounced in the text, and the possibility of permission to visit UK mentioned but he needed some reassurance. I was able to convey to him of the British authorities' lenient attitude in respect of his circumstances and urged him to take all necessary action to facilitate his departure from East Germany.

My mind was working on other things. Pte. S was either genuine and wanted to clear up his desertion, see his family and hopefully in time be able to bring his wife and children to Scotland on a visit *or* he had been briefed by the East German authorities to indulge in some minor espionage activities during his visit and this was the price he had to pay for his holiday. In addition he may have been promised further leave with his wife and then his children but probably never together; this way there would always be a 'hostage'. All these probabilities passed through my mind and when at last a date had been promised and the mother informed I submitted a report.

By midsummer of 1969 I knew I was destined to join HQ 6 Infantry Brigade at Barnard Castle and they were due to go to BAOR for prolonged training from July to November. So my report suggested that when Pte. S arrived in West Berlin his initial interview should be reasonably superficial and that on arrival in Scotland I should be sent for. With the co-operation of the mother I should be introduced as the person who was implicitly trusted by her, and he should be told that it was my involvement that had helped him with the desertion problem and other things. Then, man to man, I would want to know what prerequisites the East Germans had demanded from him. It may then have been possible for us to furnish him with some information and so eventually gain his help and co-operation for the future. If he was considered to be a bad risk maybe we could eventually, if desired, facilitate the family's transfer to the UK.

I received no reply to the report. I moved to Barnard Castle and five days later I was in Sennelager. Before we moved to Soltau, I had to help organize a Top Secret briefing to be conducted by our Commander. It was during our initial six weeks that I read a brief account in a UK newspaper to the effect that Pte. S had been sentenced to six months imprisonment in West Berlin for espionage. A brief resumé in the paper stated that Pte. S had been a deserter and to allow him to visit the UK and guarantee the safety of his wife and family, the East German Intelligence Service had tasked him in the following way. Whilst on leave in Scotland, he should visit the area of Holy Loch and endeavour to gleam information in conversation with sailors from the Nuclear Submarine Depot. When he returned to Berlin he should also attempt to obtain certain information from British soldiers stationed there, and this is when he made his mistake. Troops in Berlin are well versed in action to be taken should they suspect that they are being subjected to suspicious questioning. In this particular case the questioning was, to put it bluntly, childish and infantile. Subsequently Pte. S was arrested and he admitted all the facts. I must admit that I felt sorry for Pte. S; he was obviously a person of limited intellect, no doubt coerced into accepting his leave of absence for the minor intelligence tasks he was asked to perform and the guarantee that he could return to his family when his 'mission' was completed. I felt even sorrier for Pte. S's mother and family; they trusted me to do my best to protect this unfortunate individual who was obviously going to be used. I felt I had let them down and yet it was out of my hands.

It will no doubt never been proved, but I think that if my solution had been accepted and followed, this guileless individual would have eventually returned to Scotland and I wonder if he is unfortunately still languishing unhappily in the restrictive confines of the former East Germany.

My short tour in Scotland was rather uneventful though the unit was probably more effective and a higher standard of security awareness achieved. I had been fortunate, with the exception of the far north, to have visited a great deal of Scotland, a very beautiful country. We had spent a wonderful holiday at the Army Ski Hut near Aviemore and acquired a Golden Labrador bitch which we named Dusty. We had her for fourteen years; she was an excellent animal in every way and a great companion, especially to Chris who had a great affection for her.

With two Army friends we watched a great deal of Scottish football during the 68/69 season, and even at the age of forty-five years I played Major Unit football for HQ Scotland. This was rather disconcerting at times when you would repossess a ball after a tackle and then within yards find your seventeen or eighteen-year-old opponent facing you yet again. It became a reality about the age difference. I also represented Combined Services at cricket against St Andrews University, and HQ Scotland against a couple of other teams but Scottish weather is rarely amenable for cricket enthusiasts.

I classed this year in Scotland as a very relaxed but interesting introduction to life in UK following the years in BAOR, Cyprus, Borneo and Hong Kong.

CHAPTER 35

HQ 6 Infantry Brigade (Barnard Castle)

6 Brigade was a rather unique formation which had previously been stationed in Germany, were now resident in the Catterick area of Yorkshire and still had a BAOR emergency commitment with certain equipment held in reserve and a rapid redeployment plan in operation. On receipt of my posting and immediate promotion I visited HQ 6 Brigade to meet staff and members of my unit, discuss the role and arrange accommodation. I was also told that within days of joining I would leave for Germany for approximately five months.

In order to facilitate a 'quick getaway' the colleague I was to relieve ensured that a house in Churchill Road, Barnard Castle was available for me. If he knew there were problems he ignored them when he accepted the house, because the previous occupant, a former soldier, had had to be evicted. It was dirty and untidy, carpets were stained and there were holes in some interior doors. My erstwhile colleague, following our rapid unit handover, made good his escape before I saw the house. Jean was obviously upset, the Housing Commandant apologised for the action of his staff and promised me all the help he could offer. Eventually, during my absence abroad, Jean's persistence ensured that all the obvious repairs, exchanges, and complete re-decoration were completed. These houses were rented from the local Council and they were disgraceful in their design and situation. However we enjoyed the area in our free time, we made friends outside the Army, the journey to Preston could be achieved in a couple of hours, and we also spent another enjoyable holiday at the Army Ski Hut at Glenmore near Aviemore.

In between the arguments about the house I had to prepare to move my unit and make hurried preparation for a very high level briefing that was to take place when we were at Sennelager and for which 6 Brigade were responsible for the presentation. Needless to say my colleague had made little preparation for this, especially as it was classified TOP SECRET. The whole of BAOR's senior ranks were involved and I was responsible for the safe custody en route of all relevant documents, plus the temporary housing in the Secure complexes of Nuclear and Signal Units when the documents were not in use. 6 Bde were to use the excellent facilities of the Sennelager training area for six weeks to enable our Infantry and Gunner Units to practise preparatory field training and live firing, then move to the Soltau training area where exercises as a Brigade would take place until late November when the three Infantry and the Gunner Regiments would return to UK.

Now to personalities. The Brigade Commander was General Scott Barratt, a former Scots Guards officer who extended a warm welcome. His Brigade Major was a competent, demanding but charming officer. All the other Staff Officers on the Operations and Quartermaster's staff were helpful and greeted me warmly. However the two officers with whom I would work most closely were the most unco-operative, demanding, unhelpful individuals I met during my service with the Corps! The responsibilities, control and employment of Intelligence Corps personnel attached to Formations was laid down by an Order promulgated by HQ Intelligence and Security Group (BAOR) which was specific in its contents. It was obvious that these two officers, the OC of the Brigade Signal Squadron (Major), and the GIII (Intelligence), a Captain, were unaware of the document or chose to ignore it. The former was newly appointed and intended to create the right impression to everyone in the Headquarters; in this he failed miserably and during my year with the HQ this charming but misguided officer antagonised a large percentage of the personnel which affected atmosphere of the Headquarters. The GIII (Int) was due to leave the Headquarters on return from Germany and he intended to leave in a blaze of glory, and our small unit was to be used to ensure his Confidential Report was excellent, irrespective of the orders contained in the edict issued to formations by Intelligence and Security Group (BAOR).

To continue this sad saga, both these officers within their own spheres of responsibility attempted to employ me in particular and my unit as well, in jobs outside our responsibilities. We were a very convenient asset to them and also removed in many ways, without consultation, my authority. I had the responsibility for personnel of an attached unit that had a certain expertise to offer the Commander and his staff; we were not to be misemployed, hence the reason for the order. My predecessor had made no attempt to protect his personnel from unnecessary interference, and I spent the next twelve months in a never ending battle ensuring that my unit did the job they were trained to do and were not to be the dogsbodies of any officer or senior rank who desired a job done. Sadly, in the case of the G3 (Int) during a period at Soltau he treated us quite disgracefully and in private we came close to violence, and he backed down. This seemed to clear the air and in the final days and weeks his attitude changed for the better.

All this had stemmed from yet another altercation with the OC Signal Squadron who, with the connivance of the G3 (Int), detailed me to do a specific movement job which was the responsibility of a Signal Squadron senior rank. Again I had to protest as I had my own work to deal with, and my protest was upheld. It was such an unnecessary state of affairs: everyone has a job to do and this stupid interference just affected my unit's morale and efficiency and I was not prepared to accept any individual's quest for 'Brownie points' on the backs of the personnel of my unit. I knew I was in the right and was prepared to stick my neck out. During the arduous months in Germany and at home we did our job well with no complaints. The lads were clean, tidy and efficient; I only had cause to discipline one soldier for not shaving, otherwise they were a good and willing team.

So with the minimum of preparation we packed and commenced the movement in pre-arranged 'Packets', first staying at Colchester, then taking the ferry from Harwich to Europort then the long road journey to Sennelager. On arrival it doesn't take long to settle in, as every field soldier is aware. The TOP SECRET documents were deposited in the secure room of one of the Royal Artillery Nuclear Regiments and for the next six weeks we prepared for the classified briefing and numerous other tasks. The weather was in the main sunny and warm, despite the occasional interference I settled in well and our work was never questioned. Our hours were long but full of interest.

As a break I was visited by Pat and Jack Pitt, Royal Military Police friends from Minden days. They were currently stationed at HQ 4 Division at Herford and I spent at least a couple of weekends with them and was treated, like always, as one of the family. The classified briefing passed without problems; the Staff including ourselves were congratulated so my initiation was successful.

The move to Soltau was uneventful yet again we settled in very quickly. The whole Brigade with the exception of our affiliated Armoured Regiment were allocated space on this vast area of flat ground. A collection of buildings in the shape of a U held the offices of the Brigade Staff, my little outfit and the RMP Unit. During the week our hours were long but weekends were relatively quiet.

One evening with two other Senior Ranks we walked for a few kilometres along an adjacent country road in search of a convenient Gasthaus. When we found one a notice on the door stated 'Out of Bounds', but taking a chance we entered and were served. When the premises appeared to be ready for closure we quietly paid the bill. The landlord came to the door with us and said in English, 'You gentlemen are welcome any time,' and smiled. So for the next few weeks when on free time we would saunter down the road and enjoy the pleasant atmosphere and chat to the locals; it was a welcome break. In fact on the Sunday when the German elections took place one rather large gentleman took the three of us to a large Schloss to meet some friends, then on to another lively Gasthaus where we were royally entertained. The three of us were definitely under the weather by the end of the evening, made more hilarious when our friend insisted he would take us back to camp in his Volkswagen. We returned to our normal Gasthaus, had another drink and when we came to enter the car, sitting on the back seat was an enormous German Shepherd dog who eyed us up most curiously. My two companions, although not as heavy as our German friend weighed in at fifteen or sixteen stone apiece. The dog would not move off the back seat despite the commands of its master, it really was a laugh; the dog behaved impeccably. We filled our friend up with whisky in our Mess and, despite offers, he insisted that he would drive himself home. It was a great day.

The final Exercise was long and arduous and all my lads did well. I even received an apology from the G3 (Int) who was about to leave and rejoin his Regiment. He had had a drink and the gesture, although accepted, did not change my opinion of him; he was indiscriminate and unreasonable in his use of us: we were a springboard for his future and final report. On completion of the Exercise the tedious job of packing up and leaving the area began and we as the Headquarters Staff were among the last to leave. It was now mid November and I can assure you that the Soltau Plain is not the warmest of places to sleep outdoors at that time of the year but for the last couple of days we had to exist on the bare essentials. The long tedious journey to Europort began. Staying overnight at RAF Bruggen, the following day we continued into Holland, loaded the vehicles on board the ferry and I very sensibly, having driven all the way from Soltau, went to bed. My last recollection before sleep was a violent 45° list to starboard as we left Europort and entered the North Sea. What I didn't know was that a Force 10 gale was forecast and did occur, but I blissfully slept throughout until we arrived at Hull in bright early morning sunshine and a calm sea. Home again, a quieter routine then existed, Christmas came and went and I commenced the year as President of the Warrant Officers and Sergeants Mess (PMC).

For the next six or seven months I visited Germany each month on various matters which kept me very busy. My lads were extremely reliable and carried on with the normal tasks they had to perform. The new G3

(Int) did not interfere with them and as long as they did the work that he required he was more than content.

I must now recount a matter that occurred when I and five other senior Corps Warrant Officers who commanded Formation Intelligence Sections attended a Seminar at Bielefeld. It was highly classified and the remainder of the audience consisted of American, British and Canadian formation and unit commanders and the officers commanding Intelligence Units in their respective formations. We six Warrant Officers sat some rows behind this large gaggle of officers. One of our group I had known well for a long time but I always had the feeling that he considered me as a rival as we had joined the Corps at approximately the same time. I suppose in terms of job experience I was far ahead. I didn't really consider this but I think he did.

Throughout the day various speakers covered the whole gamut of Operational Intelligence involving the Russian and East German military forces facing 1 British Corps and some Counter Intelligence aspects. Emphasis was placed on our existing defensive plans in order to contest the calculated intelligence appraisal of the enemy's intended advance into West Germany. The appraisal and the main plan had been in existence for some time approaching twenty years with some minor alterations made by individual Commanders with the advent of new equipment, or his personal preference for defending particular areas of ground. With 11 Brigade at Minden I spent many hours in the Operations Room with General King who used to throw problems at me which I would answer, then he would shoot me down in a constructive manner, because with a grin he would tell me of alterations by other formations etc. which of course I was unaware of. I had a better understanding of high level thinking because of these 'contests'; I found them interesting, beneficial and stimulating. The General placed great trust in his staff, and rank made no difference to him.

Therefore when question time arrived in the late afternoon I was hoping that some senior officer would have the courage to stand up and present alternatives. Views and questions were tendered by officers of all three Armies, and by this time I had made up my mind that I would offer an alternative for consideration. I had the feeling that it would cause some derision and scepticism. When the senior officer in charge asked for further questions, none was offered, so I stood up.

As I started to speak, because of my accent, the whole of the officer audience turned round to gaze at the interloper. My 'rival' sitting in front of me had an amused and cynical smile on his face, and after the first few words I felt that a large hole was appearing in the floor below me and I was about to fall in it. I can assure you that to be placed in that position is extremely embarrassing, and your initial reaction is to crawl away and die.

After the first couple of sentences I began to establish my confidence. Some of my colleagues started to nod in agreement, the more sceptical and amused officers had already turned round and faced the stage, though a small complement still gazed at me. After some minutes I had stated historical and practical facts in my argument, also current changes in Soviet Army Tactical Training which every army engages in, very often enforced by political and fiscal priorities. There were also some international connotations of a possible embarrassing nature which certain people would hesitate to comment on.

With a dry throat and damp armpits and crotch I sat down. Four of my colleagues turned and smiled encouragingly, my 'rival' sat without comment; from the audience at the front rose a cacophony of verbosity which continued until the senior Intelligence Staff Officer in charge called order. I must confess I was ready for the axe to fall and that I would be dismissed with ignominy.

'Gentlemen despite your obvious comments, I must inform you that some two weeks ago the Commander BAOR was asked to consider at the request of his two senior Generals *a situation as proposed by the previous speaker,* and serious consideration would be given to all the facts as given.'

A high note of comment from the assembled officers then ensued. Some turned round to gaze in my direction. Was this in amazement or incredibility at my humble perception of a situation that in some aspects had troubled two senior British Army Generals and I, as a mere Warrant Officer, had put forward a comprehensive case to change the whole concept of the defensive plan of the whole of NATO forces, because one weak limb could affect the plans of the American and Canadian formations. I experienced a great feeling of relief, later followed by silent elation, the four colleagues nudged and smiled encouragingly, the fifth looked straight ahead and made no comment. Some weeks later the HQ staff plus my Int/NBC Cell set up stall in a designated area with other similar Formation groups in order to carry out a top level NATO Staff Exercise in Germany following my return to UK. After my assessment of a change of British plans, I made an additional indent for certain maps as a matter of urgency in anticipation of a radical change of strategy, and subsequent events proved me right.

Some quarter of an hour before the Exercise was due to commence our maps etc. had been marked accordingly to our existing knowledge, when the order came over the radio for our whole area of operations to be changed, which was exactly what the two Generals and I had considered in our submissions. I had taken a chance and made several additional 'runs' of maps. It was therefore a relatively simple job to make the necessary adjustments to our Staff maps and within ten minutes we were way ahead of all the other Staffs in our readiness to proceed. HQ 6 Brigade could afford to smirk.

By this time it had been decided that as the Canadians had opted out of the orbit of 1 (British) Corps to join the Americans, 6 Brigade should return to Germany and take over the various Barrack and Married Quarter accommodation to be vacated by the Canadians. I was not bothered about returning to the routine of BAOR and I was quite pleased when someone else wished to undergo another foreign tour and I was asked to replace an old colleague, Pat Patrick, as the Staff Instructor to the Reserve Interrogation Company who had a BAOR commitment. Pat was leaving on promotion to HQ Intelligence Centre. During our year in 'Barny' I spent at least seven months in Germany which from Jean's point of view was quite unsatisfactory, and she was pleased that we could look forward to a settled life for at least two years with only infrequent foreign trips.

Barnard Castle is a pleasant place to live, Darlington and Richmond were within easy reach for shopping and we enjoyed pleasant walks in the area, which is quite picturesque, but Jean hated all my absences.

Carolyn had passed her 11 plus, and Christopher's boarding school was about to close at the end off his 'O' Level exams, so with his agreement we were fortunate to obtain a transfer to the De La Salle College at Southsea which turned out to be an excellent move. Within six months he was a Prefect, played Rugby for Hampshire under 19s, and accordingly he forged ahead in leaps and bounds. His reports were very good and encouraging; as I recall he also acquired a girlfriend, probably his first. So we began to pack and prepare ourselves for the interest and excitement of our capital city.

CHAPTER 36

22 Interrogation Coy, London 1970-73

The arrangements to facilitate my move to London progressed extremely well. As I was was replacing a former colleague I had worked with before, our personal handover should present no problems and it didn't. The house at 213 Long Bridge Road, Barking, that my colleague had occupied would be taken over by me. It was not ideal but clean and adequate; it later presented certain problems but we coped. A great deal of work was done in the large garden but I enjoyed that and my outdoor tomatoes were extremely successful. My colleague's posting was to the Intelligence Centre, his family moved out, we moved in and the handover at Barnard Castle presented no headaches and that was the biggest hurdle completed. Local shopping was adequate, we registered with a dentist and an excellent Polish doctor. Two Catholic churches were within a mile of us, so I was ready to start.

22 Interrogation Company was a Reserve Army Unit with a most unusual training role and its recruitment status likewise. Under the wing of MI9 its role was to form and train Interrogation Teams to support the various formations stationed in Germany and also to afford training support to JSIU (Joint Services Interrogation Unit) in the training of the SAS, SBS, other specialist units and aircrew, in Escape Evasion, and Resistance to Interrogation. We also had an exchange programme with personnel from the Dutch School of Military Intelligence at Harderwijk. Our two visits and exercises at Lydd and in Holland were successful and most enjoyable. During the year we also enjoyed several weekends at the Army School of Languages, Beaconsfield, taking advantage of their excellent facilities for our Russian and German speakers.

In the few days before he left my colleague explained the rudiments of the job, and as is my wont I asked all the wrong questions. The answers I received were, 'Oh they won't do that,' 'You can't insist on that,' etc. I formed the opinion that if the job was to be done properly I was about to ruffle a few feathers and my forecast proved to be correct. I had worked with Reserve Army Units in the field and admired their dedication and enthusiasm, but in the UK their attitude to security matters was often misguided and considered a hindrance, so to actually train and administer an unusual unit of this nature was about to require a great deal of patience, tact, diplomacy and firmness.

Our Group was divided into three Companies: Photographic Interpretation, Counter Intelligence and Interrogation, the whole commanded by a regular Lt. Colonel assisted by a Training Major. A specialist Warrant Officer was the Staff Instructor for P1; a regular Captain supervised the other two. I was the Staff Instructor for Interrogation, two regular NCOs assisted in the clerical and Stores support with a regular Captain Quartermaster; civilian clerks, typists, drivers and cleaners made up the remainder. The P1 Coy was based in Birmingham, therefore many of our personnel had considerable distances to travel for training on evenings and weekends. Each member had a training commitment to fulfil. When I started to check this, certain anomalies were revealed and when I began to insist on compliance, this is when a small percentage of ill trained linguists left us; they were not missed.

We had two Majors as OC and 2 I/C. The former was a senior 'Whitehall Warrior' who owing to commitments had to resign a few months after my arrival. His replacement during my time was an academic at a military establishment who was also a very charming and competent person. The contribution of the 2 I/C was very limited. He was a 'fiscal Civil Servant' and his great claim to fame was that he had never trained abroad with the unit because his wife would not let him! What would have happened in the event of war? I soon began to categorise personnel as follows:

1) The large percentage who were natural volunteers, excellent soldiers, keen, dedicated, willing to train, help and serve.
2) Those who were not necessarily excellent soldiers, but who could fault their enthusiasm and dedication?
3) The odd ones who had ability, produced limited commitment, enjoyed the rank and its status! 'Could do better.'
4) Those with limited ability, no moral fibre, no commitment, untrustworthy, enjoyed rank and status.

I like to think that during my time all the ones in Category 4 left, and they were not missed. As the unit was made up mainly of officers one needed to physically encourage them to become actively involved in the preparation for the various home and overseas exercises we were involved in. They appeared to consider that linguistic skills were of sole importance, but a live Interrogator has got to be in the right location to be effective and should be capable of a team effort of self preservation and sufficiency.

With this in mind training changed with the OCs blessing. We won the Annual Company Competition two years running which involved other skills, more field exercises were composed by me and everybody loved it; it was fun and totally different and we usually had 100 per cent turnout. It was hard work for me but appreciated and well worthwhile. It was normal procedure for our unit to be invited to Germany to partake in a particular BAOR field exercise. This formed the basis of the two weeks Annual Camp. Those who were committed elsewhere had to be found a suitable alternative; this was always a problem but somehow we managed. As previously mentioned we also had a exchange visit and exercise with the Dutch, which required a great deal of work, administration and socializing in UK.

Our main exercise commitments concerned the contribution to JSIU, when with our assistance we were involved with the SAS, SBS, other specialist troops and RN, RAF aircrew. This took us to various UK venues and countries overseas. It was very time consuming for me but what never failed to amaze me was the fact that volunteers always filled our vacancies when they were required and most of them held very responsible positions in life. This type of person was the backbone of the Reserve Army. I felt I must give them 110 per cent support; they were wonderful people and hopefully this high percentage runs through the whole of the Reserve Army. (One volunteer is worth ten pressed men.)

When I was at home I left the house at 7.45a.m. each day and walked the mile to Barking Station, catching the special train on the Metropolitan Line to Kings Cross, then had a short walk to Bloomsbury. Finishing around 5p.m. the journey home, usually standing, was made in reverse order with the exception of Wednesday (a work night). The ten-mile journey by car was quite horrendous and could take over an hour and a half; this was only attempted at the weekend. To work in London is an endurance test in itself, I would not have enjoyed a lifetime of its miseries.

The first Christmas came and went. By now I had experienced all the problems and matters were beginning to change for the better; it was almost as though they all felt that I was really taking a serious interest in them (no reflection on my predecessors) but you really do have to show that sort of enthusiasm for their training when it becomes contagious. Doing enough is not sufficient for Volunteers, you must go over the top: then you achieve the results.

An interesting matter that occasionally occurred was the use of our premises by the following organizations for rehearsals: the BBC, ITV, Doyly Carte Opera Company and others. I did not realize what it entailed: both entertainment and annoyance. The first rehearsal I experienced was my favourite opera, *Carmen*, and the heroine was played by a delightful and diminutive Chinese lady with a lovely voice. However she was 'dwarfed' by the demeanour of the producer, a 'gay' blade with an 'on the shoulder' sheepskin coat. Shod in patent leather shoes with large silver buckles he 'pounced' up and down on a sagging Army six-foot table berating the cast with crude verbal abuse and stamping his immaculate footwear on the bending woodwork which everyone hoped would crack. Before the Colonel moved his office to the other Centre I had an office adjacent to the Main Hall and the singing was superb. I'd lay down my pen, close my eyes and thoroughly enjoy the artistes and chorus. It became annoying when voices were raised and artistic temperament prevailed, and it was not unusual to walk through the Hall to be confronted with a nubile young lady disrobing to bra and pants in order to 'slip into something more comfortable' for a five or six-hour rehearsal. The first time it was embarrassing but no one took notice so neither did I; showbiz people do not hold any inhibitions about being seen by the opposite sex in a state of undress.

The move to get rid of the 'dead legs' started when I began to check attendances at Annual Camp and training sessions and as I recall a carefully composed letter was sent to those concerned who with one exception reluctantly resigned. The odd one out suddenly attended two conveniently located exercises, left before time, falsified his claim forms which I refused to endorse (it is a Court Martial Offence) and then also resigned. We then began to recruit more linguists both young and old, who with one exception were welcome additions. I believe that now the recruitment of female linguists has been approved and I have no doubt they will enjoy the experience.

I shall now describe certain incidents that occurred on our various exercises and 'jaunts' both here and abroad. I did not travel to BAOR in 1970 because I had only arrived a few days before so the Annual Camp party departed with my colleague and I got my feet under the table, but some weeks later I and a small party crossed by Channel ferry to Belgium where we manned an Interrogation Centre with 21 SAS (TA) as 'Runners'. Our Belgian hosts as always made us extremely welcome and the Exercise was a success over the three days. The only black mark concerned a regular 22 SAS NCO (Signals) who was found drunk and unconscious on the open road in the barracks and was returned to unit *immediately*; that sort of conduct is not tolerated. It was also a parents' Open Day in the Barracks.

We next held a Company Exercise over three days in the old Intelligence Centre at Maresfield, Sussex, written by the regular Training Officer and our OC. This was to exercise personnel in night navigation, setting up in the field, self sufficiency and some interrogation. This was the first time I had had the opportunity of observing how they coped. Early on the Saturday morning the first visitor was the CO who visited the five small locations within the Camp area and he really got aboard the OC about what he had found and he wanted an improvement. By lunchtime, when I visited, it was just as bad. Although not my job I had to chase them to obtain some resemblance of cleanliness and order at each location. On the Sunday morning, as the Exercise finished, I and another officer stripped to the waist to wash and shave under running water. No one had properly slept or removed clothing since Friday, and I was quite disgusted to observe that a large percentage of personnel without removing any clothing just splashed some water on their face and that was their morning toilet. Some didn't even attempt to clean their teeth.

On our return to London I was present at the de-briefing. Various comments were made by supervising officers but were lacking in constructiveness and criticism, At the end I was unexpectedly asked to comment. My speech contained praise and some criticism, but at the end I had to make a most important point about personal hygiene, plus cleanliness and order when in location. You cannot criticize without example so I had to describe the problems of living in trenches, in the back of a Land Rover or AFV 432 or a barn, and the importance of organization to ensure the safety of issued stores and personal kit. Then came the crunch. I described the early morning scene of personal cleanliness. It was then necessary to describe the problems of an infantryman with probably only a mess tin of water to shave and wash in, how I used to insist, where possible, that my Platoon always stripped off to adequately clean themselves: they smelt fresh and importantly it boosted morale despite living conditions. I also described my own personal problems in Cyprus and Borneo and latterly on the Chinese border. I closed by saying I did not wish to see this morning's disgraceful conduct ever repeated; I saluted and left. Later one of the Captains, a barrister, said, 'Eric, that should have been said years ago, you were so right. You've offended a lot of people but don't worry about it.' He was joined by three or four others who all agreed. However the OC was not amused; he said it was his job to criticize, not mine, and he thought my comments were rude and uncalled for. I think this charming gentleman was smarting from the CO's comments early on the Saturday, and I had more forcibly rubbed salt in the wound. He knew I was right but he was too nice a person to offend. Unfortunately you cannot command without offending; we agreed to differ, but my suggestion to incorporate some of my criticisms into future training was agreed.

On the next Range weekend in bivouacs we had early morning PT and a run, the use and cooking of ten-man food packs etc. Thus began the more practical and down to earth side of soldiering, hard to inflict on part time officers, well educated and holding senior positions in professions such as civil service, law, industry and commerce. It's difficult to inform a person that if he doesn't learn to fend for himself he could starve and become ill.

Following this I wrote a weekend exercise that by night map reading would take them from London to the south of Kent calling at several check points en route. On arrival at the training area the various teams would be allocated an area to set up camp. Certain tasks had to be performed; an 'enemy' camp had to be approached and observed by day and night and mobile sentries would be in the area. This would be followed by an early morning attack on the 'enemy'. Lots of little things did go wrong, I was not attempting to create an infantryman, but as Intelligence officers and NCOs, they had to appreciate what it was like to crawl through mud and undergrowth, to be accurate in their observations and make decisions on future action. On completion one Captain said he hadn't enjoyed a weekend like that since he joined and he was one of Category 2. All of them stated they would like repeat weekends when possible.

Our home weekend with the Dutch was held in a part of Lydd Camp. Social activities had been arranged before and after the exercise which I helped to organize with our Training Captain who had sole responsibility. His exercise was totally linguistic, the prisoners did not 'run', all were Russian speakers, they had a brief and the idea was to extract information from them, they would only offer token resistance. The weather was kind and the exercise a success. I made friends with the senior Dutch Warrant Officer who really enjoyed his evenings in an English pub. The bulk of the Dutch party were Russian language graduates undergoing military service and they thoroughly enjoyed themselves 'off the leash'.

My participation the following year in Holland was purely as a visitor. I literally had nothing to do but supervise. Our participants were all Russian speaking officers and I shared a room with one of our Captains, a barrister; we also had some German Officers taking part. My Dutch friend was responsible for my activities, an interesting tour of the School and its history, an evening on the town and one at his nearby home. On completion of the Exercise each one of our party had escorts of two students and we were taken to Amsterdam. After a visit to the local Amstel Brewery and an excellent liquid lunch we had a waterborne trip around the harbour and were deposited for our evening meal in Canalstrasse, Amsterdam's den of iniquity. Needless to say the evening was highly amusing and quite an eye opener for my companion who had never been exposed to the seamier side of life or the individuals that made it up. Apart from the occasional break to partake in liquid refreshment we sauntered around the area for about 2½ hours until our escorts took us back to Hadervidj. We witnessed a knife attack, various fistic assaults and, more alarmingly, the drunken negotiations with the 'ladies of the night'. Some walked the streets but others displayed themselves behind windows, reclining on a chaise longue wearing attractive but tantalizing clothing. My companion was absolutely captivated with the atmosphere, I know Jean used to feel the same when we walked through Soho in the days before we were married; areas like that the world over seem to generate a compelling atmosphere. So it was with some reluctance that my companion came back with us, it had been a most interesting day.

One thing I found of interest on the journey to Amsterdam was some enormous plants growing on reclaimed land from the Zyder Zee. These were being harvested and roots and stubble burned. I was informed that the plants were sown annually over a period of six to eight years and when harvested were used as cattle feed, but the most important fact was that this plant extracted the salt from the former sea bed, and when the residual soil was pronounced clean a more valuable crop could be grown for a country where land available for arable crops or horticulture was at a premium. I suppose in the fullness of time that in order to satisfy the necessity of feeding and housing an increasing population the whole of this area could be reclaimed. Necessity creates inventiveness.

On return I attended one of our 'Sessions' with 22 SAS, and during a long break in the proceedings I was sitting in the Interrogators' rest area idly browsing through a book concerning life in the southern states of America: plantations, sex, bosses, blacks and so on, and was later joined by other colleagues. The boss came in and said, 'Mr Howard we have one of our American friends who has less than an hour left. [Runners could only be interrogated for a specified length of time] He's done extremely well; see what you can do in the time remaining.'

Contacting the Guard Commander I requested the prisoner by number, and the guards duly brought in, rather roughly, this tall hooded figure, dressed in shirt and trousers, bare footed. The slightly bent body shook with the cold and muscle strain of standing rigidly for long periods. The body reacted even more violently to the heat of the room and it was some minutes before I sat him on his stool and removed his hood. The eyes told you a great deal. He gazed at me through tired eyes that were filled with loathing and hate, his close cropped hair was dirty; the handsome face below was unshaven and showed strain. He identified himself with a pronounced southern accent but refused to answer subsequent questions. I went hard and soft, persuasive then demanding. I never stopped talking but kept my voice even. It was then noticed his eyelids were drooping; the necessity for sleep was overtaking his resistance. I then had an idea, remembering the book I had been reading a couple of hours earlier. Quietly leaving my chair I sat down behind him and quietly spoke his Christian name. He raised himself up but had trouble opening his eyes.

'Just imagine, it's a warm summer's night, the moon is shining through the trees, the crickets are noisy and you are relaxing quietly among the cushions on a comfortable chair. On a nearby table close to hand is a tall glass filled with iced John Collins, on the outside of the glass the condensation wets your fingers.' (More was said but I can't remember.) I waited a few seconds, 'Would you like a John Collins?'

He turned his head towards me and with pleading eyes, through dry lips, he gazed up to my face and said, 'Oh Christ, yes.'

For a few seconds there was silence. His face contorted with unrestrained anger; he half rose in his stool and cried 'You bastard!' Five little words but a crack had been opened and he knew it. I talked for the remainder of the allotted time. The only response I got was a face full of anger and hate. Placing the hood on his head I called for the guards who took him away. Some time later I was walking down the passageway with my completed Interrogation report when the American accompanied by my 'boss' faced me, he had been de-briefed. With a huge grin on his face he grabbed my hand, shook it, and slapped me across the shoulder.

'Christ, man, you really got me going then; thank God it's over; thank you very much,' and picking up his kit he strode jauntily out of the building. The 'boss' and I looked at each other and grinned; the chap was 'one tough cookie'. But what would have happened if he had been held longer? He was a member of the famous Green Berets.

That year I did another SAS trip, to Denmark. During the setting up stage I was talking to a senior Danish Air Force Officer about Hans Toksvig and my inability to contact him. This gentleman then proceeded to trace and contact Hans' former home and the new occupant; he then traced an uncle of Hans in Copenhagen who gave him an address in New York I should contact. In fact my efforts to establish correspondence failed as my letters were returned 'No longer at this address'. Through the help of the Danish Embassy in London I have since traced Hans. It transpires that Hans and Sidsell were divorced and the farm sold. Hans had a brother who was a very well known TV personality, 'The Richard Dimbleby of Denmark' as he was known, and he was based in New York and this is where Hans joined him, no doubt to assist him and carry out research.

When the brother died Hans returned to Denmark. He re-married, and is now resident near Copenhagen.

Returning to the SAS trip. The flights were by RAF Beverly aircraft and not particularly comfortable, but the job itself was a success. We were based on a Danish Air Force airfield and although the general area was relatively flat it was attractive with small inland areas of water. After a particularly busy and tiring night, one of our senior officers and I began an early morning stroll round a small lake just as the sun was beginning to rise and remove the coolness from the dawn air. This officer, who held a most important position with a well known firm in the City and later commanded the unit, turned to me and said, 'I know you may find this difficult to understand, Mr Howard, especially as a regular soldier and with your background and experience, but you have no idea of the great deal of personal satisfaction and achievement I derive from carrying out work like this. Thankfully I am not alone. It also gives my private life and work a more balanced prospective and I think I am a better person for this experience; can you understand this?'

My reply is inconsequential; maybe it was the early morning tranquillity that initiated such a profound statement. Although not quoted verbatim, certainly not wishing to be patronizing, I felt rather uplifted. Here was someone speaking on behalf of the Reserve Army; all these people who at times disrupt their family life, devote spare time, are sometimes physically extended and even injured for the possible defence of their country, deserve great credit for 100 per cent commitment.

The amusing side of this trip was the amount of pornographic literature (freely purchased in local shops) that suddenly appeared in rest areas and the size of personal hand luggage suddenly increased. As I recall when we arrived back in UK, the Customs enforced some confiscation, which was no bad thing.

An idea had been floating through my mind for some months that I would like to test not only my own Interrogators but those of JSIU, in a more investigative area of Interrogation. The whole idea is the acquisition of information. The questioning of personnel who have been well trained to resist Interrogation, in my estimation, is not conducive to enhancing the expertise of an Interrogator. I considered that apart from various ploys and a penchant for inane verbosity, this type of training was non-productive but necessary to train the specialized servicemen involved. Bearing all this in mind I offered for consideration an exercise that should encourage the Interrogators to ask questions appertaining to a set of circumstances outlined in a terrorist plot. I wrote individual briefs for each person who had to be questioned. The persons, who were volunteers from 22 Company, were given briefs early, to ensure they played the role fully, and told that they should not impart any information unless the correct questions were asked. All the Interrogators were handed the scenario outlining how a vehicle was involved in an accident in London. The driver of the vehicle was slightly injured; other passengers in the vehicle ran away from the scene. When the Police examined the vehicle documentation, arms and explosives were found. Subsequently the driver and his companions were arrested and the Interrogators had to take it from there. Others briefs were available as the plot progressed which would eventually lead the Interrogators to a 'safe house' in the Kent countryside.

All my 'actors' read the plot and their briefs. They were more than happy and enthusiastic about the roles they had to play. It made sense to them and gave them latitude to act a part. We had the 'bugged' rooms, tape recorders and Control, and at 9a.m. on the Sunday I gave the collection of Navy, Army and Air Force officers a short briefing on the initial circumstances, told them to extract as much information as possible from the prisoners about background and future intentions and told them to get on with it. By the end of the day, much to the annoyance and chagrin of the 'actors', the amount of information extracted from them was negligible and they thought it was disgraceful and lacked expertise. This proved my point; the fact that a person was a competent linguist did not necessarily make him a good interrogator. Needless to say you can imagine the reaction I got when the officers were de-briefed; all they had to do was to ask basic relevant questions, and when answered this would have led to further information: a very disappointing exercise but it gave a lot of people food for thought about the standard of training required by our 'experts'.

It was around this time when our premises were fire bombed. My office was adjacent to the main door, and on the other side was an indication board, on which was mentioned 22 Interrogation Company. The perpetrators had obviously not done their homework correctly. They fortunately chose the corresponding window to mine. The petrol bomb was thrown through a window, and the subsequent fire damaged curtains, carpet and the decorations. More than one person was seen running away from the scene, the fire was extinguished and a police enquiry commenced. The offending sign was removed, 'Closing the stable door.' The remedial action was to black out the lower parts of the windows to prevent pedestrians observing the interior of the premises from the surrounding pavement!

Our next 'job' with 22 SAS took us to France where we would be based at the French Army's Parachute School, adjacent to the lovely town of Pau in Southern France facing the Pyrenees. The SAS Advance Party commanded by the Second in Command and our party assembled at an RAF Station in southern England and flew directly to Pau. We were met by representatives of the resident Parachute Battalion and an officer of the Black Watch who acted as a Liaison Officer; he may have been a Military Attaché but I am not sure. After a meal both parties separated to commence our various administrative tasks before our support personnel arrived and the Exercise started. As guests of the French Army all our food was accompanied by a red wine of rather 'rough' vintage, and after the initial rush of blood to the head by all our personnel I was left with four water jerricans (20 gallons) of 'Rotgut'. This was accepted by two of the Rear Party travelling back to UK by road who declared it to Customs and enjoyed free booze for some time.

During World War 2 an escape route was established for airmen who had been shot down, escaped prisoners of war, or other servicemen attempting to reach the safety of neutral Spain. It was the intention of the 'Runners' from 22 SAS that they should attempt to complete the final stage through Southern France to the Spanish border. To make matters more difficult, in addition to French Army Paras and Foreign Legion troops, the local Police and the Guard Mobile, the local media urged the population within a specified area to report anything suspicious to the authorities. A large number of dogs were brought in to assist in anticipated searches. It was going to be an extremely difficult area of ground to traverse and a high proportion of 'candidates' was to be expected.

In the days prior to the commencement of the Exercise we watched with interest the almost continuous dropping of sticks of twenty parachutists throughout the daylight hours. In this particular area of France an average of three hundred 'jumping' days were possible, idyllic conditions. In a subsequent conversation with the Commanding Officer of the French Parachute Battalion, an officer and myself were given the opportunity to complete the necessary number of jumps in two days and if successful be awarded our French parachute wings. Unfortunately the Black Watch officer heard of the arrangement and expressly forbade it as we would not be covered by insurance should either of us suffer any injury. Although very disappointed the cancellation was no doubt to our benefit, but I would have liked to have sneaked one in.

The Exercise as such was a great success. All personnel involved were kept busy, the SAS troops involved gave everyone a good run for their money and I'm sure they derived great benefit from the experience. An extremely sad incident occurred at the conclusion of the Exercise when following the final de-briefing and assessment the Second in Command of 22 SAS was driving back to his HQ when he was killed outright in a tragic road accident: a rather sad end to what had been a most successful Exercise.

At this stage I must mention the Company success in the Group competition, which consisted of various written and practical skills plus a Drill Display by the three teams. Since its conception our Company, despite the academic quality of its members, had failed miserably. It was time to change this so a 'pep talk' was given and our training programme was adapted to achieve success. Enthusiasm and keenness was evident and I was asked to concentrate on the Drill aspect. On every available free period I gathered my motley crew, gently chased them around, then paid attention to the very basics of military drill that I had been successful with, in my Regiment and at Mons OCS. With some coercion mixed with praise the collective change was quite amazing in a very short time. I had to 'chivvy' the Company Sergeant Major with his words of command; other than that everyone worked hard and I knew we would win the Drill. Supervising the other aspects I was also encouraged, and it therefore came as no surprise when on the Sunday afternoon of the Group Camp 22 Company were announced as overall winners. This came as quite a surprise to many people and to rub it in we did it again the following year.

As the only qualified Range Officer in the Group at that time I organized the various practices for pistol and sub machine guns, delegating responsible officers to supervise each range and an NCO to issue ammunition under strict instructions; the importance was stressed for safety and security reasons. This is where I got into trouble. The first year shoot was held at Hythe Ranges and despite my emphasis on the issue of ammunition, I found a senior officer overriding the protests of the NCO and issuing ammunition by the handful to other officers. I was furious at this lack of discipline and contravention of instructions and I bodily threw him out of the ammunition bunker: not the correct thing to do, but in addition he had interfered in the marking of an officer's shoot I was supervising. After his removal from the bunker there was a hush. I gave instructions, the NCO smiled, nothing more was said! Later, enjoying an evening drink, the officer concerned came over, bought drinks, sat on a settee with me and chatted away as if nothing had happened. I presumed he understood his error, he made no reference to it, therefore I suppose I was lucky.

Similar conduct of a more serious nature occurred the following year at a range in Essex when once again the Group were pursuing their Annual Shoot under the same strict instructions that I had laid down the previous year. Just before lunch I had been behind the Butts to check something in the Range Stores, I verified that shooting had stopped and the Red Flag was flying on the range to my right, and started to walk to the Firing point. Suddenly, with the flag still flying, shooting started on the range to my right, automatic and single shots. To my amazement a group of officers, led on by an officer with SAS experience who should have known better, were firing indiscriminately at an object on the ground near to them and the targets; none of this was in the authorized range practice. I screamed at them in my best parade ground voice to stop firing and then followed a deathly hush. Rightly or wrongly, without using any bad language, I gave the culprits the tongue lashing of a lifetime, emphasising the utter stupidity of their actions and this included the officer in charge. I then reported the matter to the Training Officer to let him take the appropriate action. On the Monday I was sent for by the Commanding Officer who stated that he had received a report signed by several officers objecting to the disgraceful manner that they had been subjected to on the range by a person who was junior to them in rank. They had made no comment about their horrendous conduct on the range; only the fact that their dignity had been offended in front of other ranks by my verbal tirade; some had even threatened resignation.

Needless to say I was angry at the way these officers, none from 22 Company, had attempted to circumvent their conduct, so very carefully I explained that I had informed all concerned about the Range Practices and Discipline including ammunition. I also reminded the CO that because of my qualifications my word was law, irrespective of rank, when involved in Range Practices. It was pointed out that the Red Flag was still flying, the authority of the Officer in charge had not been given, the shooting was reckless and not within the scheduled practice, there was also unauthorised use of ammunition, and several other contraventions of the rules governing use of firearms.

After I had said my piece, the CO appeared to be stuck for words. To me it was apparent that he had not been informed of the full facts. After due deliberation he then stated that he appreciated the position I was in, and that my concern about Range safety was uppermost in my mind, but he could not excuse my abuse of his officers despite what they had done. He was not looking at me at this time as I recall, so I presumed that this was merely a token reprimand. To have taken this further would have placed the officers concerned in front of a Court Martial and the CO, as an experienced soldier, knew this. I have no idea if the CO spoke to all those officers concerned but quite frankly they should all have been severely reprimanded if only on an unofficial basis. A point I had to remind the CO about was that a soldier had been shot earlier in the year in a breach of range discipline but I don't think it influenced him. It has always struck me as odd that Civil Servants, the Services etc. pay more credence to breaches of protocol than to any accompanying breaches of discipline. I had a tendency to 'rock the boat' on more than one occasion.

Several family matters had occurred over this period all involving each member. The one concerning Carolyn I shall not recount. Chris at this stage was taking extra 'A' levels, and thoroughly enjoying this part of his academic career. He had been made a Prefect, was playing for Hampshire (Under 19s) at Rugby and was confident he would pass his exams. He had opted for a place at Reading University for a degree in Estate Management and I had to forcefully insist that he attended his interview decently dressed in a suit and with his hair reasonably cut (it had been very long and untidy). I had to explain to Chris that he had to impress the Board with his appearance and demeanour to offset his current lack of academic achievement. To his surprise he was successful, but later when he spent some time with a College Old Boy who explained the full ramifications of his intended future career, and the amount of time he would be expected to spend in an office, he was rather disillusioned, and without any consultation with Jean and me he contacted the Ministry of Defence and was accepted for a Selection Board and a subsequent Commission in the Army. Personally I had never pushed the Services as a career, believing that having had the benefit of a secondary boarding education he would opt for an interesting civilian career. Maybe it's the genes, the military life is obviously in the Howard blood; some volunteer while others are called. To choose to defend your country is a very proud choice.

As a mother and a military wife Jean was disappointed and somewhat noncommital; as for myself I was frank with Chris mainly in his choice of Arm (Regiment or Corps), who initially wished to follow me into the Intelligence Corps, no doubt influenced by my work which he had observed at a distance but hardly understood. I had no doubt that the Corps would accept him initially, but I thought he should wait until he had been fully informed by unit representatives during his time at Sandhurst.

I took the day off on the Monday and drove Chris to Westbury for his Selection Board. With my limited knowledge I had briefed him about his conduct and attitude during the whole of the time he was to be tested; as for the actual tests, no one but himself could accept that responsibility. On the Wednesday I went abroad until the Sunday. Jean was most apprehensive and on the Friday welcomed home a very nonchalant son who stated he had thoroughly enjoyed himself, had initially been overwhelmed by a large percentage of the other candidates who were graduates or who possessed more 'A' levels than he, but if he had failed he would try again. The following morning he remained in bed and allowed Jean to meet the postman.

'Is it a large envelope, Mum?'

'Yes,' said Jean.

'That's all right, I've passed.'

He was so confident that he had done well but it was only later that I learned just how well he had performed.

Some time later I delivered Chris to the hallowed halls of Sandhurst and later attended the tea and bun party held for parents who could question College Staff and Tutors. Two of the Tutorial Staff were members of 22 Company and as we chatted I recognised my old Brigade Commander from Minden; Major General Harman was now Commandant at Sandhurst. I felt a touch on my shoulder and as I turned General Harman stood there with his hand outstretched. The usual formalities were exchanged, then he said, 'By Christ, young Chris did well at Westbury,' and I gathered he had come close to the top of all the candidates on that particular Board. I was very proud of him.

Initially I think Chris had difficulty in adapting to the early fundamentals of military life but this is all part of the process. We spoke and removed many doubts which resulted in Chris enjoying a steady average, though undistinguished, Commissioning Course. Having weighed up all his options he chose the Intelligence Corps which insisted on newly Commissioned Officers undergoing a two-year attachment to an Infantry Regiment preferably of their own choice. With Chris's agreement and understanding there would be certain problems. He was accepted for a tour with the 1st Battalion Scots Guards who were serving in BAOR and due for a five month tour in Ulster. The Commanding Officer was a former Company Commander of mine, Lt. Col. Richard Mayfield. Chris began pre-Ulster training and on its completion, came home on a short leave then I took him to Liverpool Docks for the night ferry to Belfast. A strange farewell. I never expected to send my son on Active Service under such circumstances. I didn't linger; he was cheerful and full of confidence. I expected a glimmer of apprehension but saw none; as a father I was sure he would equip himself well as a soldier.

Soldiering got to him; he did not apply for mid tour leave – I could understand his reasons but Jean took some convincing. Some time later I attended a Scots Guards dinner in London and met Lt. Col. Mayfield, now a DSO and retired. He told me he had written a personal letter to me (presumably to our former address in Barking) which was never re-addressed to Preston, and the contents of the letter were his personal comments concerning Chris. I told him the letter had not reached me so he explained (being the gentleman he was) that he was so pleased for me that Chris had followed me into the Regiment as a Commissioned Officer. He had actually been the outstanding Subaltern during the tour, especially as he had only just left Sandhurst; he had also done extremely well during the remainder of his BAOR tour and he stated that the Regiment would willingly have accepted his permanent transfer to the Scots Guards as he considered that Chris had the makings of a first class soldier and he felt that I should know; he was very pleased for me. I was quite taken aback but felt extremely proud for Chris, that my Regiment had realized his early potential as an officer.

The next incident of a domestic nature mainly concerns Jean; it had extremely serious connotations which happily were resolved following an operation and a spell in hospital. Jean had been living for some time with the knowledge that she could feel a lump in her breast but had not disclosed the fact to me. One afternoon on the bus returning from work in Ilford the vehicle suddenly braked as she was standing waiting to alight and she was thrown against a stanchion, striking the breast that held the lump. It was only when I found her in some agony that evening that I immediately took her to our little Polish doctor who examined her and wanted a specialist opinion forthwith. The obvious solution was the Millbank Military Hospital adjacent to Westminster Hospital. The following day she was seen and X-rayed; it was cancer, but with a strong possibility it was benign. The Specialist at Westminster confirmed this; it was 50/50. She was admitted a couple of days later much to my surprise in a very composed state; mentally she was exhausted and had accepted the obvious hospitalization which would eliminate the physical pain.

As for me, I find it hard to describe my feelings. Outwardly I had put on the mask of confidence and nonchalance in order to boost the morale of Jean during those days of waiting, but inwardly I was so screwed up knowing the possibilities of what the outcome could be, a fact that Jean had never referred to, as though she had never even considered the odds could be against her and her condition revealed to be terminal; it would all depend on what the Surgeon found. One of my most uncomfortable moments was my talk with the Colonel to appraise him of the situation. As a person of sympathy and understanding his questions got to me and I found myself on the brink of breaking down and sobbing. For the first time I was having to explain the full extent of the medical problems and what the full ramifications could be if the circumstances proved terminal. I finally escaped to the toilet and my private sorrow. As previously stated, Jean's acceptance of hospitalization quite surprised me and I left her calm and resigned; for myself I spent a very restless and sleepless night. I went to work the following day but little was done and I was at Millbank Hospital at Jean's bedside when she returned to the ward from the recovery room.

My heart sank when I saw her. She had a deathly colour and her bed was tilted. However when I spoke to the Ward Sister she assured me that the tumour was benign but the operation had been quite lengthy, her blood pressure was extremely low hence the tilted bed. Sitting at the bedside holding her hand for an hour or so was really a waste of time as she was unconscious and I was not convinced but the nurses were very reassuring and I left reluctantly. The next morning when I rang she had spent a restful night, had been washed and had some breakfast. Later in the day when I saw her I was amazed: she was radiant and very cheerful, she had been told of the successful removal of the tumour, no further part was affected by the cancer and as the Surgeon jocularly remarked, she had come out of it with a good uplift but only on one! She had plenty of visitors, endured the enforced stay in hospital but the rest did her good, and when the time came to go home she was mentally relieved and grateful for the skill of the surgeons and nursing staff who were excellent; in fact I think a surgeon also attended from the nearby Westminster Hospital. We were both just grateful that all our prayers had been answered. I don't think Jean would be so foolish again to hide the inevitable, but sadly many women are reluctant to face the problem, immediately hoping it will go away; this of course rarely occurs. It was a very traumatic experience for both of us; we shared it in our own way both physically and mentally but, strange to relate, we didn't discuss at length our inner feelings; it was as though an incident had happened and now it was best forgotten. Jean was just glad it was all over and thank God there have been no further complications.

Soon after this it was decided that Group Headquarters would be better accommodated at our other residence in the vicinity of Swiss Cottage. So the Colonel and other administrative staff moved out and the Interrogation Company became the sole occupants of the current accommodation. One day I received a telephone call from a certain individual at Group who said he was aware that a posting order for me had been sent to Group but the proposed move was being resisted because apparently I was required *now*! Nothing further was heard for some weeks when the matter was resurrected on the visit to our location by the Director of Military Intelligence (a senior RAF Officer); he was accompanied by our Brigadier (the Inspector of Intelligence). We were introduced and questions were asked of a relevant nature by the DMI. The Brigadier appeared to hang back and when he faced me he said, 'So you're Howard eh, do you realize the problems you have given me in the past two months with your postings? I hope the matter has finally been concluded.'

He was looking very hard at me and my puzzled look must have shown my lack of understanding of his words. After a few moments silence he walked on.

I cannot recall accurately if it was the same night or some nights later when the Annual Meeting of ICCA (Intelligence Corps Old Comrades Association) took place at our location. Our Corps Lieutenant Colonel, Colonel D, took me on one side at the conclusion of the meeting, sat me down and purchased for me a double Scotch and ginger. He explained that he wished to offer an apology and an explanation concerning the matters of my postings, and was he right in suspecting that I was completely unaware of the background which prompted the Brigadier's remarks to me? I agreed that I had no idea about the posting problems; I had been most surprised and astonished at the Colonel's statement and later when I had time to reflect on this I was rather 'chuffed'. In retrospect I often wondered why the Corps never took any suitable remedial action!

It is not possible to relate exactly the words spoken but it would appear that from somewhere in the depths of the Ministry of Defence an order came for me to go to Northern Ireland forthwith to organize Operation 'Four Square Laundry'. (A male and female member of this team were later shot and killed in Belfast.) The removal of me from London was opposed at the highest level and my posting was cancelled. Some weeks later the MOD desired my presence in the Middle East to organize and run an Interrogation Centre; again my immediate posting was opposed from our Centre on the grounds of my retention in London and that my standard of Arabic was outdated and insufficient for the job on hand, and the posting was cancelled. Not to be outdone, the MOD, still persistent in their endeavours, tried again; yet another immediate posting to Northern Ireland for another unspecified 'job', which also was eventually cancelled. All of these postings, so I was told, occurred within two months or so. It is therefore no wonder that the Brigadier was annoyed at the persistent and obstinate action within the section of the MOD of one Senior Field Operator of the Intelligence Corps. Normal postings of personnel under usual circumstances were promulgated from the Intelligence Centre, the unusual requests for personnel direct from the MOD was exceptional, and due to strong objections from the Posting Section and my current unit, eventually involved the intervention of the Brigadier on no fewer than three occasions.

Having explained all this, the Colonel paused and said in way of explanation that it was 'considered by the higher echelon of the Intelligence

Corps that I was probably the outstanding Field Operator the Corps had had in their ranks since World War Two, if not the best. It was considered that the Corps had at that time three senior Operators who could be given any task to complete and I was one of those three. 'If it is any consolation that is no doubt the reason why the MOD required your background and expertise to carry out these very sensitive posts.' To conclude, he felt that I had a right to know what had transpired and to remove any doubts about my immediate future, I would remain in London until I completed my tour.

Realizing that I had a limited time to serve, Jean and I discussed the possibility of buying a house and putting down roots in an area compatible with a satisfactory job and an affordable residence, so we decided to opt for the Preston district where we had close relatives, friends and contacts. I tendered an application to our Posting Section informing them that I was in the process of a house purchase so I was not particularly interested in further overseas postings and that I would like to be considered for any posting with reasonable access to Preston.

In 1971 Jean and I made certain friends aware of our interest in settling down, preferably in the Penwortham/Longton area. Jean's mother had suffered a leg injury which brought on further complications and subsequently she was confined to hospital. This problem necessitated frequent visits and we both viewed several properties in the Preston area. One Sunday however on my return from overseas I read a *Lancashire Evening Post* provided by my namesake who lived in Longton. I saw an advertisement for a bungalow in Hutton, made a telephone call and spoke to a former Captain in the ACC. As a very kind and understanding person he said the premises were mine subject to approval by Jean, who made a visit the following Thursday, and the house was ours with no complications whatsoever; we were so grateful. At forty-five years of age I was not at the right age to start a mortgage but it all worked out fine in the subsequent years.

Considering what had happened previously you can imagine my feelings when I received a telephone message from the Centre asking me if I would like a posting. My reply was cautious. 'How would Preston suit?' I was assured it was not a joke, the General at HQ North West District had requested as a matter of some urgency a Section of Counter Intelligence personnel in his District owing to the increase of terrorist activity and the obvious danger to military and military associated establishments. I was told that the posting would offer quite a challenge, long hours and hard work, but of course the added carrot was the fact that I could now reside in my own house and it was doubtful if I would be considered for another posting before I finished my time. After a few more questions I accepted the job, knowing that I had to make a visit to the HQ at Preston to obtain more details about the task, accommodation, office equipment, vehicles and so on. It was also explained that in the initial weeks I would be on my own until further personnel were made available. Arrangements were made for a visit to Preston and when this had been completed successfully, the posting was accepted and arrangements made for my move.

The intervening period passed quickly. Workwise I was up to date with all tasks completed and my replacement fully in the picture. The Christmas holiday helped us to pack most of our belongings and prepare the house for handing over. I then had to say farewell to the Members of 22 Company and attend my presentation. As previously stated I had mixed feelings about the Reserve Army, and I had been involved with certain persons whom I would not wish to serve with under Active Service conditions. Conversely there were many others who I would consider it a privilege to serve with; they were a credit to themselves and their unit. In fact the personal sacrifices made by most of these people was indicative of their loyal and total commitment; I had nothing but the greatest admiration for them. So farewells were made to staff and personnel, the handover was painlessly completed and I left the family to undertake a very interesting and important $3^1/2$ years of extremely hard work.

Leaving London gave me no regrets. It is not my ideal place to reside although the city holds many attractions which we enjoyed when I was free, but lifelong residence in London or its suburbs holds no attraction. My work was interesting and I travelled abroad quite frequently which gave me very welcome breaks. All in all it was a very satisfactory tour of duty which was an experience, despite certain drawbacks, I wouldn't have missed.

CHAPTER 37

Preston North-West District HQ 1973-6

When I made my introductory visit to Preston I had arranged to spend the couple of nights with my brother John and his family at Whittle-le-Woods. I also found time to visit our bungalow and acquire the assistance in many ways of our adjacent neighbours who were so helpful, not only with the central heating but also the reception of various items of furniture, even before our personal effects arrived from London.

During the day I had to arrange for office equipment, stationery, furniture, transport, telephone, doctor, dentist, school and the transfer of any relevant files from West Midland District on units within North-West England. My area of responsibility stretched from Crewe to Carlisle involving six police forces: Cheshire, Manchester, Liverpool, Lancashire, Cumbria and the Isle of Man. The Section Office (known as the Eagle's Nest) was situated at the highest point within the most charming environment of Cuerden Hall, the home of HQ NW District, and also the Commanding General.

He was a very competent, efficient and physically fit senior officer with a distinguished war record. He knew what he wanted. I told him what I thought the job should entail; he looked at me a bit old fashioned and said, 'Come and see me if you have any problems.' This was good. I did ask him to contact Chief Constables for obvious SB Liaison, also all units warning them that things were going to change. Money was short but all help would be given. We both knew what my priorities were.

So in January 1973 I moved to Preston, being temporarily accommodated with John until the arrival of Jean and our effects. The G2 (Int) with whom I had to work was a most charming retired Colonel, who had no practical or Staff experience in Intelligence work, but was more than adept at processing the vast amount of paperwork equated with various Security Regulations. Apart from a couple of hiccups we got on extremely well. He welcomed the fact that people contacted us, and took most of the stress away from him.

After a short time we had a welcome increase in the establishment, a

Junior NCO who fortuitously lived in the general area. He had some experience in Ulster, was a competent driver and mechanic, efficient in the office, and showed great enthusiasm for the job as I outlined it. He was married with no family, and in his time with me I was more than satisfied with his performance. It was only after he had left for BAOR and my newly arrived Staff Sergeant from Northern Ireland attended to a query from a unit, that certain matters manifested themselves, then I found others. Sadly he had blotted his copybook, and I could find no obvious reason for his lapses. By this time he had decided to leave the Service voluntarily. I met him once before my discovery and I know where he is currently employed; I hope he doesn't let anyone down.

In the years I spent in Intelligence work, these years before retirement were probably my most demanding period. Unlike Borneo or Cyprus with their discomfort and possible dangers, this job had no element of danger, but it was the fact that there were not enough hours to do the job as I wanted to do it. We screeched around the roads of North-West England from morning till night, visiting units and SB Officers, making enquiries following letters, information and intuition and when I made rough drafts late at night to my horror and shame some of the drafts were absolute rubbish when I checked them the following morning. The reasons were long hours; tiredness; a domestic problem (we now had Jean's father living with us who was in the early stages of senility); and on odd occasions, alcohol and that is an accepted part of good liaison. It was most essential to drink especially when associating with known terrorists; luckily these meetings were rare.

We began our routine work of security surveys with major units both regular and Reserve Army, then Cadets, concentrating on security of arms and access equating to the security climate at the time. In four years we had few or no problems from any unit; close supervision and dedication helped to keep the sheet clean. As our presence became well known throughout North-West England so the volume of other work escalated and the unit produced more security reports than any other Intelligence Corps Unit in UK. We had some difficulty coping, and it was only over some time when the establishment was substantially increased that a degree of normality prevailed. By that time I was ready to terminate my service. Although he was not averse to working late, my first partner, only recently married, was not a happy night owl, so any work in those hours was usually done by me and as previously stated it was not only my rough drafts that suffered, so did my health; I was burning the candle at both ends and it showed more than I was aware of. My involvement was complete 100 per cent and it was only when I began to lose my appetite and develop stomach pains that I was forced to see my doctor and the problem solved, although it took time. Too much work, not enough hours in a day, and too much of a one man band. It had always been so.

It would be foolish to enlarge on this period in all aspects; suffice to say it was a most gratifying, and fascinating four years of my life. The element of danger has recently reared its ugly head again. It is very real, hopefully it will pass.

In 1975 it was decided to move HQ NW District into more secure quarters at Fulwood Barracks. I had several options for the unit's new quarters and I think decided well, Adequate security precautions were taken: new office equipment, civilian secretary, more staff, things were looking up. It was also noted that retiring Warrant Officers could remain in post as civilians dealing with Counter Intelligence matters and SB Liaison maintaining the most essential part of the job in UK, continuity, especially with SB. For whatever reason this idea was never pursued. I suspect, looking at it realistically, that this person would have demeaned the authority of the Officer Commanding. To all intents and purposes the 'civilian' would have been the fount of all knowledge, not good for discipline, but the unit would have been extremely efficient with the right person *in situ*.

The move was eventually made and in a relatively short period of time everything was up and working as normal. Personally I found it difficult to accept the vast amount of space we now enjoyed in comparison to the small cloistered environment we had had to endure at Cuerden Hall where we were far enough away from the HQ area to enjoy a certain amount of freedom without undue interference. Our first job was to carry out a survey of the Barracks and Armoury, with strong recommendations towards the Control of Access. In the spring of 1976 we received notification that our unit was to be upgraded and commanded by an officer. Unfortunately this person's reputation was well known but not by me. Prior to and on his arrival I gave him as much help as possible; I did not wish to pre-judge. It soon became obvious that we had opposing views on how the work should continue. His ideas were totally contrary to the way I had been working and frankly I became most apprehensive for the outcome after all the hard work and long hours I had put in. So, less said soonest mended.

Having handed over command I could then attend to everyday security work until the time came to attend my Release Course on Safety and Security at a Polytechnic; this was both interesting and instructive. This was now the time to begin job hunting and what a revealing exercise that was. It certainly opened my eyes as to how ill mannered, inefficient and ill informed parts of British industry and commerce were. With the experience of the Civil Service, the Law, Education, Sales, Industry, Agriculture and the verbal comments of friends and associates, I find it sad that the country tolerates so many 'deadlegs' within our society. No one seems to have the desire to shake us out of our lethargy and to assume strong ethics of discipline, responsibility and common sense.

I returned to Fulwood and one day in the gym I fell heavily. Some days later Jean and I were about to leave on holiday and I was leaning over the bookcase to remove the TV plug. I then stood up, felt a sudden pain throughout my body and fell unconscious. My passing out could only have been momentarily but when Jean found me I could not move for pain. Hours later, following help from male neighbours, I was carried to bed and when the doctor arrived and gave me morphine she was still perplexed as to the reason for my collapse and severe pain.

Two days later I was removed to Catterick Military Hospital and placed in traction. A week later I awoke in a terrible state. Five consecutive X-Rays followed and an emergency operation removed the problem. In 1969, also at Catterick, I had been told that I had a kidney stone lying dormant in an awkward place. It had now decided to move, hence my collapse and subsequent pain. As it moved (it had spikes on) it finally left the kidney but became stuck in the urethra, causing a severe blockage and intense pain. The operation over and under constant surveillance in a single room, my biggest post operative problem was constipation. I hadn't been to the loo for over a week. Those events to assume the 'Relief of Mafeking' can only be described as hilarious as the nurse, 'at panic stations', careered from one ward to another with me in a wheelchair, to find a vacant WC.

As I convalesced I answered the door one morning and in walked the new OC. He asked how I was feeling, followed by a few other inane statements, said he couldn't stay, then left. And that was the farewell to my military service. Even the most thick, idiotic, scruffy Guardsman on completion of his service was offered some form of address from his most senior officer at the end of his service. My so-called peers had an awful lot to learn about man management, a sad and disappointing end to a job I enjoyed so much.

Post service employment became a problem. I refused the appointment of Security Director of Liverpool Airport because of the disgraceful terms of employment, typical of a Council owned facility. There then followed short tours with Customs and Excise, contract labour manager, working for a friend as a horticultural labourer, a UK Sales Rep (Midlands, York and South), a social worker with teenage problem children, and latterly until retirement ten years in the Lord Chancellor's Department in the

County and Crown Courts. Altogether this was a period that offered great satisfaction, frustration and instances of disgust with my fellow man, but I did meet and work with some wonderful people and so ended my working life.

To keep the old brain ticking over I returned to Preston College, part of the University of Central Lancashire and obtained 2 'B's ('A' Levels) and 2 'A's ('O' Levels) in two years. The third year I took Law but could not take the exam as I was in Borneo; that too was enjoyable. I was the 'oldest swinger in town'. The sad thing was the gradual loss of students as the Course progressed, and this without explanation. Sadly, this is the youth of today. Maybe I should be glad I'm reaching the end of my God-given span of life; in retrospect he has been so good to me.

Conclusion

In conclusion I must look back on a long period of my life which has been extremely interesting, a variation of military and civilian employment, initially as a single person and later as a married family man.

There were very few periods from 1944-76 which could be described as idle times. Those thirty-two years were full of hard work with significantly long hours in the period of Intelligence work, much to Jean's chagrin, who in general coped with great patience and tolerance considering that during my frequent absences she had to be father and mother. For all the problems she faced and overcame, she deserves the greatest credit especially as she has always maintained that she was never the ideal military or intelligence wife. She always had expectations of a more tranquil, settled life but she bore it all with fortitude.

The Scots Guards were responsible for forming many characteristics of my makeup for which I have always been grateful. I list the following: fitness, personal cleanliness, smart appearance, bearing, acceptance of responsibility, obedience to and use of authority, tremendous confidence in my own ability and above all a sense of humour. I was taught and learned all the fundamentals of an infantry soldier, aggression and self preservation, and had an excellent attainment in the use of all arms. In my seven years or so with the Regiment I was extremely fortunate to be associated with many worthy characters, Officer Cadets and Other Ranks, all of whom helped in forming my personal character and for that I have always been most grateful to my Regiment and its members. I would always advise any young man of the right inclination to serve his country and develop many personal attributes that normal civilian employment would fail to manifest. National Service had many drawbacks, and was not popular, but speaking to men who underwent this service, an extremely high percentage were grateful for the experience.

My service with the Palestine Police was a follow-on to my initial time in the Scots Guards. Being a highly disciplined, para military organization it initially introduced me to the Law, to be followed by bomb disposal training. Promotion to Sergeant gave me the responsibility of being in charge of the Police Control Room supervising a mixed race town of

Two proud parents outside Buckingham Palace where
Chris received his well earned MBE from HM the Queen.

120,000 persons when inter-racial troubles were at a high point; all 999 emergency calls came through this Control Room. Later, with four patrol cars and their crews I took over responsibility for patrolling the very dangerous and volatile area of Eastern Haifa plus other duties.

On completion of service at the age of twenty-two years I was a very confident and competent young man, I had held responsibilities far and above the normal for a person of my age and felt quite capable of tackling any problem I might be confronted with. I was extremely fortunate that I left Palestine in one piece, 'Someone up there loves me'; therefore I was a grateful and very mature person on my return to the UK.

My UK Police and Scots Guards service further developed me as a person of wide and responsible experience, and when I became engaged in Intelligence work, though lacking in academic achievement and linguistic skills, I had other talents that many of my contemporaries lacked, and this was mainly due to my age and experience. As a former Police Officer with some CID background I had a natural flair for painstaking investigation and a suspicious mind. Throughout my Intelligence Service this enabled me to unearth at particular times numerous undiscovered serious breaches of security, and in later years involvement in top level anti-terrorist investigations in which I was particularly successful. I received no acknowledgement from my superiors despite the fact that I was sent to North-West England at the request of the General Commanding, because of the potential increase in terrorist activity and that in the years 1973-6 my unit produced more work of a security or anti-terrorist nature than any equivalent or larger military intelligence unit in UK, excepting Ulster. It must also be accepted, especially between the years 1973-5, that the total work of my unit was carried out with only two or three operators; this entailed extremely hard work and long hours. I do not wish to emphasise unnecessarily my personal involvement, but over the three years 1973-5 I frequently worked a seven-day week, and many of these days lasted eighteen or nineteen hours. I cannot offer an explanation for this dedication to duty: my health suffered but I was completely fascinated, if that's the correct expression, by this work of utmost importance and great interest. My involvement with the six Police Forces in North-West England was excellent in the degree of co-operation and exchange of information; mutual trust was established from the beginning and almost without exception I personally knew every Special Branch Officer in the area. With the exception of one Head of Special Branch (not his staff) who was blatantly unhelpful and parochial, my hard work for liaison was first class, and as any Police Officer would tell you, that was no mean achievement.

The sixteen years I spent in the nefarious world of Intelligence bore no resemblance to the epics of James Bond and Smiley. With Special Branch we did the ground work, the patient, tedious, repetitive, painstaking grind of acquiring information and processing it into sensible intelligence. Not for us the glamour of diplomatic parties, casinos, fast cars, good food and excellent restaurants, just hard work and long hours. At this level all credit should be given to the patience, tolerance and support given by wives and families of the Operators and Police Officers engaged in this type of work.

Early in 1975 I was taken to one side with a long serving Merseyside SB Officer who said, 'Eric, you look bloody rough and we've watched you since you first came here; use your loaf, it's not worth it. If anything should happen to you they'd have a replacement in no time. I know you do a good job, but don't kill yourself for it; they won't thank your widow.' He placed a friendly hand on my shoulder and walked away. I was touched by his comment and the feelings of his colleagues. He was right, of course, but it was only when we moved to Fulwood Barracks and my staff increased considerably, that the pressure decreased slightly.

Looking back, despite my frustration and disappointment in my Police Service, I would not have changed a thing. I reflect on a life span of thirty-two years of service to my country. Humbly I consider that this was achieved with honour and dedication; what more can any man say?